Street by Street

NOTTING̲H̲A̲M̲

HEANOR, HUCKNALL, ILKESTON, LONG EATON, WEST BRIDGFORD

Beeston, Bingham, Burton Joyce, Clifton, Cotgrave, Eastwood, Keyworth, Kimberley, Radcliffe on Trent, Ruddington, Stapleford

Reprinted October 2003
2nd edition December 2002
Original edition 2001

© Automobile Association Developments Limited 2003

Published by AA Publishing (a trading name of Automobile Association Developments Limited, whose registered office is Millstream, Maidenhead Road, Windsor, Berkshire SL4 5GD. Registered number 1878835).

The Post Office is a registered trademark of Post Office Ltd. in the UK and other countries.

Schools address data provided by Education Direct.

One-way street data provided by:

Tele Atlas © Tele Atlas N.V.

Mapping produced by the Cartographic Department of The Automobile Association. A01988

A CIP Catalogue record for this book is available from the British Library.

Printed by GRAFIASA S.A., Porto, Portugal

The contents of this atlas are believed to be correct at the time of the latest revision. However, the publishers cannot be held responsible for loss occasioned to any person acting or refraining from action as a result of any material in this atlas, nor for any errors, omissions or changes in such material. This does not affect your statutory rights. The publishers would welcome information to correct any errors or omissions and to keep this atlas up to date. Please write to Publishing, The Automobile Association, Fanum House (FH17), Basing View, Basingstoke, Hampshire, RG21 4EA.

Ref: ML085z

Key to map pages	ii-iii
Key to map symbols	iv-1
Enlarged scale pages	2-3
Street by Street	4-83
Index – towns & villages	84
Index – streets	85-109
Index – featured places	109-112

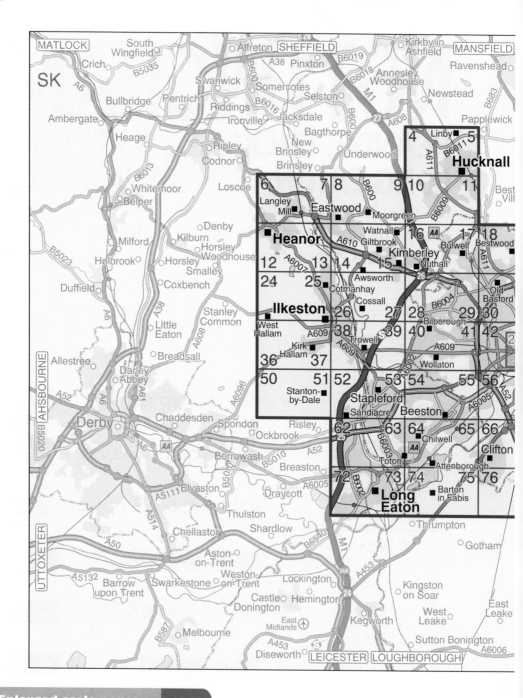

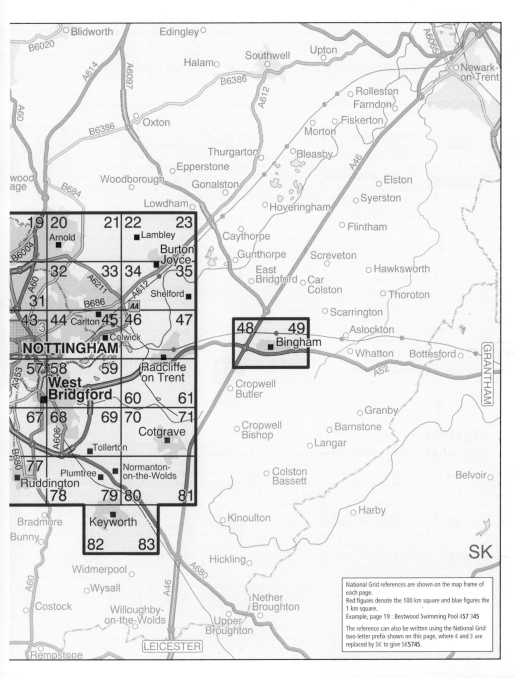

Junction 9 Motorway & junction	Underground station
Services Motorway service area	Light railway & station
Primary road single/dual carriageway	++++++++ Preserved private railway
Services Primary road service area	*LC* Level crossing
A road single/dual carriageway	•—•—•—• Tramway
B road single/dual carriageway	- - - - - - - Ferry route
Other road single/dual carriageway	·················· Airport runway
Minor/private road, access may be restricted	— · — · — County, administrative boundary
← ← One-way street	Mounds
Pedestrian area	**17** Page continuation 1:15,000
Track or footpath	**3** Page continuation to enlarged scale 1:10,000
Road under construction	River/canal, lake, pier
Road tunnel	Aqueduct, lock, weir
AA AA Service Centre	465 ▲ Winter Hill Peak (with height in metres)
P Parking	Beach
P+ Park & Ride	Woodland
Bus/coach station	Park
Railway & main railway station	Cemetery
Railway & minor railway station	Built-up area

	Featured building		Abbey, cathedral or priory
	City wall	X	Castle
A&E	Hospital with 24-hour A&E department		Historic house or building
PO	Post Office	Wakehurst Place NT	National Trust property
	Public library		Museum or art gallery
i	Tourist Information Centre		Roman antiquity
	Petrol station Major suppliers only		Ancient site, battlefield or monument
†	Church/chapel		Industrial interest
	Public toilets	❄	Garden
	Toilet with disabled facilities		Arboretum
PH	Public house AA recommended		Farm or animal centre
	Restaurant AA inspected		Zoological or wildlife collection
	Theatre or performing arts centre		Bird collection
	Cinema		Nature reserve
	Golf course	V	Visitor or heritage centre
▲	Camping AA inspected		Country park
	Caravan Site AA inspected		Cave
	Camping & caravan site AA inspected		Windmill
	Theme park		Distillery, brewery or vineyard

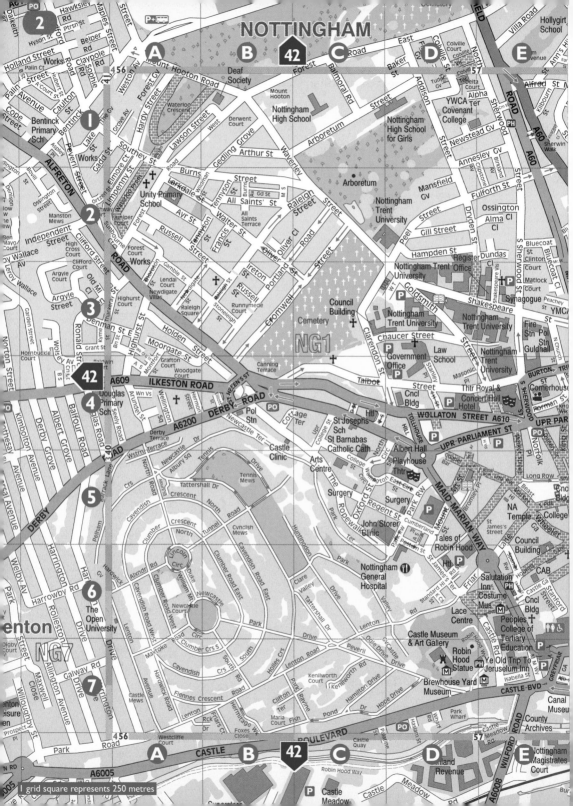

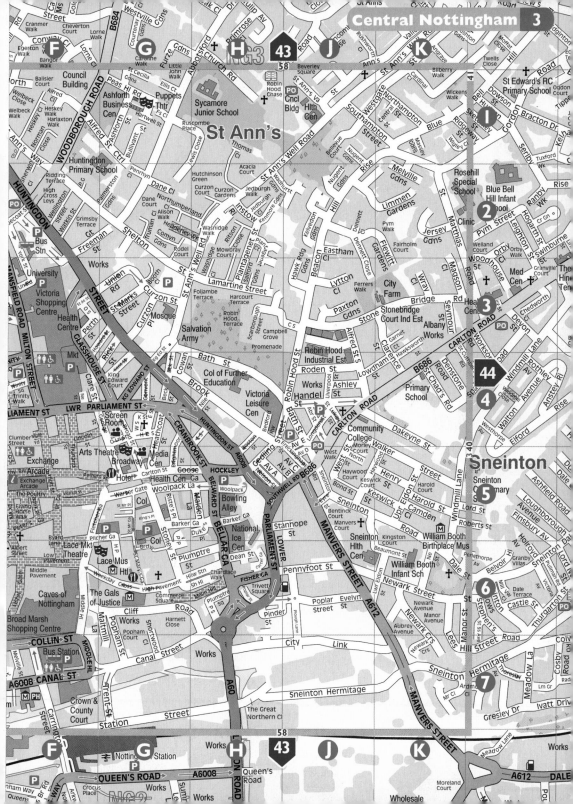

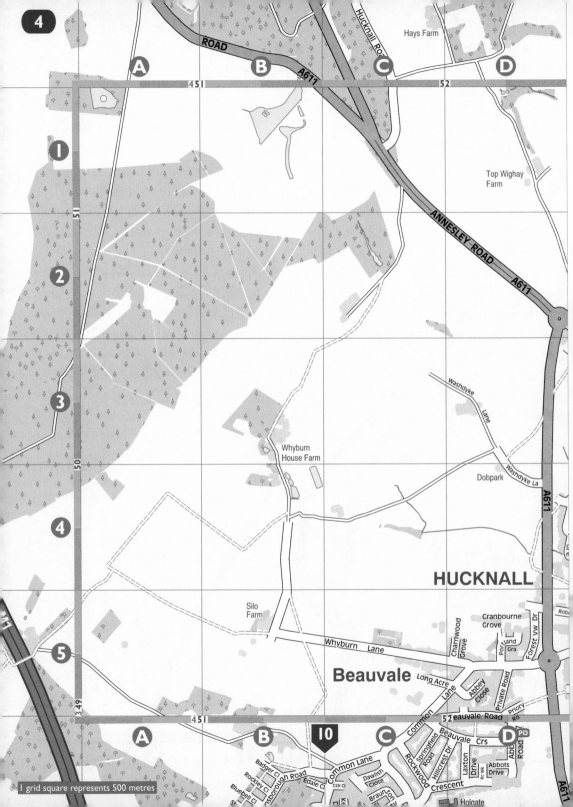

4

A B ROAD A611 C Hucknall Rd D

Hays Farm

451 52

1

Top Wighay
Farm

2

ANNESLEY ROAD A611

3

Washdyke
Lane

Whyburn
House Farm

Dobpark Washdyke La

4

HUCKNALL

Silo
Farm

Cranbourne
Grove

5

Charnwood Grove
Portland Gra
Forest vw Dr

Whyburn Lane

Beauvale Long Acre Abbey Close
Private Road
Priory Rd

349 451 52 Beauvale Road Abb Road

A B 10 C D PO

Badger Cl Road
Rockley Cl Common Lane Springfield Road Beauvale Crs
Bluebell Cl Edale Cl Dawlish Close Rockwood Hillcrest Dr Laxton Drive Abbots Drive
Braunton Crescent
Holgate

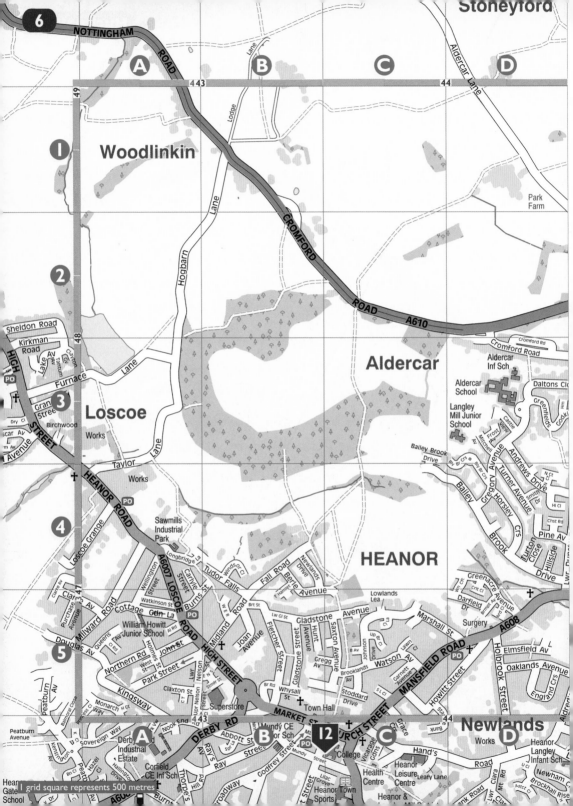

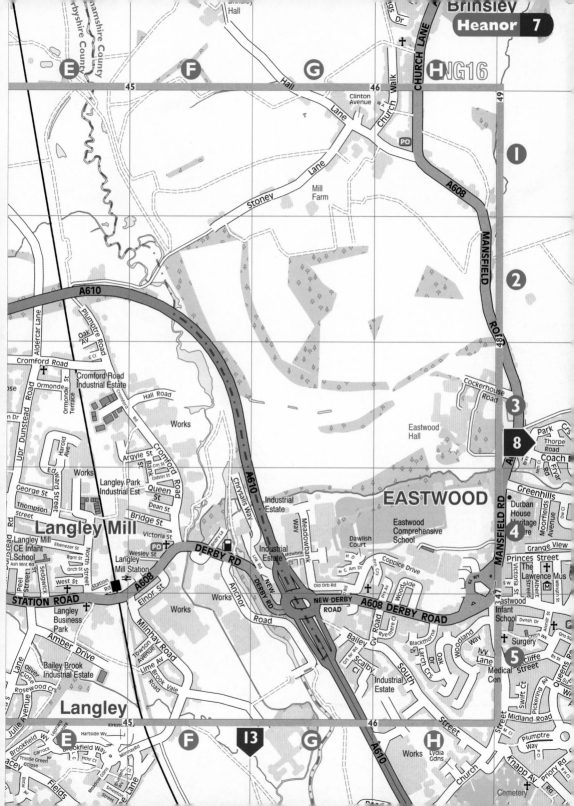

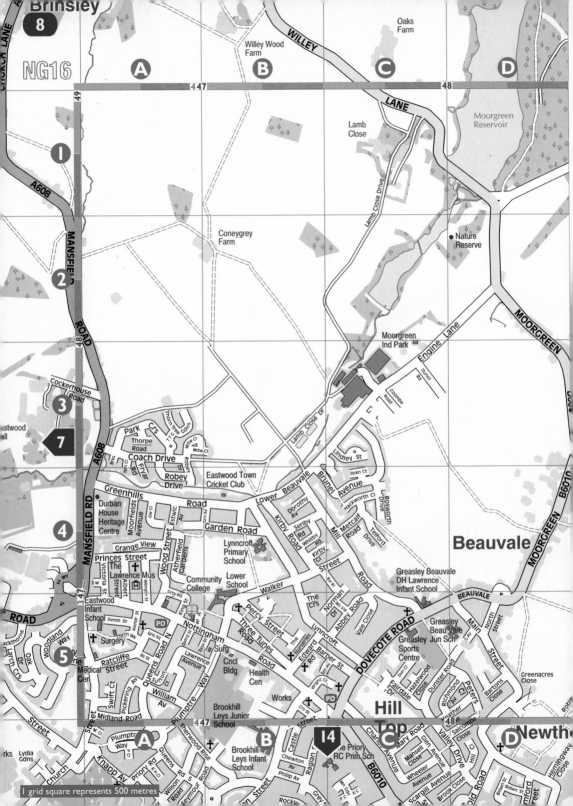

Beauvale House

Robin Hood's Well

E

F

G

H

I

2

3

10

4

5

New Road

Beauvale Manor Farm

Crowhill Farm

M1

Moorgreen

CHURCH ROAD

Cemetery

Greasley

Church Road

Bogend

Robin Hood Way

Robin Hood Way

B600

Narrow Lane

Littlefields Farm

LONG

E

F

15

G

H

B6009

Reckoning House Farm

orpe

Robin Hood Way

MAIN RD

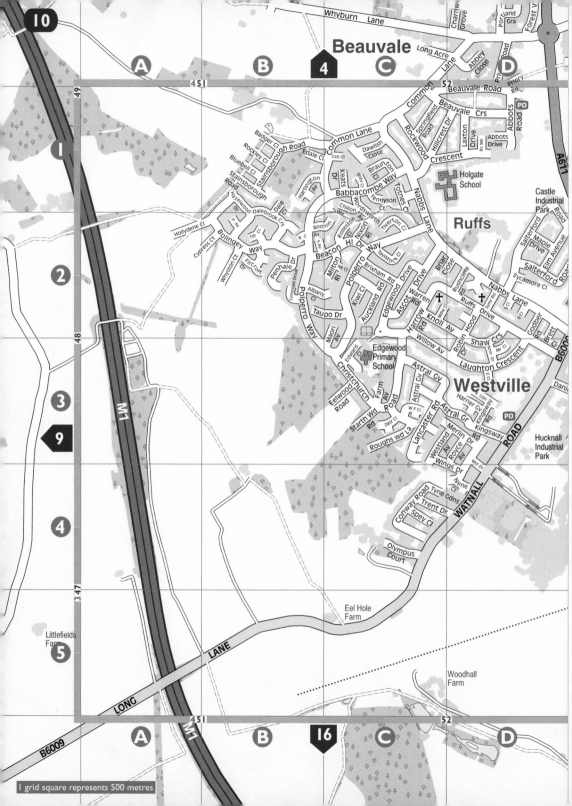

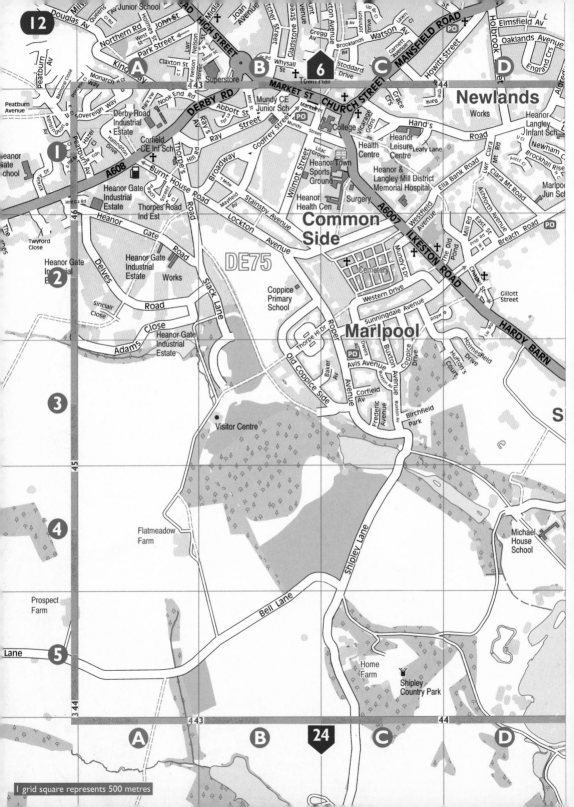

12

Douglas Av
Northern Rd
John St
Park Street
King
A
Claxton St
B
Whysall St
Superstore
Joan Avenue
Midla
Gladstone Street
Market St
Town Hall
6
Church Street
Gregg
Brooklands
Watson
Garnett Avenue
C
Mansfield Road
Howitt Street
Holbrook
Elmsfield Av
Oaklands Avenue
D
Engl

Peatburn Av
Peatburn Avenue
Monarch
Sovereign Way
Hazel
Peatburn
Derby Road Industrial Estate
Corfield CE Inf Sch
I
443
Derby Rd
Abbott St
Ray's
Mundy CE Junior Sch
Godfrey Street
Wilmot Street
Market Pl
Mundy Street
PO
College
Lilac Grove
Vicarage Gdns
Hand's
Health Centre
Heanor Leisure Centre
Leafy Lane
Road
Works
Newlands
Heanor Langley Infant Sch
Heanor Langley
Newham
Brockhall Rise

Heanor ate chool
Twyford Close
Heanor Gate Industrial Estate
Thorpes Road Ind Est
Heanor Gate Industrial Estate
2
Broadway
Thorpe's Road
Hill
Burnt House Road
Stainsby Avenue
Mayfield Av
Lockton
Heanor Town Sports Ground
Heanor Health Cen
Heanor & Langley Mill District Memorial Hospital
Surgery
A6007
Westfield Avenue
Ella Bank Road
Ashforth Avenue
Lwr Clara
East St
Mill Rd
Clara Mt Rd
The Old Pond
Breach Road
PO
Marlpool Jun Sch
Gillott Street

Sinclair Close
Heanor Gate Industrial Estate
Delves
Road
Works
Slack Lane
DE75
Coppice Primary School
Cemetery
Western Drive
Ilkeston Road
Hardy Barn

Adams Close
Heanor Gate Industrial Estate
3
Thorpe Hl Dr
Sunningdale Avenue
Roper
Marlpool
Avis Avenue
Owers
Buxton Avenue
Coppice Drive
Hutton's Court
Holmesfield Drive

Visitor Centre
Old Coppice Side
Baker Av
PO
Frederic Avenue
Corfield Av
Birchfield Park
4
Flatmeadow Farm
Shipley Lane
Michael House School

Prospect Farm
Bell Lane
5
Lane
Home Farm
Shipley Country Park

A
443
B
24
C
D

I grid square represents 500 metres

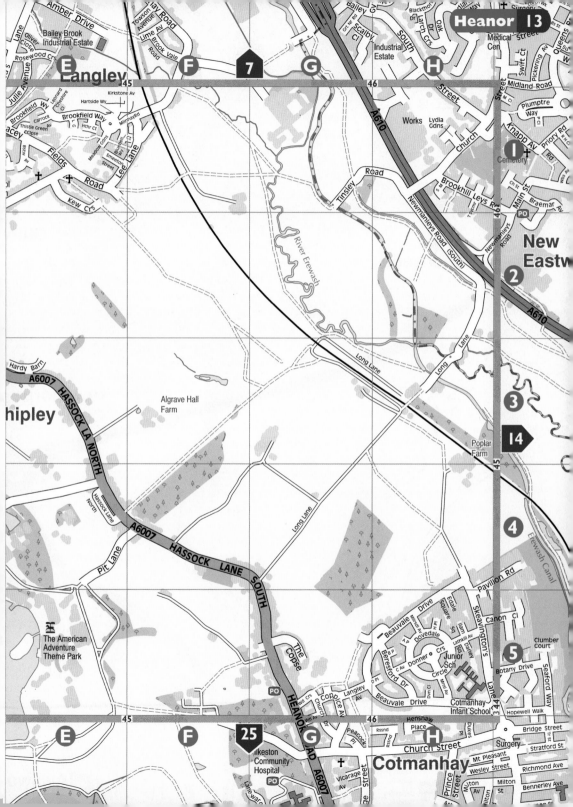

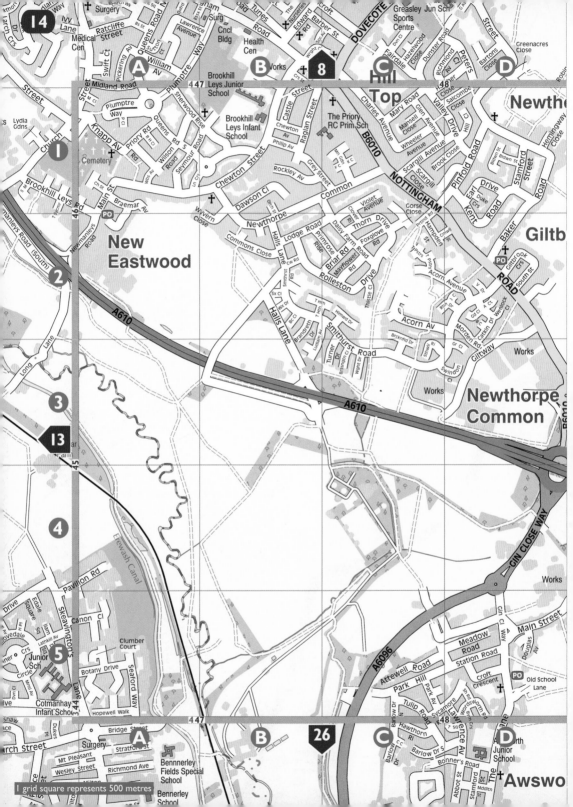

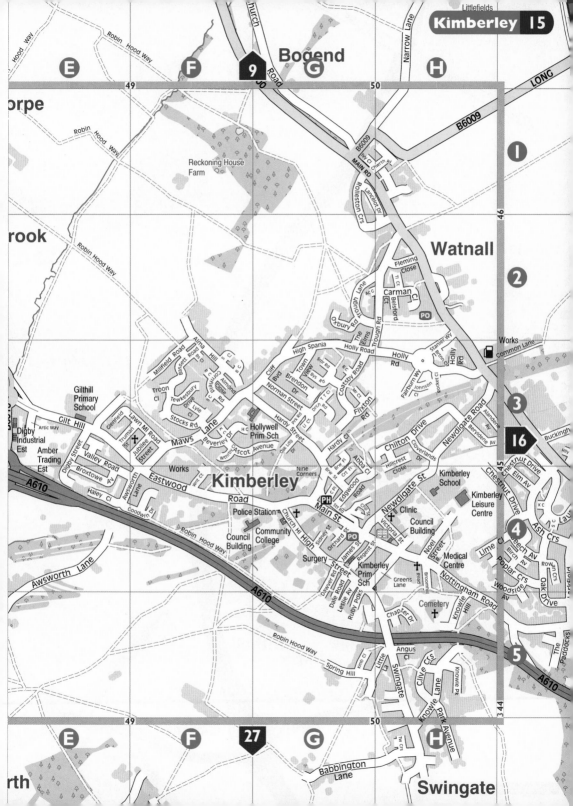

16

Littlefields

A B **10** C D

LONG LANE

451 52

Woodhall Farm

B6009

M1

1

46

Centurion Business Park

Bl...

Watnall

2

New Farm

Dabell

Blenheim Industrial Estate

PO

Works

common Lane

Sellers

Nature Reserve

WOO...

Newdigate

3

15

Buckingham Way

Osbourne Close

Bishopdale Dr

Hilly Gv

Cemetery

M1

Kimberley School

Chestnut Drive

Elm Av

Chestnut Drive

Albert Avenue

Spencer Dr

Holden Crs

Ayscough

New Farm Lane

Kimberley Leisure Centre

KC

Laurel Crs

Philip Av

St Patrick's Rd

Modtn Cl

Boden Dr

WATNALL ROAD

uncil ding

4

Ash Crs

Beech Av

Hazel Dr

Queen's Drive

Back La

Lime Cl

Birch Av

Maple Dr

Row... Av

Medical Centre

Poplar Crs

Woodside Av

Larkfield

Oak Drive

Larkfields Junior School

Sedley Av

Glebe Rd

Nottingham Road

Coronation Road

Cemetery

Knowle Hill

Kimberley

Road

PO

M1

NOTTINGHAM ROAD

The Paddocks

Edw... Rd

Nuthall

5

Knowle Crs

A610

Knowle Pk

Knowle Lane

Park Avenue

451 52

A B **28** Junction 26 C A610 D

3 4 4

WAY

Roland Avenue

Drive

Temple Crs

Temple

...field

S...

1 grid square represents 500 metres

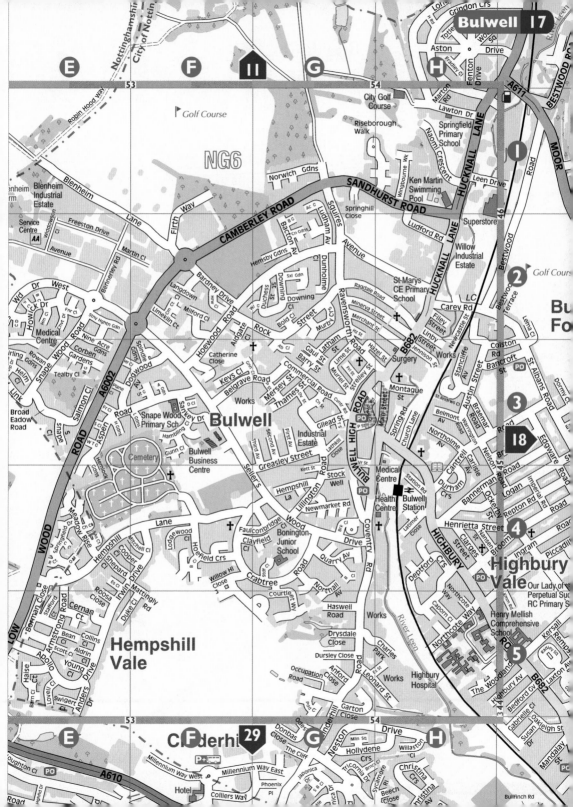

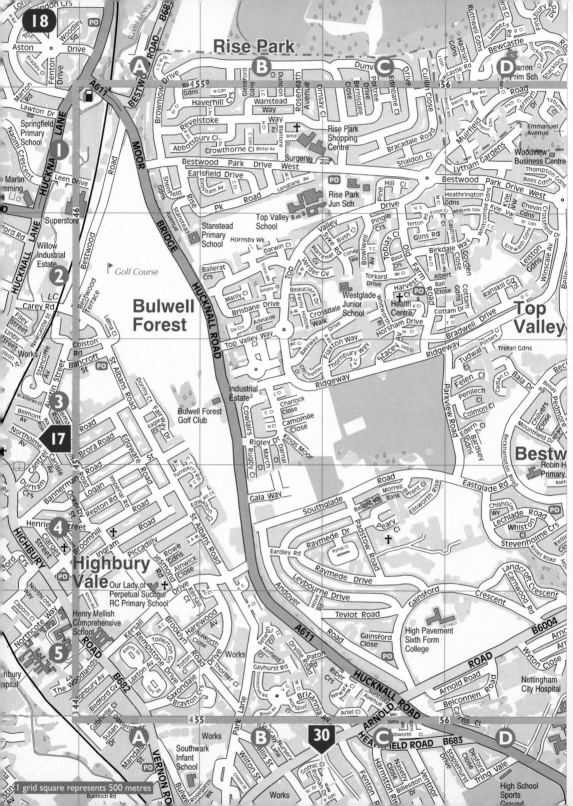

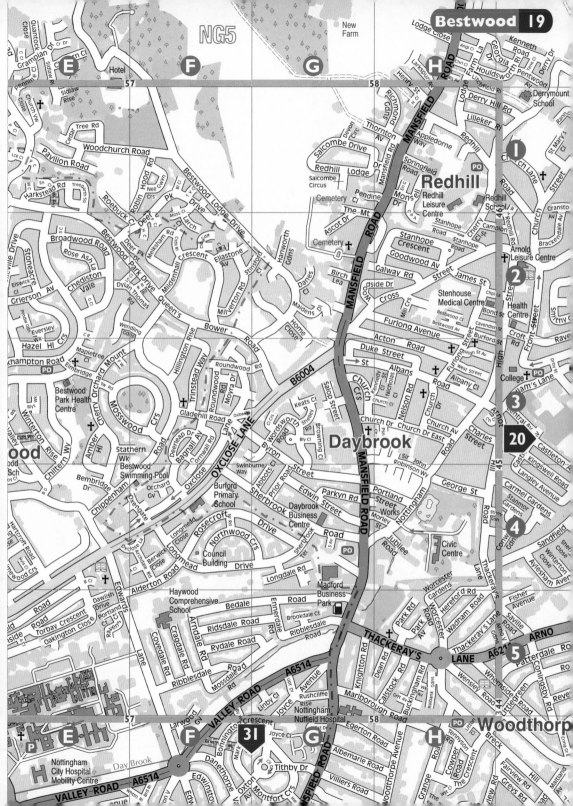

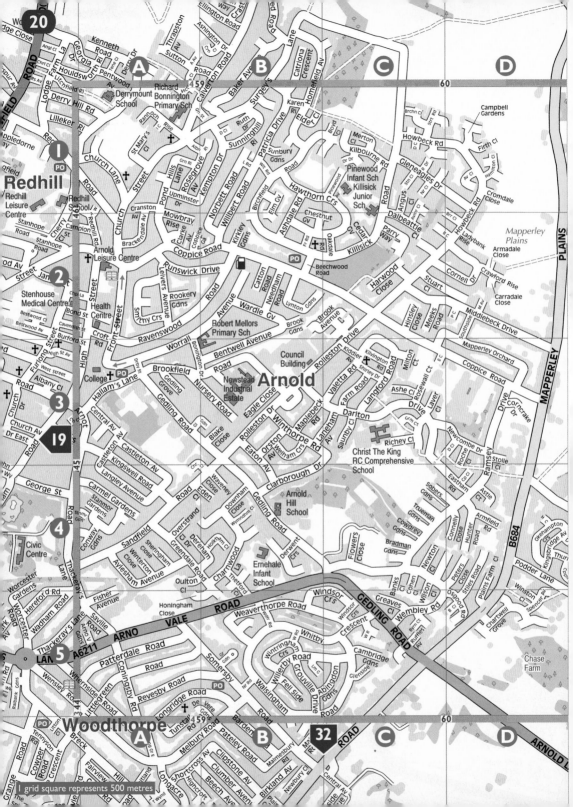

E F G H

Barn Farm

Lambley House

Hungerhill Lane

61 62

I

Playworld

Catfoot Lane

Cottage Farm

Lambley Dumble

The Dumble

2

Lambley Primary School

3

Lambley Dumble

22

Flams Av

4

Crimea Farm

Dunsford Dr

Chedington Av

Limestone Dr

Lapford Close

Ash Dr

Wi Cl

Spring Lane

Wood Farm

5

Lambley Lane

45

46

344

E F 33 G H

61 62

LANE

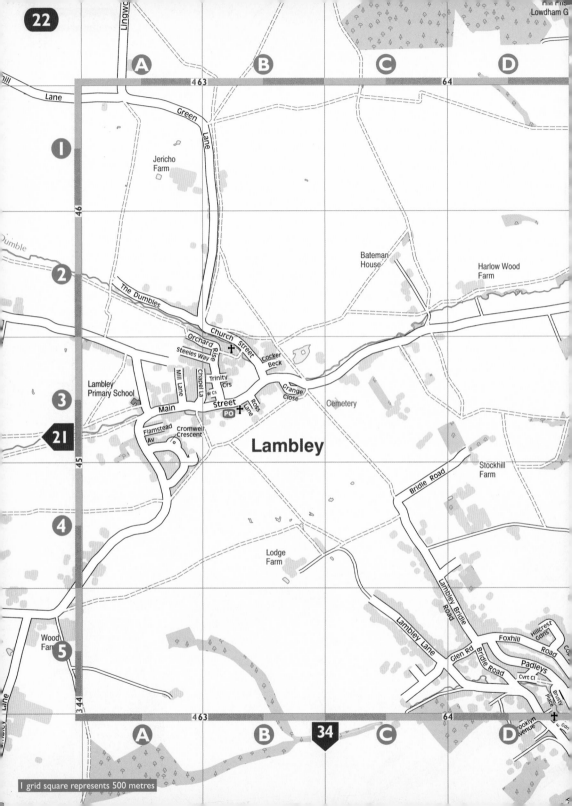

22

A   B   C   D

463   64

HM Prison
Lowdham G

Lingwo

Lane

Green Lane

Jericho
Farm

1

46

Dumble

2

The Dumbles

Bateman
House

Harlow Wood
Farm

Church Street

Orchard Rise

Steeles Way

Cocker Beck

Lambley
Primary School

Mill Lane

Chapel La

Trinity
Crs

W CS

Main Street

PO

Ross Lane

Grange
Close

Cemetery

3

Flamstead
AV

Cromwell
Crescent

45

21

Lambley

Bridle Road

Stockhill
Farm

4

Lodge
Farm

Lambley Bridle Road

Lambley Lane

Glen Rd

Bridle Road

Foxhill

Hillcrest
Gdns

Road

Padleys

Cvrt Cl

Wood
Far

5

344

463   64

A   B   **34**   C   D

Brooklyn Avenue

Brusby Place

Gdn

1 grid square represents 500 metres

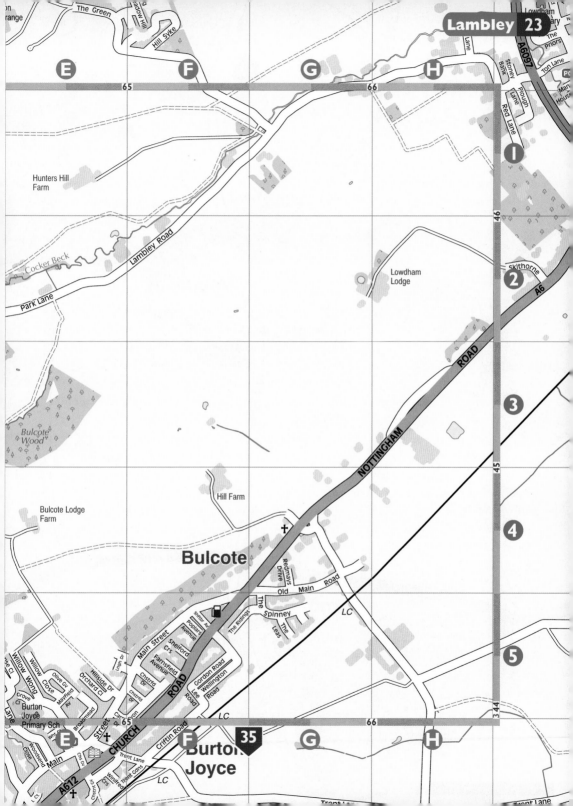

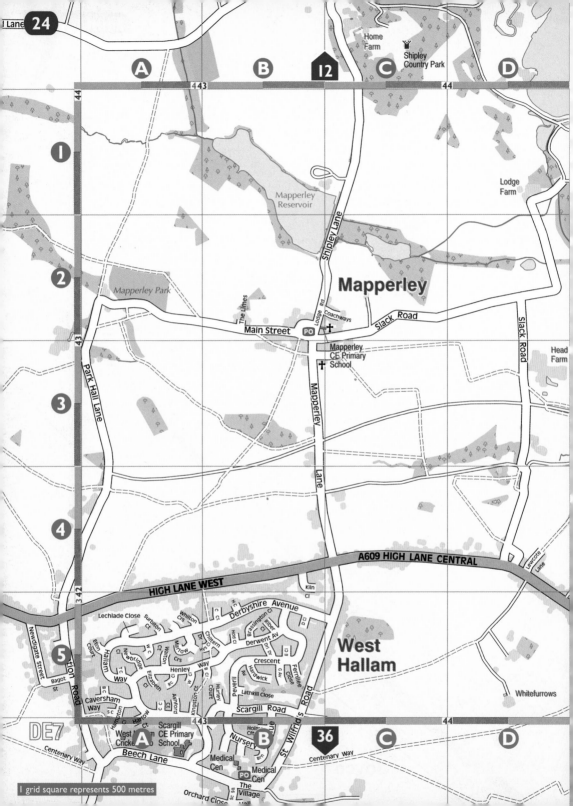

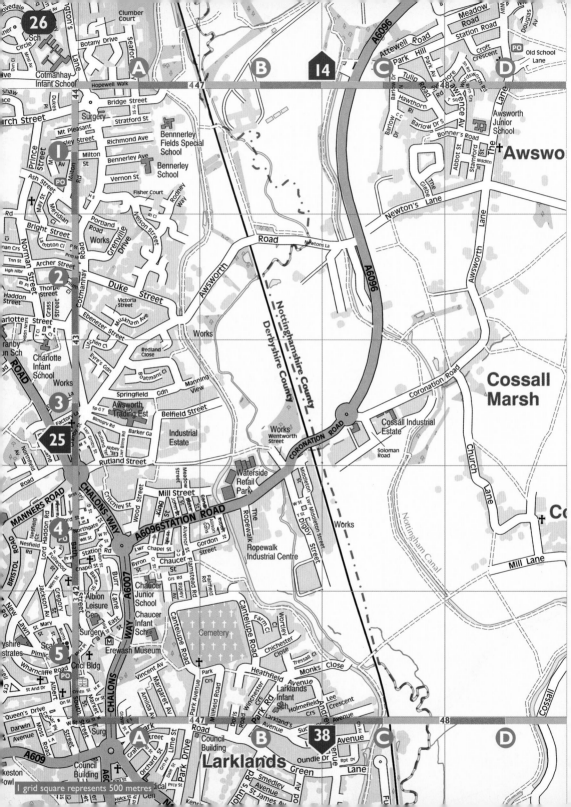

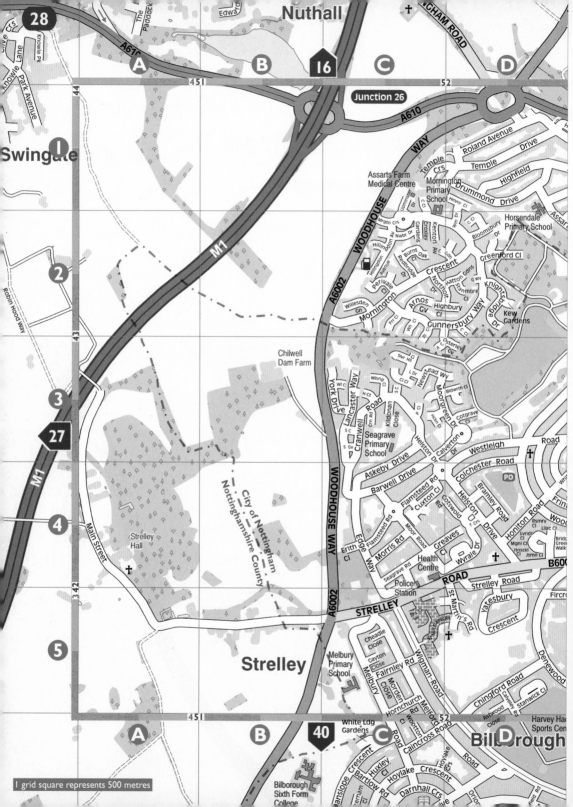

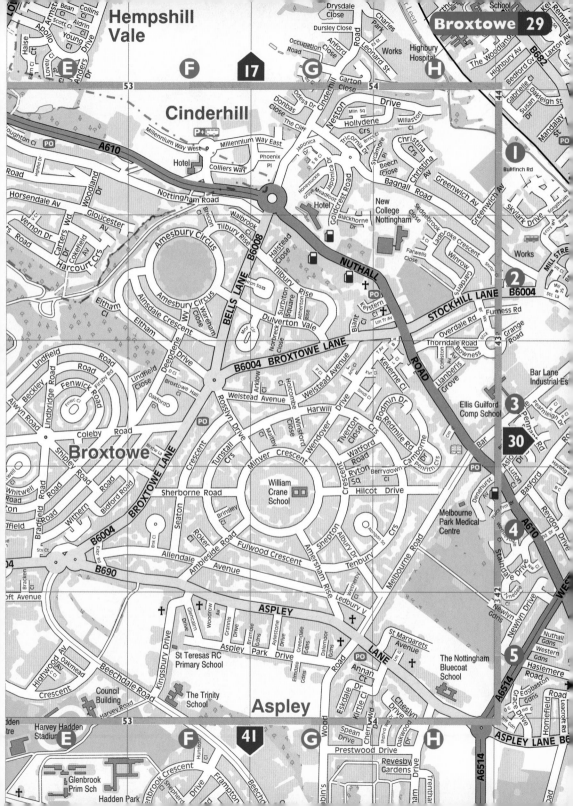

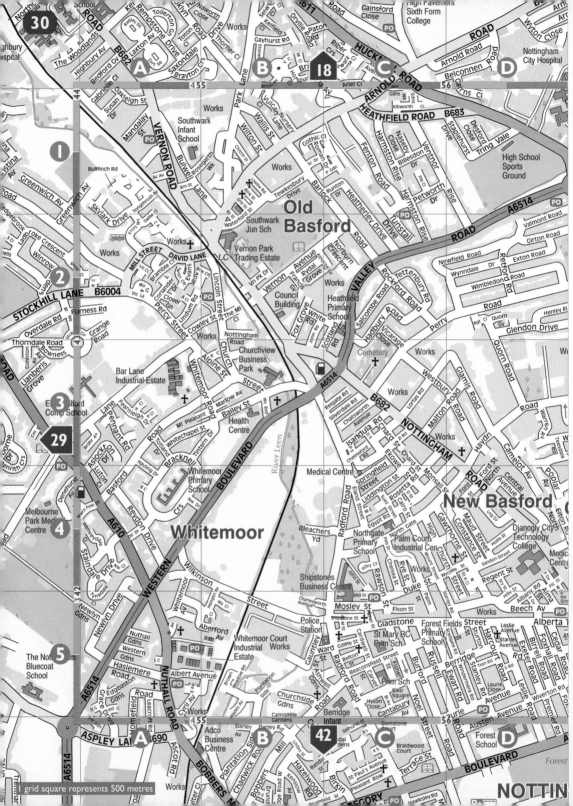

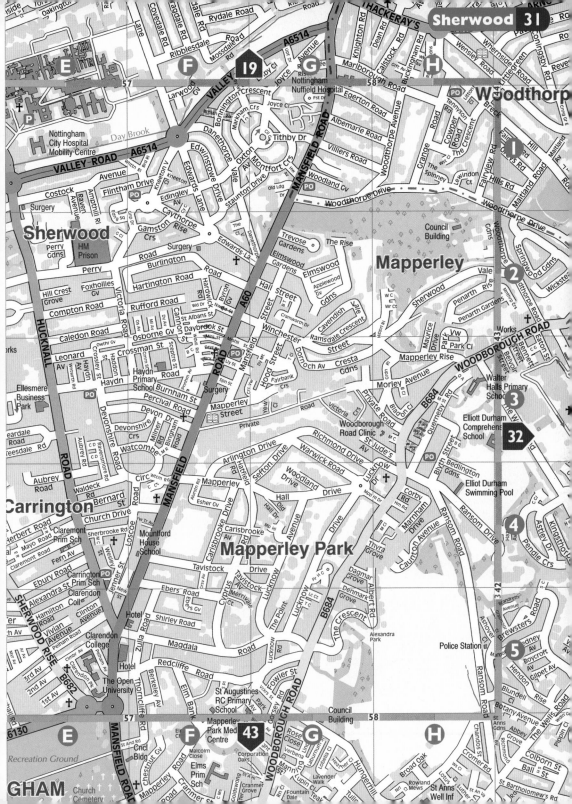

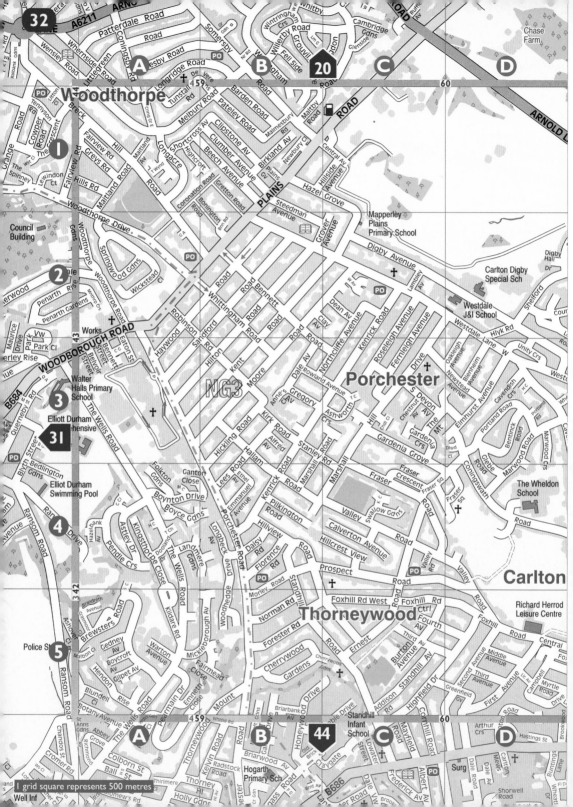

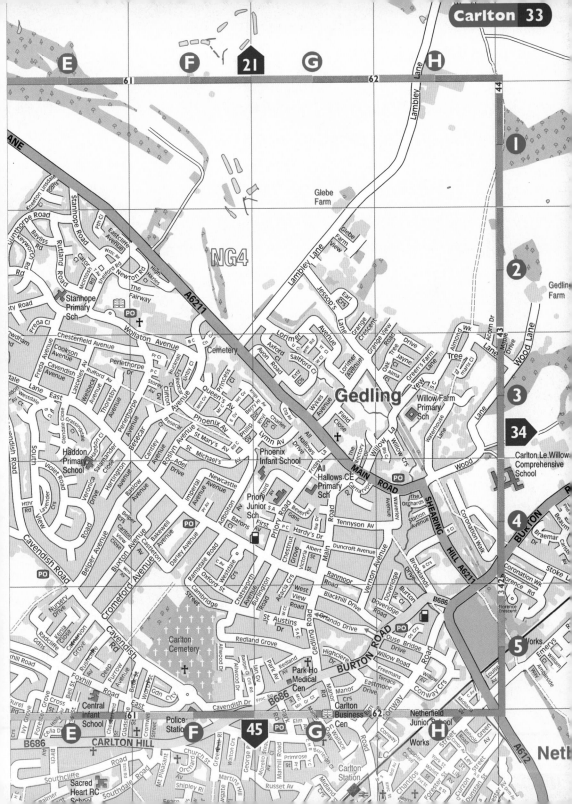

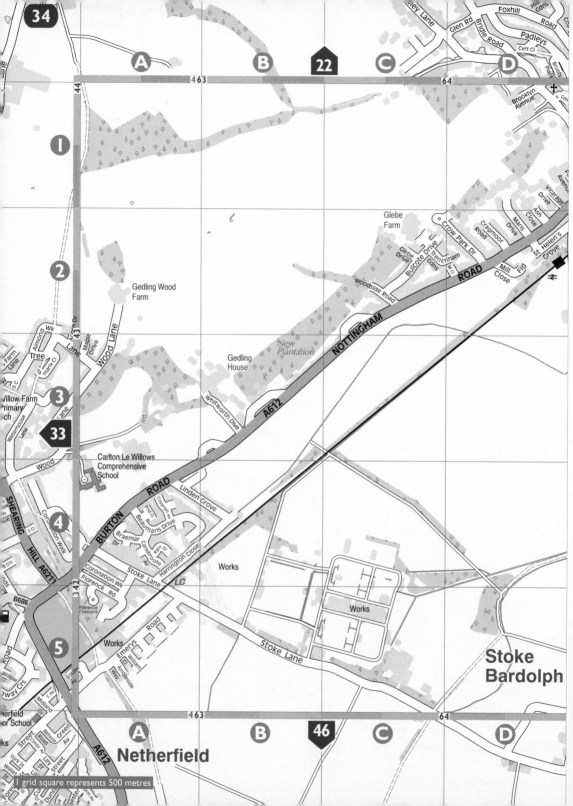

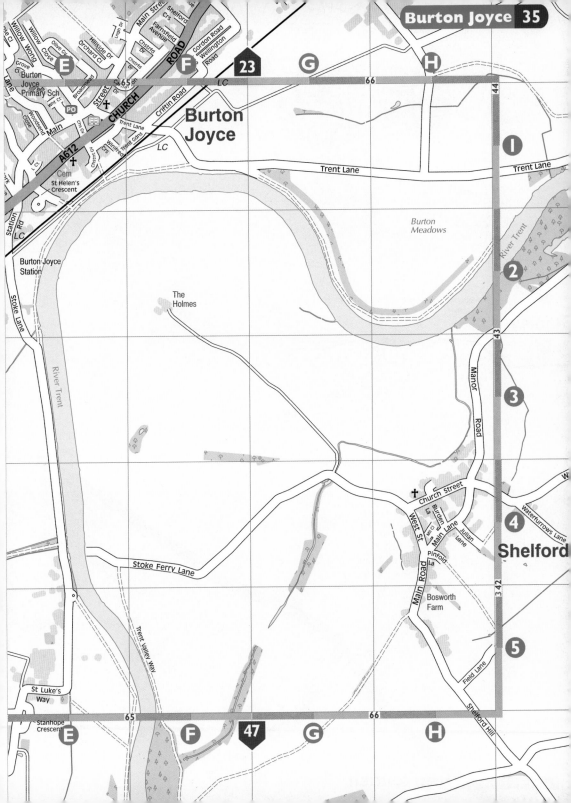

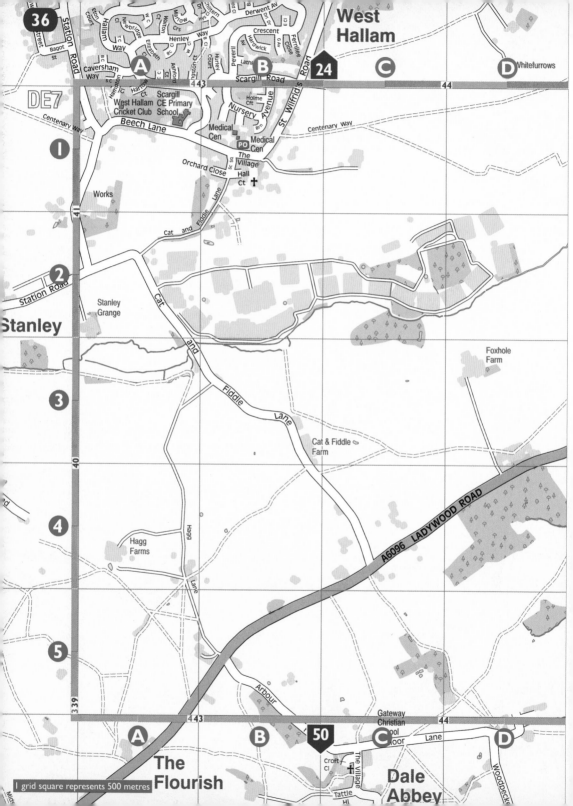

36

WEST HALLAM

24

Whitefurrows

DE7

Centenary Way

West Hallam Cricket Club

Scargill CE Primary School

Scargill Road

St Wilfrid's Road

Nursery Avenue

Centenary Way

Beech Lane

Medical Cen

Medical Cen

PO

The Village Hall

Orchard Close

Works

Cat and Fiddle Lane

Station Road

Stanley

Stanley Grange

Cat and Fiddle Lane

Foxhole Farm

Cat & Fiddle Farm

A6096 LADYWOOD ROAD

Hagg Farms

Hagg Lane

Arbour

Gateway Christian School

The Village

Woodpecker Lane

A **B** **50** **C** **D**

The Flourish

Croft Cl

Dale Abbey

Tattle Hill

1 grid square represents 500 metres

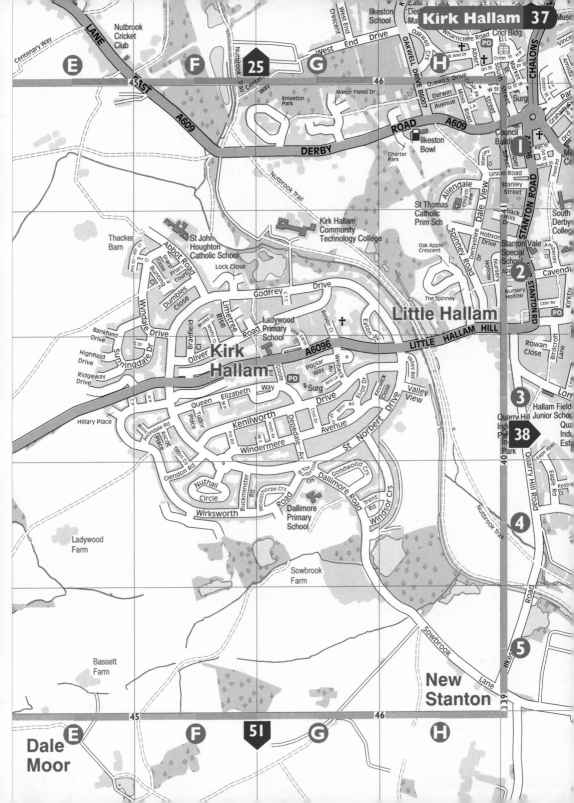

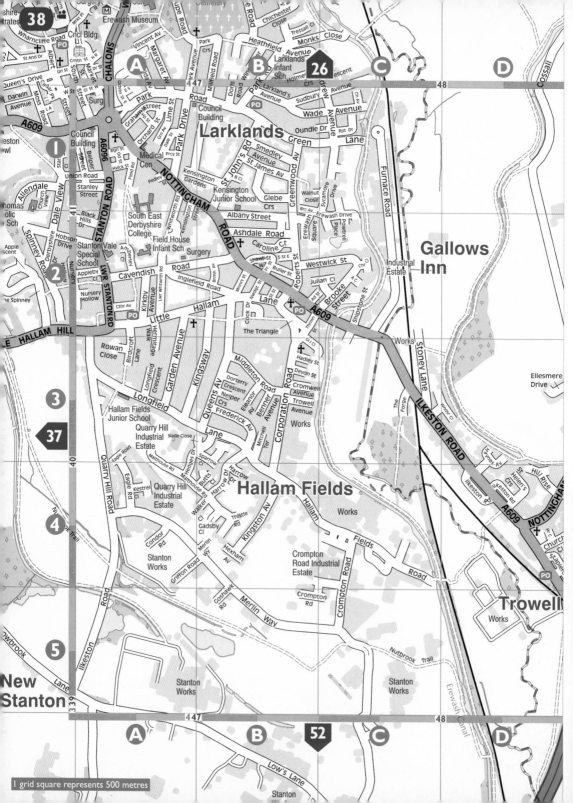

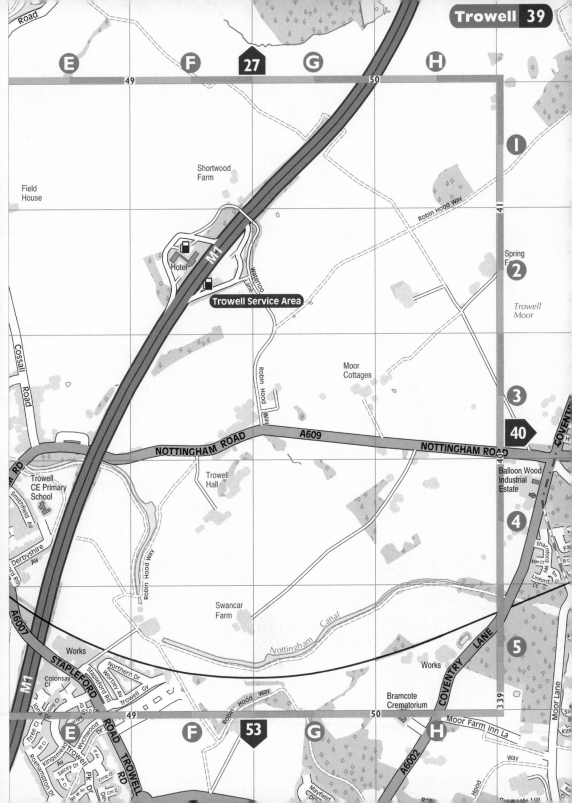

E F 27 G H

I

Road

Shortwood
Farm

Field
House

Robin Hood Way

M1

Spring F
2

Trowell
Moor

Hotel

Waterloo Lane

🏨 Trowell Service Area

Robin Hood Way

Moor
Cottages

3

40

COVENTRY

Cossall Road

NOTTINGHAM ROAD   A609   NOTTINGHAM ROAD

Balloon Wood
Industrial
Estate

Trowell
CE Primary
School

Trowell
Hall

4

Shacebord Rd
Edin Ct
Linford

RD

Smithfield Av

Derbyshire Av

Robin Hood Way

Swancar
Farm

Canal

Works

Nottingham

5

COVENTRY LANE

Moor Lane

A6007

Works

Bramcote
Crematorium

STAPLEFORD

M1

Colonsay Cl

Northern Dr
Wortley Av
Stapleford Rd
Trowell Cv

Robin Hood Way

Moor Farm Inn La

Iona Dr

Kingsmead Av
Wynchwood Dr
Saicey Dr

E F 53 G H

ROAD TROWELL RD

A6002

Mayfield

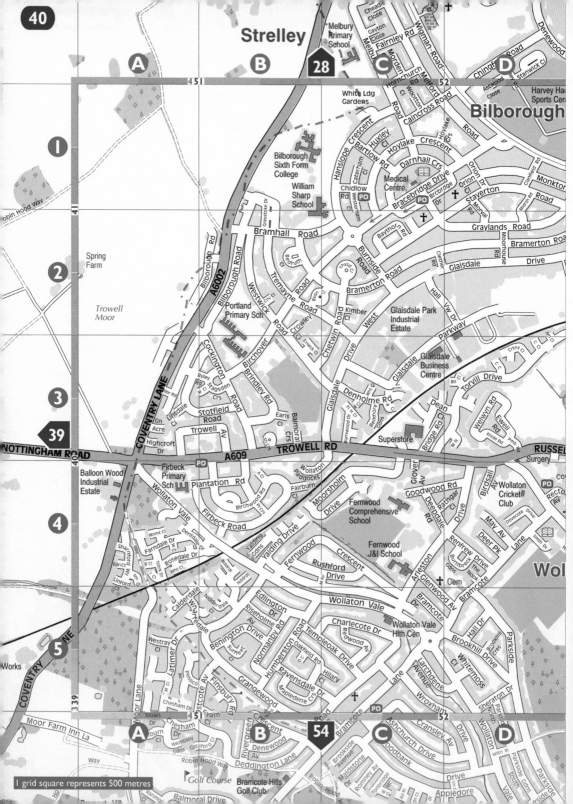

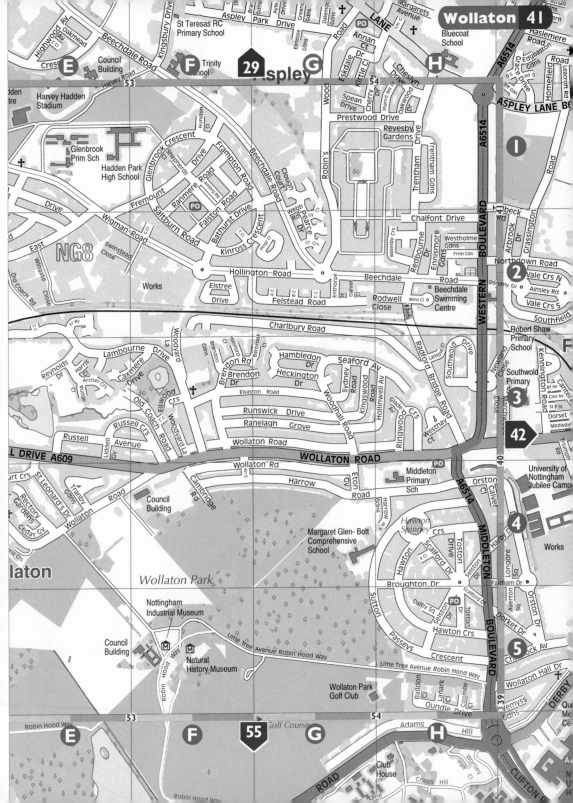

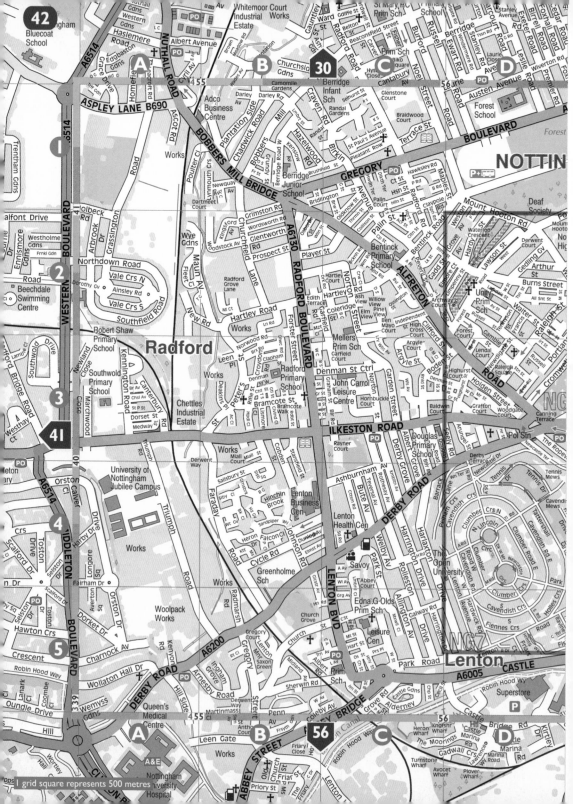

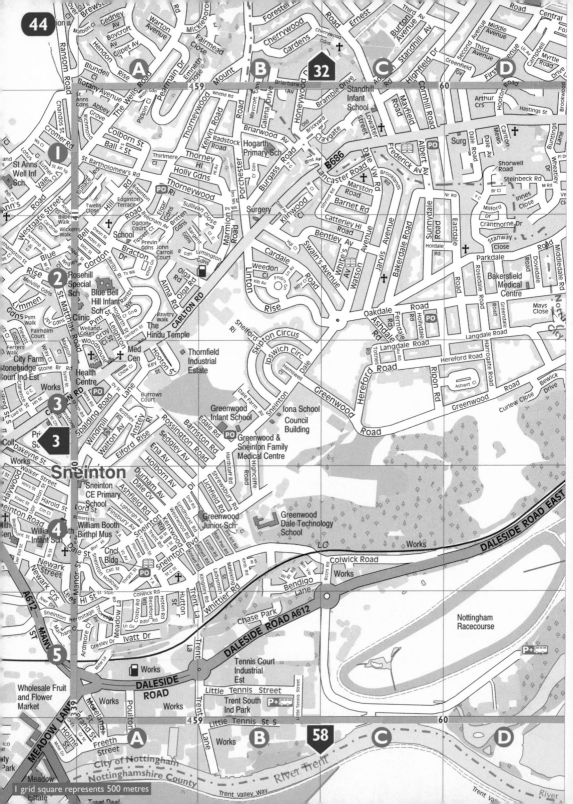

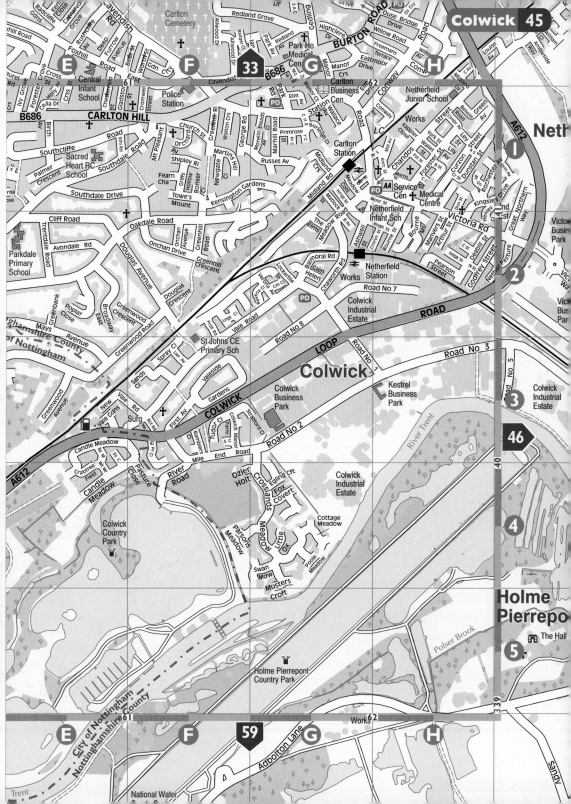

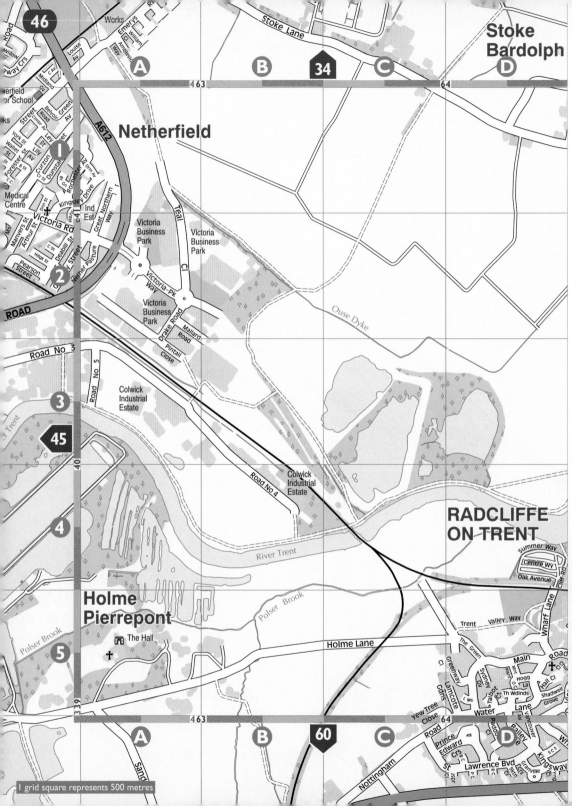

46

Stoke Lane

Stoke Bardolph

A B **34** C D

4 63 64

Netherfield

A612

1

Medical Centre

Victoria Rd

Victoria Business Park

Teal Cl

Victoria Business Park

2

ROAD

Victoria Pk Way

Victoria Business Park

Drake Road

Mallard Road

Pintail Close

Ouse Dyke

Road No 3

Road No 5

3

Colwick Industrial Estate

River Trent

45

40

Road No 4

Colwick Industrial Estate

RADCLIFFE ON TRENT

4

Summer Way

Centre Wy

Oak Avenue

Cliff Rd

5

Holme Pierrepont

The Hall

Polser Brook

Polser Brook

339

Holme Lane

Trent Valley Way

Wharf Lane

The Green

Main

Road

Hall Cl

Shadwell Grove

Lane

A 4 63 B **60** C D

64

Yew Tree Close

Water

Lawrence Blvd

Prince Edward Crs

Kingsway

Nottingham

Sandhu

St Luke's Way **E**

Stanhope Crescent

F

35

G

H

Field Lane

Shelford Hill

65

66

41

1

2

Shelford Lodge Farm

Ridge Lane

Valley Road

Shelford Road

Trent Valley Way

River Trent

Trent Vw Cdns

Cliff Drive

Hopewell Close

Welbeck Rd

Chatsworth Av

Clumber Drive

3

40

Spellow Farm

4

ROAD

Rockley Park Road

Cliff Av

Cliff Crs

Grandfield Gdns

Grandfield Av

Cliff Way

Westcliffe Avenue

Wakefield Av

Butler Av

Birkin Av

Penrith Avenue

Newstead

H Wy

Thoresby Dr

Newton Av

Thoresby Cl

Trent Valley Way

Hamilton Drive

Stanford Gdns

Oak Tree Av

Fernwood Drive

Chestnut Grove

Shelford Road

Queen's Road

Malkin Av

The Crescent

Works

South Avenue

GRANTHAM

Nursery Cl

Nursery Rd

Woodside Av

Harlequin Mews

Thomas Av

Northfield

Avenue

Morton Close

Morton Gdns

Rushcliffe Avenue

Radcliffe Stn

New Rd

Lorne Gv

Brookfield Cl

Bingham Road

Eastwood Road

Palm Gdns

Breydon

Golf Road

Gatcombe Close

Harewood Close

A52(T)

Johns Road

Carter Av

Brickyard La

Marl Rd

Blakeney Road

Woodside Rd

Dormy Cl

Woodland Cl

Covert Crs

Meadow End

Harlequin

5

339

Mayfair

Walnut Grove

Station Terr

Botton Cl

Health Centre

PO

Walker's Yd

Richmond Dr

Albert St

Lincoln St

Victoria St

Vers Gv

Cropwell Road

Glebe Lane

Radcliffe on Trent Infant School

Dayncourt School

Hillside Rd

Lime Cl

Maple Cl

Beech Cl

Sycamore Cl

Willow Cl

Cherry Tree Close

Cropwell Gardens

Radcliffe on Trent Junior School

Cemetery

Carnarvon La

Avenue

Wentworth

E

65

F

61

G

Radcliffe on Trent Golf Club

Dewberry Lane

H

A52(T)

Cropwell Road

◤ *Golf Course*

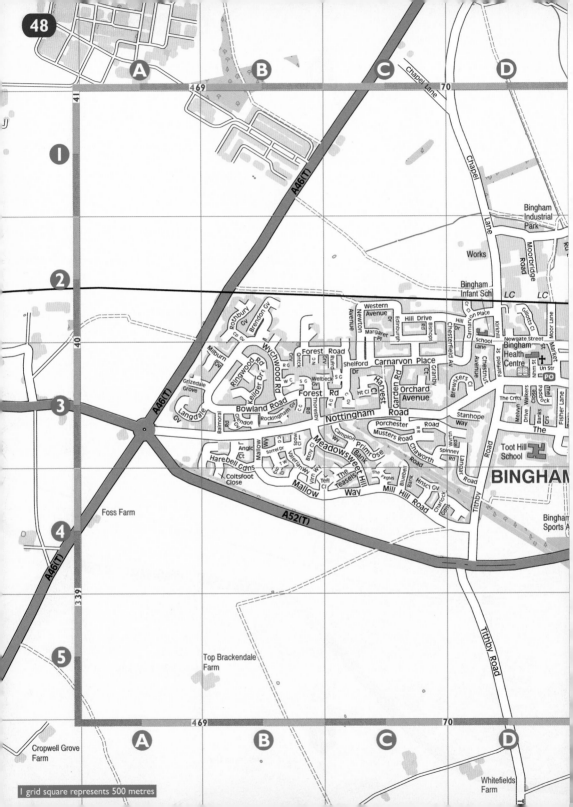

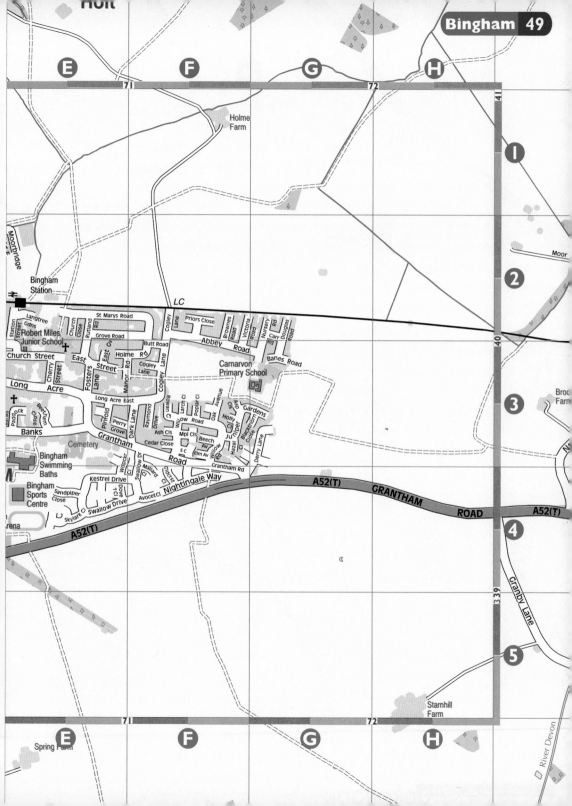

Holt

E F G H

71 72 41

I

Holme
Farm

Moor

2

Moorbridge Lane

Bingham
Station

LC

Bingham
Station

40

Langtree Gdns
Station Street
Robert Miles
Junior School
Church Street

St Marys Road
Church Close
Rutland
Grove Road

Cogley Lane
Priors Close
Browne Road
Victoria Road
Nursery Rd
Carr Rd
Douglas Road

Butt Road
Abbey Road
Banes Road

3

Brook
Farm

East Street
Fosters Lane
East Gv
Holme Rd
Manor Rd
Cogley Lane
Cogley Lane
Carnarvon
Primary School

East Street
Cherry Street

Long Acre
Beck Dam Close
Paddock Close
Banks

Long Acre East
Pinfold
Perry Grove
Dark Lane
Ash Cls
Cedar Close
Mpl Cls
Raymond Drive
Willow Road
Larch Cl
Poplar Cl
Oak Avenue
Beech Av
S C
Holly Cl
Juniper
Hazel Cl
Blackthorn Close
Gardens
Derry Lane

Cemetery
Grantham
Road
Grantham Rd

Bingham
Swimming
Baths

Bingham
Sports
Centre

Kestrel Drive
Sandpiper Close
Skylark Cl
Swallow Drive
Dove Cl
Mallard
Swallow Dr
Wdcck Cl
Avocet Cl
Nightingale Way
Chfnce

A52(T) GRANTHAM ROAD A52(T)

4

Granby Lane

A339

Arena
A52(T)

5

Starnhill
Farm

Spring Farm E F G H

71 72

River Devon

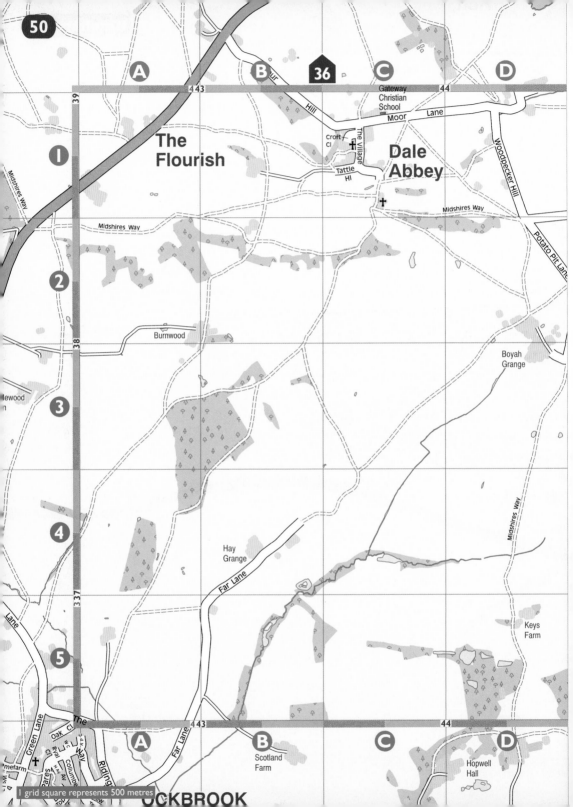

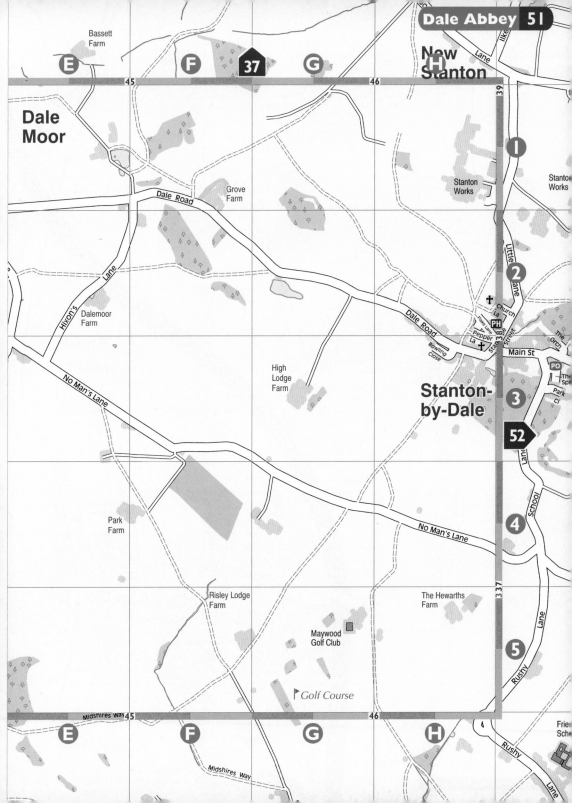

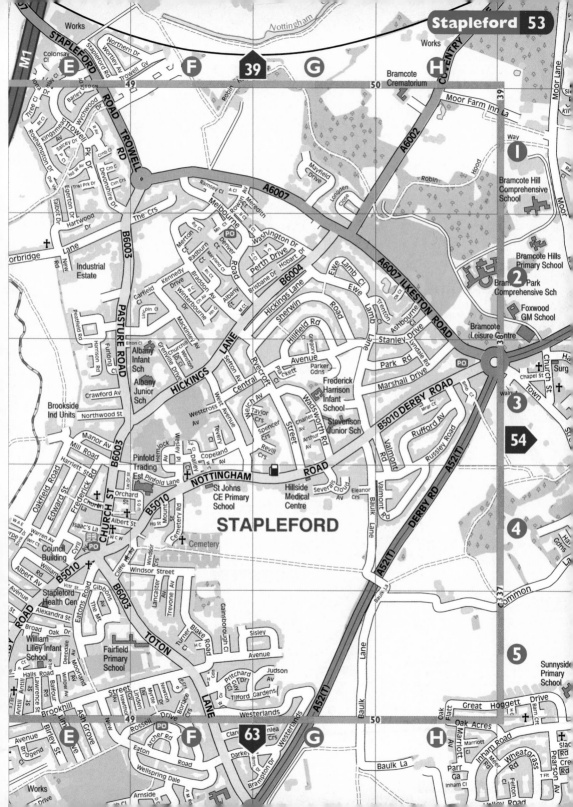

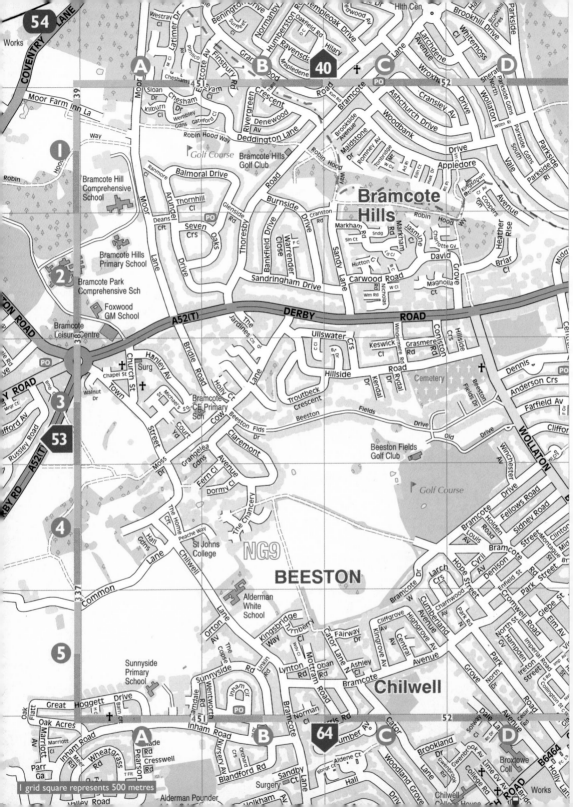

Grid references: 54 · 40 · 53 · 64

Major roads and features:
- COVENTRY LANE
- Moor Farm Inn La
- DERBY ROAD / A52(T)
- WOLLATON
- Robin Hood Way

Schools and institutions:
- Bramcote Hill Comprehensive School
- Bramcote Hills Primary School
- Bramcote Park Comprehensive Sch
- Foxwood GM School
- Bramcote Leisure Centre
- Bramcote CE Primary Sch
- St Johns College
- Alderman White School
- Sunnyside Primary School
- Chilwell College House
- Broxtowe Coll

Place names:
- Bramcote Hills
- BEESTON
- Chilwell
- NG9

Golf courses:
- Bramcote Hills Golf Club
- Beeston Fields Golf Club
- Golf Course

Selected street names:
- Latimer Dr, Westray Cl, Chesham, Eyam Cl, Denewood, Rivergreen, Balmoral Drive, Thornhill Cl, Seven Oaks Crs, Arundel Drive, Thoresby, Burnside Drive, Bankfield Drive, Warrender Close, Sandringham Drive, Deddington Lane, Benington Drive, Normanby, Humberston, Ravensdale, Hilary, Wroxham, Cransley Av, Ashchurch Drive, Woodbank, Maldstone, Romney Av, Torbridge, Appledore, Parkside Gdns, Wollaton Vale, Parkside Rd, Markham, Jasmine Cl, Carwood Road, Magnolia Ct, David Grove, Heather Rise, Briar Cl
- Ullswater, Keswick Cl, Grasmere Rd, Coniston Rd, Hillside Road, Rydal Dr, Kendal Dr, Windermere Rd, Dennis, Anderson Crs, Farfield Av, Troutbeck Crescent, Beeston Flds Dr, Claremont Avenue, Fern Cl, Dormy Cl, The Chancery, Beeston Fields, Winchester Drive, Bramcote Dr, Holden Road, Fellows Road, Sidney Road, Louis Av, Cyril Av, Denison St, Enfield St, Montague, Clinton, Park Street, Cromwell Road, Glebe St, Elm Av, North St, Hampden St, Imperial Road, Ireton St, Collington
- Hanley Av, Bridle Road, Holly Ct, Church St, Walnut Dr, Town St, Cow Lane, Moss Dr, Grangelea Gdns, Hall Gdns, Chilwell Lane, Common, Otton Av, Kingsbridge Way, Turnberry Cl, Mottram Rd, Lynton Rd, Oban Rd, Ashley Cl, Fairway Dr, Kingrove Av, Cumberland Av, Highgrove Av, Central Avenue, Charnwood, Bramcote Av, Hope Drive, Larch Crs
- Wheatgrass Rd, Cresswell Rd, Great Hoggett Drive, Oak Flatt, Oak Acres, Marriott Cl, Parr Ga, Inham Road, Nursey Av, Blandford Rd, Sandby Ct, Sunnyside Rd, Wentworth, Holkham Av, Norman Cl, Humber Av, Aldene Ct, Woodland Grove, Brookland Dr, Gwenbrook Av, Lime Gv, College Rd, Cedar Rd, Solway, Dale La, B6464, Valley Road, Alderman Pounder

Works (top left, Coventry Lane)

Scale: 1 grid square represents 500 metres

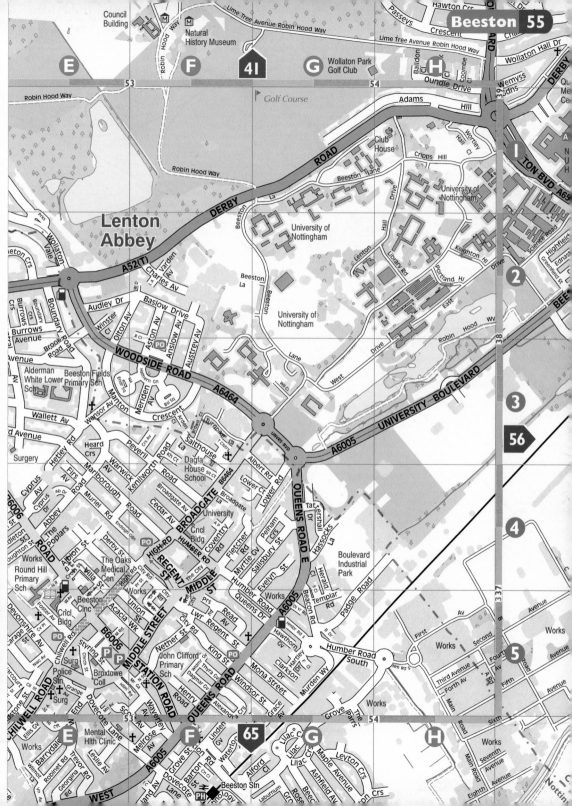

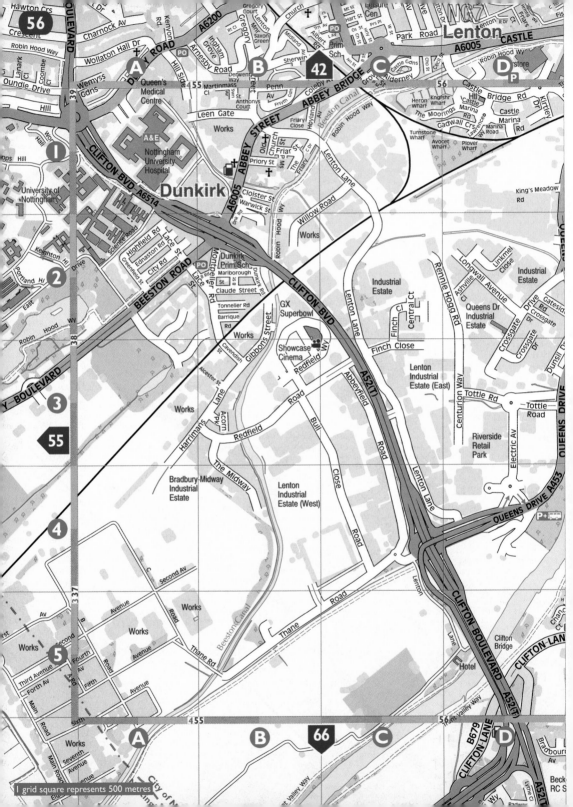

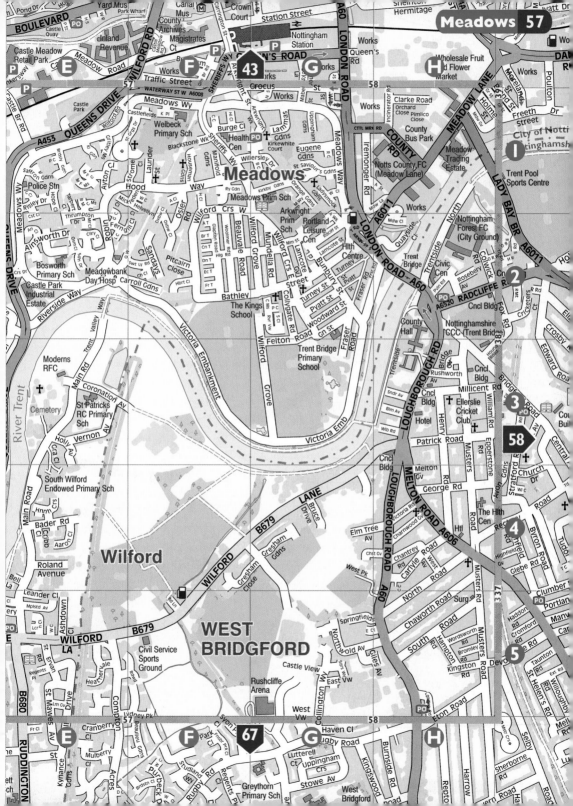

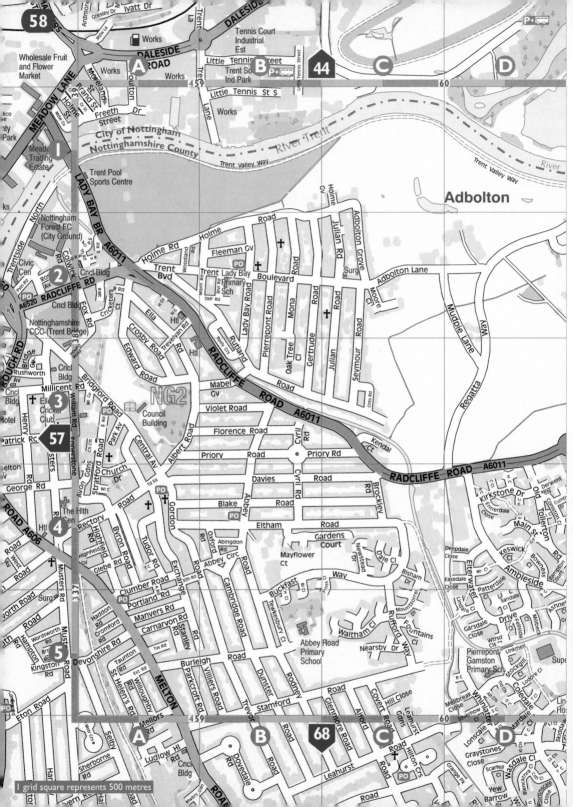

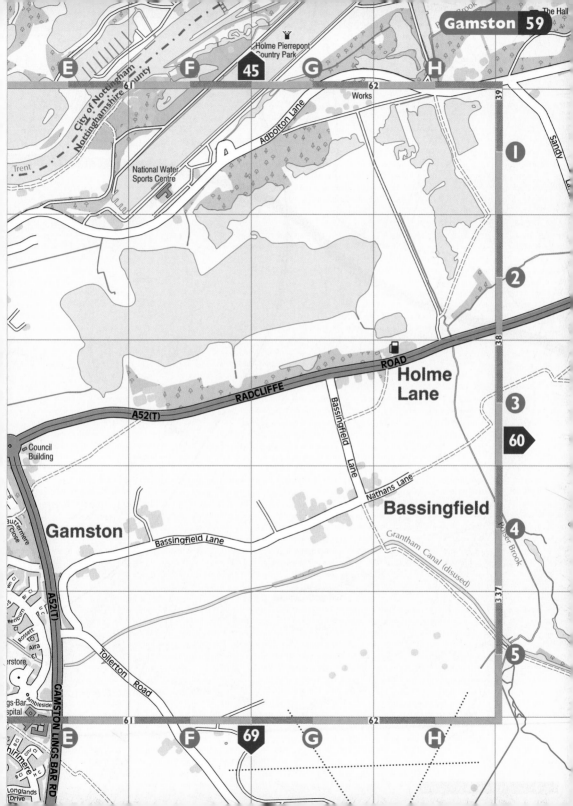

The Hall

E

F

45

G

H

City of Nottingham
Nottinghamshire County

Holme Pierrepont
Country Park

Works

Adbolton Lane

I

Sandy

Trent

National Water
Sports Centre

2

ROAD

Holme
Lane

RADCLIFFE

A52(T)

Bassingfield Lane

3

60

Council
Building

Nathans Lane

Bassingfield

Grantham Canal (disused)

4

Posser Brook

Gamston

Buttermere Close

Bassingfield Lane

5

A52(T)

Tollerton Road

rstore

GAMSTON LINGS BAR RD

Ambleside

ngs Bar
spital

Longlands
Drive

E

61

F

69

G

H

62

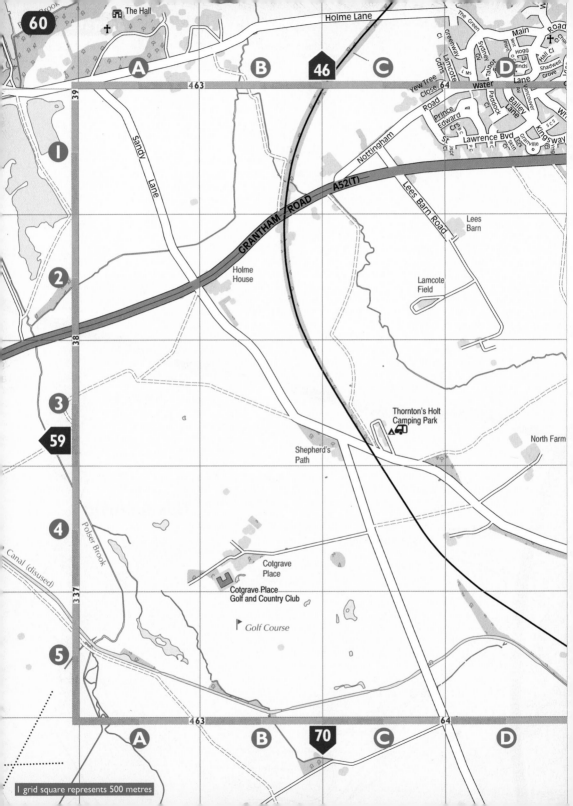

60

The Hall

Holme Lane

A **B** **46** **C** **D**

The Green

greenway
Sydney
Main Road

Hogg
Mnt

Lamcote Gdns

Talbot
Linds
Hall Cl
Shadwell

46
Yew Tree
Close 64
Water
Lane

Bailey
Lane
Kingsway

1

39

Sandy
Lane

Road
Prince
Edward
Crs
Lawrence Bvd

Paddock

SCS

St

Nottingham

2

38

GRANTHAM ROAD A52(T)

Holme
House

Lees Barn Road

Lees
Barn

Lamcote
Field

3

Thornton's Holt
Camping Park

North Farm

59

Shepherd's
Path

4

Polser Brook

Canal (disused)

Cotgrave Place

Cotgrave Place
Golf and Country Club

5

337

Golf Course

A 463 **B** **70** **C** 64 **D**

1 grid square represents 500 metres

A52(T)

Bingham
Eastwood Road
Gatcombe close
Golf Road
Harew Close
A52(T)
Johns Road
Marl Rd
Blakeney Road
Woodland Cl
Cove
Crs
Mayfair

PO
Health
Centre
Cemetery
Richmond
Walker's Cl
Albert St
Lincoln St
Victoria St
Glebe
Lane
Cropwell
Gardens
Radcliffe on
Trent Infant
School
Daycourt
School

E   **F**   **47**   **G**   **H**

Hmrstn

Lime Cl
Maple
Beech Cl
Sycamore Cl
Willow Cl
Radcliffe on
Trent Junior
School
Cherry Tree Close
Cropwell Road

66

39

1

Cropwell Road
Dewberry Lane
Radcliffe on Trent
Golf Club
Golf Course

A52(T)

2

38
Cropw

Hall
Farm

New B
Farm

3

4

3337

5

Hollygate
Farm

Grantham Canal (disused)

65   66

E   **F**   **71**   **G**   **H**

Hollygate Lane

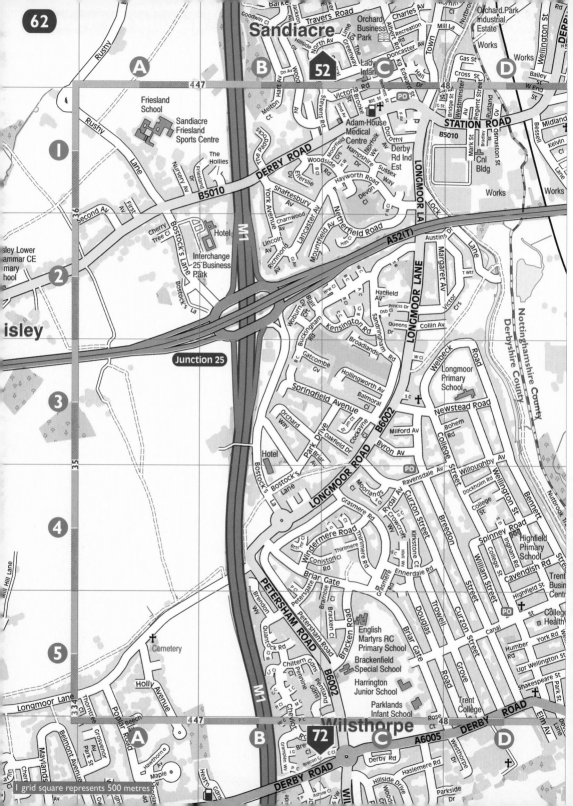

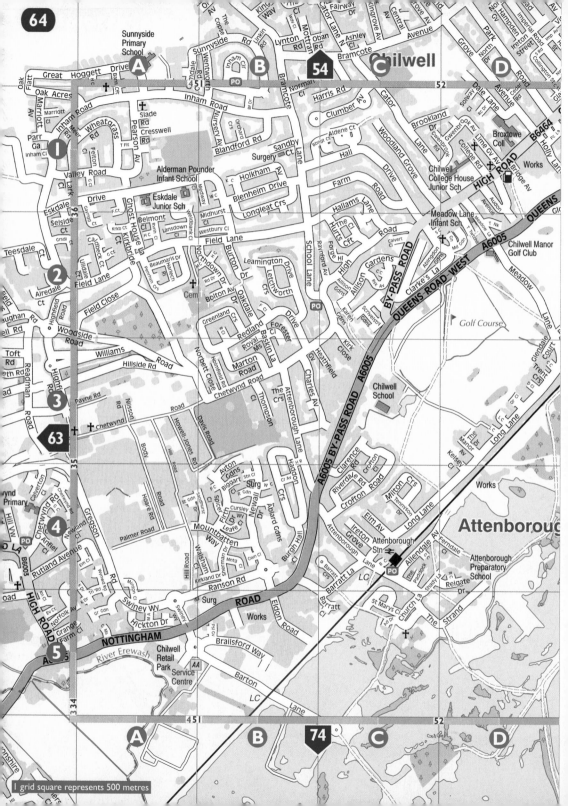

I grid square represents 500 metres

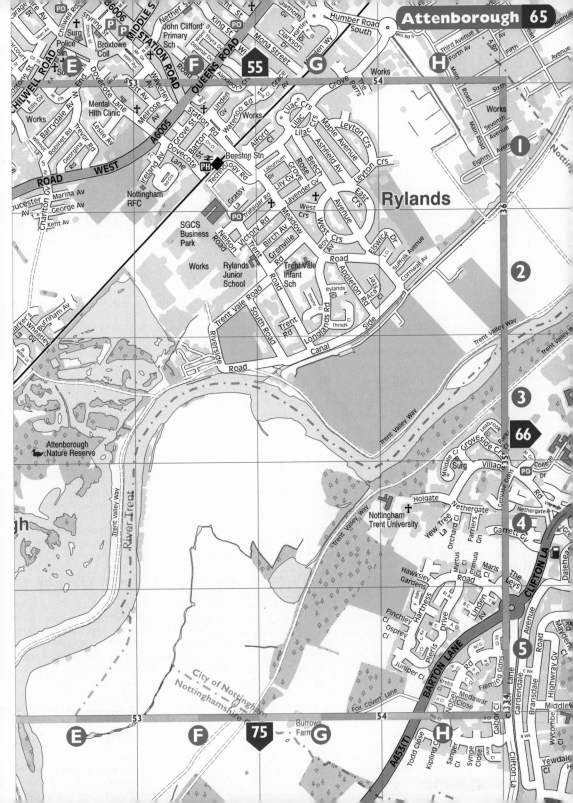

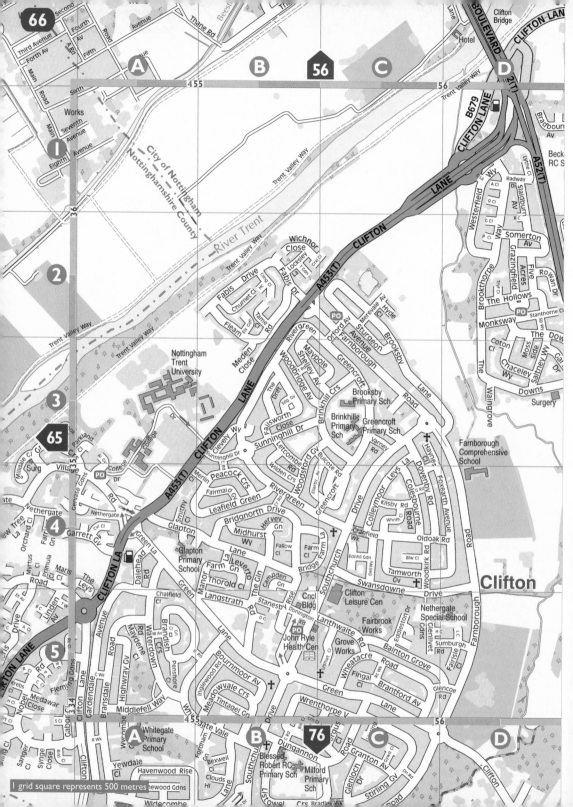

1 grid square represents 500 metres

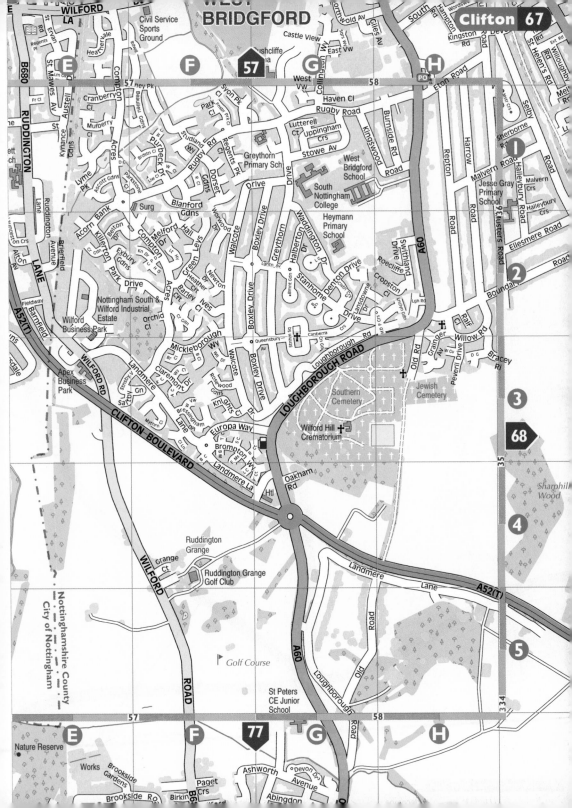

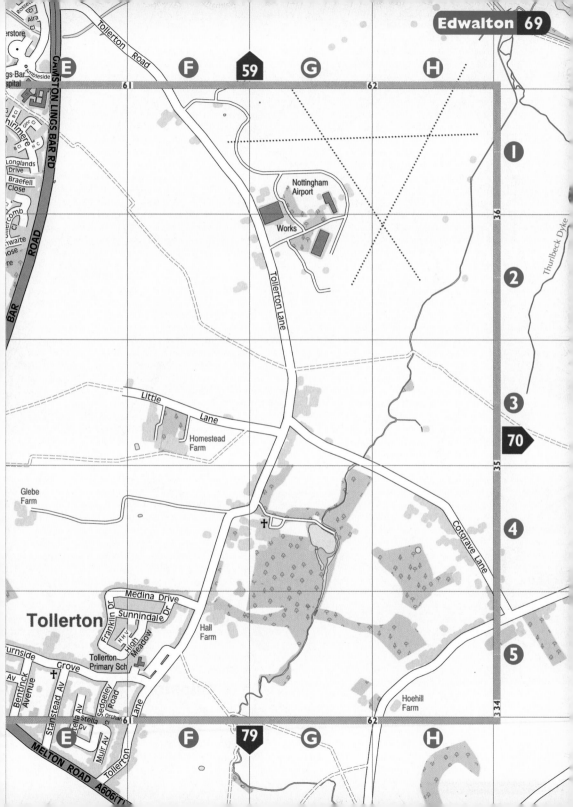

E
F
59
G
H

I

2

3

70

4

5

36

35

34

61

62

Tollerton Road

Nottingham
Airport

Works

Tollerton Lane

Thurlbeck Dyke

Little

Lane

Homestead
Farm

Glebe
Farm

Cotgrave Lane

Medina Drive

Sunnindale

Franklin Dr

High Meadow

Tollerton

Tollerton
Primary Sch

Grove

Hall
Farm

Hoehill
Farm

Burnside

Bentinck

Avenue

Ranstead Av

Stella Av

Stella Cv

Seddeley Road

Orchard

Muir Av

Tollerton Lane

E
F
79
G
H

MELTON ROAD A606(T)

GAMSTON LINGS BAR RD

BAR
ROAD

Gamston
Hospital

Longlands
Drive

Braefell
Close

Ambleside

Thirlmere

Rossett

Alra
Cl

erstore

ings Bar

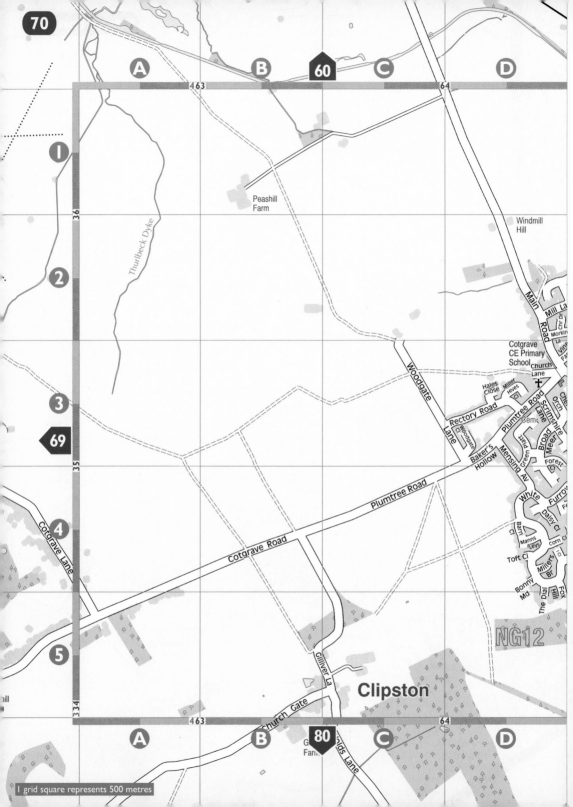

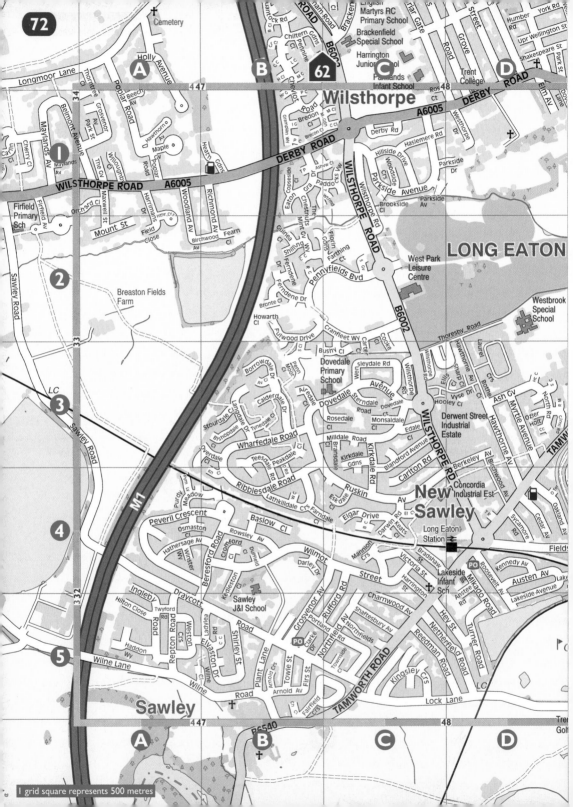

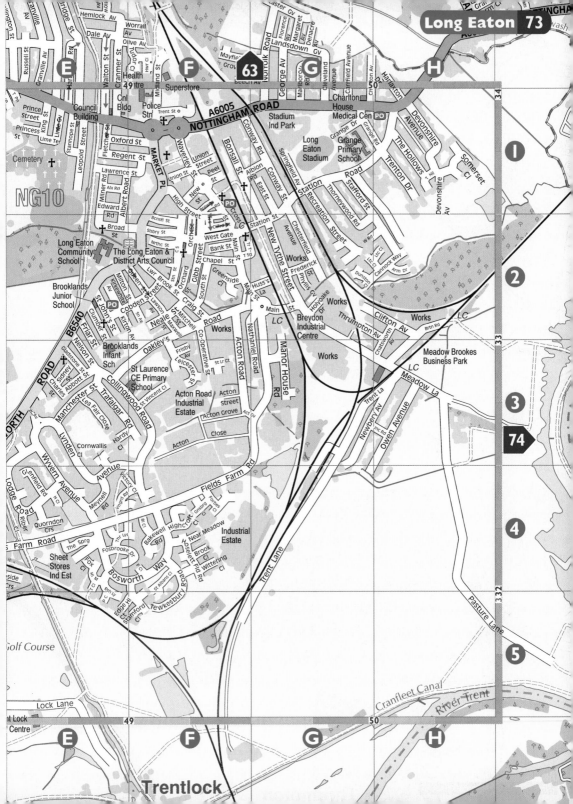

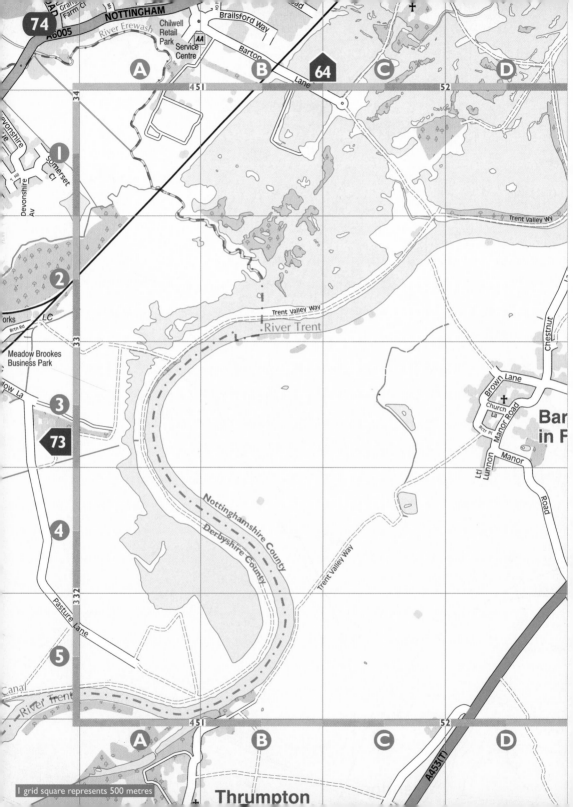

74
A6005

NOTTINGHAM

River Erewash

Graham Farm Cl

Brailsford Way

Chilwell Retail Park

Barton Lane

AA Service Centre

A   **B**   **64**   **C**   **D**

34   451   52

Devonshire

Somerset Cl

1

T. Hill

Devonshire Av

2

orks   Brtn Rd   LC

33

Meadow Brookes Business Park

w La

3

73

4

332

Pasture Lane

5

Canal

River Trent

Trent Valley Wy

Trent Valley Way

River Trent

Nottinghamshire County

Derbyshire County

Trent Valley Way

Chestnut

Brown Lane

Church La

Rctr Pl

Manor Road

**Bar
in F**

Ltl Lunnon

Manor

Road

A   **B**   **C**   **D**

451   52

A453(T)

Thrumpton

I grid square represents 500 metres

E F **65** G **H**

City of Nottingham
Northamptonshire County

I

53 54

Juniper Cl

BARTON

Clifton Lane

Fox Covert Lane

Fleming Gdns
Cardendale
Bransdale
Highway Ct
Middlefel

Medawar
Close
Nobel

Wycombe
Cl

R Wk

Yewdale
Cl

Hav
Pir
W

PO

Farnbo

Avebury

Burrows
Farm

Todd Close
Kipling Cl

Sanger
Cl

Synge
Close

Chisbury
Cl Gn
Chernil Cl

Scafell

Summerwood La

Barbury Dr Silbury Cl

2

A453(T)

Nottingham Road

STREET

Barton
Lodge

Brown

Lane

3

76 Clifton
Pasture

ton
FABIS

GREEN

Barton

Lane

4

A453(T)

Barton
Moor

Glebe
Farm

5

53 54

E F G Nottingham Road **H**

Trent Valley Way

33

332

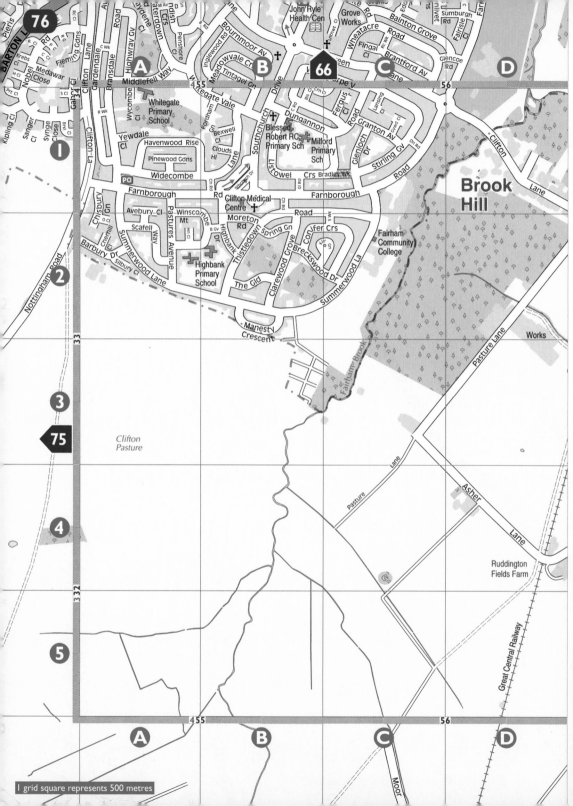

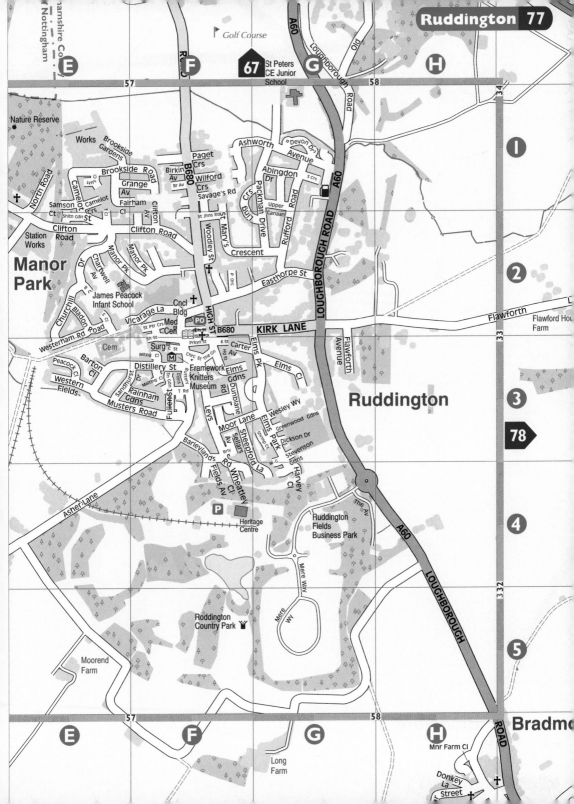

Golf Course

67 St Peters CE Junior School

E   F   G   H

Nottinghamshire Co.
Nottingham

Nature Reserve

Works   Brookside Gardens

Paget Crs

Birkin Av   Wilford Crs

Br Av   Savage's Rd

Brookside Road

Grange Av

Fairham Cl

Camelot Crs

Samson Ct   Camelot St

Shltn Gdn

North Road

Clifton Road

Clifton Road   Clifton Road

Station Works

Manor Park

Chartwell Av   Manor Pk Dr   Manor Pk

James Peacock Infant School

Churchill   Bladon Road

Westerham Rd

Cem

Barton Cl

Peacock Cl   Sandhurst

Western Fields

Rainham Gdns

Musters Road

Vicarage La   Cncl Bldg

St Ptr Crs   Med Cen

Surg

Distillery St

Framework Knitters Museum

Fulham St   Leys

Malting   Bramery

Moor Lane

Barleylands Rd

Wheatley Cl

Sheepfold La

Fields Av

Ashworth   Avenue

Devon Dr

Abingdon Dr   S Crs

Packman Drive

Upper Canaan

Rufford Road

Loughborough Road

St Mary's

Woodley St

Crescent

Easthorpe St

KIRK LANE   B680

Carter Av

Elms Pk

Elms Cl

Elms Gdns

Dunblane Rd

Wesley Wy

Greenwood Gdns

Dickson Dr

Stevenson Gdns

Harvey Cl

Elms Park

LOUGHBOROUGH ROAD

Flawforth

Flawforth Avenue

Flawford House Farm

Ruddington

78

The Av

A60

Asher Lane

P

Heritage Centre

Ruddington Fields Business Park

Mere Way

Roddington Country Park

Mere Wy

Moorend Farm

E   F   G   H

Bradmo

Long Farm

Mnr Farm Cl

Donkey La Street

ROAD

I

2

3

4

5

57   58

33

332

34

Farm

Tollerton
Primary Sch

Turnside

Grove

High Meadow

Bentinck Avenue

Av

Stanstead Av

Stella Gv

Stella Av

Orchard Cl

Sedgeley Road

Muir Av

Tollerton Lane

E

F

69

G

Hoehill
Farm

H

62

34

MELTON ROAD A606(T)

I

Main Road

Cotgrave Road

Clipston
Lane

The Levs

2

33

Saddlers
Yard

Church La

Fellows Yard

Bradley's Yard

Melton Road

Old Road

Cotgrave Road

A606(T)

Normanton-

Plumtree School

Plumtree

Back Lane

3

Chestnut
Farm

Station Road

80

Bradmore Lane

A606(T)

33 2

4

**Plumtree
Park**

Park Road

Park Ter

Park Avenue

Platt Lane

62

5

Normanto
Wolds

Crossdale
Drive Primary
School

Green
Cl

Poplars Cl

Parkside

Brockdale Gdns

Briar Close

Hillcrest
Rd

Highbury Road

Delville Avenue

Rancliffe Av

Bennet Cl

Belvedere Cl

Highfield Road

Abbot
Close

Bishops
Close

S C

Crossdale Drive

Brockwood

Rose Gv

Villa Road

Adams Hill

Clifford Close

Normanton Lane

Lowlands Drive

Wolds Cl

Covert Cl

Drive

E

Debdale

61

Spinney Road

Gorse Rd

Hayes Road

Plantation Road

Intake Road

Fairham Rd

Rose

Thelda Avenue

Debdale
La

Dale Road

Lane

F

82

Ashley Road

Uncombe Cl

Walton Drive

Wynbreck Drive

Ashley Crs

Crantock Gdns

Rannock Gardens

G

Wolds
Ri

Cherry Hl

Mount

High View Avenue

ow Drive

K H worth

Nich

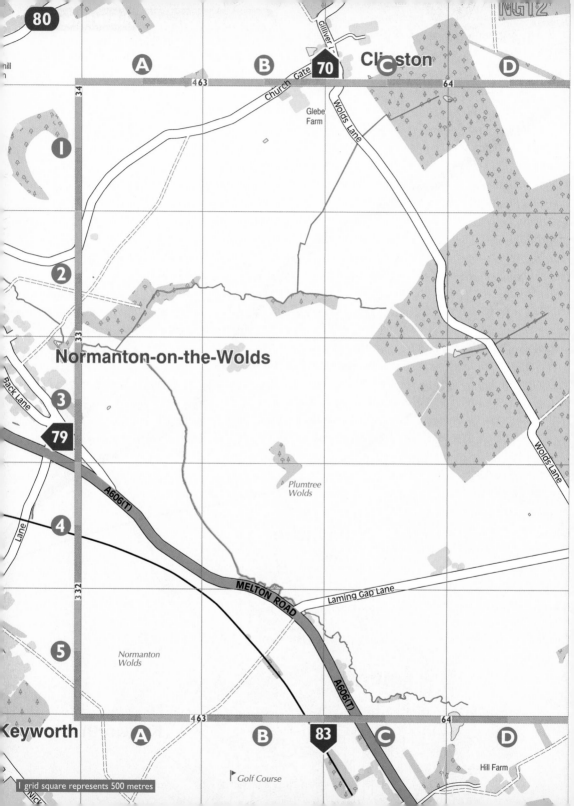

NG12

A 463 **B** Church Gate **70** **C** Cli ston **D** 64

Gillivel La

1

Glebe
Farm

Wolds Lane

2

Normanton-on-the-Wolds

Back Lane

3

79

A606(T)

Lane

4

Plumtree
Wolds

MELTON ROAD

Laming Gap Lane

5

Normanton
Wolds

A606(T)

Keyworth

A 463 **B** **83** **C** 64 **D**

Hill Farm

Golf Course

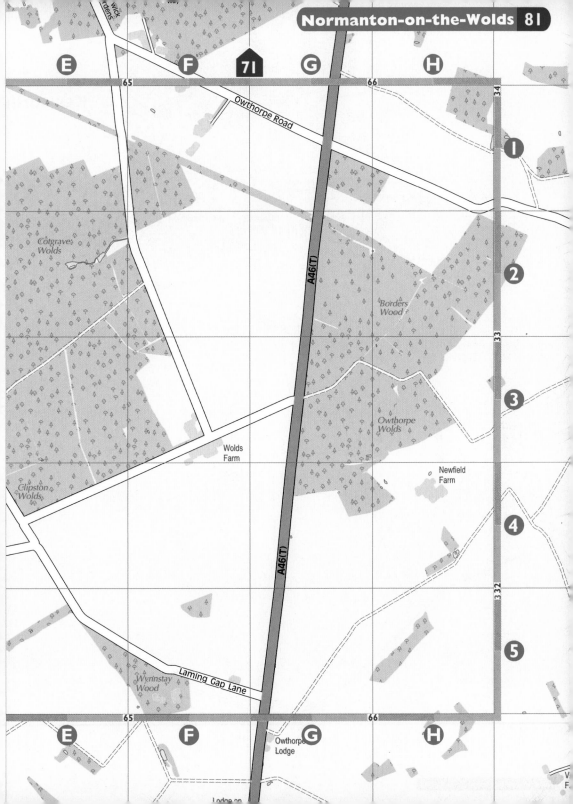

E F 71 G H

65 66 34

Owthorpe Road

I

Cotgrave
Wolds

A46(T)

Borders
Wood

2

33

3

Owthorpe
Wolds

Wolds
Farm

Newfield
Farm

Clipston
Wolds

4

A46(T)

332

5

Laming Gap Lane

Wyrinstay
Wood

65 66

E F G H

Owthorpe
Lodge

Lodge on

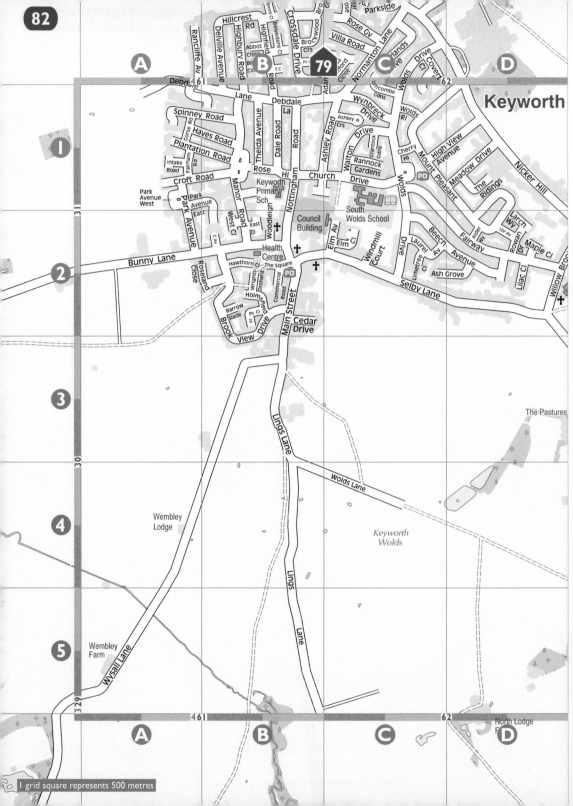

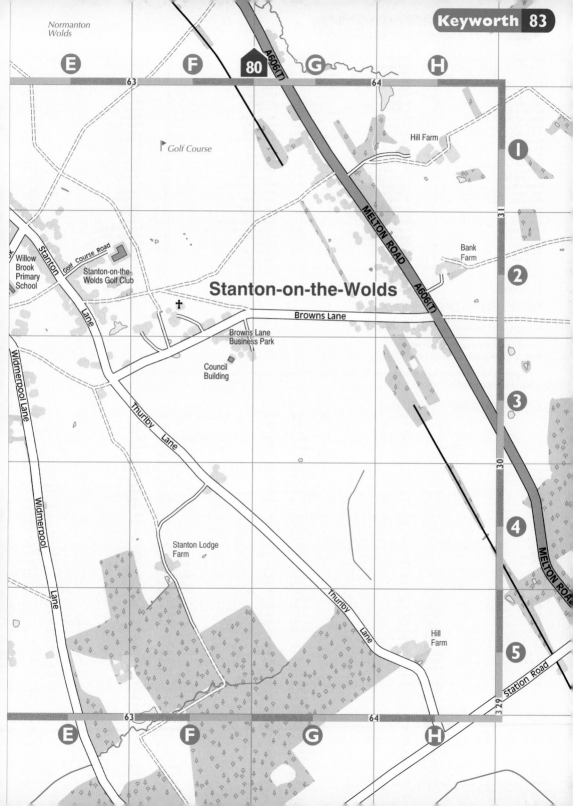

Normanton Wolds

E 63 F 80 A606(T) G 64 H

I

31

▶ *Golf Course*

Hill Farm

Willow
Brook
Primary
School

Stanton

Golf Course Road

Stanton-on-the-
Wolds Golf Club

†

Bank
Farm

2

Stanton-on-the-Wolds

Browns Lane

MELTON ROAD

A606(T)

Widmerpool Lane

Browns Lane
Business Park

Council
Building

Thurlby Lane

3

30

Widmerpool Lane

Stanton Lodge
Farm

Thurlby Lane

4

MELTON ROAD

Hill
Farm

5

Station Road

32 29

E 63 F 64 G H

Adbolton 58 C1	Cossall 26 D4	Langley Mill 7 E4	Redhill 19 H1
Aldercar 6 C3	Cossall Marsh 26 D3	Larklands 38 B1	Ruddington 77 G3
Arnold 20 B3	Cotgrave 71 G4	Lenton 42 D5	Ruffs 10 D2
Aspley 29 G5	Cotmanhay 25 H1	Lenton Abbey 55 E2	Rylands 65 H1
Attenborough 64 D4	Dale Abbey 50 C1	Linby 5 F1	St Ann's 3 H1
Awsworth 26 D1	Dale Moor 51 E1	Little Hallam 37 H2	Sandiacre 52 B5
Babbington 27 F1	Daybrook 19 G3	Long Eaton 72 D2	Sawley 72 A5
Barton in Fabis 74 D3	Dunkirk 56 A1	Loscoe 6 A3	Sherwood 31 E2
Bassingfield 59 H4	Eastwood 7 H4	Manor Park 77 E2	Shipley 12 D3
Beauvale 4 C5	Edwalton 68 B3	Mapperley 24 C2	Shipley Common 25 G2
Beauvale 8 D4	The Flourish 50 A1	Mapperley 31 H2	Stanton-by-Dale 51 H3
Beeston 54 B4	Gallows Inn 38 C2	Mapperley Park 31 F4	Stanton Gate 52 D3
Bestwood 18 D3	Gamston 59 E4	Maripool 12 C2	Stanton-on-the-Wolds 83 F2
Bilborough 40 D1	Gedling 33 G3	Meadows 57 F1	Stapleford 53 F4
Bingham 48 D4	Giltbrook 14 D2	Moorgreen 9 E3	Stoke Bardolph 34 D5
Bogend 9 G5	Greasley 9 F4	Netherfield 46 A1	Strelley 28 B5
Bramcote Hills 54 C1	Hallam Fields 38 B4	New Basford 30 C4	Swingate 27 H1
Brook Hill 76 D1	Harlequin Mews 47 H5	New Eastwood 14 A2	Thorneywood 32 B5
Broomhill 11 G2	Hazelgrove 11 F2	Newlands 12 D1	Tollerton 69 E5
Broxtowe 29 E3	Heanor 6 C4	New Sawley 72 C4	Top Valley 18 D2
Bulcote 23 F4	Hempshill Vale 17 E5	New Stanton 37 H5	Toton 63 H4
Bulwell 17 F3	Highbury Vale 17 H4	Newthorpe 14 D1	Trowell 38 D5
Bulwell Forest 18 A2	Hill Top 8 C5	Newthorpe Common 14 D3	Watnall 15 H2
Burton Joyce 35 F1	Holme Lane 59 H3	Normanton-on-the-Wolds 79 H3	West Bridgford 57 F5
Carlton 32 D4	Holme Pierrepont 46 A5	Nottingham 42 D1	West Hallam 24 C5
Carrington 30 D4	Hucknall 4 C4	Nuthall 16 B5	Westville 10 D3
Chilwell 54 C5	Ilkeston 25 G3	Old Basford 30 B1	Whitemoor 30 A4
Cinderhill 29 F1	Keyworth 82 D1	Plumtree 79 G3	Wilford 57 E4
Clifton 66 D4	Kimberley 15 F4	Plumtree Park 79 F4	Wilsthorpe 72 B1
Clipston 70 C5	Kirk Hallam 37 F3	Porchester 32 C3	Wollaton 40 D4
Colwick 45 G3	Lambley 22 B3	Radcliffe on Trent 46 D4	Woodlinkin 6 A1
Common Side 12 B2	Langley 7 E5	Radford 42 A3	Woodthorpe 31 H1

USING THE STREET INDEX

Street names are listed alphabetically. Each street name is followed by its postal town or area locality, the Postcode District, the page number, and the reference to the square in which the name is found.

Standard index entries are shown as follows:

Aaron Cl *CFTN/RUD* NG11 ....**57** E4

Street names and selected addresses not shown on the map due to scale restrictions are shown in the index with an asterisk:

Aeneas Ct *MAPPK/POR/STA* * NG3....**31** E5

GENERAL ABBREVIATIONS

ACC ....ACCESS	DEPT ....DEPARTMENT	HWY ....HIGHWAY	PH ....PUBLIC HOUSE
ALY ....ALLEY	DL ....DALE	IMP ....IMPERIAL	PK ....PARK
AP ....APPROACH	DM ....DAM	IN ....INLET	PKWY ....PARKWAY
AR ....ARCADE	DR ....DRIVE	IND EST ....INDUSTRIAL ESTATE	PL ....PLACE
ASS ....ASSOCIATION	DRO ....DROVE	INF ....INFIRMARY	PLN ....PLAIN
AV ....AVENUE	DRY ....DRIVEWAY	INFO ....INFORMATION	PLNS ....PLAINS
BCH ....BEACH	DWGS ....DWELLINGS	INT ....INTERCHANGE	PLZ ....PLAZA
BLDS ....BUILDINGS	E ....EAST	IS ....ISLAND	POL ....POLICE STATION
BND ....BEND	EMB ....EMBANKMENT	JCT ....JUNCTION	PR ....PRINCE
BNK ....BANK	EMBY ....EMBASSY	JTY ....JETTY	PREC ....PRECINCT
BR ....BRIDGE	ESP ....ESPLANADE	KG ....KING	PREP ....PREPARATORY
BRK ....BROOK	EST ....ESTATE	KNL ....KNOLL	PRIM ....PRIMARY
BTM ....BOTTOM	EX ....EXCHANGE	L ....LAKE	PROM ....PROMENADE
BUS ....BUSINESS	EXPY ....EXPRESSWAY	LA ....LANE	PRS ....PRINCESS
BVD ....BOULEVARD	EXT ....EXTENSION	LDG ....LODGE	PRT ....PORT
BY ....BYPASS	F/O ....FLYOVER	LGT ....LIGHT	PT ....POINT
CATH ....CATHEDRAL	FC ....FOOTBALL CLUB	LK ....LOCK	PTH ....PATH
CEM ....CEMETERY	FK ....FORK	LKS ....LAKES	PZ ....PIAZZA
CEN ....CENTRE	FLD ....FIELD	LNDG ....LANDING	QD ....QUADRANT
CFT ....CROFT	FLDS ....FIELDS	LTL ....LITTLE	QU ....QUEEN
CH ....CHURCH	FLS ....FALLS	LWR ....LOWER	QY ....QUAY
CHA ....CHASE	FLS ....FLATS	MAG ....MAGISTRATE	R ....RIVER
CHYD ....CHURCHYARD	FM ....FARM	MAN ....MANSIONS	RBT ....ROUNDABOUT
CIR ....CIRCLE	FT ....FORT	MD ....MEAD	RD ....ROAD
CIRC ....CIRCUS	FWY ....FREEWAY	MDW ....MEADOWS	RDG ....RIDGE
CL ....CLOSE	FY ....FERRY	MEM ....MEMORIAL	REP ....REPUBLIC
CLFS ....CLIFFS	GA ....GATE	MKT ....MARKET	RES ....RESERVOIR
CMP ....CAMP	GAL ....GALLERY	MKTS ....MARKETS	RFC ....RUGBY FOOTBALL CLUB
CNR ....CORNER	GDN ....GARDEN	ML ....MALL	RI ....RISE
CO ....COUNTY	GDNS ....GARDENS	ML ....MILL	RP ....RAMP
COLL ....COLLEGE	GLD ....GLADE	MNR ....MANOR	RW ....ROW
COM ....COMMON	GLN ....GLEN	MS ....MEWS	S ....SOUTH
COMM ....COMMISSION	GN ....GREEN	MSN ....MISSION	SCH ....SCHOOL
CON ....CONVENT	GND ....GROUND	MT ....MOUNT	SE ....SOUTH EAST
COT ....COTTAGE	GRA ....GRANGE	MTN ....MOUNTAIN	SER ....SERVICE AREA
COTS ....COTTAGES	GRG ....GARAGE	MTS ....MOUNTAINS	SH ....SHORE
CP ....CAPE	GT ....GREAT	MUS ....MUSEUM	SHOP ....SHOPPING
CPS ....COPSE	GTWY ....GATEWAY	MWY ....MOTORWAY	SKWY ....SKYWAY
CR ....CREEK	GV ....GROVE	N ....NORTH	SMT ....SUMMIT
CREM ....CREMATORIUM	HGR ....HIGHER	NE ....NORTH EAST	SOC ....SOCIETY
CRS ....CRESCENT	HL ....HILL	NW ....NORTH WEST	SP ....SPUR
CSWY ....CAUSEWAY	HLS ....HILLS	O/P ....OVERPASS	SPR ....SPRING
CT ....COURT	HO ....HOUSE	OFF ....OFFICE	SQ ....SQUARE
CTRL ....CENTRAL	HOL ....HOLLOW	ORCH ....ORCHARD	ST ....STREET
CTS ....COURTS	HOSP ....HOSPITAL	OV ....OVAL	STN ....STATION
CTYD ....COURTYARD	HRB ....HARBOUR	PAL ....PALACE	STR ....STREAM
CUTT ....CUTTINGS	HTH ....HEATH	PAS ....PASSAGE	STRD ....STRAND
CV ....COVE	HTS ....HEIGHTS	PAV ....PAVILION	SW ....SOUTH WEST
CYN ....CANYON	HVN ....HAVEN	PDE ....PARADE	TDG ....TRADING

85

TER	TERRACE	TWR	TOWER	VIL	VILLA	WHF	WHARF
THWY	THROUGHWAY	U/P	UNDERPASS	VIS	VISTA	WK	WALK
TNL	TUNNEL	UNI	UNIVERSITY	VLG	VILLAGE	WKS	WALKS
TOLL	TOLLWAY	UPR	UPPER	VLS	VILLAS	WLS	WELLS
TPK	TURNPIKE	V	VALE	VW	VIEW	WY	WAY
TR	TRACK	VA	VALLEY	W	WEST	YD	YARD
TRL	TRAIL	VIAD	VIADUCT	WD	WOOD	YHA	YOUTH HOSTEL

POSTCODE TOWNS AND AREA ABBREVIATIONS

ARN	Arnold
BING/VBLV	Bingham/Vale of Belvoir
BLWL	Bulwell
BSTN/STPLFD	Beeston/Stapleford
BWSH/BRSTN	Borrowash/Breaston
CALV/BJ	Calverton/Burton Joyce
CARL	Carlton
CFTN/RUD	Clifton/Ruddington
COT/KEY/RAD	Cotgrave/Keyworth/Radcliffe on Trent
EWD/SEL/PNX	Eastwood/Selston/Pinxton
HEANOR	Heanor
HUCK/RAV	Hucknall/Ravenshead
ILK	Ilkeston
LGEAT	Long Eaton
MAPPK/POR/STA	Mapperley Park/Porchester/St Ann's
NOTT	Nottingham
NOTTE	Nottingham east
WBRGFD	West Bridgford
WOL/BIL/BRX	Wollaton/Bilborough/Broxtowe

Index - streets

1st - Arm

1

1st Av NOTTE NG7 31 E5
2nd Av NOTTE NG7 31 E5
3rd Av NOTTE NG7 31 E5
4th Av NOTTE NG7 30 D5

A

Aaron Cl CFTN/RUD NG11 57 E4
Abba Cl EWD/SEL/PNX NG16 15 G3
Abbey Br NOTTE NG7 56 B1
Abbey Circ WBRGFD NG2 58 B4
Abbey Cl HUCK/RAV NG15 4 D5
Abbey Ct NOTTE NG7 42 C4
Abbey Dr BSTN/STPLFD NG9 55 E4
Abbeyfield Rd NOTTE NG7 56 C3
Abbey Gv
MAPPK/POR/STA NG3 44 A1
Abbey Rd BING/VBLV NG13 49 F3
BSTN/STPLFD NG9 55 E4
EWD/SEL/PNX NG16 8 C5
WBRGFD NG2 58 B4
Abbey St ILK DE7 26 A3
NOTTE NG7 56 B1
Abbot Cl COT/KEY/RAD NG12 79 F5
Abbot Rd ILK DE7 37 F2
Abbotsbury Cl ARN NG5 18 A1
Abbots Cl ARN NG5 19 G4
Abbots Dr HUCK/RAV NG15 10 D1
Abbotsford Dr
MAPPK/POR/STA NG3 3 H1
Abbotsford Ms ILK DE7 25 G2
Abbots Rd HUCK/RAV NG15 10 D1
Abbot St EWD/SEL/PNX NG16 26 D1
Abbots Wy WOL/BIL/BRX NG8 41 H4
Abbott St HEANOR DE75 12 B1
LGEAT NG10 73 E3
Abercarn Cl BLWL NG6 17 G3
Aberdeen St
MAPPK/POR/STA NG3 3 J4
Aberford Av WOL/BIL/BRX NG8 30 A5
Abingdon Dr CFTN/RUD NG11 77 G1
Abingdon Gdns ARN NG5 20 B5
BSTN/STPLFD NG9 64 C2
Abingdon Rd WBRGFD NG2 58 B4
Abingdon Sq
WOL/BIL/BRX NG8 29 G4
Ablard Gdns BSTN/STPLFD NG9 64 B4
Acacia Cl HUCK/RAV NG15 11 G2
Acacia Ct MAPPK/POR/STA NG3 3 H2
Acacia Crs CARL NG4 33 G5
Acacia Gdns
EWD/SEL/PNX NG16 15 G2
Acacia Wk BSTN/STPLFD NG9 55 E5
Acaster Cl BSTN/STPLFD NG9 65 G2
Acle Gdns BLWL NG6 17 G1
Acorn Av EWD/SEL/PNX NG16 14 C2
Acorn Bank CFTN/RUD NG11 67 E2
Acorn Dr CARL NG4 33 H3
Acorn Pk NOTTE NG7 56 B3
A'court St NOTTE NG7 42 C2
Acton Av BLWL NG6 30 A1
Acton Cl LGEAT NG10 73 F3
Acton Gv LGEAT NG10 73 F3
Acton Rd ARN NG5 19 G2
LGEAT NG10 73 F2
Acton St LGEAT NG10 73 F3
Adams Cl HEANOR DE75 12 A3
Adams Ct ILK DE7 25 H2
Adams Hl COT/KEY/RAD NG12 82 C1
NOTTE NG7 55 H1
Adam St ILK DE7 38 B2
Ada Pl HUCK/RAV NG15 5 G4
Adbolton Av CARL NG4 33 F4
Adbolton Gv WBRGFD NG2 58 C1
Adbolton La WBRGFD NG2 58 C2
Addington Rd NOTTE NG7 42 C2
Addison Dr HUCK/RAV NG15 4 D4
Addison Rd CARL NG4 32 C5
Addison St NOTT NG1 2 D1
Adelaide Cl BSTN/STPLFD NG9 53 G2
Adelaide Gv ARN NG5 18 B2
Adel Dr CARL NG4 33 F4
Adenburgh Dr
BSTN/STPLFD NG9 64 C5
Admiral Cl HEANOR DE75 6 A5
Adrian Cl BSTN/STPLFD NG9 63 G5
Aeneas Ct MAPPK/POR/STA * NG3 31 E5
Aerial Wy HUCK/RAV NG15 11 E2
Agnes Vls
MAPPK/POR/STA NG3 31 H3
Ainsdale Crs WOL/BIL/BRX NG8 29 F2
Ainsley Rd WOL/BIL/BRX NG8 42 A2
Ainsworth Dr WBRGFD NG2 57 E2
Aira Cl WBRGFD NG2 59 E5
Airedale Cl LGEAT NG10 72 B3
Airedale Ct BSTN/STPLFD NG9 63 H2
Aitchison Av HUCK/RAV NG15 5 E5
Alandene Av
EWD/SEL/PNX NG16 15 H3
Albany Cl ARN NG5 19 H3
HUCK/RAV NG15 10 B2
Albany Ct BSTN/STPLFD NG9 53 F2
Albany Rd NOTTE NG7 30 D5
Albany St ILK DE7 38 B2
Albemarle Rd ARN NG5 31 G1
Alberta Ter NOTTE NG7 30 D5
Albert Av BSTN/STPLFD NG9 53 E4
CARL NG4 44 C1
EWD/SEL/PNX NG16 16 B4
WOL/BIL/BRX NG8 30 A5
Albert Ball Cl ARN NG5 18 C2
Albert Gv NOTTE NG7 42 C3
Albert Rd BSTN/STPLFD NG9 55 F3
LGEAT NG10 52 C5
LGEAT NG10 73 E2
MAPPK/POR/STA NG3 31 G4
NOTTE NG7 42 B5
WBRGFD NG2 58 A3
Albert St BSTN/STPLFD NG9 53 E4
CARL NG4 33 G4
COT/KEY/RAD NG12 47 E5
EWD/SEL/PNX NG16 8 A4
HUCK/RAV NG15 5 G5
ILK DE7 25 H5
NOTT NG1 3 F6
Albion Ri ARN NG5 20 A1
Albion Rd LGEAT NG10 73 F1
Albion St BSTN/STPLFD NG9 55 E4
ILK DE7 26 A4
NOTT NG1 2 E7
Albion Ter ILK * DE7 26 A4
Albury Dr WOL/BIL/BRX NG8 29 G4
Albury Sq NOTTE NG7 2 A5
Alcester St NOTTE NG7 56 B3
Aldene Ct BSTN/STPLFD NG9 64 C1
Aldercar La EWD/SEL/PNX NG16 7 E3
Alder Gdns BLWL NG6 17 F3
Aldermens Cl WBRGFD NG2 57 F1
Alderney St NOTTE NG7 42 C5
Alderton Rd ARN NG5 19 F5
Alder Wy COT/KEY/RAD NG12 82 D2
Aldgate Cl BLWL NG6 17 F3
Aldred's La HEANOR DE75 12 D1
Aldridge Cl BSTN/STPLFD NG9 63 F4
Aldrin Cl BLWL NG6 17 E5
Aldworth Cl ARN NG5 19 F4
Aldwych Cl WOL/BIL/BRX NG8 28 C3
Alexander Cl HUCK/RAV NG15 5 G3
Alexander Rd NOTTE NG7 2 A6
Alexandra Crs
BSTN/STPLFD NG9 55 F5
Alexandra Pk
MAPPK/POR/STA NG3 31 G5
Alexandra Rd LGEAT NG10 73 E1
Alexandra St ARN NG5 31 E5
BSTN/STPLFD NG9 53 E5
EWD/SEL/PNX NG16 8 A5
Alford Cl BSTN/STPLFD NG9 65 F1
Alford Rd COT/KEY/RAD NG12 68 C2
WBRGFD NG2 58 C5
Alfred Av MAPPK/POR/STA NG3 32 B3
Alfred Cl MAPPK/POR/STA NG3 3 F1
Alfred St Central
MAPPK/POR/STA NG3 3 F1
Alfred St North
MAPPK/POR/STA NG3 2 E1
Alfred St South
MAPPK/POR/STA NG3 3 J3
Alfreton Rd NOTTE NG7 42 C2
Alison Av HUCK/RAV NG15 5 H3
Alison Wk
MAPPK/POR/STA NG3 3 G2
Allandale Rd HEANOR DE75 6 A5
Allendale ILK DE7 37 H1
Allendale Av BSTN/STPLFD NG9 64 C4
WOL/BIL/BRX NG8 29 F4
Allen St HUCK/RAV NG15 5 F4
Allen's Wk ARN NG5 20 A2
All Hallows Dr CARL NG4 33 G3
Allington Av NOTTE NG7 42 C5
Allison Gdns BSTN/STPLFD NG9 64 C2
ILK DE7 26 B4
All Saints' St NOTTE NG7 2 B2
All Saints Ter NOTTE NG7 2 B2
Allwood Dr CARL NG4 33 F5
Allwood Gdns HUCK/RAV NG15 11 G1
Alma Cl CARL NG4 33 H3
NOTT NG1 2 E2
Alma Hl EWD/SEL/PNX NG16 15 F2
Alma Rd MAPPK/POR/STA NG3 44 A2
Alma St NOTTE NG7 30 D4
Almond Cl EWD/SEL/PNX NG16 15 F3
HUCK/RAV NG15 11 G2
Almond Wk CARL NG4 33 H3
Alnwick Cl BLWL NG6 18 A4
Alpha Ter NOTT NG1 2 D1
Alpine St BLWL NG6 30 A3
Althorpe St NOTTE NG7 2 A4
Alton Av CFTN/RUD NG11 67 E2
Alton Cl CFTN/RUD NG11 67 F3
Alvenor St ILK DE7 26 A4
Alverstone Rd
MAPPK/POR/STA NG3 31 F4
Alvey Ter NOTTE * NG7 42 B3
Alwood Gv CFTN/RUD NG11 66 A3
Alwyn Rd WOL/BIL/BRX NG8 29 E3
Amber Ct HEANOR * DE75 12 B1
Amber Dr EWD/SEL/PNX NG16 7 E5
Ambergate Rd
WOL/BIL/BRX NG8 41 F1
Amber Hl ARN NG5 19 E3
Amberley Cl ILK DE7 38 A2
Amberley St NOTT NG1 2 D5
Ambleside WBRGFD NG2 58 D4
Ambleside Dr
EWD/SEL/PNX NG16 7 G4
Ambleside Rd
WOL/BIL/BRX NG8 29 F4
Ambleside Wy CARL NG4 34 A5
Amersham Ri WOL/BIL/BRX NG8 29 G4
Amesbury Circ
WOL/BIL/BRX NG8 29 F2
Amilda Av ILK DE7 26 A5
Ampthill Ri ARN NG5 31 E1
Ancaster Gdns
WOL/BIL/BRX NG8 41 F4
Anchor Cl WOL/BIL/BRX NG8 29 G3
Anchor Rd EWD/SEL/PNX NG16 7 F4
Anders Dr BLWL NG6 17 E5
Anderson Crs
BSTN/STPLFD NG9 54 D3
Andover Cl WOL/BIL/BRX NG8 41 G2
Andover Rd ARN NG5 18 B4
Andrew Av ILK DE7 26 B5
Andrews Dr EWD/SEL/PNX NG16 6 D3
Anfield Cl BSTN/STPLFD NG9 63 H4
Anford Cl BLWL NG6 17 G5
Angelica Ct BING/VBLV NG13 48 B3
Angel Rw NOTT NG1 2 E5
Angel Rw West NOTT NG1 2 D5
Angletarn Cl WBRGFD NG2 58 D5
Angrave Cl
MAPPK/POR/STA NG3 43 H1
Angus Cl ARN NG5 20 C1
EWD/SEL/PNX NG16 15 H5
Anmer Cl WBRGFD NG2 57 E2
Annan Ct WOL/BIL/BRX NG8 29 G5
Anne's Cl MAPPK/POR/STA NG3 32 B3
Annesley Gv NOTT NG1 2 D1
Annesley Rd HUCK/RAV NG15 4 C2
WBRGFD NG2 58 A4
Anslow Av BSTN/STPLFD NG9 55 F3
Anstee Rd LGEAT NG10 72 D5
Anstey Ri MAPPK/POR/STA NG3 44 A3
Antill St BSTN/STPLFD NG9 53 E5
Apollo Dr BLWL NG6 17 E5
Appleby Cl ILK DE7 38 A2
Appledore Av
WOL/BIL/BRX NG8 54 C1
Appledorne Wy ARN NG5 19 H1
Appleton Rd BSTN/STPLFD NG9 65 G2
Apple Tree Cl
COT/KEY/RAD * NG12 68 B2
Applewood Gv ARN NG5 31 G2
Arboretum St NOTT NG1 2 C1
Arbour Hl ILK DE7 36 B5
Arbrook Dr WOL/BIL/BRX NG8 42 A2
Arbutus Cl CFTN/RUD NG11 65 H5
Archdale Rd ARN NG5 19 F4
Archer Crs WOL/BIL/BRX NG8 41 E3
Archer Rd BSTN/STPLFD NG9 63 F1
Archer St ILK DE7 25 H2
Archway Ct NOTTE NG7 42 C2
Arden Cl BSTN/STPLFD NG9 55 F3
HUCK/RAV NG15 11 H2
Ardleigh Cl ARN NG5 18 A1
Ardmore Cl WBRGFD NG2 3 K7
Ardsley Cl HEANOR DE75 6 D5
Argyle Ct NOTTE NG7 42 C3
Argyle St EWD/SEL/PNX NG16 7 E3
NOTTE NG7 42 C3
Ariel Cl ARN NG5 18 C5
Arkers Cl BLWL NG6 30 A2
Arklow Cl WOL/BIL/BRX NG8 29 G3
Arkwright St WBRGFD * NG2 43 F5
Arkwright St North
WBRGFD NG2 43 F5
Arkwright St South
WBRGFD NG2 57 G2
Arkwright Wk WBRGFD NG2 57 G2
Arleston Dr WOL/BIL/BRX NG8 40 C4
Arlington Dr
MAPPK/POR/STA NG3 31 F4
Armadale Cl ARN NG5 20 D2

Armfield Rd *ARN* NG5 ....20 D4
Armitage Dr *LGEAT* NG10 ....73 H2
Armstrong Rd *BLWL* NG6 ....17 E5
Arncliff Cl *WOL/BIL/BRX* NG8 ....40 B4
Arndale Rd *ARN* NG5 ....19 F5
Arnesby Rd *NOTTE* NG7 ....42 A5
Arno Av *NOTTE* NG7 ....31 E5
Arnold Av *LGEAT* NG10 ....72 B5
Arnold Crs *LGEAT* NG10 ....72 B5
Arnold La *MAPPK/POR/STA* NG3 ..32 D1
Arnold Rd *ARN* NG5 ....30 C1
Arnos Gv *WOL/BIL/BRX* NG8......28 C2
Arnot Hill Rd *ARN* NG5 ....19 H3
Arno Vale Gdns *ARN* NG5 ....20 A5
Arno Vale Rd *ARN* NG5 ....20 A5
Arnside *BSTN/STPLFD* NG9 ....53 F1
Arnside Cl *ARN* NG5 ....19 E5
Arnside Rd *ARN* NG5 ....19 E5
A Rd *BSTN/STPLFD* NG9................55 H5
Arran Cl *BSTN/STPLFD* NG9 ....53 F1
Arthur Av *BSTN/STPLFD* NG9........53 G3
  NOTTE NG7 ....42 C4
Arthur Crs *CARL* NG4 ....44 D1
Arthur Mee Rd
  BSTN/STPLFD NG9......................63 F1
Arthur St *CARL* NG4 ....45 H2
  NOTTE NG7 ....2 B1
Artic Wy *EWD/SEL/PNX* NG16......15 E3
Arundel Cl *LGEAT* NG10 ....62 C2
Arundel Dr *BSTN/STPLFD* NG9......54 A1
Arundel St *NOTTE* NG7 ....2 A4
Ascot Av *EWD/SEL/PNX* NG16......15 E3
Ascot Dr *ARN* NG5 ....19 G2
  HUCK/RAV NG15 ....10 C2
Ascot Pl *ILK* DE7 ....37 F3
Ascot Rd *WOL/BIL/BRX* NG8........42 A1
Ascott Gdns *WBRGFD* NG2 ....67 E1
Ashbourne Cl *BSTN/STPLFD* NG9..53 H2
Ashbourne Ct *BLWL* NG6 ....17 E4
Ashburnham Av *NOTTE* NG7 ....54 C1
Ashchurch Dr
  WOL/BIL/BRX NG8......................54 C1
Ash Cl *BING/VBLV* NG13 ....49 F3
  CALV/BJ NG14 ....34 D1
Ash Crs *EWD/SEL/PNX* NG16........16 A4
Ashdale Av *HUCK/RAV* NG15 ......11 E2
Ashdale Rd *ARN* NG5 ....20 B2
  ILK DE7 ....38 B2
  MAPPK/POR/STA NG3 ....44 C2
Ashdown Cl *CFTN/RUD* NG11......57 E5
Ashdown Gv *BING/VBLV* NG13 ....48 C3
Ashe Cl *ARN* NG5 ....20 C3
Asher La *CFTN/RUD* NG11 ....76 D4
Ashfield Av *BSTN/STPLFD* NG9 ....65 G1
Ashfield Rd *WBRGFD* NG2 ....44 A4
Ashford Ct *ILK* DE7 ....24 A5
Ashford Pl *ILK* DE7 ....13 H5
Ashford Ri *WOL/BIL/BRX* NG8......54 C1
Ashforth Av *HEANOR* DE75 ....12 D1
Ashforth St
  MAPPK/POR/STA NG3 ....3 G1
Ashgate Rd *HUCK/RAV* NG15 ......11 H1
Ash Gv *BSTN/STPLFD* NG9 ....53 E5
  COT/KEY/RAD NG12 ....82 C2
  LGEAT NG10 ....52 B4
  LGEAT NG10 ....72 B3
Ash Lea Cl *COT/KEY/RAD* NG12 ..71 E4
Ashley Cl *BSTN/STPLFD* NG9........54 C5
Ashley Crs *COT/KEY/RAD* NG12....82 C1
Ashley Rd *COT/KEY/RAD* NG12....82 C1
Ashley St *MAPPK/POR/STA* NG3 ....3 J4
Ashling St *WBRGFD* NG2 ....57 H1
Ash Mount Rd
  EWD/SEL/PNX NG16......................7 E4
Ashness Cl *WBRGFD* NG2 ....58 D5
Ashover Cl
  MAPPK/POR/STA NG3 ....31 H5
Ashridge Wy
  COT/KEY/RAD NG12 ....68 D2
Ash St *ILK* DE7 ....25 H1
Ash Vw *NOTTE* NG7 ....42 C2
Ashview Cl *LGEAT* NG10 ....72 B1
Ashville Cl *WBRGFD* NG2 ....56 D2
Ashwater Dr
  MAPPK/POR/STA NG3 ....21 E4
Ashwell Gdns *NOTTE* NG7 ....30 B5
Ashwell St *CARL* NG4 ....45 G2
Ashwick Cl *CFTN/RUD* NG11........66 D1
Ashworth Av *CFTN/RUD* NG11......77 F1
Ashworth Crs
  MAPPK/POR/STA NG3 ....44 D3
Askeby Dr *WOL/BIL/BRX* NG8......28 C4
Aslockton Dr *WOL/BIL/BRX* NG8..30 A4
Aspen Cl *BING/VBLV* NG13 ....49 F3
Aspen Rd *BLWL* NG6 ....17 E3
Asper St *CARL* NG4 ....45 H1

Aspley La *WOL/BIL/BRX* NG8........29 G5
Aspley Park Dr
  WOL/BIL/BRX NG8......................29 F5
Aspley Pl *NOTTE* NG7 ....42 C2
Assarts Rd *EWD/SEL/PNX* NG16 ..28 D2
Astcote Cl *ARN* NG5 ....20 C3
Astle Ct *ARN* NG5 ....19 G3
Astley Dr *MAPPK/POR/STA* NG3 ..32 A4
Aston Av *BSTN/STPLFD* NG9........55 F3
Aston Dr *BLWL* NG6 ....11 H5
Aston Gn *BSTN/STPLFD* NG9........63 F3
Astral Gv *HUCK/RAV* NG15 ....10 C3
Astwood Cl *WOL/BIL/BRX* NG8 ....40 D1
Atherfield Gdns
  EWD/SEL/PNX NG16......................8 A4
Atherton Ri *WOL/BIL/BRX* NG8 ....29 G2
Atherton Rd *ILK* DE7 ....25 F2
Athorpe Gv *BLWL* NG6 ....30 B2
Attenborough La
  BSTN/STPLFD NG9......................64 B3
Attercliffe Ter *WBRGFD* NG2 ....57 F2
Attewell Rd
  EWD/SEL/PNX NG16....................14 C5
Aubrey Av *WBRGFD* NG2 ....3 K6
Aubrey Rd *ARN* NG5 ....31 E4
Auckland Cl *NOTTE* NG7 ....42 B3
Auckland Rd *HUCK/RAV* NG15 ....10 C2
Audley Cl *ILK* DE7 ....25 G2
Audley Dr *BSTN/STPLFD* NG9......55 E2
Audon Av *BSTN/STPLFD* NG9........64 D1
Augustine Gdns *ARN* NG5............18 D1
Austen Av *LGEAT* NG10 ....72 D4
  NOTTE NG7 ....42 D1
Austins Dr *LGEAT* NG10 ....62 C2
Austin St *BLWL* NG6 ....17 H3
Austrey Av *BSTN/STPLFD* NG9......55 F3
Avalon Cl *BLWL* NG6 ....18 B5
Avebury Cl *CFTN/RUD* NG11........76 A2
Aveline Cl *ARN* NG5 ....18 C2
The Avenue *CFTN/RUD* NG11......77 G4
Avenue A *NOTT* NG1 ....3 H5
Avenue B *NOTT* NG1 ....3 H5
Avenue C *NOTT* NG1 ....3 J5
Avenue D *NOTT* NG1 ....3 J5
Avenue E *NOTT* NG1 ....3 J5
Averton Sq *HUCK/RAV* NG15........42 A5
Aviemore Cl *ARN* NG5 ....20 C2
Avis Av *HEANOR* DE75 ....12 C3
Avocet Cl *BING/VBLV* NG13 ....49 F4
Avocet Whf *WBRGFD* NG2 ....56 C1
Avonbridge Cl *ARN* NG5 ....20 D1
Avondale *COT/KEY/RAD* NG12 ....71 F3
Avondale Cl *LGEAT* NG10............72 B3
Avondale Rd *CARL* NG4 ....45 E2
  ILK DE7 ....37 F3
Avon Gdns *WBRGFD* NG2 ....58 A4
Avonlea Cl *ILK* DE7 ....38 C2
Avon Pl *BSTN/STPLFD* NG9..........55 F4
Avon Rd *CARL* NG4 ....33 G3
  MAPPK/POR/STA NG3 ....44 C3
Awsworth La
  EWD/SEL/PNX NG16....................15 E4
  EWD/SEL/PNX NG16....................26 D2
Awsworth Rd *ILK* DE7 ....26 B2
Axford Cl *CARL* NG4 ....33 G3
Aylesham Av *ARN* NG5 ....20 A4
Aylestone Dr *WOL/BIL/BRX* NG8 ..29 G5
Ayr St *NOTTE* NG7 ....2 A2
Ayscough Av
  EWD/SEL/PNX NG16....................16 B4
Ayton Cl *WBRGFD* NG2 ....57 E1
Ayton Gdns *BSTN/STPLFD* NG9....64 B4
Azalea Ct *EWD/SEL/PNX* NG16....14 D2

B

Babbacombe Cl *ARN* NG5............19 E4
Babbacombe Wy
  HUCK/RAV NG15 ....10 C1
Babbington Crs *CARL* NG4 ....33 F3
Babbington La
  EWD/SEL/PNX NG16....................27 G1
Babington Ct *BSTN/STPLFD* NG9..64 B1
The Babington *NOTTE* NG7 ....56 B1
Back La *COT/KEY/RAD* NG12........79 H3
  EWD/SEL/PNX NG16....................16 C4
  ILK DE7 ....25 H3
Bacon Cl *EWD/SEL/PNX* NG16 ....14 B2
Bacton Av *BLWL* NG6 ....17 G2
Bacton Gdns *BLWL* NG6 ....17 G2
Baden Powell Rd *WBRGFD* NG2 ..44 A4
Bader Rd *CFTN/RUD* NG11 ....57 E4
Badger Cl *CARL* NG4 ....33 F5
  HUCK/RAV NG15 ....10 B1
Bagnall Av *ARN* NG5 ....19 F3
Bagnall Rd *BLWL* NG6 ....29 H1

Bagthorpe Cl *ARN* NG5 ....30 D2
Baildon Cl *WOL/BIL/BRX* NG8......41 H5
Bailey Brook Crs
  EWD/SEL/PNX NG16......................6 D3
Bailey Brook Dr
  EWD/SEL/PNX NG16......................6 C3
Bailey Cl *ARN* NG5 ....19 G3
Bailey Grove Rd
  EWD/SEL/PNX NG16......................7 C5
Bailey La *COT/KEY/RAD* NG12......60 D1
Bailey St *BLWL* NG6 ....30 B3
  BSTN/STPLFD NG9......................52 D5
  CARL NG4 ....45 H1
Bainton Gv *CFTN/RUD* NG11........66 C5
Baker Av *ARN* NG5 ....20 B1
  HEANOR DE75 ....12 C3
Bakerdale Rd
  MAPPK/POR/STA NG3 ....44 C2
Baker Rd *EWD/SEL/PNX* NG16 ....14 D2
Baker's Hollow
  COT/KEY/RAD NG12 ....70 D3
Bakewell Av *CARL* NG4 ....33 F4
Bakewell Dr *ARN* NG5 ....18 B3
Bakewell Rd *LGEAT* NG10 ....73 F4
Bala Dr *ARN* NG5 ....18 D3
Baldwin Ct *NOTTE* NG7 ....42 C3
Baldwin St *EWD/SEL/PNX* NG16 ..14 D1
  NOTTE NG7 ....2 A3
Balfour Rd *BSTN/STPLFD* NG9 ....53 E5
  NOTTE NG7 ....42 C3
Balisier Ct *MAPPK/POR/STA* NG3 ..3 F1
Ballantrae Cl *ARN* NG5 ....20 C2
Ballerat Crs *ARN* NG5 ....18 B2
Ball St *MAPPK/POR/STA* NG3......44 A1
Balmoral Av *WBRGFD* NG2 ....57 H3
Balmoral Cl *LGEAT* NG10 ....62 C3
Balmoral Crs *WOL/BIL/BRX* NG8 ..40 B3
Balmoral Dr *BSTN/STPLFD* NG9 ..54 A1
Balmoral Gv *HUCK/RAV* NG15 ......5 G4
Balmoral Rd *BING/VBLV* NG13 ....48 B3
  CARL NG4 ....45 G2
  ILK DE7 ....37 G3
  NOTT NG1 ....43 E1
Bamkin Cl *HUCK/RAV* NG15 ....11 G1
Bampton Ct *WBRGFD* NG2 ....58 D4
Banbury Av *BSTN/STPLFD* NG9 ....63 G3
Bancroft St *BLWL* NG6 ....17 H3
Banes Rd *BING/VBLV* NG13 ....49 G3
Bangor Wk
  MAPPK/POR/STA NG3 ....43 F1
Bankfield Dr *BSTN/STPLFD* NG9 ..54 B3
Bank Pl *NOTT* NG1 ....3 F5
Banks Cl *ARN* NG5 ....20 C5
Banks Crs *BING/VBLV* NG13 ....48 D3
Banks Paddock
  BING/VBLV NG13 ....49 E3
Banks Rd *BSTN/STPLFD* NG9........63 F4
Bank St *EWD/SEL/PNX* NG16 ....7 F3
  LGEAT NG10 ....73 F2
Bankwood Cl *WOL/BIL/BRX* NG8 ..29 F4
Bannerman Rd *BLWL* NG6 ....17 H4
Barbara Sq *HUCK/RAV* NG15........5 F5
Barber Cl *ILK* DE7 ....25 H2
Barber St *EWD/SEL/PNX* NG16......8 B5
Barbrook Cl *WOL/BIL/BRX* NG8 ..41 G3
Barbury Dr *CFTN/RUD* NG11........76 A2
Barclay Ct *ILK* DE7 ....25 G2
Barden Rd *ARN* NG5 ....32 B1
Bardney Dr *BLWL* NG6 ....17 F2
Barent Cl *ARN* NG5......................18 C4
Barent Wk *ARN* NG5 ....18 C4
Barker Av East *LGEAT* NG10 ....52 C5
Barker Av North *LGEAT* NG10 ......52 B5
Barker Ga *ILK* DE7 ....26 A3
  NOTT NG1 ....3 H5
Barker's La *BSTN/STPLFD* NG9 ....64 D2
Barkla Cl *CFTN/RUD* NG11..........75 H1
Bar La *WOL/BIL/BRX* NG8 ....29 H3
Barley Cft *WBRGFD* NG2 ....67 F2
Barley Dale Dr
  BSTN/STPLFD NG9......................53 E1
Barleylands *CFTN/RUD* NG11......77 F3
Barling Dr *ILK* DE7 ....25 F4
Barlock Rd *BLWL* NG6 ....30 B1
Barlow Dr *EWD/SEL/PNX* NG16....26 C1
Barlow Dr North
  EWD/SEL/PNX NG16....................26 C1
Barlow Dr South
  EWD/SEL/PNX NG16....................26 C1

Barn Cft *BSTN/STPLFD* NG9..........54 A5
Barndale Cl *WBRGFD* NG2 ....67 F3
Barnes Rd *ARN* NG5 ....18 C2
Barnet Rd
  MAPPK/POR/STA NG3 ....44 C1
Barnfield *CFTN/RUD* NG11..........67 F5
Barnsley Ter *WBRGFD* NG2 ....57 F2
Barnston Rd *WBRGFD* NG2 ....44 A3
Barons Cl *CARL* NG4 ....33 F4
Barrack La *NOTTE* NG7 ....42 C4
Barra Ms *WBRGFD* NG2 ....57 E1
Barratt Cl *BSTN/STPLFD* NG9 ......64 C5
Barratt Crs *BSTN/STPLFD* NG9......64 C4
Barratt La *BSTN/STPLFD* NG9......64 C5
Barrhead Cl *ARN* NG5..................18 B1
Barrington Cl
  COT/KEY/RAD NG12 ....60 D1
Barrique Rd *NOTTE* NG7 ....56 B2
Barrow Slade
  COT/KEY/RAD NG12 ....82 B2
Barrydale Av *BSTN/STPLFD* NG9..65 E1
Barry St *BLWL* NG6 ....17 H3
Bartlow Rd *WOL/BIL/BRX* NG8 ....40 C1
Barton Cl *CFTN/RUD* NG11..........77 E3
Barton La *BSTN/STPLFD* NG9......64 B5
  CFTN/RUD NG11 ....65 H5
Barton Rd *LGEAT* NG10 ....73 H2
Bartons Cl *EWD/SEL/PNX* NG16....26 B1
Barton St *BSTN/STPLFD* NG9 ......65 F1
Barwell Dr *WOL/BIL/BRX* NG8 ....28 C4
Basa Crs *ARN* NG5 ....18 C2
Basford Rd *BLWL* NG6 ....30 A4
Baskin La *BSTN/STPLFD* NG9 ......64 B2
Baslow Av *CARL* NG4 ....33 E4
Baslow Cl *LGEAT* NG10 ....72 B4
Baslow Dr *BSTN/STPLFD* NG9......53 E2
Bassett Cl *EWD/SEL/PNX* NG16 ..15 F3
  ILK DE7 ....25 H2
Bassett Rd *EWD/SEL/PNX* NG16 ..15 F3
Bassford Av *HEANOR* DE75 ....6 C5
Bassingfield La
  COT/KEY/RAD NG12 ....59 F4
Bastion St *NOTTE* NG7 ....42 B3
Bateman Gdns *NOTTE* NG7 ....42 C1
Bathley St *WBRGFD* NG2 ....57 F2
Baths La *HUCK/RAV* NG15 ....5 G5
Bath St *ILK* DE7 ....25 H4
  NOTT NG1 ....3 H4
Bathurst Dr *WOL/BIL/BRX* NG8 ....41 F2
Baulk La *BSTN/STPLFD* NG9 ....53 G4
Bawtry Wk
  MAPPK/POR/STA NG3 ....44 A2
The Bayley *NOTTE* NG7 ....56 B1
Bayliss Rd *CARL* NG4 ....33 E2
Bayswater Rd
  EWD/SEL/PNX NG16....................15 G3
Baythorn Rd *WOL/BIL/BRX* NG8 ..40 C2
Beacon Hill Dr *HUCK/RAV* NG15 ..10 C2
Beacon Hill Ri
  MAPPK/POR/STA NG3 ....3 J3
Beacon Rd *BSTN/STPLFD* NG9......55 G5
Beaconsfield St *LGEAT* NG10 ......73 F2
  NOTTE NG7 ....30 C5
Bean Cl *BLWL* NG6 ....17 E5
Beardall St *HUCK/RAV* NG15........11 G1
Beardsley Gdns *WBRGFD* NG2 ....57 E1
Beardsmore Gv *HUCK/RAV* NG15 ..5 E3
Beast Market Hl *NOTT* NG1 ....2 E5
Beauclerk Dr *ARN* NG5 ....18 B2
Beaufort Cl *CFTN/RUD* NG11 ......67 G4
Beaufort Dr *BSTN/STPLFD* NG9 ..64 B1
Beaulieu Gdns *WBRGFD* NG2 ......67 F1
Beaumaris Dr
  BSTN/STPLFD NG9......................64 A2
  CARL NG4 ....34 A4
Beaumont Cl *BSTN/STPLFD* NG9 ..53 F2
  COT/KEY/RAD NG12 ....79 F5
Beaumont Gdns *WBRGFD* NG2 ....67 G2
Beaumont St *WBRGFD* NG2 ....3 J6
Beauvale *EWD/SEL/PNX* NG16......8 D5
Beauvale Crs *HUCK/RAV* NG15 ....10 C1
Beauvale Dr *ILK* DE7 ....13 H5
Beauvale Ri *EWD/SEL/PNX* NG16 ..8 B4
Beauvale Rd *HUCK/RAV* NG15 ....10 D1
  WBRGFD NG2 ....57 F2
Beckenham Rd *NOTTE* NG7 ....42 C2
Beckford Rd *WBRGFD* NG2 ....44 A5
Beckhampton Rd *ARN* NG5 ....18 C4
Beckley Rd *WOL/BIL/BRX* NG8 ....29 E3
Beckside *COT/KEY/RAD* NG12......68 D2
Beck St *CARL* NG4 ....33 F5
  NOTT NG1 ....3 H4
Bedale Ct *BSTN/STPLFD* NG9......63 H2
Bedale Rd *ARN* NG5 ....19 F5
Bedarra Gv *NOTTE* NG7 ....42 B4
Bede-ling *WBRGFD* NG2 ....57 F5
Bedford Ct *BSTN/STPLFD* NG9 ....53 H4

NOTTE * NG7 ....30 C5
Bedford Gv *BLWL* NG6 ....18 A5
Bedford Rw *NOTT* NG1 ....3 H4
Bedlington Gdns
  MAPPK/POR/STA NG3 ...31 H4
Beecham Av
  MAPPK/POR/STA NG3 ......44 A1
Beech Av *BING/VBLV* NG13 ..49 F3
  BSTN/STPLFD NG9 ....65 G1
  BWSH/BRSTN DE72 ......72 A1
  CARL NG4 ....45 G2
  COT/KEY/RAD NG12 ....82 C2
  EWD/SEL/PNX NG16 ....16 A4
  HUCK/RAV NG15 ....5 F5
  LGEAT NG10 ....52 C4
  LGEAT NG10 ....63 F5
  MAPPK/POR/STA NG3 ...32 B1
  NOTTE NG7 ....30 D5
Beech Cl *BLWL* NG6 ....29 H1
  COT/KEY/RAD NG12 ....61 E1
  COT/KEY/RAD NG12 ....68 B2
Beechdale Rd
  WOL/BIL/BRX NG8 ....29 E5
Beech La *ILK* DE7 ....36 A1
Beechwood Rd *ARN* NG5 ......20 B2
Beeston Ct *BLWL* NG6 ....18 A3
Beeston Fields Dr
  BSTN/STPLFD NG9 ....54 B3
Beeston La *NOTTE* NG7 ....55 F2
Beeston Rd *NOTTE* NG7 ....56 A4
Beetham Cl *BING/VBLV* NG13..49 E3
Belconnen Rd *ARN* NG5 ....18 C5
Belfield St *ILK* DE7 ....26 A3
Belford Cl *BLWL* NG6 ....17 E2
Belfry Wy *COT/KEY/RAD* NG12 ..68 D2
Belgrave Ms *CFTN/RUD* NG11 ..67 F3
Belgrave Rd *BLWL* NG6 ....17 F3
Bellar Ga *NOTT* NG1 ....3 H5
Belle-Isle Rd *HUCK/RAV* NG15 ..11 F1
Belleville Dr *ARN* NG5 ....18 D2
Bellevue Ct
  MAPPK/POR/STA NG3 ......3 J1
Bell La *CFTN/RUD* NG11 ....57 E4
Bellmore Gdns
  WOL/BIL/BRX NG8 ....40 C5
Bells La *WOL/BIL/BRX* NG8 ...29 F2
Bell St *CARL* NG4 ....33 E5
Belmont Av *BLWL* NG6 ....17 H3
Belmont Cl
  BSTN/STPLFD NG9 ....64 A2
  HUCK/RAV NG15 ....11 F1
Belper Av *CARL* NG4 ....33 E4
Belper Crs *CARL* NG4 ....33 E4
Belper Rd *NOTTE* NG7 ....42 C1
Belper St *ILK* DE7 ....38 A1
Belsay Rd *ARN* NG5 ....18 D3
Belsford Ct
  EWD/SEL/PNX NG16 ....15 H2
Belton Cl *LGEAT* NG10 ....62 C2
Belton Dr *WBRGFD* NG2 ....67 E2
Belton St *NOTTE* NG7 ....30 C5
Belvedere Av *NOTTE* NG7 .....30 C5
Belvedere Cl
  COT/KEY/RAD NG12 ....79 F5
Belvoir Cl *ILK* DE7 ....37 G2
  LGEAT NG10 ....73 F4
Belvoir Hl *WBRGFD* NG2 ....44 A4
Belvoir Rd *CARL* NG4 ....45 H1
  WBRGFD NG2 ....58 B2
Belvoir St *HUCK/RAV* NG15 ....5 E4
  MAPPK/POR/STA NG3 ...32 A3
Belward St *NOTT* NG1 ....3 H5
Belwood Cl *CFTN/RUD* NG11 ..66 C1
Bembridge Ct
  BSTN/STPLFD NG9 ....53 H4
Bembridge Dr *ARN* NG5 ....19 E4
Bendigo La *WBRGFD* NG2 ......44 B5
Benington Dr
  WOL/BIL/BRX NG8 ....40 B5
Ben Mayo Ct *NOTTE* NG7 ......42 C2
Benner Av *ILK* DE7 ....38 B3
Bennerley Av *ILK* DE7 ....26 A1
Bennerley Rd *BLWL* NG6 ....17 E2
Bennett Rd
  MAPPK/POR/STA NG3 ...32 B2
Bennett St *LGEAT* NG10 ....52 C5
  MAPPK/POR/STA NG3 ...32 B2
Bennworth Cl *HUCK/RAV* NG15 ..11 E2
Bentinck Av
  COT/KEY/RAD NG12 ....69 E5
Bentinck Ct *WBRGFD* NG2 ......3 J5
Bentinck Rd *CARL* NG4 ....32 D3
  NOTTE NG7 ....42 C2
Bentinck St *HUCK/RAV* NG15 ...5 E4
Bentley Av
  MAPPK/POR/STA NG3 ...44 B2
Bentwell Av *ARN* NG5 ....20 B3
Beresford Dr *ILK* DE7 ....13 H5

Beresford Rd *LGEAT* NG10 ....72 B4
Beresford St *NOTTE* NG7 ....42 B3
Berkeley Av *LGEAT* NG10 ......72 C4
  MAPPK/POR/STA NG3 ...31 F5
Berle Av *HEANOR* DE75 ....6 B4
Bernard Av *HUCK/RAV* NG15 ...5 C3
Bernard St *ARN* NG5 ....31 E4
Berridge Rd *NOTTE* NG7 ....30 C5
Berridge Rd West *NOTTE* NG7 ..42 B1
Berriedale Cl *ARN* NG5 ....20 D2
Berrydown Cl
  WOL/BIL/BRX NG8 ....29 G3
Berry Hill Gv *CARL* NG4 ....33 F3
Berwick Cl *ARN* NG5 ....19 F4
Berwin Cl *LGEAT* NG10 ....62 B5
Beryldene Av
  EWD/SEL/PNX NG16 ....15 H3
Besecar Av *CARL* NG4 ....33 F3
Besecar Cl *CARL* NG4 ....33 F3
Bessell La *BSTN/STPLFD* NG9 ..64 A1
Bestwick Av *HEANOR* DE75 ...13 E1
Bestwood Av *ARN* NG5 ....19 H2
Bestwood Cl *ARN* NG5 ....19 H2
Bestwood Lodge Dr *ARN* NG5 ..19 F1
Bestwood Park Dr *ARN* NG5 ...19 E2
Bestwood Park Dr West
  ARN NG5 ....18 A1
Bestwood Rd *BLWL* NG6 ....18 A1
  HUCK/RAV NG15 ....11 H1
Bestwood Ter *BLWL* NG6 ....18 A1
Bethel Gdns *HUCK/RAV* NG15 ..10 B2
Betony Cl *BING/VBLV* NG13 ...48 B3
Betula Cl *CFTN/RUD* NG11 .....65 H5
Beverley Dr
  EWD/SEL/PNX NG16 ....15 F3
Beverley Gdns *CARL* NG4 ......33 G4
Bewcastle Rd *ARN* NG5 ....18 D1
Bewick Dr
  MAPPK/POR/STA NG3 ...44 D3
Bexwell Cl *CFTN/RUD* NG11 ...76 B1
Biant Cl *WOL/BIL/BRX* NG8 ....29 E4
Bidford Rd *WOL/BIL/BRX* NG8 ..29 E4
Biggart Cl *BSTN/STPLFD* NG9 ..64 B4
Biko Sq *NOTTE* NG7 ....30 C5
Bilberry Wk
  MAPPK/POR/STA NG3 ......3 K1
Bilborough Rd
  WOL/BIL/BRX NG8 ....40 A3
Bilby Gdns
  MAPPK/POR/STA NG3 ...44 A3
Billesdon Dr *ARN* NG5 ....30 C1
Bingham Rd *ARN* NG5 ....31 F3
  COT/KEY/RAD NG12 ....47 E5
  COT/KEY/RAD NG12 ....71 E3
Bingley Cl *WOL/BIL/BRX* NG8 ..41 G2
Birch Av *BSTN/STPLFD* NG9 ...65 G2
  CARL NG4 ....45 E1
  EWD/SEL/PNX NG16 ....16 A4
  ILK DE7 ....38 B1
Birchdale Av *HUCK/RAV* NG15 ..11 F2
Birchfield Pk *HEANOR* DE75 ...12 C3
Birchfield Rd *ARN* NG5 ....20 B2
Birchover Pl *ILK* DE7 ....13 H5
Birchover Rd *WOL/BIL/BRX* NG8 ..40 B3
Birchwood Av
  BWSH/BRSTN DE72 ......72 A2
  LGEAT NG10 ....72 D3
Birchwood Rd
  WOL/BIL/BRX NG8 ....40 B4
Bircumshaw's Rd *HEANOR* DE75 ...6 B5
Birdcroft La *ILK* DE7 ....38 A3
Birdsall Av *WOL/BIL/BRX* NG8 ..40 D4
Birkdale Cl *COT/KEY/RAD* NG12 ..68 D4
Birkdale Wy *ARN* NG5 ....18 C2
Birkin Av *BSTN/STPLFD* NG9 ..63 H4
  CFTN/RUD NG11 ....77 F1
  COT/KEY/RAD NG12 .....47 F1
  NOTTE NG7 ....42 C1
Birkland Av
  MAPPK/POR/STA NG3 ...32 B1
  NOTT NG1 ....3 G3
Birley St *BSTN/STPLFD* NG9 ..63 E1
Birling Cl *BLWL* NG6 ....16 D3
Birrell Rd *NOTTE* NG7 ....30 D5
Bisham Dr *WBRGFD* NG2 ....58 C4
Bishopdale Cl *LGEAT* NG10 ...72 B3
Bishopdale Dr
  EWD/SEL/PNX NG16 ....15 F3
Bishops Cl *COT/KEY/RAD* NG12 ..79 F5
Bishops Rd *BING/VBLV* NG13 ..48 C2
Bishop St *EWD/SEL/PNX* NG16 ..8 A5
Bishops Wy *HUCK/RAV* NG15 ...5 G3
Bispham Dr *BSTN/STPLFD* NG9 ..63 G3
Blackburn Pl *ILK* DE7 ....25 H2
Blackfriars Cl *WOL/BIL/BRX* NG8 ..28 C3

Blackhill Dr *CARL* NG4 ....33 G5
Black Hills Dr *ILK* DE7 ....38 A2
Blackrod Cl *BSTN/STPLFD * NG9 ..63 H4
Blackstone Wk *WBRGFD* NG2 ..57 F1
Blackthorn Cl *BING/VBLV* NG13 ..49 F3
Blackthorne Dr *BLWL* NG6 .....29 G2
  EWD/SEL/PNX NG16 .....21 H5
Bladon Cl *MAPPK/POR/STA* NG3 ..31 H3
Bladon Rd *CFTN/RUD* NG11 ...77 E2
Blair Gv *LGEAT* NG10 ....62 B2
Blaise Cl *CFTN/RUD* NG11 .....76 B1
Blake Cl *ARN* NG5 ....20 B3
Blake Ct *LGEAT* NG10 ....72 C4
Blakeney Rd
  COT/KEY/RAD NG12 ....47 G5
Blake St *BSTN/STPLFD* NG9 ...53 F5
  WBRGFD NG2 ....58 B4
Blake St *ILK* DE7 ....26 A4
Blandford Av *LGEAT* NG10 .....72 C4
Blandford Rd *BSTN/STPLFD* NG9 ..64 A1
Blanford Gdns *WBRGFD* NG2 ..67 F1
Blankney St *BLWL* NG6 ....30 B1
Blantyre Av *ARN* NG5 ....18 B1
Bleaberry Cl *WBRGFD* NG2 ....68 D1
Bleachers Yd *NOTTE* NG7 ......30 B4
Bleasby St *WBRGFD* NG2 ....44 A4
Bleasdale Cl *CARL* NG4 ....33 H3
Blencathra Cl *WBRGFD* NG2 ...68 D1
Blenheim Av
  MAPPK/POR/STA NG3 ...32 D3
Blenheim Cl *CFTN/RUD* NG11 ..77 F2
Blenheim Dr *BSTN/STPLFD* NG9 ..64 B1
Blenheim La *BLWL* NG6 ....17 E1
Blenhiem Ct *LGEAT* NG10 .....62 C2
Blidworth Cl *WOL/BIL/BRX* NG8 ..28 D3
Bloomsbury Dr
  EWD/SEL/PNX NG16 ....28 D2
Bloomsgrove Rd *ILK* DE7 ......26 A3
Bluebell Bank *BING/VBLV* NG13 ..48 C4
Bluebell Cl *HUCK/RAV* NG15 ...10 B1
Blue Bell Hill Rd
  MAPPK/POR/STA NG3 ......3 K1
Bluebell Wy *HEANOR* DE75 ....13 E1
Bluecoat Cl *NOTT* NG1 ....2 E2
Bluecoat St *NOTT* NG1 ....2 E2
Blundell Cl
  MAPPK/POR/STA NG3 ...32 A5
Blyth Gdns
  MAPPK/POR/STA NG3 ...31 H3
Blyth St *MAPPK/POR/STA* NG3 ..31 H4
Blyton Wk *ARN* NG5 ....19 E3
Boatmans Cl *ILK* DE7 ....26 A1
Boatswain Dr *HUCK/RAV* NG15 ...5 G4
Bobbers Mill Br *NOTTE* NG7 ...42 A1
Bobbers Mill Rd *NOTTE* NG7 ..42 A2
Boden Dr *EWD/SEL/PNX* NG16 ..16 B4
Boden St *NOTTE* NG7 ....42 C3
Bodmin Av *HUCK/RAV* NG15 ...10 B2
Bodmin Dr *WOL/BIL/BRX* NG8 ..29 H3
Body Rd *BSTN/STPLFD* NG9 ...64 A3
Bohem Rd *LGEAT* NG10 ....62 D3
Bold Cl *BLWL* NG6 ....17 G2
Bolero Cl *WOL/BIL/BRX* NG8 ..40 D3
Bolingey Wy *HUCK/RAV* NG15 ..10 B2
Bolsover St *HUCK/RAV* NG15 ...5 G5
Bolton Av *BSTN/STPLFD* NG9 ..64 B3
Bolton Cl *WBRGFD* NG2 ....58 B4
Bolton Ter *COT/KEY/RAD* NG12 ..47 E5
Bond St *ARN* NG5 ....19 H2
  WBRGFD NG2 ....3 J5
Bonetti Cl *MAPPK/POR/STA* NG3 ..20 D5
Bonington Cl *BLWL* NG6 ....17 F4
Bonington Dr *ARN* NG5 ....20 A3
Bonington Rd
  MAPPK/POR/STA NG3 ...32 A1
Bonner's Rd
  EWD/SEL/PNX NG16 ....26 C1
Bonnington Crs *ARN* NG5 ....31 F1
Bonny Md *COT/KEY/RAD* NG12 ..70 D5
Bonsall St *LGEAT* NG10 ....73 F1
Bonser Cl *CARL* NG4 ....45 F1
Booth Cl *MAPPK/POR/STA* NG3 ...3 G3
Borlace Crs *BSTN/STPLFD* NG9 ..53 F5
Borman Cl *BLWL* NG6 ....17 E5
Borrowdale Cl *WBRGFD* NG2 ..59 E5
Borrowdale Dr *LGEAT* NG10 ...72 B5
Bosden Cl *WOL/BIL/BRX* NG8 ..40 B2
Bosley Sq *BSTN/STPLFD* NG9 ..55 F3
Bostock's La *BWSH/BRSTN* DE72 ..62 A2
  LGEAT NG10 ....62 B4
Boston Ms *ARN * NG5 ....30 C2
Boston St *NOTT* NG1 ....3 H5
Boswell St *NOTTE* NG7 ....42 B3
Bosworth Dr
  EWD/SEL/PNX NG16 ......8 A3
Bosworth Wy *LGEAT* NG10 .....73 E4
Botany Av
  MAPPK/POR/STA NG3 ...31 H3

Botany Cl *CFTN/RUD* NG11 ....67 F3
Botany Dr *ILK* DE7 ....14 A5
Bothe Cl *LGEAT* NG10 ....72 D3
Boundary Crs
  BSTN/STPLFD NG9 ....55 E2
Boundary La
  EWD/SEL/PNX NG16 ......7 F4
Boundary Rd *BSTN/STPLFD* NG9 ..55 E2
  WBRGFD NG2 ....67 H2
Bourne Cl *BSTN/STPLFD* NG9 ..54 C2
Bourne Cottages *ILK * DE7 .....25 H4
Bourne Ms *CARL* NG4 ....45 H2
Bourne St *CARL* NG4 ....45 H2
Bournmoor Av *CFTN/RUD* NG11 ..66 B5
Bovill St *NOTTE* NG7 ....42 C2
Bowden Dr *BSTN/STPLFD* NG9 ..55 G5
Bowers Av
  MAPPK/POR/STA NG3 ...43 F1
Bowes Well Rd *ILK* DE7 ....25 H3
Bowland Cl
  MAPPK/POR/STA NG3 ...44 B1
Bowland Rd *BING/VBLV* NG13 ..48 B3
Bowling Cl *ILK* DE7 ....51 H3
Bowlwell Av *ARN* NG5 ....18 C2
Bowness Av *BLWL* NG6 ....29 H3
Bowness Cl *WBRGFD* NG2 .....58 D4
Bowscale Cl *WBRGFD* NG2 ....68 D1
Boxley Dr *WBRGFD* NG2 ....67 G2
Boyce Gdns
  MAPPK/POR/STA NG3 ...32 A4
Boycroft Av
  MAPPK/POR/STA NG3 ...32 A5
Boyd Cl *ARN* NG5 ....20 C1
Boynton Dr
  MAPPK/POR/STA NG3 ...32 A4
Bracadale Rd *ARN* NG5 ....18 C1
Bracebridge Dr
  WOL/BIL/BRX NG8 ....40 C1
Bracey Ri *WBRGFD* NG2 ....67 H3
Bracken Cl *CARL* NG4 ....33 E3
  LGEAT NG10 ....62 C5
  WOL/BIL/BRX NG8 ....29 E4
Brackendale Av *ARN* NG5 ....20 A2
Brackenfield Dr
  EWD/SEL/PNX NG16 ....14 C2
Bracken Rd *LGEAT* NG10 ....62 C5
Bracknell Crs *WOL/BIL/BRX* NG8 ..30 A4
Bracton Dr
  MAPPK/POR/STA NG3 ...44 A2
Bradbourne Av *CFTN/RUD* NG11 ..66 D1
Bradbury St *WBRGFD* NG2 .....44 B4
Braddock Cl *NOTTE* NG7 ....42 B4
Braddon Av *BSTN/STPLFD* NG9 ..53 F2
Bradfield Rd *WOL/BIL/BRX* NG8 ..29 E4
Bradgate Cl *LGEAT* NG10 ....62 C5
Bradgate Rd *NOTTE* NG7 ....30 C5
Bradley St *LGEAT* NG10 ....62 D1
Bradley's Yd
  COT/KEY/RAD NG12 ....79 F2
Bradley Wk *CFTN/RUD* NG11 ..76 B1
Bradman Gdns *ARN* NG5 ....20 C4
Bradmore Av *CFTN/RUD* NG11 ..77 F1
Bradmore La
  COT/KEY/RAD NG12 ....79 E4
Bradmore Ri *ARN* NG5 ....31 F1
Bradshaw St *LGEAT* NG10 ......72 C4
Bradwell Cl *EWD/SEL/PNX* NG16 ..14 D2
Bradwell Dr *ARN* NG5 ....18 D2
Braefell Cl *COT/KEY/RAD* NG12 ..69 E1
Braefield Cl *ILK* DE7 ....37 F3
Braemar Av
  EWD/SEL/PNX NG16 ....14 A1
Braemar Dr *CARL* NG4 ....34 A4
Braemar Rd *BLWL* NG6 ....17 H3
Braidwood Ct *NOTTE* NG7 .....42 C1
Brailsford Rd *NOTTE* NG7 ......56 B2
Brailsford Wy
  BSTN/STPLFD NG9 ....64 B5
Bramber Gv *CFTN/RUD* NG11 ..77 F2
Bramble Cl *BLWL* NG6 ....30 A2
  BSTN/STPLFD NG9 ....54 A4
  LGEAT NG10 ....62 C5
Bramble Dr
  MAPPK/POR/STA NG3 ...44 B1
Bramble Gdns
  WOL/BIL/BRX NG8 ....29 C5
Brambleway
  COT/KEY/RAD NG12 ....71 F4
Bramcote Av *BSTN/STPLFD* NG9 ..54 C5
Bramcote Dr *BSTN/STPLFD* NG9 ..54 B4
  WOL/BIL/BRX NG8 ....40 C5
Bramcote Dr West
  BSTN/STPLFD NG9 ....54 B5
Bramcote La *BSTN/STPLFD* NG9 ..54 B5
  WOL/BIL/BRX NG8 ....54 C5
Bramcote Rd *BSTN/STPLFD* NG9 ..54 D4
Bramcote St *NOTTE* NG7 ....42 B3
Bramcote Wk *NOTTE* NG7 ......42 B3

Bramerton Rd WOL/BIL/BRX NG8 ...40 C2
Bramhall Rd WOL/BIL/BRX NG8 ...40 B2
Bramley Rd WOL/BIL/BRX NG8 ...28 D4
Brampton Av HEANOR DE75 ...6 D5
Brampton Dr BSTN/STPLFD NG9...63 F1
Brancaster Cl HUCK/RAV NG15...10 C1
Brandish Crs CFTN/RUD NG11 ...66 A5
Brandreth Av MAPPK/POR/STA NG3 ...32 A5
Brandreth Dr EWD/SEL/PNX NG16 ...14 B3
Brand St WBRGFD NG2 ...43 H5
Branklene Cl EWD/SEL/PNX NG16 ...15 F3
Bransdale Cl LGEAT NG10 ...72 C3
Bransdale Rd CFTN/RUD NG11 ...76 A1
Branston WBRGFD NG2 ...67 G2
Branston Wk ARN NG5 ...31 F1
Brantford Av CFTN/RUD NG11 ...66 C5
Brassington Cl EWD/SEL/PNX NG16 ...14 C3
ILK DE7 ...24 B5
Braunton Cl HUCK/RAV NG15...10 C1
Brayton Crs BLWL NG6 ...18 A5
Breach Rd HEANOR DE75 ...12 D2
Breadsall Ct ILK * DE7 ...26 A2
Brechin Cl ARN NG5 ...20 C1
Breck Hill Rd ARN NG5 ...31 H1
Breckswood Dr CFTN/RUD NG11 ...76 B2
Brecon Cl LGEAT NG10 ...72 C3
WOL/BIL/BRX NG8 ...29 F1
Bredon Cl LGEAT NG10 ...72 C3
Breedon St LGEAT NG10 ...62 C4
Brendon Ct BSTN/STPLFD * NG9 ...54 A3
Brendon Dr EWD/SEL/PNX NG16 ...15 G3
WOL/BIL/BRX NG8 ...41 F3
Brendon Gdns WOL/BIL/BRX NG8 ...41 F3
Brendon Gv BING/VBLV NG13 ...48 B2
Brendon Rd WOL/BIL/BRX NG8...41 F3
Brendon Wy LGEAT NG10 ...62 B5
Brentcliffe Av MAPPK/POR/STA NG3 ...44 B1
Bressingham Dr CFTN/RUD NG11 ...67 F3
Brett Cl HUCK/RAV NG15...10 D3
Brewery St EWD/SEL/PNX NG16...15 G4
Brewsters Cl BING/VBLV NG13...48 D3
Brewsters Rd MAPPK/POR/STA NG3 ...32 A5
Briar Av LGEAT NG10 ...62 B3
Briarbank Av MAPPK/POR/STA NG3 ...32 B5
Briar Cl BSTN/STPLFD NG9 ...54 D2
COT/KEY/RAD NG12 ...79 C5
HUCK/RAV NG15 ...10 C2
Briar Ga COT/KEY/RAD NG12 ...71 F4
LGEAT NG10 ...62 B4
Briar Rd EWD/SEL/PNX NG16...14 C2
Briarwood Av MAPPK/POR/STA NG3 ...44 B1
Brickyard Dr HUCK/RAV NG15 ...11 H2
Brickyard La COT/KEY/RAD NG12 ...47 G5
Bridge Av BSTN/STPLFD NG9 ...54 D1
Bridge Ct HUCK/RAV NG15 ...11 F2
Bridge Farm La CFTN/RUD NG11 ...66 B4
Bridge Gv WBRGFD NG2 ...57 H3
Bridgend Cl BSTN/STPLFD NG9 ...63 E1
Bridge Rd WOL/BIL/BRX NG8 ...40 C3
Bridge St EWD/SEL/PNX NG16...7 F4
ILK DE7 ...24 D1
LGEAT NG10 ...62 C1
LGEAT NG10 ...63 E5
Bridgford Rd WBRGFD NG2 ...58 A3
Bridgnorth Dr CFTN/RUD NG11...66 B4
Bridgnorth Wy BSTN/STPLFD NG9 ...63 F3
Bridle Rd BSTN/STPLFD NG9 ...54 A4
CALV/BJ NG14 ...22 C4
Bridlesmith Ga NOTT1 ...3 F5
Bridlington St NOTTE NG7 ...42 B1
Bridport Av WOL/BIL/BRX NG8 ...42 A3
Brielen Rd COT/KEY/RAD NG12 ...47 F5
Brierfield Av CFTN/RUD NG11 ...67 E2
Brierley Gn CARL NG4 ...45 H1
Brige Green Wk WOL/BIL/BRX NG8 ...28 D4
Brightmoor St NOTT * NG1 ...3 G5
Brightmoor St NOTT NG1 ...3 G5
Bright St ILK DE7 ...25 H2
Brindley Rd WOL/BIL/BRX NG8 ...40 B3
Brinkhill Crs CFTN/RUD NG11...66 C3
Brinsley Cl WOL/BIL/BRX NG8 ...29 F4

Brisbane Dr ARN NG5 ...18 B2
BSTN/STPLFD NG9 ...53 F2
Bristol Rd ILK DE7 ...25 H4
Britannia Av BLWL NG6 ...18 B5
Britannia Cl EWD/SEL/PNX NG16 ...15 H3
Britannia Rd LGEAT NG10 ...63 E5
Britten Gdns MAPPK/POR/STA NG3 ...44 A2
Brixham Rd HUCK/RAV NG15 ...10 C2
Brixton Rd NOTTE NG7 ...42 B3
B Rd BSTN/STPLFD NG9 ...56 A5
Broad Eadow Rd EWD/SEL/PNX NG16 ...17 E3
Broadgate BSTN/STPLFD NG9 ...55 F4
Broadgate Av BSTN/STPLFD NG9 ...55 F4
Broadgate La BSTN/STPLFD NG9 ...55 F4
Broadholme St NOTTE NG7 ...42 C5
Broadhurst Av WOL/BIL/BRX NG8 ...30 A3
Broadlands LGEAT NG10 ...62 C2
Broadleigh Cl CFTN/RUD NG11 ...67 F3
Broadmead CALV/BJ NG14 ...35 E1
Broad Meer COT/KEY/RAD NG12...70 D3
Broad Oak Cl MAPPK/POR/STA NG3 ...43 H1
Broad Oak Dr BSTN/STPLFD NG9 ...53 E5
Broadstairs Rd BSTN/STPLFD NG9 ...63 G4
Broadstone Cl WBRGFD NG2 ...67 F1
Broad St LGEAT NG10 ...73 E2
NOTT NG1 ...3 G4
Broad Wk BLWL NG6 ...29 H2
Broadway HEANOR DE75 ...12 B1
ILK DE7 ...25 H2
NOTT NG1 ...3 G4
Broadway East CARL NG4 ...45 E2
Broadwood Ct BSTN/STPLFD NG9 ...55 F3
Broadwood Rd ARN NG5 ...19 E2
Brockdale Gdns COT/KEY/RAD NG12 ...79 F5
Brockhall Ri HEANOR DE75...12 D1
Brockhole Cl WBRGFD NG2 ...69 E1
Brockhurst Gdns MAPPK/POR/STA NG3 ...44 A2
Brockley Rd WBRGFD NG2 ...58 C4
Brockwood Crs COT/KEY/RAD NG12 ...79 F5
Bromfield Cl MAPPK/POR/STA NG3 ...44 D1
Bromley Cl BLWL NG6 ...17 G4
Bromley Pl NOTT NG1 ...2 D5
Bromley Rd WBRGFD NG2 ...57 H5
Brompton Wy CFTN/RUD NG11...67 F3
Bronte Cl LGEAT NG10 ...72 B2
Brook Av ARN NG5 ...20 B2
Brook Cl BLWL NG6 ...17 G4
EWD/SEL/PNX NG16 ...14 C1
LGEAT NG10 ...73 F4
Brookdale Ct ARN NG5 ...19 G5
Brooke St ILK DE7 ...38 C2
LGEAT NG10 ...62 C1
Brookfield Av HUCK/RAV NG15 ...11 F2
Brookfield Cl COT/KEY/RAD NG12 ...47 E5
Brookfield Ct WBRGFD * NG2 ...57 F1
Brookfield Rd ARN NG5 ...20 A3
Brookfield Wy HEANOR DE75 ...13 E1
Brook Gdns ARN NG5 ...20 B2
Brookhill Crs WOL/BIL/BRX NG8 ...40 D5
Brookhill Dr WOL/BIL/BRX NG8 ...40 D5
Brookhill Leys Rd EWD/SEL/PNX NG16 ...13 H1
Brookhill St BSTN/STPLFD NG9...54 C1
Brookland Dr BSTN/STPLFD NG9...64 C1
Brooklands Av HEANOR DE75 ...6 C5
Brooklands Crs CARL NG4 ...33 H4
Brooklands Dr CARL NG4 ...33 H4
Brooklands Rd MAPPK/POR/STA NG3 ...44 C1
Brooklyn Av CALV/BJ NG14 ...34 D1
Brooklyn Cl BLWL NG6 ...18 A5
Brooklyn Rd BLWL NG6 ...18 A5
Brook Rd BSTN/STPLFD NG9 ...55 E3
Brooksby La CFTN/RUD NG11...66 C3
Brookside EWD/SEL/PNX NG16...8 A3
Brookside Av BSTN/STPLFD NG9...54 A1
Brookside Cl LGEAT NG10 ...72 C1
Brookside Gdns CFTN/RUD NG11 ...77 E1
Brookside Rd CFTN/RUD NG11 ...77 E1
Brook St NOTT NG1 ...3 G4
Brookthorpe Wy CFTN/RUD NG11 ...76 D2

Brook Vale Rd EWD/SEL/PNX NG16 ...7 F5
Brook View Ct COT/KEY/RAD * NG12 ...82 B2
Brook View Dr COT/KEY/RAD NG12 ...82 B2
Brookwood Crs CARL NG4 ...44 D1
Broomfield Cl LGEAT NG10 ...62 B1
Broomhill Av ILK DE7 ...38 B2
Broomhill Rd BLWL NG6 ...17 H4
EWD/SEL/PNX NG16 ...15 H4
HUCK/RAV NG15 ...11 F2
Brora Rd BLWL NG6 ...18 A3
Broughton Cl ILK DE7 ...25 G3
Broughton Dr WOL/BIL/BRX NG8 ...41 H5
Broughton St BSTN/STPLFD NG9 ...54 D4
Brownes Rd BING/VBLV NG13 ...49 F2
Browning Cl ARN NG5 ...19 G3
Brown La CFTN/RUD NG11 ...74 D3
Brownlow Dr BLWL NG6 ...18 A1
Brown Meadow Rd NOTTE NG7 ...30 B5
Browns Cft BLWL NG6 ...30 A2
Brown's Flats EWD/SEL/PNX NG16 ...15 G4
Browns La COT/KEY/RAD NG12 ...83 G2
Browns Rd LGEAT NG10 ...73 F1
Brown St NOTTE NG7 ...42 C1
Broxtowe Av EWD/SEL/PNX NG16 ...15 E4
WOL/BIL/BRX NG8 ...29 H3
Broxtowe Dr HUCK/RAV NG15 ...5 E3
Broxtowe Hall Cl WOL/BIL/BRX NG8 ...29 F3
Broxtowe La WOL/BIL/BRX NG8 ...29 F4
Broxtowe St ARN NG5 ...31 F5
Bruce Cl WBRGFD NG2 ...57 C1
Bruce Dr WBRGFD NG2 ...57 G4
Brunel Av EWD/SEL/PNX NG16 ...8 B4
Brunswick Dr BSTN/STPLFD NG9 ...63 F1
Brushfield St NOTTE NG7 ...42 B1
Brussels Ter ILK DE7 ...25 H4
Brusty Pl CALV/BJ NG14 ...22 D5
Buckfast Wy WBRGFD NG2 ...58 B5
Buckingham Av HUCK/RAV NG15 ...5 E4
Buckingham Ct LGEAT NG10 ...62 B3
Buckingham Rd ARN NG5 ...19 H5
LGEAT NG10 ...62 B3
Buckingham Wy EWD/SEL/PNX NG16 ...16 A3
Bucklow Cl WOL/BIL/BRX NG8...30 A4
Buckminster Rd ILK DE7 ...37 F4
Budby Ri HUCK/RAV NG15 ...5 C5
Bulcote Dr CALV/BJ NG14 ...34 C2
Bulcote Rd CFTN/RUD NG11 ...66 B3
Bullace Rd MAPPK/POR/STA NG3 ...44 A1
Bull Close Rd NOTTE NG7 ...56 B3
Buller St ILK DE7 ...38 B2
Buller Ter ARN NG5 ...31 G2
Bullfinch Rd BLWL NG6 ...30 A1
Bullins Cl ARN NG5 ...19 F1
Bullivant St MAPPK/POR/STA NG3 ...3 G1
Bulwell High Rd BLWL NG6 ...17 G4
Bulwell La BLWL NG6 ...30 A1
Bulwer Rd NOTTE NG7 ...42 C5
Bunbury St WBRGFD NG2 ...57 G2
Bunny La COT/KEY/RAD NG12 ...82 A2
Bunting Cl ILK DE7 ...37 F2
Buntings La CARL NG4 ...44 D1
Bunting St NOTTE NG7 ...56 B2
Burcot Cl ILK DE7 ...24 B5
Burden La COT/KEY/RAD NG12 ...35 H4
Burford Rd NOTTE NG7 ...30 C5
Burford St ARN NG5 ...19 H2
Burgass Rd MAPPK/POR/STA NG3 ...44 B1
Burge Cl WBRGFD NG2 ...57 F1
Burgh Hall Cl BSTN/STPLFD NG9 ...64 B4
Burhill CFTN/RUD NG11 ...71 F4
Burleigh Cl CARL NG4 ...45 G1
Burleigh Rd WBRGFD NG2 ...58 A5
Burleigh St ILK DE7 ...26 A4
Burlington Rd ARN NG5 ...31 F2
CARL NG4 ...33 G5
Burnaby St BLWL NG6 ...30 A1
Burnbank Cl WBRGFD NG2 ...69 E1
Burnbreck Gdns WOL/BIL/BRX NG8 ...40 D4
Burncroft ILK DE7 ...36 B1
Burndale Wk ARN NG5 ...18 B2
Burnham Av BSTN/STPLFD NG9 ...65 E2
Burnham Cl ILK DE7 ...24 A5
Burnham St ARN NG5 ...31 F3
Burnham Wy WBRGFD NG2 ...43 F5

Burns Av NOTTE NG7 ...2 B2
Burnside Dr BSTN/STPLFD NG9 ...54 B1
Burnside Gv COT/KEY/RAD NG12 ...68 D5
Burnside Rd WBRGFD NG2 ...67 H1
WOL/BIL/BRX NG8 ...40 C2
Burns St HEANOR DE75 ...6 A5
ILK DE7 ...25 H5
NOTTE NG7 ...2 A2
Burnt House Rd HEANOR DE75 ...12 A1
Burnt Oak Cl EWD/SEL/PNX NG16 ...28 C2
Burnwood Dr WOL/BIL/BRX NG8 ...40 C3
Burr La ILK DE7 ...26 A4
Burrows Av BSTN/STPLFD NG9 ...55 E2
Burrows Ct MAPPK/POR/STA NG3 ...44 A3
Burrows Crs BSTN/STPLFD NG9...55 E2
Burtness Rd CFTN/RUD NG11 ...66 A5
Burton Av CARL NG4 ...32 C5
Burton Cl CARL NG4 ...33 H5
Burton Dr BSTN/STPLFD NG9 ...64 B2
Burton Rd CARL NG4 ...33 H5
Burton St HEANOR DE75 ...6 B5
NOTT NG1 ...2 E4
Burwell St NOTTE NG7 ...42 C1
Bush Cl ARN NG5 ...18 C2
Bushy Cl LGEAT NG10 ...72 B3
Bute Av NOTTE NG7 ...42 C4
Butler Av COT/KEY/RAD NG12 ...47 F4
Butlers Cl HUCK/RAV NG15 ...11 E4
Buttermead Cl BSTN/STPLFD NG9 ...53 E1
Buttermere Cl LGEAT NG10 ...62 B4
WBRGFD NG2 ...58 D4
Buttermere Ct ARN NG5 ...31 F3
Buttermere Dr BSTN/STPLFD NG9 ...54 C3
Butterton Cl ILK DE7 ...38 B1
Buttery Gdns CFTN/RUD NG11 ...77 F3
Butt Rd BING/VBLV NG13 ...49 F3
Butts Cl ILK DE7 ...38 B4
Butt St LGEAT NG10 ...62 C1
Buxton Av CARL NG4 ...33 E4
HEANOR DE75 ...12 C3
Buxton Gn HEANOR * DE75 ...12 C3
Byard La NOTT NG1 ...3 F5
Byfield Cl NOTTE NG7 ...42 C2
Byford Cl MAPPK/POR/STA NG3 ...31 H3
Byley Rd WOL/BIL/BRX NG8 ...40 A3
By-Pass Rd BSTN/STPLFD NG9...54 A4
Byrne Ct ARN NG5 ...20 C5
Byron Av LGEAT NG10 ...62 C3
Byron Ct BSTN/STPLFD NG9 ...53 F2
WBRGFD * NG2 ...J5
Byron Crs EWD/SEL/PNX NG16 ...14 C3
Byron Gv ARN NG5 ...31 F2
Byron Rd WBRGFD NG2 ...58 A4
Byron St ARN NG5 ...19 G3
HUCK/RAV NG15 ...11 F1
ILK DE7 ...26 A4

C

Caddaw Av HUCK/RAV NG15 ...11 F1
Cadlan Cl ARN NG5 ...18 D3
Caernarvon Pl BSTN/STPLFD * NG9 ...64 A2
Caincross Rd WOL/BIL/BRX NG8 ...40 C1
Cairns Cl ARN NG5 ...18 D5
Cairnsmore Cl LGEAT NG10 ...62 B5
Cairo St NOTTE NG7 ...30 C4
Caister Rd CFTN/RUD NG11 ...76 B1
Caldbeck Cl WBRGFD NG2 ...58 D4
Caldbeck Ct BSTN/STPLFD NG9 ...64 A2
Caldbeck Wk ARN NG5 ...19 E3
Calderdale WOL/BIL/BRX NG8 ...40 A5
Calderdale Dr LGEAT NG10 ...72 B3
Calderhall Gdns ARN NG5 ...19 F2
Caledon Rd ARN NG5 ...31 E3
Calladine Rd HEANOR DE75 ...6 A5
Callaway Cl WOL/BIL/BRX NG8 ...40 D3
Calstock Rd ARN NG5 ...19 H5
Calveley Rd WOL/BIL/BRX NG8 ...28 C5
Calver Cl WOL/BIL/BRX NG8 ...41 H4
Calvert Cl BSTN/STPLFD NG9 ...64 C1
Calverton Av CARL NG4 ...32 C4
Calverton Cl BSTN/STPLFD NG9...63 H4
Calverton Dr WOL/BIL/BRX NG8 ...28 C3
Calverton Rd ARN NG5 ...20 B1
Camberley Cl BLWL NG6 ...17 F2
Camberley Rd BLWL NG6 ...17 F2
Camborne Dr WOL/BIL/BRX NG8 ...29 D4

Cambria Ms
  MAPPK/POR/STA NG3 ......43 F1
Cambridge Crs
  BSTN/STPLFD NG9 ......53 E1
Cambridge Gdns *ARN* NG5 ......20 C5
Cambridge Rd *WBRGFD* NG2 ......58 B4
  WOL/BIL/BRX NG8 ......41 F4
Cambridge St *CARL* NG4 ......33 F5
Camdale Cl *BSTN/STPLFD* NG9 ......64 A1
Camden Cl *WBRGFD* NG2 ......3 K5
Camelia Av *CFTN/RUD* NG11 ......65 H5
Camelot Av *ARN* NG5 ......30 D3
Camelot Crs *CFTN/RUD* NG11 ......77 E1
Camelot St *CFTN/RUD* NG11 ......77 E1
Cameo Cl *CARL* NG4 ......45 G2
Cameron St *ARN* NG5 ......31 F3
Camomile Cl *ARN* NG5 ......18 B3
Camomile Gdns *NOTTE* NG7 ......30 B5
Campbell Dr *CARL* NG4 ......32 D3
Campbell Gdns *ARN* NG5 ......20 D1
Campbell Gv
  MAPPK/POR/STA NG3 ......3 H3
Campbell St *EWD/SEL/PNX* NG16 ......7 H4
  MAPPK/POR/STA NG3 ......3 J3
Campden Gn *CFTN/RUD* NG11 ......66 B4
Campion St *ARN* NG5 ......19 H2
Campion Wy *BING/VBLV* NG13 ......48 C3
Camrose Cl *WOL/BIL/BRX* NG8 ......29 E5
Canal Side *BSTN/STPLFD* NG9 ......65 C3
Canal St *ILK* DE7 ......26 B4
  LGEAT NG10 ......62 C1
  LGEAT NG10 ......62 D5
  NOTT NG1 ......3 G7
Canberra Cl *BSTN/STPLFD* NG9 ......53 F2
Canberra Crs *WBRGFD* NG2 ......67 G2
Canberra Gdns *WBRGFD* NG2 ......67 G3
Candleby Cl *COT/KEY/RAD* NG12 ......71 E3
Candleby La
  COT/KEY/RAD NG12 ......71 E3
Candle Meadow *WBRGFD* NG2 ......45 E4
Canning Ter *NOTT* NG1 ......2 B4
Cannock Wy *LGEAT* NG10 ......73 H2
Cannon St *ARN* NG5 ......31 F2
Canon Cl *ILK* DE7 ......13 H5
Cantabury Av *NOTTE* NG7 ......42 C1
Cantelupe Rd *ILK* DE7 ......26 A5
Canterbury Cl
  EWD/SEL/PNX NG16 ......28 C1
Canterbury Rd
  WOL/BIL/BRX NG8 ......42 A3
Cantley Av *CARL* NG4 ......33 F3
Cantrell Rd *BLWL* NG6 ......17 H4
Canver Cl *WOL/BIL/BRX* NG8 ......40 B2
Canwick Cl *WOL/BIL/BRX* NG8 ......40 B3
Caporn Cl *BLWL* NG6 ......17 H5
Cardale Rd
  MAPPK/POR/STA NG3 ......44 B2
Cardinal Cl *MAPPK/POR/STA* NG3 ......3 K1
Cardington Cl *ARN* NG5 ......18 B1
Cardwell St *NOTTE* NG7 ......30 C5
Carew Rd *CFTN/RUD* NG11 ......66 B4
Carey Rd *BLWL* NG6 ......17 H2
Carisbrooke Av
  BSTN/STPLFD NG9 ......55 F3
  CARL NG4 ......34 A4
  MAPPK/POR/STA NG3 ......31 F3
Carisbrooke Dr
  MAPPK/POR/STA NG3 ......31 F4
Carlile Rd *CARL* NG4 ......33 F5
Carlingford Rd *HUCK/RAV* NG15 ......5 F5
Carlin St *BLWL* NG6 ......17 G3
Carlisle Av *BLWL* NG6 ......17 H3
Carlton Cl *HEANOR* DE75 ......6 D4
Carlton Fold *WBRGFD* * NG2 ......44 A5
Carlton Hl *CARL* NG4 ......45 E1
Carlton Ms *CARL* NG4 ......44 D1
Carlton Rd *LGEAT* NG10 ......72 C4
  MAPPK/POR/STA NG3 ......44 A2
Carlton St *NOTT* NG1 ......3 G5
Carlton Vale Cl *CARL* NG4 ......33 E4
Carlyle Rd *WBRGFD* NG2 ......57 H5
Carlyle Rd *WBRGFD* NG2 ......57 H4
Carlyle St *HEANOR* DE75 ......6 A4
Carman Cl *EWD/SEL/PNX* NG16 ......15 H4
Carmel Gdns *ARN* NG5 ......20 A4
Carnarvon Cl *BING/VBLV* NG13 ......48 D2
Carnarvon Gv *CALV/BJ* NG14 ......23 E5
Carnarvon Gv *CARL* NG4 ......33 E5
Carnarvon Pl *BING/VBLV* NG13 ......48 C3
Carnarvon Rd *WBRGFD* NG2 ......58 A3
Carnarvon St *CARL* NG4 ......45 E2
Carnforth Cl *BSTN/STPLFD* NG9 ......63 E1
Carnwood Rd *ARN* NG5 ......18 D4
Caroline Ct *ILK* DE7 ......38 C1
Caroline Wk
  MAPPK/POR/STA NG3 ......43 G1
Carradale Cl *ARN* NG5 ......20 D2
Carrfield Av *BSTN/STPLFD* NG9 ......63 G5

LGEAT NG10 ......73 G1
Carrington Ct *ARN* NG5 ......31 F4
Carrington St *NOTT* NG1 ......3 F7
Carrock Av *HEANOR* DE75 ......13 E1
Carroll Gdns *WBRGFD* NG2 ......57 E2
Carr Rd *BING/VBLV* NG13 ......49 G2
Cartbridge *COT/KEY/RAD* NG12 ......71 E4
Carter Av *CFTN/RUD* NG11 ......77 F3
  COT/KEY/RAD NG12 ......47 G5
Carter Ga *LGEAT* NG10 ......72 C2
Carter Ga *NOTT* NG1 ......3 H6
Carter Rd *BSTN/STPLFD* NG9 ......63 C4
Carters Wood Dr
  EWD/SEL/PNX NG16 ......29 E2
Carver St *NOTTE* NG7 ......30 C5
Carwood Rd *BSTN/STPLFD* NG9 ......54 C2
Castellan Ri *ARN* NG5 ......19 F2
Casterton Rd *ARN* NG5 ......19 E2
Castle Bvd *NOTT* NG1 ......2 E7
  NOTTE NG7 ......42 D5
Castle Bridge Rd *WBRGFD* NG2 ......56 D1
Castlefields *WBRGFD* NG2 ......57 E1
Castle Gdns *NOTTE* NG7 ......42 C5
Castle Ga *NOTT* NG1 ......2 E6
Castle Marina Rd *WBRGFD* NG2 ......56 D1
Castle Meadow *WBRGFD* NG2 ......2 E7
Castle Ms *NOTTE* NG7 ......2 A7
Castle Pk *WBRGFD* NG2 ......57 E1
Castle Quay *NOTT* NG7 ......43 E5
Castlerigg Cl *WBRGFD* NG2 ......68 D1
Castle Rd *NOTT* NG1 ......2 E6
Castle St *EWD/SEL/PNX* NG16 ......14 B1
  WBRGFD NG2 ......44 A4
Castleton Av *ARN* NG5 ......20 A4
  CARL NG4 ......33 F4
  ILK DE7 ......13 H5
Castleton Cl *HUCK/RAV* NG15 ......10 C1
  WBRGFD NG2 ......57 E2
Castleton Ct
  EWD/SEL/PNX NG16 ......17 E4
Castle Vw *EWD/SEL/PNX* NG16 ......14 B1
  WBRGFD NG2 ......57 G5
Caterham Cl *WOL/BIL/BRX* NG8 ......40 C1
Cat & Fiddle La *ILK* DE7 ......36 A2
Catfoot La *ILK* DE7 ......21 E2
Catherine Av *ILK* DE7 ......38 A2
Catherine Cl *BLWL* NG6 ......17 F3
Catkin Dr *EWD/SEL/PNX* NG16 ......14 D3
Catlow Wk *ARN* NG5 ......19 F2
Cator Cl *CARL* NG4 ......33 E2
Cator La *BSTN/STPLFD* NG9 ......64 C1
Cator La North
  BSTN/STPLFD NG9 ......54 B5
Catterley Hill Rd
  MAPPK/POR/STA NG3 ......44 C2
Cattle Market Rd *WBRGFD* NG2 ......57 G1
Catton Rd *ARN* NG5 ......20 B2
Caulton St *NOTTE* NG7 ......42 C2
Caunton Av
  MAPPK/POR/STA NG3 ......31 H1
Causeway Ms *WBRGFD* NG2 ......57 H4
Cavell Cl *CFTN/RUD* NG11 ......66 A4
Cavendish Av *CARL* NG4 ......33 E3
Cavendish Av *HUCK/RAV* NG15 ......11 H2
Cavendish Crs
  BSTN/STPLFD NG9 ......53 E1
  CARL NG4 ......33 E5
Cavendish Crs North *NOTT* NG7 ......2 A8
Cavendish Crs South *NOTT* NG7 ......2 A7
Cavendish Dr *CARL* NG4 ......33 F5
Cavendish Ms *NOTTE* NG7 ......2 B5
Cavendish Pl *BSTN/STPLFD* NG9 ......55 E5
  NOTTE * NG7 ......2 A8
Cavendish Rd *CARL* NG4 ......32 D3
  ILK DE7 ......38 A2
  LGEAT NG10 ......62 D4
Cavendish Rd East *NOTTE* NG7 ......2 B5
Cavendish Rd West *NOTTE* NG7 ......2 A6
Cavendish St *ARN* NG5 ......19 H2
  NOTTE NG7 ......56 B3
Cavendish V *ARN* NG5 ......31 G2
Caversham Wy *ILK* DE7 ......24 A5
Cawston Gdns *BLWL* NG6 ......17 G2
Caxmere Dr *WOL/BIL/BRX* NG8 ......41 E3
Caxton Cl *CARL* NG4 ......45 H1
Caythorpe Crs *ARN* NG5 ......31 F2
Caythorpe Ri *ARN* NG5 ......31 F1
Cecil St *WBRGFD* NG2 ......42 C5
Cedar Av *BSTN/STPLFD* NG9 ......55 F4
  LGEAT NG10 ......72 D4
Cedar Cl *BING/VBLV* NG13 ......49 F3
  LGEAT NG10 ......52 C4
Cedar Dr *COT/KEY/RAD* NG12 ......82 B2
Cedar Ldg *NOTTE* * NG7 ......2 B5

Cedar Pk *ILK* DE7 ......25 H5
Cedar Rd *BSTN/STPLFD* NG9 ......64 D1
  NOTTE NG7 ......30 D5
Cedar Tree Rd *ARN* NG5 ......19 E5
Celandine Cl *ARN* NG5 ......18 B3
Celandine Gdns
  BING/VBLV NG13 ......48 B3
Celia Dr *CARL* NG4 ......45 E1
Cemetery Rd *BSTN/STPLFD* NG9 ......53 F4
Centenary Wy *ILK* DE7 ......37 F1
Central Av *ARN* NG5 ......20 A3
  BSTN/STPLFD NG9 ......55 E5
  BSTN/STPLFD NG9 ......54 C5
  BSTN/STPLFD NG9 ......54 D2
  HUCK/RAV NG15 ......11 F1
  LGEAT NG10 ......52 C5
  MAPPK/POR/STA NG3 ......32 B1
  NOTTE NG7 ......30 D4
  WBRGFD NG2 ......58 A4
Central Ct *NOTTE* NG7 ......56 C2
Central St *MAPPK/POR/STA* NG3 ......3 K1
Centre Wy *COT/KEY/RAD* NG12 ......46 D4
Centurion Wy *NOTTE* NG7 ......56 D3
Cernan Ct *BLWL* NG6 ......17 E5
Cerne Cl *CFTN/RUD* NG11 ......76 D1
Chaceley Wy *CFTN/RUD* NG11 ......66 D3
The Chaddesden
  MAPPK/POR/STA * NG3 ......43 F1
Chadwick Rd *NOTTE* NG7 ......42 B1
Chain La *NOTTE* * NG7 ......56 B2
Chalfield Cl *CFTN/RUD* NG11 ......76 D1
Chalfont Dr *WOL/BIL/BRX* NG8 ......41 H2
Chalons Cl *ILK* DE7 ......26 A4
Chalons Wy *ILK* DE7 ......26 A5
Chamberlain Cl *CFTN/RUD* NG11 ......65 H5
Chambers Av *ILK* DE7 ......38 C1
Champion Av *ILK* DE7 ......25 F2
The Chancery
  BSTN/STPLFD NG9 ......54 B4
Chancery Ct *CFTN/RUD* NG11 ......56 D5
Chandos Av *CARL* NG4 ......33 H5
Chandos St *CARL* NG4 ......45 H1
  MAPPK/POR/STA NG3 ......43 H1
Chantrey Cl *BSTN/STPLFD* NG9 ......64 C2
Chantrey Rd *WBRGFD* NG2 ......57 H4
Chantry Cl *LGEAT* NG10 ......72 B5
Chapel Bar *NOTT* NG1 ......2 D5
Chapel La *ARN* NG5 ......19 H2
  BING/VBLV NG13 ......48 D1
  CARL NG4 ......22 A3
  COT/KEY/RAD NG12 ......71 E3
Chapel Mews Ct
  BSTN/STPLFD * NG9 ......54 A3
Chapel Pl *EWD/SEL/PNX* NG16 ......15 G4
Chapel St *BSTN/STPLFD* NG9 ......54 A3
  CFTN/RUD NG11 ......77 F3
  EWD/SEL/PNX NG16 ......14 A1
  EWD/SEL/PNX NG16 ......15 G4
  HEANOR DE75 ......12 D2
  ILK DE7 ......25 H4
  LGEAT NG10 ......52 C5
Chapter Dr *EWD/SEL/PNX* NG16 ......15 H5
Chardlace Wk *NOTT* NG1 ......3 H6
Chard St *NOTTE* NG7 ......30 C5
Charlbury Ct
  BSTN/STPLFD * NG9 ......40 A4
Charlbury Rd
  WOL/BIL/BRX NG8 ......41 G2
Charlecote Dr
  WOL/BIL/BRX NG8 ......40 C5
Charlecote Park Dr
  WBRGFD NG2 ......67 F2
Charles Av *BSTN/STPLFD* NG9 ......53 G3
  BSTN/STPLFD NG9 ......55 F2
  BSTN/STPLFD NG9 ......64 B3
  EWD/SEL/PNX NG16 ......14 C1
  LGEAT NG10 ......52 C5
Charles Cl *CARL* NG4 ......33 G3
  ILK DE7 ......38 C2
Charles Pk *BLWL* NG6 ......17 H5
Charles St *ARN* NG5 ......19 H3
  CFTN/RUD NG11 ......77 F2
  HUCK/RAV NG15 ......5 F5
  LGEAT NG10 ......73 E3
Charlesworth Av *NOTTE* NG7 ......30 B5
Charlock Cl *ARN* NG5 ......18 B3
Charlock Gdns *BING/VBLV* NG13 ......48 C4
Charlotte Gv *BSTN/STPLFD* NG9 ......54 C2
Charlotte St *ILK* DE7 ......25 H2
Charlton Av *LGEAT* NG10 ......73 G3
Charlton Gv *BSTN/STPLFD* NG9 ......64 C2
Charnock Av *WOL/BIL/BRX* NG8 ......42 A5
Charnwood Av
  BSTN/STPLFD NG9 ......54 C5
  COT/KEY/RAD NG12 ......82 B2
  LGEAT NG10 ......62 B2
  LGEAT NG10 ......72 C5
Charnwood Gv *BING/VBLV* NG13 ......48 C3

  HUCK/RAV NG15 ......4 D5
  WBRGFD NG2 ......57 H4
Charnwood La *ARN* NG5 ......20 B4
Charter Pk *ILK* DE7 ......37 H1
Chartwell Av *CFTN/RUD* NG11 ......77 E2
Chartwell Gv
  MAPPK/POR/STA NG3 ......20 C5
Chase Pk *WBRGFD* NG2 ......44 B5
Chatham St *NOTT* NG1 ......2 E1
Chatsworth Av
  BSTN/STPLFD NG9 ......64 B4
  CARL NG4 ......33 F5
  COT/KEY/RAD NG12 ......47 F4
  LGEAT NG10 ......73 H3
  NOTTE NG7 ......30 D5
Chatsworth Ct *LGEAT* NG10 ......62 C2
Chatsworth Ct *ILK* DE7 ......24 B5
Chatsworth Dr *HUCK/RAV* NG15 ......11 F1
Chatsworth Pl *ILK* DE7 ......37 E3
Chatsworth Rd *WBRGFD* NG2 ......58 C3
Chaucer St *ILK* DE7 ......26 A4
  NOTT NG1 ......2 C3
Chaworth Av
  EWD/SEL/PNX NG16 ......15 G1
Chaworth Rd *BING/VBLV* NG13 ......48 C3
  CARL NG4 ......45 G2
  WBRGFD NG2 ......57 H5
Cheadle Cl
  MAPPK/POR/STA NG3 ......32 C3
  WOL/BIL/BRX NG8 ......40 C3
Cheddar Cl *CFTN/RUD* NG11 ......76 B1
Chedington Av
  MAPPK/POR/STA NG3 ......21 E4
Chediston V *ARN* NG5 ......19 E2
Chedworth Cl
  MAPPK/POR/STA NG3 ......44 A3
Chelmsford Rd *NOTTE* NG7 ......30 C3
Chelsbury Ct *ARN* NG5 ......19 H3
Chelsea St *EWD/SEL/PNX* NG16 ......28 D2
Chelsea St *NOTTE* NG7 ......30 C4
Cheltenham Cl
  BSTN/STPLFD NG9 ......63 G4
Cheltenham St *BLWL* NG6 ......30 B1
Chennel Nook
  COT/KEY/RAD NG12 ......71 F4
Chepstow Rd *CFTN/RUD* NG11 ......76 B1
Cherhill Cl *CFTN/RUD* NG11 ......76 A1
Cheriton Dr *ILK* DE7 ......25 F2
Cherry Av *HUCK/RAV* NG15 ......11 G4
Cherry Cl *ARN* NG5 ......19 H2
Cherry Hl *COT/KEY/RAD* NG12 ......82 C1
Cherry Orch
  COT/KEY/RAD NG12 ......70 D3
Cherry Orchard Mt *ARN* NG5 ......19 E3
Cherry St *BING/VBLV* NG13 ......49 E3
Cherry Tree Cl
  BWSH/BRSTN DE72 ......62 A2
  COT/KEY/RAD NG12 ......61 E1
  ILK DE7 ......37 G2
Cherry Tree La
  COT/KEY/RAD NG12 ......68 C3
Cherry Wood Dr
  WOL/BIL/BRX NG8 ......41 G1
Cherrywood Gdns
  MAPPK/POR/STA NG3 ......32 B5
Chertsey Cl
  MAPPK/POR/STA NG3 ......32 A4
Chertsey Ct *ILK* DE7 ......24 A5
Cherwell Ct *BLWL* NG6 ......17 E4
Chesham Dr *ARN* NG5 ......31 E3
  BSTN/STPLFD NG9 ......40 A5
Chesil Av *WOL/BIL/BRX* NG8 ......42 A3
Cheslyn Dr *WOL/BIL/BRX* NG8 ......29 H5
Chesterfield Av
  BING/VBLV NG13 ......48 D2
  CARL NG4 ......33 E3
  LGEAT NG10 ......73 G2
Chesterfield Dr *CALV/BJ* NG14 ......23 F5
Chesterfield St *CARL* NG4 ......45 E1
Chester Gn *BSTN/STPLFD* NG9 ......63 F4
Chesterman Cl
  EWD/SEL/PNX NG16 ......26 C1
Chestnut Av *BING/VBLV* NG13 ......48 D3
  BSTN/STPLFD NG9 ......55 E5
  MAPPK/POR/STA NG3 ......32 C3
Chestnut Dr
  EWD/SEL/PNX NG16 ......15 H4
Chestnut Gv *ARN* NG5 ......20 B2
  CALV/BJ NG14 ......35 E1
  CARL NG4 ......47 E4
  COT/KEY/RAD NG12 ......47 E4
  HUCK/RAV NG15 ......11 G3
  LGEAT NG10 ......52 B4
  MAPPK/POR/STA NG3 ......43 F1
  WBRGFD NG2 ......57 G4
Chestnut La *CFTN/RUD* NG11 ......74 D3
Chestnut Rd *EWD/SEL/PNX* NG16 ......6 D4
The Chestnuts *LGEAT* NG10 ......72 B1

MAPPK/POR/STA NG3 ....32 A4
Chetwin Rd WOL/BIL/BRX NG8 ....40 C3
Chetwynd Rd
  BSTN/STPLFD NG9 ....63 H4
Cheverton Ct
  MAPPK/POR/STA NG3 ....43 F1
Chevin Gdns ARN NG5 ....18 D1
Cheviot Dr BLWL NG6 ....17 E2
Cheviot Rd LGEAT NG10 ....62 B5
Chewton Av
  EWD/SEL/PNX NG16 ....14 B1
Chewton St
  EWD/SEL/PNX NG16 ....14 B1
Cheyne Wk HUCK/RAV NG15 ....5 G4
Cheyny Cl WBRGFD NG2 ....57 F2
Chichester Cl ARN NG5 ....18 B3
  ILK DE7 ....26 B5
Chichester Dr
  COT/KEY/RAD NG12 ....70 D2
Chidlow Rd WOL/BIL/BRX NG8 .....40 C3
Chigwell Cl WOL/BIL/BRX NG8 ....28 D2
Chilion Wy HUCK/RAV NG15 ....10 C1
Chiltern Av ARN NG5 ....24 B5
Chiltern Gdns LGEAT NG10 ....62 B5
Chiltern Wy ARN NG5 ....19 E4
Chilton Dr EWD/SEL/PNX NG16 ....15 H3
Chilvers Cl ARN NG5 ....18 D3
Chilwell Ct BLWL NG6 ....18 A3
Chilwell La HUCK/RAV NG15 ....54 A4
Chilwell Rd BSTN/STPLFD NG9 ....55 E5
Chilwell St NOTTE NG7 ....42 C5
Chingford Rd WOL/BIL/BRX NG8 ..28 D5
Chippendale St NOTTE NG7 ....42 C5
Chippenham Rd ARN NG5 ....19 E4
Chisbury Gn CFTN/RUD NG11 ......76 A2
Chisholm Wy ARN NG5 ....18 D4
Christchurch Rd
  HUCK/RAV NG15 ....10 C3
Christina Av BLWL NG6 ....29 H1
Christina Crs BLWL NG6 ....29 H1
Christine Cl HUCK/RAV NG15 ....5 H3
Christopher Cl
  WOL/BIL/BRX NG8 ....41 E2
Chrysalis Wy
  EWD/SEL/PNX NG16 ....7 F4
Church Av ARN NG5 ....19 H3
  NOTTE NG7 ....42 C5
Church Cl ARN NG5 ....19 G3
  BING/VBLV NG13 ....49 E2
  BSTN/STPLFD NG9 ....38 D4
  COT/KEY/RAD NG12 ....46 D5
  MAPPK/POR/STA * NG3 ....3 F1
Church Crs ARN NG5 ....19 G3
  BSTN/STPLFD NG9 ....63 H2
Church Cft WBRGFD NG2 ....58 A3
Churchdale Av
  BSTN/STPLFD NG9 ....53 F2
Church Dr East ARN NG5 ....19 H3
Church Dr ARN NG5 ....19 H3
  ARN NG5 ....31 E4
  COT/KEY/RAD NG12 ....82 B1
  HUCK/RAV NG15 ....5 F5
  ILK DE7 ....13 G5
  LGEAT NG10 ....52 C4
  WBRGFD NG2 ....58 A4
Churchfield La NOTTE NG7 ....42 B2
Church Ga COT/KEY/RAD NG12 ...80 D1
Church Gv NOTTE NG7 ....42 B5
Church HI EWD/SEL/PNX NG16 ....15 G4
Churchill Cl ARN NG5 ....20 A4
Churchill Dr BSTN/STPLFD NG9 ...53 F3
  CFTN/RUD NG11 ....77 E2
Church La ARN NG5 ....20 A1
  BLWL NG6 ....17 H3
  BSTN/STPLFD NG9 ....53 E4
  BSTN/STPLFD NG9 ....64 C5
  CFTN/RUD NG11 ....74 D3
  COT/KEY/RAD NG12 ....70 D3
  COT/KEY/RAD NG12 ....79 F2
  EWD/SEL/PNX NG16 ....7 H1
  EWD/SEL/PNX NG16 ....26 D3
  HUCK/RAV NG15 ....5 C3
  ILK DE7 ....51 H2
Church Ms WBRGFD NG2 ....57 G2
Church Rd CALV/BJ NG14 ....35 E1
  EWD/SEL/PNX NG16 ....9 E4
Churchside Gdns NOTTE NG7 ......30 B5
Church Sq NOTTE * NG7 ....42 C5
Church St ARN NG5 ....20 A2
  BING/VBLV NG13 ....49 E3
  BLWL NG6 ....30 B3
  BSTN/STPLFD NG9 ....53 E4
  BSTN/STPLFD NG9 ....54 A3
  BSTN/STPLFD NG9 ....55 E5
  CARL NG4 ....22 B2
  CARL NG4 ....45 F3
  CFTN/RUD NG11 ....77 F3
  COT/KEY/RAD NG12 ....35 H4

EWD/SEL/PNX NG16 ....13 H1
HEANOR DE75 ....12 C1
ILK DE7 ....25 H1
LGEAT NG10 ....52 C4
NOTTE NG7 ....42 C5
Church Vw ILK DE7 ....37 H1
Church View Cl ARN NG5 ....19 E1
Churchview Ct WBRGFD NG2 ......57 H4
Church Wk EWD/SEL/PNX NG16 ..7 H1
  EWD/SEL/PNX NG16 ....8 A5
Churnet Cl CFTN/RUD NG11 ....66 B2
Churston Ct
  BSTN/STPLFD * NG9 ....55 F5
Cinderhill Gv CARL NG4 ....33 F3
Cinderhill Rd BLWL NG6 ....29 G1
Citadel St NOTTE NG7 ....42 B3
The City BSTN/STPLFD NG9 ....55 F5
City Link WBRGFD NG2 ....3 J7
City Rd BSTN/STPLFD NG9 ....55 F5
  NOTTE NG7 ....56 A2
Clandon Dr ARN NG5 ....31 E3
Clanfield Rd WOL/BIL/BRX NG8 ...40 D1
Clapham St NOTTE NG7 ....42 B3
Clara Mount Rd HEANOR DE75 ...12 D1
Clarborough Dr ARN NG5 ....20 B4
Clarehaven BSTN/STPLFD NG9 ...63 F1
Claremont Av
  BSTN/STPLFD NG9 ....54 B3
  HUCK/RAV NG15 ....11 F2
Claremont Dr CFTN/RUD NG11 ....67 F3
Claremont Rd ARN NG5 ....31 E4
Clarence Rd BSTN/STPLFD NG9 ..64 C4
  LGEAT NG10 ....72 D3
Clarence St
  MAPPK/POR/STA NG3 ....3 K3
Clarendon Pk ARN NG5 ....31 E5
Clarendon St NOTTE NG1 ....2 C3
Clare St NOTT NG1 ....3 F4
Clare Va NOTTE NG7 ....2 C6
Clarewood Gv CFTN/RUD NG11 ...76 B2
Clarges St BLWL NG6 ....17 H4
Clarke Av ARN NG5 ....20 A2
Clarke Dr LGEAT NG10 ....72 B5
Clarke Rd WBRGFD NG2 ....57 H1
Clarke's La BSTN/STPLFD NG9 ....64 C2
Clarkson Dr BSTN/STPLFD NG9 ...55 G5
Claude St NOTTE NG7 ....56 B2
Claxton St HEANOR DE75 ....6 A5
Claxton Ter HEANOR DE75 ....6 A5
Clay Av MAPPK/POR/STA NG3 ....32 B2
Claye St LGEAT NG10 ....73 F2
Clayfield Cl BLWL NG6 ....17 F4
Claygate MAPPK/POR/STA NG3 ..33 H4
Clay La HEANOR DE75 ....6 C5
Claypole Rd NOTTE NG7 ....42 C1
Claytons Dr NOTTE NG7 ....56 B1
Clether Rd WOL/BIL/BRX NG8 ....40 C2
Cleve Av BSTN/STPLFD NG9 ....63 F3
Cleveland Av LGEAT NG10 ....73 G1
Cleveland Cl NOTTE NG7 ....42 B3
Cleveleys Rd
  BSTN/STPLFD NG9 ....63 F3
Clevely Wy CFTN/RUD NG11 ....66 B3
The Cliff BLWL NG6 ....29 G1
Cliff Bvd EWD/SEL/PNX NG16 .....15 G3
Cliff Crs COT/KEY/RAD NG12 ......47 E4
Cliff Dr COT/KEY/RAD NG12 ....47 F3
Cliffe Hill Av BSTN/STPLFD NG9 ..53 E4
Cliffgrove Av
  BSTN/STPLFD NG9 ....54 C5
Cliffmere Wk CFTN/RUD NG11 ....66 A5
Clifford Av BSTN/STPLFD NG9 ....54 B3
Clifford Cl COT/KEY/RAD NG12 ...79 C5
  LGEAT NG10 ....72 B5
Clifford Ct NOTTE * NG7 ....42 C5
Clifford St LGEAT NG10 ....73 F2
  NOTTE NG7 ....42 C2
Cliff Rd CARL NG4 ....45 E2
  COT/KEY/RAD NG12 ....46 D4
  NOTT NG1 ....3 G6
Cliff Wy COT/KEY/RAD NG12 ......47 E4
Clifton Av CFTN/RUD NG11 ....77 F1
  LGEAT NG10 ....73 H2
Clifton Bvd NOTTE NG7 ....56 A1
Clifton Br CFTN/RUD NG11 ....56 D5
Clifton Crs BSTN/STPLFD NG9 ....64 D3
Clifton Gv CARL NG4 ....33 F3
Clifton La CFTN/RUD NG11 ....66 A5
  CFTN/RUD NG11 ....76 A1
  CFTN/RUD NG11 ....76 D1
Clifton Rd CFTN/RUD NG11 ....77 F2
Clifton St BSTN/STPLFD NG9 ......55 F5
Clifton Ter NOTTE NG7 ....2 B7
Clinton Av ARN NG5 ....31 E5
  EWD/SEL/PNX NG16 ....7 G1
Clinton Ct NOTTE NG1 ....2 E2
Clinton St BSTN/STPLFD NG9 .....54 D4
Clinton Ter NOTTE * NG7 ....2 A4

Clipstone Av
  MAPPK/POR/STA NG3 ....32 B1
  NOTT NG1 ....2 D1
Clipstone Cl WOL/BIL/BRX NG8 ..28 C3
Clipston La COT/KEY/RAD NG12 ..79 G2
Clive Crs EWD/SEL/PNX NG16 ....15 H5
Cliveden Gn CFTN/RUD NG11 .....66 A5
The Cloisters BSTN/STPLFD NG9 ..55 F3
Cloister St NOTTE NG7 ....56 B1
The Close ARN NG5 ....31 F2
  BSTN/STPLFD NG9 ....64 C2
Close Quarters
  BSTN/STPLFD NG9 ....54 B3
Cloud Av BSTN/STPLFD NG9 ......53 G4
Clouds HI CFTN/RUD NG11 ....76 B1
Cloudside Rd LGEAT NG10 ....52 B4
Clough Ct WOL/BIL/BRX NG8 .....41 C1
Cloverdale COT/KEY/RAD NG12 ...71 F4
Clover Gn BLWL NG6 ....30 A2
Clover Lands CFTN/RUD NG11 .....67 F3
Cloverlands Dr
  EWD/SEL/PNX NG16 ....15 H3
Clover Ri EWD/SEL/PNX NG16 ....14 C1
Clumber Av ARN NG5 ....31 E5
  BSTN/STPLFD NG9 ....54 B3
  CARL NG4 ....45 H1
  MAPPK/POR/STA NG3 ....32 B1
Clumber Ct ILK DE7 ....14 A5
Clumber Crs North NOTTE NG7 ...2 A6
Clumber Crs South NOTTE NG7 ...2 A7
Clumber Dr COT/KEY/RAD NG12 ..47 F4
Clumber Rd WBRGFD NG2 ....58 A5
Clumber Rd East NOTTE NG7 ......2 B6
Clumber Rd West NOTTE NG7 .....2 A6
Clumber St LGEAT NG10 ....73 E2
  NOTT NG1 ....3 F4
Coach Dr EWD/SEL/PNX NG16 ...8 A3
Coachmans Cft
  WOL/BIL/BRX NG8 ....41 F3
Coachways ILK DE7 ....24 B2
Coates Av HUCK/RAV NG15 ....5 E3
Coatsby Rd EWD/SEL/PNX NG16 ..15 G3
Cobden St LGEAT NG10 ....73 E2
  NOTTE NG7 ....42 B3
Cockayne Cl LGEAT NG10 ....62 C3
Cocker Beck CARL NG4 ....22 B3
Cockerhouse Rd
  EWD/SEL/PNX NG16 ....7 H3
Cockington Rd
  WOL/BIL/BRX NG8 ....40 B3
Cockleys LGEAT NG10 ....72 D3
Cogley La BING/VBLV NG13 ....49 F3
Cohen Cl ARN NG5 ....20 C5
Cokefield Av WOL/BIL/BRX NG8 ..29 E2
Colborn St
  MAPPK/POR/STA NG3 ....44 A1
Colchester Rd
  WOL/BIL/BRX NG8 ....28 D4
Coleby Av NOTTE NG7 ....56 B1
Coleby Rd WOL/BIL/BRX NG8 ....29 E3
Coledale WBRGFD NG2 ....58 D5
Coleridge Crs ARN NG5 ....19 G3
Coleridge St NOTTE NG7 ....42 C2
Colesbourne Rd
  CFTN/RUD NG11 ....66 C4
Colindale Gdns
  EWD/SEL/PNX NG16 ....28 C2
Colinwood Av ARN NG5 ....18 B1
College Dr CFTN/RUD NG11 ....66 A4
College St BSTN/STPLFD NG9 .....54 D1
College St LGEAT NG10 ....62 C3
  NOTT NG1 ....2 C5
Colleymoor Leys La
  CFTN/RUD NG11 ....66 C4
Colliers Wy EWD/SEL/PNX NG16 ..29 F1
Colliery Cl WBRGFD NG2 ....57 E2
Collin Av LGEAT NG10 ....62 C2
Collin Gn ARN NG5 ....31 C1
Collington St BSTN/STPLFD NG9 ..54 D5
Collington Wy WBRGFD NG2 ....67 C1
Collingwood Cl CFTN/RUD NG11 ..66 B2
Collingwood Rd LGEAT NG10 ......73 E3
Collins Cl BLWL NG6 ....17 E5
Collins Homes
  BSTN/STPLFD * NG9 ....54 D2
Collin St BSTN/STPLFD NG9 ....55 E5
  NOTT NG1 ....3 F7
Collison St NOTTE NG7 ....42 C2
Collygate Rd WBRGFD NG2 ....57 G2
Colmon Cl ARN NG5 ....18 D3
Colonsay Ct BSTN/STPLFD NG9 ..39 E5
Colston Crs WBRGFD NG2 ....67 C2
Colston Ga COT/KEY/RAD NG12 ..71 F3
Colston Rd BLWL NG6 ....17 H5
Coltsfoot Ct BING/VBLV NG13 .....48 B4
Colville Ct NOTTE NG1 ....43 E1
Colville St NOTT NG1 ....43 E1
Colville Ter NOTT NG1 ....2 D1

Colville Vls NOTT * NG1 ....43 E1
Colwick Loop Rd CARL NG4 ....45 F3
Colwick Manor Farm CARL NG4 ..45 F3
Colwick Park Cl WBRGFD NG2 ....45 F3
Colwick Rd WBRGFD NG2 ....57 H2
Comery Av
  MAPPK/POR/STA NG3 ....44 B1
Comfrey Cl ARN NG5 ....18 B3
Commerce Sq NOTT NG1 ....3 G6
Commercial Av
  BSTN/STPLFD * NG9 ....55 E5
Commercial Rd BLWL NG6 ....17 G3
  COT/KEY/RAD NG12 ....82 B2
Commodore Gdns
  WOL/BIL/BRX NG8 ....29 H3
Common La BSTN/STPLFD NG9 ..54 A5
  EWD/SEL/PNX NG16 ....15 H3
  HUCK/RAV NG15 ....10 C1
Commons Cl
  EWD/SEL/PNX NG16 ....14 B2
Compton Acres WBRGFD NG2 ....57 E5
Compton Rd ARN NG5 ....31 E5
Comyn Gdns
  MAPPK/POR/STA NG3 ....3 G2
Condor Rd ILK DE7 ....38 A4
Conduit Cl WBRGFD NG2 ....57 F1
Coney Wk ARN NG5 ....18 C2
Conifer Crs CFTN/RUD NG11 ......76 B2
Coningsby Gdns East ARN NG5 ...32 A1
Coningsby Rd ARN NG5 ....20 A5
Coningswath Rd CARL NG4 ....32 D3
Conisborough Ter WBRGFD NG2 ..57 F2
Conisbrough Av CARL NG4 ....34 A4
Coniston Av BLWL NG6 ....29 H3
Coniston Cl WBRGFD NG2 ....58 D4
Coniston Dr ILK DE7 ....37 G3
Coniston Rd BSTN/STPLFD NG9 ..54 C2
  HUCK/RAV NG15 ....5 E4
  LGEAT NG10 ....62 B4
Connelly Cl ARN NG5 ....20 C4
The Connery HUCK/RAV NG15 ....5 F4
Connery Ms BSTN/STPLFD NG9 ..64 A5
Constance St NOTTE NG7 ....30 A5
Convent St NOTT NG1 ....3 G4
Conway Av CARL NG4 ....45 H1
Conway Cl
  MAPPK/POR/STA NG3 ....43 F1
Conway Crs CARL NG4 ....33 H5
Conway Gdns ARN NG5 ....20 A4
Conway Rd CARL NG4 ....45 H1
  HUCK/RAV NG15 ....10 C4
  LGEAT NG10 ....73 F1
Conway St LGEAT NG10 ....73 G1
Conway Wk
  MAPPK/POR/STA * NG3 ....43 F1
Cook Dr ILK DE7 ....38 B2
Cooke Cl LGEAT NG10 ....72 C2
Cookson Av CARL NG4 ....33 E3
Coombe Cl WOL/BIL/BRX NG8 ....41 H5
Coombe Rd EWD/SEL/PNX NG16 ..8 C3
Co-operative Av HUCK/RAV NG15 ..5 G4
Co-operative St LGEAT NG10 ....73 F2
Cooper Cl ARN NG5 ....20 D4
  BLWL NG6 ....17 E4
Coopers Gn WOL/BIL/BRX NG8 ..54 D1
Cooper St CARL NG4 ....45 H1
Copeland Av BSTN/STPLFD NG9 ..53 F3
Copeland Gv BING/VBLV NG13 ...48 B3
Copeland Rd HUCK/RAV NG15 ....5 H4
Cope St NOTTE NG7 ....42 C2
Coppice Av ILK DE7 ....13 G5
Coppice Ct HEANOR * DE75 ......12 C4
Coppice Dr EWD/SEL/PNX NG16 ..7 H4
  HEANOR DE75 ....12 C3
Coppice Ga ARN NG5 ....20 A2
Coppice Gv
  MAPPK/POR/STA NG3 ....32 A3
Coppice Rd ARN NG5 ....20 A2
Copplestone Dr
  MAPPK/POR/STA NG3 ....20 D4
The Copse BSTN/STPLFD NG9 ....54 B5
  HUCK/RAV NG15 ....11 H1
  ILK DE7 ....13 G5
Copse Cl CALV/BJ NG14 ....22 D5
Copseside Cl LGEAT NG10 ....72 B1
Corben Gdns BLWL NG6 ....17 E3
Corby Rd MAPPK/POR/STA NG3 ..31 H4
Corfield Av HEANOR DE75 ....12 C3
Coriander Cl BLWL NG6 ....30 A2
Corinth Rd CFTN/RUD NG11 ....66 B3
Corn Cl COT/KEY/RAD NG12 ......70 D4
Corncrake Av BLWL NG6 ....30 A2
Corncrake Dr ARN NG5 ....20 D3
Cornell Dr ARN NG5 ....20 D2
The Cornfields ARN * NG5 ....19 E2
Cornfield Rd
  EWD/SEL/PNX NG16 ....15 F3
Cornhill Rd CARL NG4 ....32 C5

Cornwall Av BSTN/STPLFD NG9 ....65 H2
Cornwallis Cl LGEAT NG10 ....73 E3
Cornwall Rd ARN NG5 ....57 E3
Coronation Av CFTN/RUD NG11 ...57 E3
   LGEAT NG10 ....52 B4
Coronation Rd
   EWD/SEL/PNX NG16 ....16 A4
   HUCK/RAV NG15 ....5 E4
   ILK DE7 ....26 B3
   MAPPK/POR/STA NG3 ....32 A1
Coronation St ILK DE7 ....25 H5
Coronation Wk CARL NG4 ....33 H4
Corporation Oaks
   MAPPK/POR/STA NG3 ....43 F1
Corporation Rd ILK DE7 ....38 B3
Corsham Gdns
   MAPPK/POR/STA NG3 ....44 B3
Cosby Rd WBRGFD NG2 ....44 A5
Cossall Rd BSTN/STPLFD NG9 ......26 D3
Costock Av ARN NG5 ....31 E1
Cotgrave Av CARL NG4 ....33 G3
Cotgrave Cl WOL/BIL/BRX NG8 ....28 C3
Cotgrave La
   COT/KEY/RAD NG12 ....69 H4
Cotgrave Rd
   COT/KEY/RAD NG12 ....79 G2
Cotmanhay Rd ILK DE7 ....26 A2
Coton Cl CFTN/RUD NG11 ....66 D3
Cotswold Cl LGEAT NG10 ....72 C1
Cotswold Rd WOL/BIL/BRX NG8 ...28 C4
Cottage Cl ILK DE7 ....25 G2
Cottage Garden La
   HEANOR DE75 ....6 A5
Cottage Meadow CARL NG4 ....45 G4
Cottage Ter NOTT NG1 ....2 B4
Cottam Dr ARN NG5 ....18 C2
Cottam Gdns ARN NG5 ....18 D2
Cottesmore Rd NOTTE NG7 ....42 C4
County Cl BSTN/STPLFD NG9 ....65 F1
County Rd CARL NG4 ....32 D2
   WBRGFD NG2 ....57 H1
Court Crs WOL/BIL/BRX NG8 ....40 D4
Courtenay Gdns
   MAPPK/POR/STA NG3 ....43 G1
Court Gdns CFTN/RUD NG11 ....67 E2
Courtleet Wy BLWL NG6 ....17 G5
Courtney Cl WOL/BIL/BRX NG8 ....40 D3
Court St NOTTE NG7 ....42 C1
Court Yd BSTN/STPLFD NG9 ....54 A3
Covedale Rd ARN NG5 ....19 F5
Coventry La BSTN/STPLFD NG9 ....39 H5
   WOL/BIL/BRX NG8 ....40 A3
Coventry Rd BLWL NG6 ....17 G4
   BSTN/STPLFD NG9 ....55 H4
Covert Cl CALV/BJ NG14 ....22 D5
   COT/KEY/RAD NG12 ....79 G5
   HUCK/RAV NG15 ....11 H1
Covert Crs COT/KEY/RAD NG12 ...47 C5
Covert Rd WBRGFD NG2 ....58 C5
Cowan St NOTT NG1 ....3 G4
Cowdrey Gdns ARN NG5 ....20 C4
Cowlairs ARN NG5 ....18 B3
Cow La BSTN/STPLFD NG9 ....54 B3
Cowley St BLWL NG6 ....30 A2
Cowper Rd ARN NG5 ....31 H1
   EWD/SEL/PNX NG16 ....14 C2
Cowslip Cl BING/VBLV NG13 ....48 B4
Coxmoor Cl COT/KEY/RAD NG12 ..68 C2
Crabtree Fld WBRGFD NG2 ....45 E4
Crabtree Rd BLWL NG6 ....17 F4
Cragdale Rd ARN NG5 ....19 F5
Cragmoor Rd CALV/BJ NG14 ....34 D2
Craig St LGEAT NG10 ....73 F2
Crammond Rd WBRGFD NG2 ....57 E1
Crampton Ct ARN NG5 ....18 D2
Cramworth Dr ARN NG5 ....31 G2
Cranberry Cl CFTN/RUD NG11 .....67 E1
Cranbourne Cl
   BSTN/STPLFD NG9 ....53 E1
Cranbourne Gv HUCK/RAV NG15...4 D3
Cranbrook St NOTT NG1 ....3 G4
Cranfield Wk LGEAT NG10 ....66 C4
Cranfleet Wy LGEAT NG10 ....72 C2
Cranford Gdns WBRGFD NG2 ....67 F2
Cranmer Gv
   MAPPK/POR/STA NG3 ....43 F1
Cranmer St ILK DE7 ....26 A4
   LGEAT NG10 ....63 G5
   MAPPK/POR/STA NG3 ....43 F1
Cranmer Wk
   MAPPK/POR/STA NG3 ....43 F1
Cransley Av WOL/BIL/BRX NG8 ....54 C1
Cranston Av ARN NG5 ....20 A1
Cranston Rd BSTN/STPLFD NG9 ...54 B3
Cranthorne Dr
   MAPPK/POR/STA NG3 ....44 D2
Crantock Gdns
   COT/KEY/RAD NG12 ....82 C1

Cranwell Rd WOL/BIL/BRX NG8 ...28 C3
Craster Dr BLWL NG6 ....17 E2
Craven Rd NOTTE NG7 ....42 B1
Crawford Av BSTN/STPLFD NG9 ...53 E3
Crawford Cl WOL/BIL/BRX NG8 ...40 D3
Crawford Ri ARN NG5 ....20 D2
The Crescent ARN NG5 ....31 H1
   BSTN/STPLFD NG9 ....31 G4
   BSTN/STPLFD NG9 ....63 H4
   BSTN/STPLFD NG9 ....64 B3
   COT/KEY/RAD NG12 ....47 F4
   EWD/SEL/PNX NG16 ....8 B5
   MAPPK/POR/STA NG3 ....31 G5
Crescent Av CARL NG4 ....33 F4
Cresswell Rd BSTN/STPLFD NG9 ...64 A1
Cresta Gdns ARN NG5 ....31 G3
Crewe Cl NOTTE NG7 ....42 C2
Cribb Cl CFTN/RUD NG11 ....57 F2
Crich Vw ARN NG5 ....31 F3
Cricketers Ct WBRGFD NG2 ....58 A2
Criftin Rd CALV/BJ NG14 ....35 F1
Cripps Hl NOTTE NG7 ....55 H1
Critchley St ILK DE7 ....26 A4
Critch's Flats
   EWD/SEL/PNX NG16 ....15 G4
C Rd BSTN/STPLFD NG9 ....56 A4
Crocus Pl WBRGFD * NG2 ....4 F5
Crocus St WBRGFD NG2 ....57 F1
Croft Av HUCK/RAV NG15 ....11 F4
Croft Cl ILK DE7 ....50 C1
Croft Crs EWD/SEL/PNX NG16 ....14 D5
Crofton Cl BSTN/STPLFD NG9 ......64 A1
   WOL/BIL/BRX NG8 ....41 G2
Crofton Rd BSTN/STPLFD NG9 .....64 C4
Croft Rd ARN NG5 ....20 A2
   COT/KEY/RAD NG12 ....68 B2
The Crofts BING/VBLV NG13 ....48 D3
Cromarty Cl WBRGFD * NG2 ....57 E1
Cromdale Cl ARN NG5 ....20 D1
Cromeford Av CARL NG4 ....33 E5
Cromer Rd
   MAPPK/POR/STA NG3 ....43 H1
Cromford Cl EWD/SEL/PNX NG16 ....7 E3
   LGEAT NG10 ....72 B4
Cromford Rd
   EWD/SEL/PNX NG16 ....6 D3
   ILK DE7 ....38 A5
Crompton Rd ILK DE7 ....38 C5
Cromwell Av ILK DE7 ....38 B3
Cromwell Crs CARL NG4 ....22 A3
Cromwell St BSTN/STPLFD NG9 ...54 D5
Cromwell St CARL NG4 ....45 F1
   EWD/SEL/PNX NG16 ....14 C2
   NOTTE NG7 ....2 B3
Cropston Cl WBRGFD NG2 ....67 G2
Cropton Crs WOL/BIL/BRX NG8 ...41 G2
Cropton Gv BING/VBLV NG13 ....48 B3
Cropwell Gdns
   COT/KEY/RAD NG12 ....61 F1
Cropwell Gn
   MAPPK/POR/STA NG3 ....44 A2
Cropwell Rd
   COT/KEY/RAD NG12 ....47 E5
Crosby Rd WBRGFD NG2 ....58 A2
Crossdale Dr
   COT/KEY/RAD NG12 ....79 F5
Crossdale Wk ARN NG5 ....18 B2
Crossfield Dr ARN NG5 ....18 D1
Crossgate Dr WBRGFD NG2 ....56 D3
Crosshill COT/KEY/RAD NG12 ......71 F3
Crosshill ILK DE7 ....37 E3
Crosslands Meadow CARL NG4 .....45 G4
Crossley St ARN NG5 ....31 E3
Crossman St ARN NG5 ....31 E3
Cross St ARN NG5 ....19 H2
   BSTN/STPLFD NG9 ....55 E4
   CARL NG4 ....45 E1
   CARL NG4 ....45 H1
   EWD/SEL/PNX NG16 ....8 D5
   LGEAT NG10 ....52 D5
   LGEAT NG10 ....73 F1
Crowborough Av
   WOL/BIL/BRX NG8 ....54 A1
Crowcroft Wy LGEAT NG10 ....62 C4
Crow Hill Rd CARL NG4 ....45 G1
Crowley Cl WOL/BIL/BRX NG8 .....40 B2
Crown Cl LGEAT NG10 ....72 B2
Crow Park Dr CALV/BJ NG14 ....34 C2
Crowthorne Cl ARN NG5 ....18 B1
Crowthorne Gdns ARN NG5 ....18 B1
Croxall Cl CFTN/RUD NG11 ....66 B2
Croxley Gdns
   EWD/SEL/PNX NG16 ....28 C2
Croydon Rd NOTTE NG7 ....42 B4
Crummock Cl
   BSTN/STPLFD NG9 ....54 B3
Cuillin Cl LGEAT NG10 ....62 B5

Cumberland Av
   BSTN/STPLFD NG9 ....54 C5
Cumberland Cl
   CFTN/RUD * NG11 ....77 F2
Cumberland Pl NOTT NG1 ....2 D5
Cumbria Gra WBRGFD NG2 ....58 D4
Curlew Cl MAPPK/POR/STA NG3 ...44 A5
Curlew Whf WBRGFD * NG2 ....56 C1
Cursley Wy BSTN/STPLFD NG9 .....64 A4
Curtis St HUCK/RAV NG15 ....11 F1
Curzon Ct MAPPK/POR/STA NG3 ....3 H2
Curzon Gdns
   MAPPK/POR/STA NG3 ....3 H2
Curzon Pl MAPPK/POR/STA NG3 ....3 G3
Curzon St CARL NG4 ....45 H1
   LGEAT NG10 ....62 C4
   MAPPK/POR/STA NG3 ....3 G3
Cuxton Cl WOL/BIL/BRX NG8 ....28 C4
Cycle Rd NOTTE NG7 ....42 B4
Cypress Ct HUCK/RAV NG15 ....10 A2
Cyprus Av BSTN/STPLFD NG9 ....55 E4
Cyprus Dr BSTN/STPLFD NG9 ....55 E4
Cyprus Rd
   MAPPK/POR/STA NG3 ....31 F5
Cyril Av BSTN/STPLFD NG9 ....53 E4
   BSTN/STPLFD NG9 ....54 D4
   WOL/BIL/BRX NG8 ....30 A5
Cyril Rd WBRGFD NG2 ....58 B4

D

Dabell Av BLWL NG6 ....16 D2
Dagmar Gv BSTN/STPLFD NG9 .....55 F5
   MAPPK/POR/STA NG3 ....31 G4
Daisy Cl COT/KEY/RAD NG12 ......70 D4
Daisy Farm Rd
   EWD/SEL/PNX NG16 ....14 C2
Daisy Rd MAPPK/POR/STA NG3 ...32 B4
Dakeyne St
   MAPPK/POR/STA NG3 ....3 K4
Dalbeattie Cl ARN NG5 ....20 C2
Dalby Sq WOL/BIL/BRX NG8 ....41 H5
Dale Av CARL NG4 ....44 D1
   LGEAT NG10 ....63 E5
   MAPPK/POR/STA NG3 ....32 B3
Dalebrook Crs HUCK/RAV NG15 ...10 B2
Dale Cl HUCK/RAV NG15 ....10 B1
   WBRGFD NG2 ....58 C4
Dale Farm Av
   MAPPK/POR/STA NG3 ....44 B3
Dale Gv WBRGFD NG2 ....44 A4
Dalehead Rd CFTN/RUD NG11 ......66 A4
Dale La BSTN/STPLFD NG9 ....54 D5
Dalemoor Gdns
   WOL/BIL/BRX NG8 ....29 C5
   COT/KEY/RAD NG12 ....82 B1
   EWD/SEL/PNX NG16 ....15 C5
   ILK DE7 ....51 F1
Daleside COT/KEY/RAD NG12 ......71 E4
Daleside Rd WBRGFD NG2 ....44 B5
Daleside Rd East WBRGFD NG2 ....44 D4
Dale St ILK DE7 ....38 A1
   WBRGFD NG2 ....3 K6
Dale Ter WBRGFD * NG2 ....44 A4
Dale Vw ILK DE7 ....37 H2
Dale View Rd CARL NG4 ....44 C1
Dalkeith Ter NOTTE NG7 ....42 C1
Dallas York Rd
   BSTN/STPLFD NG9 ....55 G5
Dalley Cl BSTN/STPLFD NG9 ....53 F3
Dallimore Rd ILK DE7 ....37 G4
Dalton Cl BSTN/STPLFD NG9 ....63 F1
Daltons Cl EWD/SEL/PNX NG16 ...6 D3
Danbury Mt ARN NG5 ....31 G3
Dane Cl MAPPK/POR/STA NG3 ....3 G2
Dane Ct MAPPK/POR/STA NG3 ......3 G2
Danes Cl ARN NG5 ....19 G2
Danethorpe V ARN NG5 ....31 F2
Daniels Wy HUCK/RAV NG15 ....10 D3
Darfield Dr HEANOR DE75 ....6 D5
Darkey La BSTN/STPLFD NG9 ....63 F1
Dark La BING/VBLV NG13 ....49 F3
Darley Av BSTN/STPLFD NG9 ....63 F3
   CARL NG4 ....33 F4
   NOTTE NG7 ....42 B1
   LGEAT NG10 ....72 B4
Darley Rd NOTTE NG7 ....42 B1
Darley Sq ILK DE7 ....13 H5
Dariton Dr ARN NG5 ....20 C4
Darnal Cl ARN NG5 ....18 B3
Darnhall Crs WOL/BIL/BRX NG8 ....40 C1
Dartmeet Ct NOTTE NG7 ....42 A1
Darvel Cl WOL/BIL/BRX NG8 ....41 G2
Darwin Av ILK DE7 ....37 H1

Darwin Cl ARN NG5 ....18 B2
Darwin Rd LGEAT NG10 ....72 C4
David Cl ARN NG5 ....54 C2
David La BLWL NG6 ....30 A2
Davidson Cl ARN NG5 ....20 D3
Davies Rd WBRGFD NG2 ....58 B4
Davis Rd BSTN/STPLFD NG9 ....64 A3
Davy Cl HUCK/RAV NG15 ....5 C1
Dawlish Cl HUCK/RAV NG15 ....10 C1
Dawlish Ct EWD/SEL/PNX NG16 ....7 E4
Dawlish Dr ARN NG5 ....19 E5
Dawn Cl ARN NG5 ....5 C3
Dawn Vw BSTN/STPLFD NG9 ....53 E1
Dawson Cl EWD/SEL/PNX NG16 ...14 B1
Dawver Rd EWD/SEL/PNX NG16 ...15 C5
Daybrook Av ARN NG5 ....31 F2
Daybrook St ARN NG5 ....31 F2
Deabill St CARL NG4 ....45 H2
Dead La EWD/SEL/PNX NG16 ....27 E4
Deakins Pl NOTTE NG7 ....42 B3
Dean Av MAPPK/POR/STA NG3 .....32 C2
Dean Cl WOL/BIL/BRX NG8 ....40 C3
Dean Rd ARN NG5 ....19 E5
Deanscourt COT/KEY/RAD NG12 ...71 F3
Deans Cft BSTN/STPLFD NG9 ....54 A2
Dean St EWD/SEL/PNX NG16 ....7 F4
   NOTT NG1 ....3 H6
Debdale La COT/KEY/RAD NG12 ...79 E4
Deddington La
   BSTN/STPLFD NG9 ....54 B1
Deepdale Av BSTN/STPLFD NG9 ...53 E5
Deepdale Cl WBRGFD NG2 ....58 D4
Deepdale Ct HEANOR * DE75 ....12 B1
Deepdale Rd LGEAT NG10 ....72 B3
   WOL/BIL/BRX NG8 ....40 C4
Deepdene Cl WOL/BIL/BRX NG8 ...29 F3
Deepdene Wy
   WOL/BIL/BRX NG8 ....29 F3
Deep Furrow Av CARL NG4 ....33 G5
Deerleap Dr ARN NG5 ....19 F5
Deer Pk WOL/BIL/BRX NG8 ....40 D4
Deer Park Dr ARN NG5 ....19 F2
Delia Av HUCK/RAV NG15 ....5 H3
Dell Wy CFTN/RUD NG11 ....66 C4
Dellwood Cl
   MAPPK/POR/STA NG3 ....32 D3
Delta Ct NOTT NG1 ....2 D1
Delta St NOTTE NG7 ....30 C4
Delves Rd HEANOR DE75 ....12 A2
Delville Av COT/KEY/RAD NG12 ...79 F5
Denacre Av LGEAT NG10 ....63 G5
Denehurst Av
   WOL/BIL/BRX NG8 ....29 H4
Denewood Av
   BSTN/STPLFD NG9 ....54 B1
Denewood Crs
   WOL/BIL/BRX NG8 ....28 D5
Denholme Rd
   WOL/BIL/BRX NG8 ....40 C3
Denison Ct NOTTE * NG7 ....42 C2
Denison St BSTN/STPLFD NG9 ......54 D4
   NOTTE NG7 ....42 C2
Denman St Central NOTTE NG7 ....42 B3
Denman St East NOTTE NG7 ....42 C3
Denman St West NOTTE NG7 ....42 B3
Denmark Gv
   MAPPK/POR/STA NG3 ....31 G5
Dennett Cl MAPPK/POR/STA NG3 ...3 J2
Dennis Av BSTN/STPLFD NG9 ....54 D3
Dennis St CARL NG4 ....45 H1
Denstone Rd
   MAPPK/POR/STA NG3 ....3 K4
Dentale Dr WOL/BIL/BRX NG8 ......40 A4
Denton Av LGEAT NG10 ....52 B5
Denton Dr WBRGFD NG2 ....67 G2
Denver Ct BSTN/STPLFD NG9 ....53 F2
Depedale Av ILK DE7 ....37 G3
Deptford Crs BLWL NG6 ....17 H4
Derby Gv NOTTE NG7 ....42 C3
Derby Rd BSTN/STPLFD NG9 ....52 D5
   BSTN/STPLFD NG9 ....54 B2
   EWD/SEL/PNX NG16 ....7 F4
   HEANOR DE75 ....12 A1
   ILK DE7 ....37 C1
   LGEAT NG10 ....72 D1
   NOTTE NG7 ....2 B4
Derbyshire Av
   BSTN/STPLFD NG9 ....39 E4
   ILK DE7 ....24 B5
Derbyshire Cl ILK DE7 ....24 B5
Derbyshire Dr ILK DE7 ....37 H2
Derbyshire La HUCK/RAV NG15 ....5 F5
Derby St BSTN/STPLFD NG9 ....20 A3
   ILK DE7 ....26 A5
   NOTT NG1 ....2 C4
Derby Ter NOTTE NG7 ....2 A4
Dereham Dr ARN NG5 ....20 A4

Derry Hill Rd *ARN* NG5 ....19 H1
Derry La *BING/VBLV* NG13 ....49 G3
Derwent Av *ILK* DE7 ....24 B5
ILK DE7 ....25 C3
Derwent Cl *BSTN/STPLFD* NG9 ....64 D5
WBRGFD NG2 ....58 D4
Derwent Ct *NOTE* NG7 ....2 B1
Derwent Crs *ARN* NG5 ....5 C3
Derwent Dr *HUCK/RAV* NG15 .....11 F3
Derwent Wy *NOTTE* NG7 ....42 B5
NOTTE NG7 ....42 A3
Desford Cl *ARN* NG5 ....30 D1
De Vere Gdns *ARN* NG5 ....20 A5
Devitt Dr *HUCK/RAV* NG15 ....5 H3
Devon Circ *ARN* NG5 ....19 C1
Devon Cl *EWD/SEL/PNX* NG16 ......8 C5
LGEAT NG10 ....62 C1
Devon Dr *ARN* NG5 ....31 F3
CFTN/RUD NG11 ....77 C1
Devonshire Av
BSTN/STPLFD NG9 ....54 D5
LGEAT NG10 ....73 H2
Devonshire Cl *ILK* DE7 ....13 H5
Devonshire Crs *ARN* NG5 ....31 E3
Devonshire Dr
BSTN/STPLFD NG9 ....53 E1
EWD/SEL/PNX NG16 ....8 A5
Devonshire Prom *NOTTE* * NG7 ...42 B5
Devonshire Rd *ARN* NG5 ....57 H5
WBRGFD NG2 ....57 H5
Devon St *ILK* DE7 ....38 B3
MAPPK/POR/STA NG3 ....44 A3
Dewberry La *COT/KEY/RAD* NG12 ..61 G1
The Dial *COT/KEY/RAD* NG12 .....70 D5
Dickens Ct *EWD/SEL/PNX* NG16 ....8 C4
Dickson Dr *CFTN/RUD* NG11 ....77 C3
Didcot Dr *WOL/BIL/BRX* NG8 ....30 A4
Digby Av *MAPPK/POR/STA* NG3 ...32 C2
Digby Ct *NOTTE* * NG7 ....42 C5
Digby Hall Dr
MAPPK/POR/STA NG3 ....32 D2
Digby St *EWD/SEL/PNX* NG16 .....15 E4
ILK DE7 ....26 B4
Distillery St *CFTN/RUD* NG11 .....77 F3
Dockholm Rd *LGEAT* NG10 ....62 D4
Dogwood Av *BLWL* NG6 ....17 E3
Donbas Cl *BLWL* NG6 ....29 C1
Doncaster Av *LGEAT* NG10 ....52 C5
Doncaster Gv *LGEAT* NG10 ....63 G3
Doncaster Ter *WBRGFD* NG2 ....57 F2
Donington Rd *CFTN/RUD* NG11 ...66 B5
Donner Crs *ILK* DE7 ....13 H5
Dooland Dr
MAPPK/POR/STA NG3 ....32 A4
Dorchester Gdns *WBRGFD* NG2 ....67 H3
Dorchester Rd
EWD/SEL/PNX NG16 ....15 G3
Doris Rd *ILK* DE7 ....38 B1
Dorket Cl *ARN* NG5 ....31 F3
Dorket Dr *WOL/BIL/BRX* NG8 .....41 H5
Dorking Rd *NOTTE* NG7 ....42 B2
Dormy Cl *BSTN/STPLFD* NG9 ......54 B4
COT/KEY/RAD NG12 ....47 C5
Dormy Ct *BLWL* NG6 ....18 A3
Dornoch Av *ARN* NG5 ....31 G3
Dorothy Av *EWD/SEL/PNX* NG16 ...8 A4
HUCK/RAV NG15 ....5 G3
LGEAT NG10 ....62 C1
Dorothy Gv *WOL/BIL/BRX* NG8 ...41 H2
Dorset Gdns *WBRGFD* NG2 ....67 F1
Dorset St *WOL/BIL/BRX* NG8 ......42 A3
Dorterry Crs *ILK* DE7 ....38 B3
Douglas Av *CARL* NG4 ....45 E2
EWD/SEL/PNX NG16 ....14 D1
Douglas Cl *COT/KEY/RAD* NG12 ...61 E1
Douglas Crs *CARL* NG4 ....45 F2
Douglas Rd *BING/VBLV* NG13 .....49 G2
LGEAT NG10 ....52 C5
NOTTE NG7 ....42 C5
Douro Dr *ARN* NG5 ....20 C5
Dove Cl *BING/VBLV* NG13 ....49 E4
Dovecote Rd *WOL/BIL/BRX* NG8 ...40 D4
Dovecote La *BSTN/STPLFD* NG9 ...55 E5
Dovecote Rd *EWD/SEL/PNX* NG16 ..8 C5
Dovedale Av *LGEAT* NG10 ....72 B3
Dovedale Cir *ILK* DE7 ....13 H5
Dovedale Ct *LGEAT* NG10 ....72 C4
Dovedale Rd
MAPPK/POR/STA NG3 ....44 D2
WBRGFD NG2 ....68 B1
Dove La *LGEAT* NG10 ....62 B5
Dovenby Rd *CFTN/RUD* NG11 .....66 C3
Doveridge Av *CARL* NG4 ....33 H5
Doveridge Rd *CARL* NG4 ....33 C5
Dove St *BLWL* NG6 ....17 F3
Downes Ct *ARN* NG5 ....17 F3
Downham Cl *ARN* NG5 ....20 B4
Downing Cl *BLWL* NG6 ....17 G2

Downing St *BLWL* NG6 ....17 G2
The Downs *CFTN/RUD* NG11 ......66 D3
Dowson St *MAPPK/POR/STA* NG3 ..44 A2
Drakemyre Cl *ARN* NG5 ....20 C1
Drake Rd *CARL* NG4 ....46 A3
Draycott Rd *LGEAT* NG10 ....72 A4
Draymans Ct *NOTTE* NG7 ....30 C4
Drayton St *ARN* NG5 ....31 F3
The Drift *CFTN/RUD* NG11 ....66 B3
HUCK/RAV NG15 ....5 G3
The Drive *BSTN/STPLFD* NG9 .....64 D3
Dronfield Pl *ILK* DE7 ....13 H5
Drummond Av *CARL* NG4 ....46 A1
Drummond Dr
EWD/SEL/PNX NG16 ....28 D1
Drummond Rd *ILK* DE7 ....25 C4
Dryden St *NOTT* NG1 ....2 D2
Drysdale Cl *BLWL* NG6 ....17 G5
Duchess St *BLWL* NG6 ....17 G2
Duffield Cl *LGEAT* NG10 ....72 B4
Duke Cl *BLWL* NG6 ....17 E5
Duke Crs *EWD/SEL/PNX* NG16 ....14 D1
Dukes Pl *ILK* DE7 ....25 H1
NOTT NG1 ....3 H5
Duke St *ARN* NG5 ....19 G3
HUCK/RAV NG15 ....5 H5
ILK DE7 ....26 A2
NOTTE NG7 ....30 C5
Duke William Mt *NOTTE* NG7 ....2 A6
Dulverton V *WOL/BIL/BRX* NG8 ...29 G2
Dulwich Rd *NOTTE* NG7 ....42 B2
The Dumbles *CARL* NG4 ....22 A2
Dumbles Cl *ILK* DE7 ....37 F2
Dunblane Rd *CFTN/RUD* NG11 ...77 F3
Duncombe Cl
MAPPK/POR/STA NG3 ....43 H1
Duncroft Av *CARL* NG4 ....33 C4
Dundas Cl *NOTT* NG1 ....2 E2
Dungannon Rd *CFTN/RUD* NG11 ..76 D1
Dunholme Cl *BLWL* NG6 ....17 G2
Dunkery Rd *CFTN/RUD* NG11 .....76 C1
Dunkirk Rd *NOTTE* NG7 ....56 B2
Dunlin Whf *WBRGFD* * NG2 ....56 D1
Dunlop Av *NOTTE* NG7 ....42 B4
Dunsby Cl *CFTN/RUD* NG11 ....66 B5
Dunsford Dr
MAPPK/POR/STA NG3 ....20 D4
Dunsil Dr *WBRGFD* NG2 ....56 D3
Dunsil Rd *EWD/SEL/PNX* NG16 ....8 C1
Dunsmore Cl *BSTN/STPLFD* NG9 ..65 G2
Dunstan St *CARL* NG4 ....45 H1
Dunster Rd *EWD/SEL/PNX* NG16 ...8 C3
WBRGFD NG2 ....58 B5
Dunston Cl *LGEAT* NG10 ....73 G2
Durham Av *WBRGFD* NG2 ....44 A4
Durham Cl *WBRGFD* * NG2 ....44 A4
Durham Crs *BLWL* NG6 ....17 H4
Durham St *ILK* DE7 ....26 A4
Durlston Cl *WBRGFD* NG2 ....67 E1
Durnford St *NOTTE* NG7 ....30 C3
Dursley Cl *BLWL* NG6 ....17 G5
Dylan Thomas Rd *ARN* NG5 ....19 E2

E

Eagle Cl *ARN* NG5 ....20 B3
Eagle Ct *BLWL* NG6 ....18 A3
Eagle Rd *ILK* DE7 ....38 A4
Eardley Rd *ARN* NG5 ....18 B4
Earl Crs *CARL* NG4 ....33 G2
Earl Dr *EWD/SEL/PNX* NG16 ......14 D1
Earls Cl *WOL/BIL/BRX* NG8 ....40 B3
Earlsfield Dr *ARN* NG5 ....18 A1
Earlswood Dr
COT/KEY/RAD NG12 ....68 C2
Easedale Cl *WBRGFD* NG2 ....58 D4
East Acres *COT/KEY/RAD* NG12 ..71 E2
East Circus St *NOTT* NG1 ....2 D5
Eastcliffe Av *CARL* NG4 ....33 E2
East Cl *COT/KEY/RAD* NG12 ....82 B2
Eastcote Av *BSTN/STPLFD* NG9 ..54 A1
East Crs *BSTN/STPLFD* NG9 ....65 G1
Eastdale Rd
MAPPK/POR/STA NG3 ....44 D2
East Dr *NOTTE* NG7 ....55 H2
Eastglade Rd *ARN* NG5 ....18 D4
East Gv *BING/VBLV* NG13 ....49 E3
NOTTE NG7 ....30 D5
Eastham Cl
MAPPK/POR/STA NG3 ....3 J2
Eastham Rd *ARN* NG5 ....20 D4
Eastholme Cft *WBRGFD* NG2 ......45 E3
Easthorpe St *CFTN/RUD* NG11 ...77 G2
East Moor *COT/KEY/RAD* NG12 ...71 D5
Eastmoor Dr *CARL* NG4 ....33 G5
East Nelson St *HEANOR* DE75 ......6 B5

East St *BING/VBLV* NG13 ....49 E3
HEANOR DE75 ....12 D2
ILK DE7 ....26 A5
LGEAT NG10 ....73 C1
NOTT NG1 ....3 G4
Eastwold *COT/KEY/RAD* NG12 ....71 F4
Eastwood Cl *HUCK/RAV* NG15 ...10 D3
Eastwood Rd
COT/KEY/RAD NG12 ....47 F5
EWD/SEL/PNX NG16 ....15 H4
Eastwood St *BLWL* NG6 ....17 G5
Eaton Av *ARN* NG5 ....20 B3
ILK DE7 ....37 G2
Eaton Cl *BSTN/STPLFD* NG9 ....55 C5
Eaton Grange Dr *LGEAT* NG10 ....72 B1
Eatons Rd *BSTN/STPLFD* NG9 .....53 E5
Eaton St *MAPPK/POR/STA* NG3 ...32 A2
Ebenezer St *EWD/SEL/PNX* NG16 ..7 A1
ILK DE7 ....26 A2
Ebers Gv *MAPPK/POR/STA* NG3 ..31 F5
Ebers Rd *MAPPK/POR/STA* NG3 ..31 F5
Ebury Rd *ARN* NG5 ....31 E4
Eckington Cl *ILK* DE7 ....24 B5
Eckington Ter *WBRGFD* NG2 ....57 F2
Ecton Cl *ARN* NG5 ....18 C2
Edale Cl *HUCK/RAV* NG15 ....10 B1
LGEAT NG10 ....72 C3
Edale Rd *BSTN/STPLFD* NG9 ....63 F2
MAPPK/POR/STA NG3 ....44 A3
Edale Sq *ILK* DE7 ....13 H5
Eddleston Dr *CFTN/RUD* NG11 ...66 C5
Edenbridge Ct
WOL/BIL/BRX NG8 ....54 C1
Eden Cl *ARN* NG5 ....20 A4
Edenhall Gdns *CFTN/RUD* NG11 ..66 C4
Edern Cl *ARN* NG5 ....18 D3
Edgbaston Gdns
WOL/BIL/BRX NG8 ....30 A5
Edge Hill Ct *LGEAT* NG10 ....73 E5
Edge Wy *WOL/BIL/BRX* NG8 ....28 C4
Edgewood Dr *HUCK/RAV* NG15 ..10 C2
Edgington Cl
COT/KEY/RAD NG12 ....71 F4
Edginton St
MAPPK/POR/STA NG3 ....44 A1
Edginton Ter
MAPPK/POR/STA NG3 ....44 A1
Edgware Rd *BLWL* NG6 ....18 A3
Edgwood Rd
EWD/SEL/PNX NG16 ....15 C4
Edinburgh Dr *BING/VBLV* NG13 ...48 C2
Edingale Ct *BSTN/STPLFD* NG9 ...40 A4
Edingley Av *ARN* NG5 ....31 F1
Edingley Sq *ARN* NG5 ....31 F1
Edith Ter *NOTTE* NG7 ....42 B2
Edlington Dr *WOL/BIL/BRX* NG8 ..40 B5
Edmond Gv *HUCK/RAV* NG15 ......5 H4
Edmonton Ct *WBRGFD* NG2 ....57 C5
Ednaston Rd *NOTTE* NG7 ....56 A2
Edwald Rd *COT/KEY/RAD* NG12 ..68 C3
Edwalton Cl
COT/KEY/RAD NG12 ....68 C3
Edwalton Ct *BLWL* NG6 ....18 A4
Edwalton Lodge Cl
COT/KEY/RAD NG12 ....68 B3
Edward Av *WOL/BIL/BRX* NG8 .....30 A5
Edward Cl *HUCK/RAV* NG15 ....10 C3
Edward Rd *EWD/SEL/PNX* NG16 ...8 B5
EWD/SEL/PNX NG16 ....16 B5
LGEAT NG10 ....73 E1
WBRGFD NG2 ....58 A3
Edwards La *ARN* NG5 ....19 E4
Edward St *BSTN/STPLFD* NG9 .....53 E4
EWD/SEL/PNX NG16 ....7 A4
Edwinstowe Dr *ARN* NG5 ....31 F1
Edwin St *ARN* NG5 ....19 G4
Eelwood Rd *HUCK/RAV* NG15 ....10 C3
Egerton Dr *BSTN/STPLFD* NG9 ....53 E1
Egerton Rd *ARN* NG5 ....31 G1
Egerton St
MAPPK/POR/STA NG3 ....43 F1
Egerton Wk
MAPPK/POR/STA * NG3 ....43 F1
Egling Cft *CARL* NG4 ....45 G4
Egypt Rd *NOTTE* NG7 ....30 C4
Eighth Av *BSTN/STPLFD* NG9 .....65 H1
Eisele Cl *BLWL* NG6 ....17 E4
Ekowe St *NOTTE* NG7 ....30 C3
Eland St *NOTTE* NG7 ....30 C3
Elder Av *ARN* NG5 ....20 B4
Elder Gv *HUCK/RAV* NG15 ....11 G3
Eldon Rd *BSTN/STPLFD* NG9 ......64 B5
Eleanor Av *ILK* DE7 ....38 B3
Eleanor Crs *BSTN/STPLFD* NG9 ..53 G4
Electric Av *WBRGFD* NG2 ....56 D4
Eley Cl *ILK* DE7 ....25 F3
Elford Ri *MAPPK/POR/STA* NG3 ...44 A3

Elgar Dr *LGEAT* NG10 ....72 C4
Elgar Gdns
MAPPK/POR/STA NG3 ....44 A2
Eliot Cl *LGEAT* NG10 ....72 C4
Eliot Dr *ILK* DE7 ....37 G3
Elizabeth Cl *HUCK/RAV* NG15 ....10 D2
ILK DE7 ....24 A5
Elizabeth Gv *CARL* NG4 ....33 C4
Elizabeth Rd *BSTN/STPLFD* NG9 ..63 H3
Ella Bank Rd *HEANOR* DE75 ....12 C1
Ella Rd *WBRGFD* NG2 ....58 A2
Ellastone Av *ARN* NG5 ....19 F2
Ellerby Av *CFTN/RUD* NG11 ....66 B4
Ellerslie Gv *LGEAT* NG10 ....62 B1
Ellesmere Cl *ARN* NG5 ....20 C3
Ellesmere Dr *BSTN/STPLFD* NG9 ..38 D3
Ellesmere Rd *WBRGFD* NG2 ....68 A2
Elliott St *NOTTE* NG7 ....2 B4
Ellis Av *HUCK/RAV* NG15 ....11 G1
Ellis Cl *LGEAT* NG10 ....72 C3
Ellis Ct *MAPPK/POR/STA* NG3 ......3 G1
Ellis Gv *BSTN/STPLFD* NG9 ....65 E1
Ellsworth Ri *ARN* NG5 ....18 C4
Ellwood Crs *WOL/BIL/BRX* NG8 ..41 F3
Elm Av *BING/VBLV* NG13 ....49 F3
BSTN/STPLFD NG9 ....54 D5
BSTN/STPLFD NG9 ....64 C4
CARL NG4 ....45 G1
COT/KEY/RAD NG12 ....82 C2
EWD/SEL/PNX NG16 ....16 A4
HUCK/RAV NG15 ....10 D2
LGEAT NG10 ....52 C4
LGEAT NG10 ....62 B5
Elm Bank *MAPPK/POR/STA* NG3 ..31 F5
Elmbridge *ARN* NG5 ....19 E3
Elm Cl *COT/KEY/RAD* NG12 ....82 C2
MAPPK/POR/STA NG3 ....43 F1
Elmdale Gdns
WOL/BIL/BRX NG8 ....29 G5
Elm Dr *CARL* NG4 ....45 G1
Elm Gv *ARN* NG5 ....20 B2
Elmhurst Av
MAPPK/POR/STA NG3 ....32 D3
Elmore Ct *NOTTE* NG7 ....2 A2
The Elms *CARL* NG4 ....45 G2
Elms Cl *CFTN/RUD* NG11 ....77 G3
Elmsdale Gdns *CALV/BJ* NG14 ....34 D1
Elmsfield Av *HEANOR* DE75 ....6 D5
Elms Gdns *CFTN/RUD* NG11 ....77 F3
Elmsham Av *ARN* NG5 ....18 A1
Elms Pk *CFTN/RUD* NG11 ....77 G3
EWD/SEL/PNX NG16 ....15 G3
Elmsthorpe Av *NOTTE* NG7 ....42 B4
Elmswood Gdns *ARN* NG5 ....31 G2
Elm Tree Av *WBRGFD* NG2 ....57 G4
Elm Vw *NOTTE* NG7 ....42 C2
Elnor St *EWD/SEL/PNX* NG16 ......7 F5
Elson St *NOTTE* NG7 ....30 C5
Elston Gdns *CFTN/RUD* NG11 ....66 B2
Elstree Dr *WOL/BIL/BRX* NG8 .....41 F2
Elswick Cl *ARN* NG5 ....19 E2
Elswick Dr *BSTN/STPLFD* NG9 ....65 G2
Elterwater Dr *WBRGFD* NG2 ....58 D4
Eltham Cl *WOL/BIL/BRX* NG8 .....29 E2
Eltham Dr *WOL/BIL/BRX* NG8 .....29 F2
Eltham Rd *WBRGFD* NG2 ....58 B4
Elton Cl *BSTN/STPLFD* NG9 ....53 E3
Elton Rd *ARN* NG5 ....31 E4
Elton Rd North *ARN* NG5 ....30 D4
Elton Ter *NOTTE* * NG7 ....42 C1
Elvaston Dr *LGEAT* NG10 ....72 A5
Elvaston Rd *WOL/BIL/BRX* NG8 ..41 H4
Elveden Dr *ILK* DE7 ....25 F1
Emerys Rd *CARL* NG4 ....34 A5
Emmanuel Av *ARN* NG5 ....18 D1
MAPPK/POR/STA NG3 ....32 B4
Emneth Cl
MAPPK/POR/STA NG3 ....32 A3
Empingham Cl
BSTN/STPLFD NG9 ....64 A4
Emsworth Cl *ILK* DE7 ....25 C2
Ena Av *WBRGFD* NG2 ....44 A3
Enderby Gdns *ARN* NG5 ....19 H1
Enderby Sq *BSTN/STPLFD* NG9 ...55 E3
Endsleigh Gdns
BSTN/STPLFD NG9 ....55 E4
COT/KEY/RAD NG12 ....68 B2
Enfield St *BSTN/STPLFD* NG9 .....54 D5
Engine La *EWD/SEL/PNX* NG16 ...2 D5
England Crs *HEANOR* DE75 ....6 D5
Ennerdale Cl *WBRGFD* NG2 ....58 D4
Ennerdale Rd *ARN* NG5 ....19 G5
LGEAT NG10 ....62 D5
Ennismore Gdns
WOL/BIL/BRX NG8 ....41 H2
Ennismore Ms *CFTN/RUD* NG11 ..67 F4
Enthorpe St *WOL/BIL/BRX* NG8 ..41 G2
Epperstone Rd *WBRGFD* NG2 ......57 H3

Epsom Rd BSTN/STPLFD NG9..........63 F3
Erdington Wy
　BSTN/STPLFD NG9 ....63 F3
Erewash Dr ILK DE7.....................38 B2
Erewash Gdns BSTN/STPLFD NG5.....18 D2
Erewash Gv BSTN/STPLFD NG9.........63 G5
Erewash Sq ILK DE7.....................38 B2
Eric Av HUCK/RAV NG15 ....5 E3
Erith Cl WOL/BIL/BRX NG8 ....28 C4
Ernest Rd CARL NG4 ....32 C5
Erskine Rd ARN NG5 ....31 E4
Esher Gv MAPPK/POR/STA NG3.....31 F4
Eskdale Cl LGEAT NG10 ....72 C4
Eskdale Ct WBRGFD NG2 ....58 D4
Eskdale Dr BSTN/STPLFD NG9 ....63 H2
　WOL/BIL/BRX NG8 ....29 G5
Esk Hause Cl
　COT/KEY/RAD NG12 ....68 D2
Essex St EWD/SEL/PNX NG16.........8 A5
Estwic Av EWD/SEL/PNX NG16 ....8 A4
Ethel Av HUCK/RAV NG15 ....5 G3
　MAPPK/POR/STA NG3 ....32 B4
Ethel Rd WBRGFD NG2 ....58 A4
Eton Cl ILK DE7 ....24 A5
Eton Gv WOL/BIL/BRX NG8 ....41 G4
Eton Rd WBRGFD NG2 ....67 H1
Eucalyptus Av CFTN/RUD NG11 .....65 H5
Eugene Gdns WBRGFD NG2 ....57 G1
Eugene St WBRGFD NG2 ....43 G5
Europa Wy CFTN/RUD NG11 ....67 F5
Evans Rd BLWL NG6 ....30 A2
Evedon Wk ARN NG5.....................19 E1
Evelyn St BSTN/STPLFD NG9 ....55 G5
　WBRGFD NG2.............................3 J6
Eversley Wk ARN NG5 ....19 E2
Evesham Ct BSTN/STPLFD NG9 ....63 H5
Ewart Rd NOTTE NG7 ....30 D5
Ewe Lamb Cl BSTN/STPLFD NG9.....53 G2
Ewe Lamb La BSTN/STPLFD NG9.....53 G2
Ewell Rd WOL/BIL/BRX NG8 ....40 D3
Exbourne Rd WOL/BIL/BRX NG8 ....29 E4
Exbury Gdns WBRGFD NG2 ....67 G2
Exchange Ar NOTT NG1 ....3 F5
Exchange Rd WBRGFD NG2 ....58 A4
Exchange Wk NOTT NG1 ....3 F5
Exeter Cl CARL NG4 ....33 G3
Exeter Rd NOTTE NG7 ....30 D5
　WBRGFD NG2 ....58 A5
Extension St ILK DE7 ....38 A1
Exton Rd ARN NG5.......................30 D2
Eyam Cl BSTN/STPLFD NG9 ....54 B1
Eyre's Gdn ILK DE7 ....26 A3
Eyre St WBRGFD NG2 ....3 J5

F

Fabis Dr CFTN/RUD NG11 ....66 B2
Factory La BSTN/STPLFD NG9 ....64 D1
　ILK DE7 ....25 H3
Failsworth Cl CFTN/RUD NG11 ....66 B3
Fairbank Crs ARN NG5 ....31 C3
Fairburn Cl WOL/BIL/BRX NG8 ....40 B4
Fairburn Wy
　EWD/SEL/PNX NG16 ....15 H3
Faircroft Av LGEAT NG10 ....62 C1
Fairdale Dr EWD/SEL/PNX NG16 .....8 C5
Fairfield Cl CFTN/RUD NG11...........67 E1
Fairfield Crs LGEAT NG10 ....72 B5
Fairfield Rd ILK DE7 ....26 B4
Fairham Cl CFTN/RUD NG11...........67 E1
Fairham Ct CFTN/RUD * NG11 ....66 D3
Fairham Dr WOL/BIL/BRX NG8 ....41 H4
Fairham Rd COT/KEY/RAD NG12 ....82 A1
Fairholm Ct
　MAPPK/POR/STA NG3 ....3 K2
Fairisle Cl CFTN/RUD NG11 ....66 D5
Fairland Crs WBRGFD NG2 ....67 H2
Fair Lea Cl LGEAT NG10 ....73 E3
Fairlight Wy ARN NG5 ....19 E3
Fairmaid Gv CFTN/RUD NG11 ....66 B4
Fairmead Cl
　MAPPK/POR/STA NG3 ....32 A5
Fairnley Rd WOL/BIL/BRX NG8 ......28 C3
Fairview Ct CFTN/RUD NG11 ....67 G4
Fairview Rd ARN NG5 ....31 H1
The Fairway CARL NG4 ....33 F2
Fairway COT/KEY/RAD NG12 ....82 D2
Fairway Dr BLWL NG6 ....18 A3
　BSTN/STPLFD NG9......................54 C3
Falcon Cl ARN NG5 ....42 B4
Falcon Gv NOTTE NG7 ....30 D4
Falcon St NOTTE NG7 ....30 D4
Falconwood Gdns
　CFTN/RUD NG11 ....65 H5
Fallow Cl CFTN/RUD NG11 ....66 B4

Fall Rd HEANOR DE75 ....6 B4
Falstaffe Ms NOTTE * NG7 ....30 D4
Falston Rd WOL/BIL/BRX NG8 ....41 F2
Faraday Rd NOTTE NG7 ....42 B4
Farfield Av BSTN/STPLFD NG9........54 D3
Farfield Gv BSTN/STPLFD NG9........54 D3
Farleys La HUCK/RAV NG15 ....11 F2
Farley St BLWL NG6 ....17 G3
Farm Av HUCK/RAV NG15 ....10 C3
Farm Cl CFTN/RUD NG11 ....66 B4
　ILK DE7 ....26 B5
　LGEAT NG10 ....73 F4
Farm Rd ARN NG5 ....20 C3
　BSTN/STPLFD NG9......................64 C1
Farnborough Rd
　CFTN/RUD NG11 ....76 B1
Farndale Cl LGEAT NG10 ....72 B4
Farndale Dr WOL/BIL/BRX NG8 ......40 A4
Farndon Dr BSTN/STPLFD NG9 ....63 C3
Far New Cl LGEAT NG10 ....62 C2
Farnsfield Av CALV/BJ NG14 ....23 F5
Far Pastures Cl
　COT/KEY/RAD NG12 ....82 B2
Farriers Cft ILK DE7 ....25 F2
Farriers Gn CFTN/RUD NG11 ....65 H4
Farringdon Cl
　WOL/BIL/BRX NG8 ....28 C2
Far Rye WOL/BIL/BRX NG8 ....41 E2
Farthing Ct LGEAT NG10 ....72 C2
Farwells Cl BLWL NG6 ....29 H1
Faulconbridge Cl BLWL NG6 ....17 G4
Fearn Cha CARL NG4 ....45 F1
Fearn Cl BWSH/BRSTN DE72 ....72 B2
Fearnleigh Dr BLWL NG6 ....30 A3
Featherstone Cl CARL NG4.............33 E2
Felen Cl ARN NG5 ....18 D3
Fellbarrow Cl WBRGFD NG2 ....68 D1
Fellows Rd BSTN/STPLFD NG9 ....54 D4
Fellows Yd COT/KEY/RAD NG12 ....79 F2
Fell Side ARN NG5 ....20 B5
Fellside Cl WBRGFD NG2 ....58 D5
Felstead Ct BSTN/STPLFD NG9 ....54 B2
Felstead Rd WOL/BIL/BRX NG8 ......41 G2
Felton Cl BSTN/STPLFD NG9...........64 A1
Felton Rd WBRGFD NG2 ....57 G3
Fenchurch Cl ARN NG5 ....18 D1
Fenimore Ct
　COT/KEY/RAD * NG12 ....47 G5
Fenroth Cl BLWL NG6 ....17 E2
Fenton Dr BLWL NG6.....................11 H5
Fenton Rd ARN NG5 ....30 C1
Fenwick Cl WOL/BIL/BRX NG8 ....29 E3
Fenwick Rd WOL/BIL/BRX NG8 ......29 E3
Fergus Cl CFTN/RUD NG11 ....76 C1
Ferguson Cl BSTN/STPLFD NG9......64 B4
Fern Av ARN NG5 ....31 E4
Fern Cl BSTN/STPLFD NG9 ....54 A4
Fern Crs EWD/SEL/PNX NG16 ....7 G4
Ferndale Cl BSTN/STPLFD NG9 ....64 C4
Ferndale Rd
　MAPPK/POR/STA NG3 ....44 C2
Ferndene Dr LGEAT NG10 ....72 B4
Ferngill Cl WBRGFD NG2 ....57 E2
Fernilee Cl ILK DE7 ....24 B5
Fern Lea Av
　COT/KEY/RAD NG12 ....70 D4
Fernleigh Av
　MAPPK/POR/STA NG3 ....32 C3
Fernwood Crs
　WOL/BIL/BRX NG8 ....40 B4
Fernwood Dr
　COT/KEY/RAD NG12 ....47 E4
Ferny Hollow Cl ARN NG5 ....18 B2
Ferrers Wk
　MAPPK/POR/STA NG3 ....3 J3
Ferriby Ter WBRGFD NG2 ....57 F2
Festival Rd ILK DE7 ....37 F3
Festus Cl MAPPK/POR/STA * NG3 ...3 G1
Festus St CARL NG4 ....45 H1
Field Cl BSTN/STPLFD NG9.............64 A2
　BWSH/BRSTN DE72 ....72 A2
　CARL NG4 ....33 G3
Field House Cl
　WOL/BIL/BRX NG8 ....40 C3
Field La BSTN/STPLFD NG9.............63 H2
　COT/KEY/RAD NG12 ....35 H5
Field Rd ILK DE7 ....38 A1
Fields Av CFTN/RUD NG11 ....77 F4
Fields Farm Rd LGEAT NG10...........72 D4
Fieldway CFTN/RUD NG11 ....67 E2
Fiennes Crs NOTTE NG7 ....2 A7
Fifth Av BSTN/STPLFD NG9 ....56 D5
Filey St BLWL NG6 ....17 H2
Finch Cl NOTTE NG7 ....56 C3
Finchley Cl CFTN/RUD NG11...........65 H5
Findern Gn
　MAPPK/POR/STA NG3 ....44 B2
Fingal Cl CFTN/RUD NG11..............66 C5

Finsbury Av WBRGFD NG2 ....44 A4
Finsbury Park Cl WBRGFD NG2 .....67 F1
Finsbury Rd BSTN/STPLFD NG9......40 B5
Firbank Ct BSTN/STPLFD NG9 ....64 A2
Firbeck Rd ARN NG5.....................20 B2
　WOL/BIL/BRX NG8 ....40 B4
Fir Cl BLWL NG6 ....17 E2
Fircroft Av BSTN/STPLFD NG9.........28 D5
Fircroft Dr HUCK/RAV NG15 ....10 B2
Fir Dl COT/KEY/RAD NG12 ....71 F3
Firecrest Wy BLWL NG6 ....30 A2
Firs Av BSTN/STPLFD NG9..............55 E4
Firsby Rd WOL/BIL/BRX NG8 ....29 E3
Firs Rd COT/KEY/RAD NG12 ....68 C1
Firs St LGEAT NG10 ....72 B5
First Av BLWL NG6 ....17 G3
　BSTN/STPLFD NG9......................55 H5
　BWSH/BRSTN DE72 ....62 A1
　CARL NG4 ....32 D5
　CARL NG4 ....33 G4
　CARL NG4 ....45 F3
Firth Cl ARN NG5 ....20 D1
Firth Dr BSTN/STPLFD NG9............64 B4
Firth Wy BLWL NG6 ....17 F2
Fisher Av ARN NG5 ....20 A5
Fisher Cl ILK DE7 ....26 A1
Fisher Ga NOTT NG1 ....3 H6
Fisher La BING/VBLV NG13 ....48 D3
Fisher St NOTTE NG7 ....30 C5
Fish Pond Dr NOTTE NG7 ....2 B7
Five Acres CFTN/RUD NG11 ....65 H4
Flagholme COT/KEY/RAD NG12......71 E4
Flake La ILK DE7 ....51 H2
Flamingo Ct WBRGFD * NG2 ....56 D1
Flamstead Av CARL NG4 ....22 A3
Flamstead Rd ILK DE7 ....26 A4
Flamsteed Rd
　WOL/BIL/BRX NG8 ....28 C4
The Flatts BSTN/STPLFD NG9.........64 A1
Flawborough Ri
　CFTN/RUD * NG11 ....67 F3
Flawforth Av CFTN/RUD NG11 ....77 G2
Flawforth La
　COT/KEY/RAD NG12 ....77 H2
Flaxendale COT/KEY/RAD NG12 ....71 F4
Flaxton Wy ARN NG5 ....18 C3
Fleam Rd CFTN/RUD NG11 ....66 B2
Fleeman Gv WBRGFD NG2 ....58 B2
Fleet Cl NOTTE NG7 ....42 A2
Fleetway Cl
　EWD/SEL/PNX NG16 ....14 C1
Fleetwith Cl WBRGFD NG2 ....68 D1
Fleming Cl EWD/SEL/PNX NG16 .....15 H1
Fleming Dr CARL NG4 ....34 C1
Fleming Gdns CFTN/RUD NG11 ......65 H5
Fletcher Ga NOTT NG1 ....3 G5
Fletcher Rd BSTN/STPLFD NG9 ......55 F4
Fletcher St HEANOR DE75 ....6 B5
　LGEAT NG10 ....73 E1
Flewitt Gdns
　MAPPK/POR/STA NG3 ....3 K2
Flintham Dr ARN NG5 ....31 E1
Flixton Rd EWD/SEL/PNX NG16......15 G3
Florence Av LGEAT NG10 ....63 G5
Florence Ct ILK * DE7 ....26 A4
Florence Crs CARL NG4 ....34 A5
Florence Gv
　MAPPK/POR/STA NG3 ....44 B1
Florence Rd CARL NG4 ....34 A4
　MAPPK/POR/STA NG3 ....32 B4
　WBRGFD NG2............................58 B3
Florence St HUCK/RAV NG15 ....11 F2
Florin Gdns LGEAT NG10 ....72 C2
Flowers Cl ARN NG5 ....20 C4
Flying Horse Wk NOTT NG1..............3 F5
Foljambe Ter
　MAPPK/POR/STA NG3 ....3 H3
Folkton Gdns
　MAPPK/POR/STA NG3 ....32 A4
Forbes Cl LGEAT NG10 ....73 F4
Fordham Gn CFTN/RUD NG11 ....76 B1
Ford St NOTTE NG7 ....30 D4
Ford St North NOTTE NG7 ....30 D4
Forest Cl COT/KEY/RAD NG12 ....70 D3
Forest Cl NOTTE NG7 ....2 A2
Forester St BSTN/STPLFD NG9 ....64 D1
Forester Gv CARL NG4 ....45 E1
Forester Rd
　MAPPK/POR/STA NG3 ....32 B5
Forester St CARL NG4 ....45 H1
Forest Gv NOTT NG1 ....43 E1
　NOTTE NG7.................................2 A1
Forest Rd BING/VBLV NG13 ....48 B3
Forest Rd East NOTT NG1................2 C1
Forest Rd West NOTT NG1...............2 B1
Forest View Dr HUCK/RAV NG15......4 D5
The Forge BSTN/STPLFD NG9.........38 C3
Forge Hl BSTN/STPLFD NG9...........64 C2

Forman St NOTT NG1 ....2 E4
Forster St NOTTE NG7 ....42 B2
Forsythia Gdns NOTTE NG7 ....56 B1
Forth Av BSTN/STPLFD NG9 ....55 H5
Fosbrooke Dr LGEAT NG10 ....73 E4
Foster Av BSTN/STPLFD NG9 ....55 E5
Fosters Dr ARN NG5 ....31 G1
Fosters La BING/VBLV NG13 ....49 E3
Fountain Dale Ct
　MAPPK/POR/STA NG3 ....43 G1
Fountains Cl WBRGFD NG2.............58 C5
Fourth Av BSTN/STPLFD NG9 ....55 H5
　CARL NG4 ....32 C5
Fowler St MAPPK/POR/STA NG3 ....31 G5
Fox Cl LGEAT NG10 ....73 E4
Fox Covert CARL NG4 ....45 G4
Fox Covert La CFTN/RUD NG11 ......65 G4
Foxearth Av CFTN/RUD NG11 ....66 C4
Foxes Cl NOTTE NG7 ....2 B7
Foxglove Rd
　EWD/SEL/PNX NG16 ....14 C2
The Foxgloves BING/VBLV NG13 ....48 C4
Fox Gv BLWL NG6 ....30 B4
Foxhall Rd NOTTE NG7 ....30 D5
Fox Hl COT/KEY/RAD NG12 ....70 D1
Foxhill Rd CALV/BJ NG14 ....22 D5
　CARL NG4 ....32 D5
Foxhill Rd Central CARL NG4 ....32 D5
Foxhill Rd East CARL NG4 ....33 E5
Foxhill Rd West CARL NG4 ....32 C5
Foxhollies Gv ARN NG5 ....31 E2
Fox Meadow HUCK/RAV NG15.......11 E4
Fox Rd WBRGFD NG2 ....58 A2
Foxton Cl BLWL NG6 ....17 E2
　ILK DE7 ....25 F2
Fradley Cl BLWL NG6 ....11 H5
Frampton Rd WOL/BIL/BRX NG8.....41 F1
Frances Gv HUCK/RAV NG15 ....5 G3
Francis Gv BLWL NG6 ....30 B2
Francis Rd CARL NG4 ....33 G5
Francis St NOTTE NG7 ....2 B2
Franklin Cl ARN NG5 ....19 F2
Franklin
　COT/KEY/RAD NG12 ....69 E5
Franklyn Gdns
　COT/KEY/RAD NG12 ....79 F5
　WOL/BIL/BRX NG8 ....41 H2
Fraser Crs CARL NG4 ....32 C4
Fraser Rd CARL NG4 ....32 C4
　WBRGFD NG2............................57 G3
Fraser Sq CARL NG4 ....32 D4
Frearson Farm Ct
　EWD/SEL/PNX * NG16 ....14 A4
Freckingham St NOTT NG1 ....3 H4
Freda Av CARL NG4 ....33 E3
Freda Cl CARL NG4 ....33 E2
Frederic Av HEANOR DE75 ....12 C3
Frederick Av CARL NG4 ....44 C1
　ILK DE7 ....38 B3
Frederick Gv NOTTE NG7 ....42 C5
Frederick Rd BSTN/STPLFD NG9 ....53 E4
Frederick St LGEAT NG10 ....73 G2
Freeland Cl BSTN/STPLFD NG9 ......63 G3
Freemans Ter CARL NG4 ....33 H5
Freemantle Wk ARN NG5 ....18 B2
Freeston Dr BLWL NG6 ....17 E2
Freeth Cl WBRGFD * NG2 ....58 A1
Freeth St WBRGFD NG2 ....58 A1
Fremount Dr WOL/BIL/BRX NG8 .....41 F1
French St ILK DE7 ....38 B3
Fretwell St NOTTE NG7 ....42 B1
Friar Ct WBRGFD * NG2 ....57 E2
Friar La NOTT NG1 ....2 D6
Friars Ct ILK DE7 ....37 F2
　NOTTE NG7.................................2 B7
Friar St LGEAT NG10 ....73 E2
　NOTTE NG7...............................56 B1
The Friary NOTTE NG7..................56 B1
Friary Cl NOTTE NG7 ....56 B1
Friday La CARL NG4 ....33 C4
Friesland Dr BWSH/BRSTN DE72 ....62 B1
Frinton Rd WOL/BIL/BRX NG8 ....28 D4
Frisby Av LGEAT NG10 ....73 F3
Frogmore St NOTT NG1 ....2 E1
Front St ARN NG5 ....20 A3
Frost Av EWD/SEL/PNX NG16 ....6 D3
Fryar Rd EWD/SEL/PNX NG16 ....8 A3
Fulforth St NOTT NG1 ....2 D2
Fuller St CFTN/RUD NG11 ....77 F3
Fullwood Av ILK DE7 ....25 H4
Fullwood Cl BSTN/STPLFD NG9 ......64 B2
Fullwood St ILK DE7 ....25 H4
Fulwood Crs WOL/BIL/BRX NG8 .....28 C4
Fulwood Dr LGEAT NG10 ....72 B2
Furlong Av ARN NG5 ....19 H2
Furlong Cl BSTN/STPLFD NG9 ....53 E3
Furlong St ARN NG5 ....19 H3
Furnace Rd ILK DE7 ....38 C1

Furness Cl *WBRGFD* NG2......................58 C5
Furness Rd *BLWL* NG6.........................29 H2
Furzebrook St *CARL* NG4....................45 F2
Furze Gdns
  MAPPK/POR/STA NG3.................43 G1
Fylde Cl *BSTN/STPLFD* NG9.................63 F4

G

The Gables *NOTTE* * NG7....................30 D5
Gabor Cl *CFTN/RUD* NG11..................75 H1
Gabrielle Cl *BLWL* NG6......................30 A1
Gadd St *NOTTE* NG7...........................42 C2
Gadsby Cl *ILK* DE7............................38 B4
Gadwall Crs *WBRGFD* NG2.................56 C1
Gainsborough Cl
  BSTN/STPLFD NG9...................53 F5
  LGEAT NG10.............................73 F4
Gainsborough Ct
  BSTN/STPLFD * NG9..................55 F4
Gainsford Cl *ARN* NG5.......................18 C5
Gainsford Crs *ARN* NG5.....................18 C5
Gala Wy *ARN* NG5.............................18 B4
The Galeb *NOTTE* * NG7.....................56 B1
Gale Cl *BSTN/STPLFD* * NG9...............55 C5
Galena Dr
  MAPPK/POR/STA NG3.................44 B1
Gallows Inn Cl *ILK* DE7......................38 A3
Galway Rd *ARN* NG5..........................19 H2
  NOTTE NG7..............................42 C5
Gamble St *NOTTE* NG7......................2 A3
Gamston Crs *ARN* NG5.......................31 F2
Gamston Lings Bar Rd
  COT/KEY/RAD NG12..................68 B5
Ganton Cl
  MAPPK/POR/STA NG3.................32 A4
Garden Av *ILK* DE7............................38 A3
Garden City *CARL* NG4.......................33 F5
Gardendale Av *CFTN/RUD* NG11.......76 A1
Gardeners Wk *ARN* NG5....................30 C1
Gardenia Crs
  MAPPK/POR/STA NG3.................32 C3
Gardenia Gv
  MAPPK/POR/STA NG3.................32 C3
Garden Rd *BING/VBLV* NG13.............48 C3
  EWD/SEL/PNX NG16...................5 B4
  HUCK/RAV NG15.......................5 E5
Gardens Ct *WBRGFD* NG2.................58 B4
Garden St *NOTTE* NG7.......................42 C4
Gardinia Cl *BSTN/STPLFD* NG9...........63 H4
Garfield Cl *NOTTE* NG7......................42 C4
Garfield Rd *NOTTE* NG7....................42 B2
Garforth Cl *WOL/BIL/BRX* NG8..........30 D5
The Garland *NOTTE* * NG7.................56 B1
Garnet Cl *MAPPK/POR/STA* NG3.......3 A3
Garnet St *CARL* NG4..........................45 G1
Garnett Av *HEANOR* DE75..................6 C5
Garrett Gv *CFTN/RUD* NG11..............65 H4
Garsdale Cl *WBRGFD* NG2.................58 D5
Garsdale Dr *CFTN/RUD* NG11............66 D3
Garton Cl *BLWL* NG6.........................17 G5
  BSTN/STPLFD NG9...................64 A1
Gas St *LGEAT* NG10...........................52 D5
Gatcombe Cl
  COT/KEY/RAD NG12..................47 F5
Gatcombe Gv *LGEAT* NG10...............62 B3
Gateford Cl *BSTN/STPLFD* NG9..........54 A1
Gateside Rd *WBRGFD* NG2...............58 D2
Gatling St *NOTTE* NG7.......................42 B3
Gaul St *BLWL* NG6............................17 G3
Gauntley St *NOTTE* NG7...................30 B5
Gauntley St *NOTTE* NG7...................30 B5
Gautries Cl *ARN* NG5.........................18 D2
Gawthorne St *NOTTE* NG7................30 C4
Gayhurst Rd *BLWL* NG6.....................18 B5
Gaynor Ct *WOL/BIL/BRX* NG8...........41 G2
Gayrigg Ct *BSTN/STPLFD* NG9...........64 A1
Gayton Cl *WOL/BIL/BRX* NG8............28 C5
Gaywood Cl *CFTN/RUD* NG11...........76 C1
Gedling Gv *ARN* NG5.........................20 A3
  NOTTE NG7..............................42 C5
Gedling Rd *ARN* NG5.........................20 A3
  CARL NG4................................33 C5
Gedling St *NOTT* NG1.......................3 H5
Gedney Av
  MAPPK/POR/STA NG3.................32 A5
Gell Rd *BSTN/STPLFD* NG9.................65 E2
George Av *BSTN/STPLFD* NG9............65 H2
  LGEAT NG10.............................73 C1
George Green Ct *WBRGFD* * NG2....44 A4
George Rd *CARL* NG4........................45 F1
  WBRGFD NG2...........................57 H4
George St *ARN* NG5..........................19 H4
  EWD/SEL/PNX NG16...................7 E4
  HUCK/RAV NG15.......................5 F4

NOTT NG1...3 F4
Georgina Rd *BSTN/STPLFD* NG9........65 E1
Gertrude Rd *WBRGFD* NG2...............58 B3
Gervase Gdns *CFTN/RUD* NG11.......66 A4
Ghost House La
  BSTN/STPLFD NG9....................64 A1
Gibbons Av *BSTN/STPLFD* NG9.........63 H4
Gibbons St *NOTTE* NG7....................56 B3
Gibb St *LGEAT* NG10.........................73 F2
Gibson Rd *NOTTE* NG7.....................30 D5
Gilbert Gdns
  MAPPK/POR/STA NG3.................44 B3
Gilead St *BLWL* NG6..........................17 G3
Giles Av *WBRGFD* NG2......................57 G5
Giles Ct *WBRGFD* * NG2....................58 A4
Gillercomb Cl
  COT/KEY/RAD NG12..................69 E2
Gilliver La *COT/KEY/RAD* NG12.........70 B5
Gillotts Cl *BING/VBLV* NG13..............48 D3
Gillott St *HEANOR* DE75....................12 C2
Gill St *NOTT* NG1..............................2 D1
Gilpet Av *MAPPK/POR/STA* NG3.......32 A5
Giltbrook Crs
  EWD/SEL/PNX NG16...................14 D2
Gilt Hi *EWD/SEL/PNX* NG16...............15 E3
Giltway *EWD/SEL/PNX* NG16.............14 D3
Gimson Cl *ILK* DE7............................25 F2
Gin Close Wy
  EWD/SEL/PNX NG16...................14 D5
Girton Rd *ARN* NG5..........................30 D2
Gisburn Cl *CFTN/RUD* NG11..............66 D2
The Glade *CFTN/RUD* NG11..............76 B2
Glade Av *WOL/BIL/BRX* NG8.............41 H3
Gladehill Rd *ARN* NG5......................19 F3
Gladstone Av *HEANOR* DE75............6 A5
Gladstone St *BSTN/STPLFD* NG9.......64 D1
  CARL NG4................................45 E1
  EWD/SEL/PNX NG16...................7 E4
  HEANOR DE75.........................6 B5
  LGEAT NG10............................73 E5
  NOTTE NG7.............................30 C5
Gladstone St East *ILK* DE7.................26 A5
Gladstone St West *ILK* DE7...............38 A1
Glaisdale Dr East
  WOL/BIL/BRX NG8....................40 D2
Glaisdale Dr West
  WOL/BIL/BRX NG8....................40 C3
Glaisdale Pkwy
  WOL/BIL/BRX NG8....................40 C3
Glamis Rd *ARN* NG5..........................30 D3
Clapton La *CFTN/RUD* NG11.............66 A4
Clapton Rd *WBRGFD* NG2.................57 F2
Claramara Cl *WBRGFD* NG2..............57 E2
Glasshouse St *NOTT* NG1..................3 F3
The Glebe *EWD/SEL/PNX* NG16........26 C1
Glebe Crs *ILK* DE7.............................38 B1
Glebe Dr *CALV/BJ* NG14...................34 C2
Glebe Farm Cl *WBRGFD* * NG2.........67 F2
Glebe Farm Vw *CARL* NG4................33 G2
Glebe La *COT/KEY/RAD* NG12..........47 E5
Glebe Rd *CARL* NG4..........................32 D3
  EWD/SEL/PNX NG16...................16 B4
  WBRGFD NG2...........................58 A4
Glebe St *BSTN/STPLFD* NG9..............54 D5
  HUCK/RAV NG15.......................5 F4
The Glen *CFTN/RUD* NG11...............66 B5
Glen Av *EWD/SEL/PNX* NG16............14 C1
Glenbrook *COT/KEY/RAD* NG12.......71 F3
Glenbrook Crs
  WOL/BIL/BRX NG8....................41 F1
Glencairn Dr *WOL/BIL/BRX* NG8......29 F5
Glencoe Rd *CFTN/RUD* NG11............66 C5
Glencoyne Rd *CFTN/RUD* NG11........76 B1
Glendale Cl *CARL* NG4......................33 C3
Glendale Ct *BSTN/STPLFD* NG9.........64 D3
Glendale Gdns *ARN* NG5...................20 A3
Glendoe Gv *BING/VBLV* NG13...........48 B3
Glendon Dr *ARN* NG5.......................30 D2
  HUCK/RAV NG15.......................11 F2
Glendon Rd *ILK* DE7.........................37 F4
Gleneagles Ct
  COT/KEY/RAD NG12..................68 C3
Gleneagles Dr *ARN* NG5....................20 C1
Glenfield Av
  EWD/SEL/PNX NG16...................15 E3
Glenfield Rd *LGEAT* NG10..................73 E4
Glen Helen *CARL* NG4.......................45 G2
Glenlivet Gdns *CFTN/RUD* NG11.......66 A5
Glenloch Dr *CFTN/RUD* NG11............76 C1
Glenmore Rd *WBRGFD* NG2..............58 C5
Glenorchy Crs *WOL/BIL/BRX* NG8....18 B2
Glen Parva Av *ARN* NG5....................19 H1
Glenridding Cl *WBRGFD* NG2............69 E1
Glen Rd *CALV/BJ* NG14......................22 D5
Glensford Gdns *ARN* NG5.................18 B1
Glenside *ARN* NG5............................20 C5
Glenside Rd *BSTN/STPLFD* NG9........54 B1
Glenstone Ct *NOTTE* NG7.................42 C1

Glentworth Rd *NOTTE* NG7..............42 B2
Glenwood Av
  WOL/BIL/BRX NG8....................40 C4
Glins Rd *ARN* NG5.............................18 C2
Gloucester Av
  BSTN/STPLFD NG9....................64 D1
  EWD/SEL/PNX NG16...................29 E1
  LGEAT NG10.............................62 B2
  NOTTE NG7.............................42 B4
Glover Av *WOL/BIL/BRX* NG8...........40 C4
Goathland Cl *ARN* NG5.....................19 E2
Godber Rd *HUCK/RAV* NG15.............10 D2
Godfrey Dr *ILK* DE7..........................37 F2
Godfrey St *CARL* NG4.......................45 H1
  HEANOR DE75.........................12 B1
Godkin Dr *EWD/SEL/PNX* NG16........6 D1
Goldcrest Cl *BING/VBLV* NG13...........49 F4
Goldcrest Rd *BLWL* NG6....................29 C2
Goldsmith St *NOTT* NG1...................2 D1
Goldswong Ter
  MAPPK/POR/STA NG3.................43 F1
Golf Club Dr *ILK* DE7.........................52 B2
Golf Course Rd
  COT/KEY/RAD NG12..................83 E2
Golf Rd *COT/KEY/RAD* NG12............47 F5
Goodall Crs *HUCK/RAV* NG15............11 H1
Goodall St *NOTTE* NG7.....................42 C1
Goodliffe St *NOTTE* NG7...................30 C5
Goodman Cl
  EWD/SEL/PNX NG16...................14 D2
Goodwin Cl *LGEAT* NG10..................52 B5
Goodwin Dr
  EWD/SEL/PNX NG16...................15 E4
Goodwin St *NOTTE* NG7...................2 E4
Goodwood Av *ARN* NG5...................19 H2
Goodwood Crs *ILK* DE7.....................37 C4
Goodwood Dr
  BSTN/STPLFD NG9....................63 G4
Goodwood Rd
  WOL/BIL/BRX NG8....................40 C4
Goole Av *ILK* DE7..............................37 C3
Goose Ga *NOTT* NG1........................3 C5
Gordon Cl *BSTN/STPLFD* NG9............64 C4
Gordon Ri *MAPPK/POR/STA* NG3.....31 H3
Gordon Rd *CALV/BJ* NG14.................23 F5
  MAPPK/POR/STA NG3................44 A2
  WBRGFD NG2..........................58 A4
Gordon St *ILK* DE7............................26 A4
Gorman Ct *ARN* NG5.........................20 C3
Gorse Cl *EWD/SEL/PNX* NG16...........14 C1
  LGEAT NG10............................62 C4
Gorse Ct *ARN* NG5............................18 B5
Gorse Rd *COT/KEY/RAD* NG12..........82 A1
Gorsey Rd
  MAPPK/POR/STA NG3.................43 G1
Goshawk Rd *ILK* DE7.........................38 B5
Gothic Cl *BLWL* NG6.........................30 B1
Goverton Sq *BLWL* NG6....................18 A5
Gowan Cl *BSTN/STPLFD* NG9.............64 B4
Goyden Cl *ARN* NG5.........................18 D2
Grace Av *BSTN/STPLFD* NG9..............65 C1
Grace Crs *HEANOR* DE75..................12 C1
Grace Dr *WOL/BIL/BRX* NG8.............30 A5
Grafton Av *ARN* NG5.........................19 H5
Grafton Ct *NOTTE* NG7.....................2 A4
Graham St *ILK* DE7............................38 A1
  NOTTE NG7............................42 C5
Grainger Av *WBRGFD* NG2................67 H3
Grainger St *NOTTE* NG7...................57 H1
Grampian Wy *LGEAT* NG10...............72 B1
Granby Cl *BING/VBLV* NG13.............48 C3
Granby St *ILK* DE7............................25 H3
Granby Vls *WBRGFD* * NG2..............44 A4
Grandfield Av
  COT/KEY/RAD NG12..................47 E4
Grandfield Crs
  COT/KEY/RAD NG12..................47 E4
Grange Av *BSTN/STPLFD* NG9...........55 E5
  CFTN/RUD NG11.....................77 E1
Grange Cl *CARL* NG4.........................22 B3
  CFTN/RUD NG11.....................57 E3
Grange Ct *CFTN/RUD* NG11..............67 F4
Grange Crs *CARL* NG4.......................33 C3
Grange Dr *LGEAT* NG10.....................73 C1
Grange Farm *WBRGFD* NG2..............58 D4
Grange Farm Cl
  BSTN/STPLFD NG9...................63 H5
Grangelea Gdns
  BSTN/STPLFD NG9....................54 A4
Grange Pk *WBRGFD* NG2..................68 D1
Grange Rd *ARN* NG5.........................31 H1
  BLWL NG6..............................30 A2
  COT/KEY/RAD NG12................68 B2
  LGEAT NG10...........................73 C1
Grange Vw *EWD/SEL/PNX* NG16.......4 A1
Grange View Rd *CARL* NG4...............33 C3
Grangewood Av *ILK* DE7...................38 A1

Grangewood Rd
  WOL/BIL/BRX NG8....................40 B5
Grannis Dr *WOL/BIL/BRX* NG8..........29 F5
Grantham Cl
  EWD/SEL/PNX NG16...................14 D3
Grantham Rd *BING/VBLV* NG13.........49 E3
Grantham Rd *BING/VBLV* NG13.........49 F4
  COT/KEY/RAD NG12................47 F5
  LGEAT NG10...........................60 B2
Granton Av *CFTN/RUD* NG11............76 C1
Granville Av *LGEAT* NG10..................63 E5
Granville Ct
  MAPPK/POR/STA * NG3.............44 A3
Granville Crs
  COT/KEY/RAD NG12..................60 D1
Grasmere Cl *HUCK/RAV* NG15...........5 E4
Grasmere Rd *BSTN/STPLFD* NG9.......54 C3
  LGEAT NG10...........................62 C5
Grasmere St *LGEAT* NG10.................62 C1
Grasmoor Cl
  MAPPK/POR/STA NG3.................31 H5
Grassingdale Cl *CARL* NG4................33 C3
Grassington Rd
  WOL/BIL/BRX NG8....................40 A2
Grassmere *COT/KEY/RAD* NG12.......71 F3
Grass St *ILK* DE7...............................25 H2
Grassy La *BSTN/STPLFD* NG9............65 F1
Graylands Rd *WOL/BIL/BRX* NG8......40 D2
Graystones Cl *WBRGFD* NG2............68 D1
Grazingfield *CFTN/RUD* NG11...........66 D2
Greasley Av
  EWD/SEL/PNX NG16...................8 D5
Greasley St *BLWL* NG6......................17 G4
Great Freeman St
  MAPPK/POR/STA NG3.................3 F2
Great Hoggett Dr
  BSTN/STPLFD NG9....................53 H5
The Great Northern Cl
  WBRGFD NG2...........................3 H7
Great Northern Rd
  EWD/SEL/PNX NG16...................7 G5
Great Northern Wy *CARL* NG4..........46 A2
Greaves Cl *ARN* NG5.........................20 C5
  WOL/BIL/BRX NG8...................28 C4
Greek St *NOTTE* NG7........................2 A4
The Green *BSTN/STPLFD* NG9............64 D2
  CFTN/RUD NG11.....................77 F3
  COT/KEY/RAD NG12................68 D2
Green Acre *COT/KEY/RAD* NG12.......68 C2
  WOL/BIL/BRX NG8...................40 A3
Greenacre Av *HEANOR* DE75...........6 D4
Greenacres Cl
  EWD/SEL/PNX NG16...................8 D5
Green Av *CARL* NG4..........................45 H1
Greenbank *CARL* NG4.......................45 E1
Greenburn Cl *WBRGFD* NG2.............58 D5
Green Cl *COT/KEY/RAD* NG12...........79 G5
  HUCK/RAV NG15.....................11 H2
Greencroft *CFTN/RUD* NG11.............66 C4
Greendale Gdns
  WOL/BIL/BRX NG8....................29 G5
Greendale Rd *ARN* NG5....................20 A4
  MAPPK/POR/STA NG3...............44 D2
Greenfield Gv *CARL* NG4...................32 D5
Greenfields *EWD/SEL/PNX* NG16......6 D3
Greenfields Dr
  COT/KEY/RAD NG12..................71 E4
Greenfield St *NOTTE* NG7.................56 A2
Greenford Cl
  WOL/BIL/BRX NG8....................28 D2
Greengates Av
  MAPPK/POR/STA NG3.................32 A2
Greenhill Crs *CARL* NG4....................45 F2
Greenhill Ri *CARL* NG4......................45 F1
Greenhill Rd *CARL* NG4....................45 F1
Greenhills Av
  EWD/SEL/PNX NG16...................8 B4
Greenhills Rd
  EWD/SEL/PNX NG16...................8 A4
Greenland Crs
  BSTN/STPLFD NG9....................64 B2
Green La *CARL* NG4...........................22 A1
  CFTN/RUD NG11.....................66 A4
  ILK DE7...................................38 B1
Green Leys *WBRGFD* NG2.................67 F2
Green Platt
  COT/KEY/RAD NG12..................70 D4
Green's Farm La *CARL* NG4...............33 H3
Greenside Cl *LGEAT* NG10.................73 F4
Greens La *EWD/SEL/PNX* NG16.........15 H4
Green St *CFTN/RUD* NG11.................75 E4
  WBRGFD NG2.........................57 G2
The Greenway *LGEAT* NG10..............52 C5
Greenway Cl
  COT/KEY/RAD NG12..................46 C5
Greenwich Av *BLWL* NG6..................29 H2
Greenwich Park Cl
  WBRGFD * NG2........................67 F1

Greenwood Av
HUCK/RAV NG15 ....5 E4
ILK DE7 ....38 B1
MAPPK/POR/STA NG3 ....45 E3
Greenwood Crs CARL NG4 ....45 E2
Greenwood Gdns
CFTN/RUD NG11 ....77 G3
Greenwood Rd
MAPPK/POR/STA NG3 ....44 B3
Greenwood V HUCK/RAV NG15 ....4 D4
Greetwell Cl WOL/BIL/BRX NG8 ....41 F2
Gregg Av HEANOR DE75 ....6 B5
The Gregory NOTTE * NG7 ....56 B1
Gregory Av EWD/SEL/PNX NG16 ....6 D4
MAPPK/POR/STA NG3 ....32 B3
NOTTE NG7 ....42 C5
Gregory Bvd NOTTE NG7 ....42 C1
Gregory Cl BSTN/STPLFD NG9 ....53 G2
Gregory Ct BSTN/STPLFD NG9 ....64 A2
NOTTE NG7 ....42 B5
Gregory St ILK DE7 ....25 H4
NOTTE NG7 ....42 B5
Gregson Gdns
BSTN/STPLFD NG9 ....64 A5
Gregson Rd BSTN/STPLFD NG9 ....64 A4
Grenville Dr BSTN/STPLFD NG9 ....53 F3
ILK DE7 ....26 A2
Grenville Ri ARN NG5 ....20 A1
Grenville Rd BSTN/STPLFD NG9 ....65 G2
Gresham Cl WBRGFD NG2 ....57 F4
Gresham Gdns ARN NG5 ....20 B5
WBRGFD NG2 ....57 G1
Gresley Rd WBRGFD NG2 ....44 A5
Gresley Rd ILK DE7 ....26 A4
Gressy Rd CFTN/RUD NG11 ....66 C4
Gretton Rd
MAPPK/POR/STA NG3 ....32 B1
Greyfriar Ga NOTT NG1 ....2 E7
Greyhound St NOTT NG1 ....2 E6
Greys Rd ARN NG5 ....32 A1
Greystoke Dr WOL/BIL/BRX NG8 ....40 B2
Grey St EWD/SEL/PNX NG16 ....14 B1
Greythorn Dr WBRGFD NG2 ....67 G2
Grierson Av ARN NG5 ....19 E2
Griffon Rd ILK DE7 ....38 A4
Griffs Hollow CARL NG4 ....45 F1
Grimsby Ter
MAPPK/POR/STA NG3 ....3 F2
Grimston Rd NOTTE NG7 ....42 B2
Grindon Crs BLWL NG6 ....11 H5
Grindslow Av ILK DE7 ....24 B5
Grinsbrook NOTTE NG7 ....42 B4
Gripps Common
COT/KEY/RAD NG12 ....71 E5
Grisedale Ct BSTN/STPLFD NG9 ....63 H2
Gritley Ms WBRGFD NG2 ....57 E1
Grizedale Gv BING/VBLV NG13 ....48 A3
The Grove BWSH/BRSTN DE72 ....72 A1
Grosvenor Av
BWSH/BRSTN DE72 ....72 A1
LGEAT NG10 ....72 B2
MAPPK/POR/STA NG3 ....31 F5
Grosvenor Rd
EWD/SEL/PNX NG16 ....8 A4
Grouville Dr ARN NG5 ....20 B5
Grove Av BSTN/STPLFD NG9 ....54 D5
NOTTE NG7 ....2 A1
Grove Cl CALV/BJ NG14 ....23 E5
Grover Av MAPPK/POR/STA NG3 ....32 B2
Grove Rd BING/VBLV NG13 ....49 G4
NOTTE NG7 ....2 A1
Groveside Crs CFTN/RUD NG11 ....65 H4
Grove St BSTN/STPLFD NG9 ....65 F1
Grundy St NOTTE NG7 ....42 B2
Guinea Cl LGEAT NG10 ....72 B2
Gunn Cl BLWL NG6 ....17 F3
Gunnersbury Wy
WOL/BIL/BRX NG8 ....28 D2
Gunthorpe Cl ARN NG5 ....31 E2
Gunthorpe Dr ARN NG5 ....31 F1
Gunthorpe Rd CARL NG4 ....33 G2
Guy Cl BSTN/STPLFD NG9 ....53 F5
Gwenbrook Av
BSTN/STPLFD NG9 ....64 C1
Gwenbrook Rd
BSTN/STPLFD NG9 ....64 C1

H

Hackworth Cl
EWD/SEL/PNX NG16 ....8 C4
Hadbury Rd ARN NG5 ....30 C3
Haddon Cl CARL NG4 ....33 E3
ILK DE7 ....24 B5
Haddon Crs BSTN/STPLFD NG9 ....64 B4
Haddon Nurseries ILK DE7 ....25 H3

Haddon Rd WBRGFD NG2 ....58 A5
Haddon St ARN NG5 ....31 E3
ILK DE7 ....25 H2
Haddon Wy COT/KEY/RAD NG12 ....47 F4
LGEAT NG10 ....72 A5
Hadleigh Cl BSTN/STPLFD NG9 ....63 F4
Hadley St ILK DE7 ....38 B3
Hadstock Cl LGEAT NG10 ....62 C2
Hagg La ILK DE7 ....36 A4
Hagley Cl MAPPK/POR/STA NG3 ....44 B2
Haileybury Rd WBRGFD NG2 ....68 A2
Haileybury Rd WBRGFD NG2 ....68 A1
Haise Ct BLWL NG6 ....17 E5
The Gregory NOTTE * NG7 ....56 B1
Halberton Dr WBRGFD NG2 ....68 A1
Hales Cl COT/KEY/RAD NG12 ....70 D3
Haley Cl EWD/SEL/PNX NG16 ....15 E4
Halifax Ct WOL/BIL/BRX NG8 ....28 C3
Halifax Pl NOTT NG1 ....3 G6
Hallam Fields Rd ILK DE7 ....38 B4
Hallam Rd BSTN/STPLFD NG9 ....55 E5
MAPPK/POR/STA NG3 ....31 H3
Hallam's La ARN NG5 ....20 A3
BSTN/STPLFD NG9 ....64 C1
Hall Cl COT/KEY/RAD NG12 ....46 D5
ILK DE7 ....36 B1
Hall Cft BSTN/STPLFD NG9 ....65 E1
Hallcroft Rd ILK DE7 ....26 A5
Hall Dr BSTN/STPLFD NG9 ....64 C1
LGEAT NG10 ....52 C5
WOL/BIL/BRX NG8 ....40 D5
Hall Farm Cl
COT/KEY/RAD * NG12 ....69 E5
Hallfields COT/KEY/RAD NG12 ....68 D3
Hall Gdns BSTN/STPLFD NG9 ....54 A4
Hallington Dr HEANOR DE75 ....12 A1
Hall Rd EWD/SEL/PNX NG16 ....7 F3
Halls La EWD/SEL/PNX NG16 ....14 B2
Halls Rd BSTN/STPLFD NG9 ....52 D5
Hall St ARN NG5 ....31 G2
Hall View Dr WOL/BIL/BRX NG8 ....40 C2
Halstead Cl BSTN/STPLFD NG9 ....64 B2
WOL/BIL/BRX NG8 ....29 G2
Hambledon Dr
WOL/BIL/BRX NG8 ....41 G3
Hambleton Cl LGEAT NG10 ....62 B5
Hambling Cl BLWL NG6 ....17 F3
The Hamilton NOTTE * NG7 ....56 B1
Hamilton Cl ARN NG5 ....20 D1
BSTN/STPLFD NG9 ....63 G4
Hamilton Dr
COT/KEY/RAD NG12 ....47 E4
NOTTE NG7 ....2 C7
Hamilton Rd ARN NG5 ....31 E5
LGEAT NG10 ....73 E1
The Hamlet HEANOR DE75 ....6 B5
Hammersmith Cl
EWD/SEL/PNX NG16 ....28 D1
Hampden Gv
BSTN/STPLFD NG9 ....54 D5
Hampden St
EWD/SEL/PNX NG16 ....14 C2
NOTT NG1 ....2 D2
Hampshire Dr LGEAT NG10 ....62 C1
Hampstead Rd
MAPPK/POR/STA NG3 ....31 H4
Hampton Cl BSTN/STPLFD NG9 ....63 F3
ILK DE7 ....36 A1
Hampton Ct HEANOR DE75 ....6 A5
Hampton Rd WBRGFD NG2 ....57 H5
Handel St MAPPK/POR/STA NG3 ....3 J4
Hand's Rd HEANOR DE75 ....12 C1
Hankin St HUCK/RAV NG15 ....11 H1
Hanley Av BSTN/STPLFD NG9 ....54 A3
Hanley St NOTT NG1 ....2 D4
Hannah Crs CFTN/RUD NG11 ....57 E4
Hanslope Crs WOL/BIL/BRX NG8 ....40 C1
Hanson Crs HUCK/RAV NG15 ....5 F5
Hanworth Gdns ARN NG5 ....19 G2
Harberton Cl ARN NG5 ....19 H1
Harby Dr WOL/BIL/BRX NG8 ....41 H4
Harcourt Crs WOL/BIL/BRX NG8 ....29 E2
Harcourt Rd NOTTE NG7 ....30 D5
Harcourt St BSTN/STPLFD NG9 ....54 D5
Harcourt Ter
MAPPK/POR/STA NG3 ....3 H3
Hardstaff Rd WBRGFD NG2 ....44 B3
Hardwick Av ILK DE7 ....24 B5
Hardwicke Rd
BSTN/STPLFD NG9 ....64 B3
Hardwick Gv WBRGFD NG2 ....58 A2
Hardwick Pl ILK DE7 ....37 F3
Hardwick Rd ARN NG5 ....31 F2
NOTTE NG7 ....2 A7
Hardwood Cl BLWL NG6 ....17 E3
Hardy Barn HEANOR DE75 ....12 D2
Hardy Cl EWD/SEL/PNX NG16 ....15 G3
LGEAT NG10 ....73 E3

Hardy's Dr CARL NG4 ....33 G4
Hardy St EWD/SEL/PNX NG16 ....15 G3
NOTTE NG7 ....2 A1
Harebell Gdns BING/VBLV NG13 ....48 B3
Harewood Av BLWL NG6 ....18 A5
Harewood Cl
COT/KEY/RAD NG12 ....47 F5
LGEAT NG10 ....62 C2
Harkstead Rd MAPPK/POR/STA NG5 ....19 E1
Harlaxton Dr LGEAT NG10 ....63 H5
NOTTE NG7 ....42 C4
Harlaxton Wk
MAPPK/POR/STA NG3 ....3 F1
Harlech Cl ILK DE7 ....25 F3
Harlech Ri BSTN/STPLFD NG9 ....64 A2
Harlequin Cl
COT/KEY/RAD NG12 ....47 G5
Harlequin Ct
EWD/SEL/PNX NG16 ....7 G4
Harlequin Ms
COT/KEY/RAD NG12 ....47 H4
Harley St NOTTE NG7 ....42 C5
Harlow Ct ILK DE7 ....36 A1
Harlow Gv CARL NG4 ....33 F3
Harmston Ri ARN NG5 ....30 C1
Harnett Cl NOTT NG1 ....3 G6
Harold Av EWD/SEL/PNX NG16 ....7 E3
Harold Ct WBRGFD NG2 ....3 K5
Harold St WBRGFD NG2 ....3 K5
Harpenden Sq
WOL/BIL/BRX NG8 ....29 F2
Harrier Gv HUCK/RAV NG15 ....10 D3
Harriett St BSTN/STPLFD NG9 ....53 E3
Harrimans Dr
BWSH/BRSTN DE72 ....72 A1
Harrimans La NOTTE NG7 ....56 A3
Harrington Cl CARL NG4 ....34 A4
Harrington Dr NOTTE NG7 ....42 C5
Harrington St LGEAT NG10 ....72 C4
Harris Cl WOL/BIL/BRX NG8 ....41 E3
Harrison Rd BSTN/STPLFD NG9 ....53 E3
Harris Rd BSTN/STPLFD NG9 ....64 B1
Harrogate Rd
MAPPK/POR/STA NG3 ....44 D3
Harrogate St CARL NG4 ....45 G1
Harrowby Rd NOTTE NG7 ....42 C4
Harrow Dr ILK DE7 ....38 B4
Harrow Gdns WOL/BIL/BRX NG8 ....41 H4
Harrow Rd HUCK/RAV NG15 ....10 C2
WBRGFD NG2 ....67 H1
WOL/BIL/BRX NG8 ....41 G4
Hart Av LGEAT NG10 ....62 B1
Hartcroft Rd ARN NG5 ....19 E4
Hartford Cl MAPPK/POR/STA * NG3 ....3 G1
Hartington Av HUCK/RAV NG15 ....10 B1
CARL NG4 ....33 E4
Hartington Cl ILK DE7 ....24 B5
Hartington Pl ILK DE7 ....37 G3
Hartington Rd ARN NG5 ....31 F2
Hartley Ct NOTTE NG7 ....42 C2
Hartley Dr BSTN/STPLFD NG9 ....55 G5
Hartley Rd NOTTE NG7 ....42 C2
Hartness Rd CFTN/RUD NG11 ....65 H5
Hartside Cl WBRGFD NG2 ....58 D4
Hartside Gdns LGEAT NG10 ....72 B1
Hartside Wy HEANOR DE75 ....13 E1
Hart St NOTTE NG7 ....42 C5
Hartwell St
MAPPK/POR/STA NG3 ....3 G1
Hartwood Dr BSTN/STPLFD NG9 ....53 E2
Harvest Cl ARN NG5 ....18 C2
BING/VBLV NG13 ....48 C3
Harvey Cl CFTN/RUD NG11 ....77 G4
Harvey Cft BSTN/STPLFD NG9 ....38 D4
Harvey Rd WOL/BIL/BRX NG8 ....41 E1
Harwich Cl WOL/BIL/BRX NG8 ....29 G3
Harwill Crs WOL/BIL/BRX NG8 ....29 G3
Harwood Cl ARN NG5 ....20 C2
Haslam St NOTTE NG7 ....2 D7
Haslemere Rd LGEAT NG10 ....72 C1
WOL/BIL/BRX NG8 ....30 A5
Hassock La North
HEANOR DE75 ....13 E4
Hassock La South
HEANOR DE75 ....13 F4
Hassocks La BSTN/STPLFD NG9 ....55 E4
Hastings St CARL NG4 ....44 D1
Haswell Rd BLWL NG6 ....17 G5
Hatfield Av LGEAT NG10 ....62 C4
Hatfield Dr WBRGFD NG2 ....67 F2
Hatfield Rd
MAPPK/POR/STA NG3 ....31 H3
Hatherleigh Cl
MAPPK/POR/STA NG3 ....20 D4
Hathern Cl LGEAT NG10 ....73 E4
Hathern Gn BSTN/STPLFD NG9 ....55 F3
Hathersage Av LGEAT NG10 ....72 A4
Hatley Cl WBRGFD * NG2 ....57 E2

Hatton Crofts LGEAT NG10 ....72 D3
Hatton Gdns WOL/BIL/BRX NG8 ....28 D2
Havelock St ILK DE7 ....38 A1
Haven Cl WBRGFD NG2 ....67 G1
Havenwood Ri CFTN/RUD NG11 ....76 A1
Haverhill Crs ARN NG5 ....18 A1
Haversham Cl BLWL NG6 ....30 A3
Hawarden Ter NOTTE NG7 ....42 C1
Hawkhurst Dr
WOL/BIL/BRX NG8 ....54 C1
Hawkins Ct ILK * DE7 ....26 A1
Hawk Ridge Gdns
MAPPK/POR/STA NG3 ....3 J3
Hawkshead Cl
COT/KEY/RAD NG12 ....69 E1
Hawksley Gdns CFTN/RUD NG11 ....65 H4
Hawksley Rd NOTTE NG7 ....42 C1
Hawkswood Cl
BSTN/STPLFD NG9 ....64 A2
Hawksworth Av ARN NG5 ....31 E4
Hawksworth Rd WBRGFD NG2 ....58 A2
Hawksworth St
MAPPK/POR/STA NG3 ....3 K4
Hawthorn Av
BWSH/BRSTN DE72 ....72 A1
COT/KEY/RAD NG12 ....71 E4
HUCK/RAV NG15 ....11 E1
Hawthorn Cl
COT/KEY/RAD NG12 ....68 C2
COT/KEY/RAD NG12 ....82 B2
Hawthorn Crs ARN NG5 ....20 B1
Hawthorne Av
BSTN/STPLFD NG9 ....53 E5
LGEAT NG10 ....72 D3
Hawthorn Gv BSTN/STPLFD NG9 ....55 G5
Hawthorn Ri
EWD/SEL/PNX NG16 ....26 C1
Hawton Crs WOL/BIL/BRX NG8 ....41 H4
Hayden La HUCK/RAV NG15 ....5 G2
Haydn Av ARN NG5 ....31 E3
Haydn Rd ARN NG5 ....30 D3
Haydock Cl EWD/SEL/PNX NG16 ....15 F4
Hayes Cl ILK DE7 ....24 A5
Hayes Rd COT/KEY/RAD NG12 ....82 A1
Hayles Ct ARN NG5 ....19 E4
Hayling Cl ILK DE7 ....25 F2
Hayling Dr BLWL NG6 ....30 A3
Haynes Av BSTN/STPLFD NG9 ....38 D3
Haynes Cl CFTN/RUD NG11 ....66 C3
Hays Cl ILK DE7 ....25 C3
Haywood Ct WBRGFD NG2 ....3 J5
Haywood Rd
MAPPK/POR/STA NG3 ....32 A3
Haywood St WBRGFD NG2 ....3 J5
Hayworth Rd LGEAT NG10 ....62 C1
Hazelbank Av
MAPPK/POR/STA NG3 ....32 A4
Hazel Cl BING/VBLV NG13 ....49 F3
HEANOR DE75 ....12 A1
Hazel Dr EWD/SEL/PNX NG16 ....16 A4
Hazel Gv HUCK/RAV NG15 ....11 E2
MAPPK/POR/STA NG3 ....32 B1
Hazel Hill Crs ARN NG5 ....19 E3
Hazel Mdw HUCK/RAV NG15 ....11 F2
Hazelmere Gv NOTTE NG7 ....42 B4
Hazel St BLWL NG6 ....17 G2
Hazel Wy HUCK/RAV NG15 ....5 G2
Hazelwood COT/KEY/RAD NG12 ....71 E5
Hazelwood Cl
EWD/SEL/PNX NG16 ....8 C5
Hazelwood Dr HUCK/RAV NG15 ....10 B1
Hazelwood Rd NOTTE NG7 ....42 B1
Headingley Gdns
WOL/BIL/BRX NG8 ....30 A5
Healey Cl WBRGFD NG2 ....57 F1
Heanor Gate Rd HEANOR DE75 ....12 A2
Heanor Rd HEANOR DE75 ....6 A4
ILK DE7 ....25 H2
Heard Crs BSTN/STPLFD NG9 ....55 E3
The Heath EWD/SEL/PNX NG16 ....14 B2
Heathcoat St NOTT NG1 ....3 G5
Heather Cl EWD/SEL/PNX NG16 ....14 C1
MAPPK/POR/STA NG3 ....43 C1
Heather Ct HEANOR DE75 ....13 E1
Heather Crs BWSH/BRSTN DE72 ....72 A1
Heather Cft WBRGFD NG2 ....67 F2
Heatherley Dr BLWL NG6 ....30 C1
Heather Ri BSTN/STPLFD NG9 ....54 D2
Heather Rd CARL NG4 ....33 G4
Heathervale CFTN/RUD NG11 ....57 G5
Heathfield Av ILK DE7 ....26 B5
Heathfield Gv
BSTN/STPLFD NG9 ....64 B3
Heathfield Rd ARN NG5 ....30 C1
Heath Gdns BWSH/BRSTN DE72 ....72 B1
Heathrington Gdns ARN NG5 ....18 C1
Heaton Cl MAPPK/POR/STA NG3 ....32 A4

Heckington Dr
WOL/BIL/BRX NG8 ....41 G3
Hedderley Wk
MAPPK/POR/STA NG3 ....3 G2
Hedges Dr *ILK* DE7 ....38 A4
Hedley St *NOTTE* NG7 ....30 D5
Helen Cl *BSTN/STPLFD* * NG9 ....54 C5
Hellebore Cl *ARN* NG5 ....18 B3
Helm Cl *BLWL* NG6 ....17 E3
Helmsdale Gdns *ARN* NG5 ......18 C1
Helston Dr *WOL/BIL/BRX* NG8 ....28 C3
Helvellyn Cl *WBRGFD* NG2 ......57 F1
Helvellyn Wy *LGEAT* NG10 ......62 C4
Hemingway Cl *CARL* NG4 ....45 E1
EWD/SEL/PNX NG16 ....14 D1
LGEAT NG10 ....63 E5
Hemlock Av *BSTN/STPLFD* NG9 ..53 F3
LGEAT NG10 ....63 E5
Hemlock La *ILK* DE7 ....37 C3
Hemphill La *BLWL* NG6 ....17 E4
Hemsby Gdns *BLWL* NG6 ....17 F2
Hemscott Cl *BLWL* NG6 ....17 E3
Hemsley Dr *EWD/SEL/PNX* NG16 ....7 G4
Hemswell Cl
MAPPK/POR/STA NG3 ....44 B3
Hendon Ri
MAPPK/POR/STA NG3 ....32 A5
Henley Cl *CARL* NG4 ....45 H2
Henley Gdns *BSTN/STPLFD* NG9 ..53 F2
Henley Ri *ARN* NG5 ....30 D2
Henley Wy *ILK* DE7 ....24 A5
Henrietta St *BLWL* NG6 ....17 H4
Henry Rd *BSTN/STPLFD* NG9 ....55 F5
NOTTE NG7 ....42 B5
WBRGFD NG2 ....57 H3
Henry St *HUCK/RAV* NG15 ......11 G1
WBRGFD NG2 ....3 K5
Henshaw Av *ILK* DE7 ....37 C3
Henshaw Pl *ILK* DE7 ....25 H1
Hepple Dr *BLWL* NG6 ....16 D3
Herald Cl *BSTN/STPLFD* NG9 ....55 C4
Herbert Rd *ARN* NG5 ....30 D4
Hereford Rd *ARN* NG5 ....19 H5
CARL NG4 ....33 C3
MAPPK/POR/STA NG3 ....44 C3
Hermitage Wk *ILK* DE7 ....38 A2
NOTTE 2 B7
Hermon St *NOTTE* NG7 ....2 A4
Heron Dr *NOTTE* NG7 ....42 B4
Herons Ct *WBRGFD* NG2 ....68 D2
Heron Whf *WBRGFD* NG2 ....56 C1
Hervey Gn *CFTN/RUD* NG11 ....66 B4
Heskey Cl *MAPPK/POR/STA* NG3 ..3 F1
Heskey Wk *MAPPK/POR/STA* NG3 ..3 F1
Heslington Av
WOL/BIL/BRX NG8 ....38 B5
Hetley Rd *BSTN/STPLFD* NG9 ..55 F4
Hexham Av *ILK* DE7 ....38 B4
Hexham Cl *WBRGFD* NG2 ....58 B5
Heyford Ct *HEANOR* DE75 ......12 D1
Hey St *LGEAT* NG10 ....72 C5
Hickings La *BSTN/STPLFD* NG9 ..53 F3
Hickling Rd
MAPPK/POR/STA NG3 ....32 B3
Hickling Wy *COT/KEY/RAD* NG12 ..71 F5
Hickton Dr *BSTN/STPLFD* NG9 ..64 A5
Highbank Dr *CFTN/RUD* NG11 ..76 B2
Highbury Av *BLWL* NG6 ....17 H5
Highbury Cl *WOL/BIL/BRX* NG8 ..28 C2
Highbury Rd *BLWL* NG6 ....17 H4
COT/KEY/RAD NG12 ....79 F5
High Church St *NOTTE* NG7 ....30 C4
Highclere Dr *CARL* NG4 ....33 C5
Highcliffe Rd *WBRGFD* NG2 ....44 B3
Highcroft *MAPPK/POR/STA* NG3 ..32 A1
Highcroft Cl *LGEAT* NG10 ......73 F4
Highcroft Dr *WOL/BIL/BRX* NG8 ..40 A3
High Cross Ct *NOTTE* NG7 ......42 C2
High Cross Leys
MAPPK/POR/STA NG3 ....3 F2
High Cross St *NOTT* NG1 ....3 G4
Highfield Dr *CARL* NG4 ....32 C5
EWD/SEL/PNX NG16 ....29 E1
ILK DE7 ....37 E3
Highfield Gv *WBRGFD* NG2 ....58 A4
Highfield Rd *BSTN/STPLFD* NG9 ..63 H3
COT/KEY/RAD NG12 ....79 F5
EWD/SEL/PNX NG16 ....28 C1
NOTTE NG7 ....56 A2
WBRGFD NG2 ....58 A4
Highfield St *LGEAT* NG10 ......62 D5
Highgate Cl *CARL* NG4 ....32 D3
Highgate Dr *ILK* DE7 ....25 H1
Highgrove Av
BSTN/STPLFD NG9 ....54 C5
Highgrove Gdns
COT/KEY/RAD NG12 ....68 B3
High Hazles Cl *CARL* NG4 ......33 F2

High Hazles Rd
COT/KEY/RAD NG12 ....71 E2
High Holborn *ILK* DE7 ....25 H2
High Lane Central *ILK* DE7 ....24 C4
High La East *ILK* DE7 ....25 E5
High La West *ILK* DE7 ....24 A5
High Leys Rd *HUCK/RAV* NG15 ..11 E2
High Meadow
COT/KEY/RAD NG12 ....69 F5
High Pavement *NOTT* NG1 ......3 G6
High Rd *BSTN/STPLFD* NG9 ....55 F4
BSTN/STPLFD NG9 ....63 H5
BSTN/STPLFD NG9 ....64 C2
High Spania
EWD/SEL/PNX NG16 ....15 G3
High St *ARN* NG5 ....20 A3
BSTN/STPLFD NG9 ....53 F4
CFTN/RUD NG11 ....77 F3
EWD/SEL/PNX NG16 ....15 G4
HEANOR DE75 ....6 A5
HUCK/RAV NG15 ....5 G5
ILK DE7 ....26 A5
LGEAT NG10 ....73 F1
NOTT NG1 ....3 F5
High Street Av *ARN* NG5 ......19 H3
Highurst St *NOTTE* NG7 ....2 A3
Highurst St *NOTTE* NG7 ....2 A4
High View Av
COT/KEY/RAD NG12 ....82 C1
Highwood Av
WOL/BIL/BRX NG8 ....29 E5
Highway Gv *CFTN/RUD* NG11 ..66 A5
Hilary Cl *WOL/BIL/BRX* NG8 ....40 C5
Hilcot Dr *WOL/BIL/BRX* NG8 ....29 G4
Hillary Pl *ILK* DE7 ....37 E3
Hill Cl *EWD/SEL/PNX* NG16 ....14 D1
WBRGFD NG2 ....58 C5
Hillcrest Cl *EWD/SEL/PNX* NG16 ..15 H4
Hillcrest Dr *HUCK/RAV* NG15 ..10 C1
Hillcrest Gdns *CALV/BJ* NG14 ..22 D5
Hill Crest Gv *ARN* NG5 ....31 E2
Hillcrest Rd *COT/KEY/RAD* NG12 ..79 F5
Hillcrest Vw *CARL* NG4 ....32 B4
Hill Dr *BING/VBLV* NG13 ....48 D2
Hill Farm Ct *COT/KEY/RAD* NG12 ..68 B4
Hillfield Gdns *ARN* NG5 ....18 B1
Hillfield Rd *BSTN/STPLFD* NG9 ..53 G3
Hillingdon Av
EWD/SEL/PNX NG16 ....28 C2
Hillington Ri *ARN* NG5 ....19 F3
Hill Ri *BSTN/STPLFD* NG9 ......38 D4
Hill Rd *BSTN/STPLFD* NG9 ......64 A4
HEANOR DE75 ....12 A1
Hillsford Cl *WOL/BIL/BRX* NG8 ..41 F2
Hillside *EWD/SEL/PNX* NG16 ....6 D4
Hill Side *NOTTE* NG7 ....42 A5
Hillside Av
MAPPK/POR/STA NG3 ....32 B1
Hillside Crs *BSTN/STPLFD* NG9 ..54 D2
Hillside Dr *CALV/BJ* NG14 ......23 E5
LGEAT NG10 ....72 C1
Hillside Gv *LGEAT* NG10 ......52 B5
Hillside Rd *BSTN/STPLFD* NG9 ..54 C3
BSTN/STPLFD NG9 ....64 A3
COT/KEY/RAD NG12 ....47 F5
Hills Rd *ARN* NG5 ....31 H1
Hill View Rd *BSTN/STPLFD* NG9 ..63 H4
Hillview Rd
MAPPK/POR/STA NG3 ....32 B4
Hilton Cl *LGEAT* NG10 ....72 A5
Hilton Crs *WBRGFD* NG2 ....68 C1
Hilton Rd *MAPPK/POR/STA* NG3 ..32 B3
Hinchin Brook *NOTTE* NG7 ......42 B4
Hinsley Cl *ARN* NG5 ....20 C2
Hirst Ct *NOTTE* * NG7 ....2 A3
Hirst Crs *WOL/BIL/BRX* NG8 ....40 A4
Hixon's La *ILK* DE7 ....51 E2
Hoare Rd *BSTN/STPLFD* NG9 ..64 A1
Hobart Cl *WBRGFD* NG2 ....57 F2
Hobart Dr *BSTN/STPLFD* NG9 ..53 G2
Hobson Dr *ILK* DE7 ....37 H2
Hockerwood *CFTN/RUD* NG11 ..66 B2
Hockley *NOTT* NG1 ....3 H5
Hodgkin Cl *CFTN/RUD* NG11 ....65 H5
Hodgkinson St *CARL* NG4 ......45 H2
Hoefield Crs *BLWL* NG6 ....16 F4
Hoe Hill Vw *COT/KEY/RAD* NG12 ..69 E5
Hoewood Rd *BLWL* NG6 ....17 F3
Hogarth Cl *BSTN/STPLFD* NG9 ..53 F5
Hogarth St
MAPPK/POR/STA NG3 ....44 A2
Hogbarn La *HEANOR* DE75 ......6 A2
Hoggetts Cl *BSTN/STPLFD* NG9 ..54 A5
Hogg La *COT/KEY/RAD* NG12 ..46 D5
Holbeck Rd *HUCK/RAV* NG15 ..5 F4
WOL/BIL/BRX NG8 ....41 H2
Holborn Av *WBRGFD* NG2 ......44 A3
Holbrook St *HEANOR* DE75 ......6 D5

Holby Cl *ARN* NG5 ....18 C2
Holcombe Cl *WOL/BIL/BRX* NG8 ..29 G3
Holdale Rd
MAPPK/POR/STA NG3 ....44 C2
Holden Ct *NOTTE* * NG7 ....2 A5
Holden Crs *EWD/SEL/PNX* NG16 ..16 B4
Holden Gdns *BSTN/STPLFD* NG9 ..53 F5
Holden Rd *BSTN/STPLFD* NG9 ..54 D4
Holden St *NOTTE* NG7 ....2 A3
Holgate *CFTN/RUD* NG11 ....65 H4
Holgate Rd *WBRGFD* NG2 ......57 F2
Holkham Av *BSTN/STPLFD* NG9 ..64 B1
Holkham Cl *ARN* NG5 ....20 B4
ILK DE7 ....25 F2
Holland Meadow *LGEAT* NG10 ..73 E4
Holland St *NOTTE* NG7 ....42 C1
Holles Crs *WBRGFD* NG2 ....2 B7
The Hollies *BWSH/BRSTN* DE72 ..62 B2
Hollies Dr *COT/KEY/RAD* NG12 ..68 B2
Hollington Rd
WOL/BIL/BRX NG8 ....41 F2
Hollingworth Av *LGEAT* NG10 ..62 C3
Hollinwell Av *WOL/BIL/BRX* NG8 ..41 H3
Hollinwell Ct
COT/KEY/RAD NG12 ....68 C3
Hollis St *NOTTE* NG7 ....42 C1
The Hollows *CFTN/RUD* NG11 ..66 D2
LGEAT NG10 ....73 H1
Hollow Stone *NOTT* NG1 ....3 G6
Holly Av *BWSH/BRSTN* DE72 ..62 A5
CARL NG4 ....45 E1
CFTN/RUD NG11 ....57 E3
MAPPK/POR/STA NG3 ....44 B1
Hollybrook Gv
EWD/SEL/PNX NG16 ....16 A3
Holly Cl *BING/VBLV* NG13 ......49 F3
HUCK/RAV NG15 ....11 G2
Holly Ct *BSTN/STPLFD* NG9 ....54 B3
Hollycroft *WBRGFD* NG2 ....68 B2
Hollydale Rd
MAPPK/POR/STA NG3 ....44 C2
Hollydene Cl *HUCK/RAV* NG15 ..10 A2
Hollygate Crs *BLWL* NG6 ......29 C1
Holly Gdns
MAPPK/POR/STA NG3 ....44 A1
Hollygate La
COT/KEY/RAD NG12 ....71 C1
Holly La *BSTN/STPLFD* NG9 ....64 D1
Holly Rd *EWD/SEL/PNX* NG16 ..15 H3
Holme Cl *ILK* DE7 ....25 C3
Holme Cft *ILK* DE7 ....36 B1
Holmefield Crs *ILK* DE7 ....26 B5
Holme Gv *WBRGFD* NG2 ....58 C1
Holme La *COT/KEY/RAD* NG12 ..46 C5
Holme Rd *BING/VBLV* NG13 ....49 E3
WBRGFD NG2 ....58 B2
Holmes Cl *EWD/SEL/PNX* NG16 ..6 D4
Holmesfield Dr *HEANOR* DE75 ..12 D2
Holmes St *HEANOR* DE75 ......6 A5
Holme St *WBRGFD* NG2 ....57 H1
Holmewood Crs *ARN* NG5 ......18 D4
Holmewood Dr
EWD/SEL/PNX NG16 ....14 C2
Holmfield Rd *BSTN/STPLFD* NG9 ..64 B3
Holmfield *COT/KEY/RAD* NG12 ..82 B2
Holroyd Av *WBRGFD* NG2 ......44 A4
Holyoake Dr *LGEAT* NG10 ......73 G2
Holyoake Rd
MAPPK/POR/STA NG3 ....32 D2
Holywell Rd *ILK* DE7 ....25 F2
Home Cl *ARN* NG5 ....19 G2
The Home Cft
BSTN/STPLFD NG9 ....54 A4
Home Dr *BSTN/STPLFD* NG9 ....67 H2
Homefield Av *ARN* NG5 ....20 B1
Homefield Rd
WOL/BIL/BRX NG8 ....42 A1
Homestead *EWD/SEL/PNX* NG16 ..6 D3
Honeysuckle Cl
WOL/BIL/BRX NG8 ....28 D4
Honeysuckle Gv
BING/VBLV NG13 ....48 C4
BLWL NG6 ....29 C1
Honeywood Dr
MAPPK/POR/STA NG3 ....44 B1
Honingham Cl *ARN* NG5 ....20 A5
Honingham Rd *ILK* DE7 ....25 F2
Honister Cl *CFTN/RUD* NG11 ..76 A2
WBRGFD NG2 ....58 D4
Honiton Cl *BSTN/STPLFD* NG9 ..53 H4
Honiton Rd *WOL/BIL/BRX* NG8 ..28 D4
Hood St *ARN* NG5 ....31 G3
Hooley Cl *LGEAT* NG10 ....72 C5
Hooton Rd *CARL* NG4 ....44 D1
Hooton St
MAPPK/POR/STA NG3 ....44 A3
Hope Cl *WBRGFD* NG2 ....57 E1
Hopedale Cl *NOTTE* NG7 ....42 B3

Hope Dr *NOTTE* NG7 ....2 C7
Hope St *BSTN/STPLFD* NG9 ....54 D4
ILK DE7 ....38 A1
Hopewell Cl *COT/KEY/RAD* NG12 ..47 F3
Hopewell Wk *ILK* DE7 ....14 A5
Horace Av *BSTN/STPLFD* NG9 ..52 D4
Hornbuckle Ct *NOTTE* NG7 ......42 C3
Hornchurch Rd
WOL/BIL/BRX NG8 ....40 C1
Hornsby Wk *ARN* NG5 ....18 B2
Horridge St *ILK* DE7 ....26 A1
Horsecroft Cl *ILK* DE7 ....25 F3
Horsendale Av
EWD/SEL/PNX NG16 ....29 E1
Horsham Dr *ARN* NG5 ....18 C2
Horsley Crs *EWD/SEL/PNX* NG16 ..6 D4
Hoselett Field Rd *LGEAT* NG10 ..73 F4
Hoten Rd *WBRGFD* NG2 ....44 A5
Hotspur Cl *BLWL* NG6 ....18 B5
Houghton Av *ILK* DE7 ....25 F2
Houghton Cl
EWD/SEL/PNX NG16 ....28 C1
Hound Rd *WBRGFD* NG2 ....57 H3
Hounds Ga *NOTT* NG1 ....2 E6
Houseman Gdns *WBRGFD* NG2 ..57 F1
Houston Cl *ARN* NG5 ....18 B1
Hovenden Gdns *NOTTE* * NG7 ..42 B1
Hove Rd *ARN* NG5 ....18 B5
Howard Cl *LGEAT* NG10 ....63 F5
Howard St *NOTT* NG1 ....3 F4
Howarth Cl *LGEAT* NG10 ....72 B3
Howbeck Rd *ARN* NG5 ....20 C1
Howden Rd *BLWL* NG6 ....11 H5
Howell-Jones Rd
BSTN/STPLFD NG9 ....64 A3
Howells Cl *ARN* NG5 ....19 F2
Howick Dr *BLWL* NG6 ....17 E2
Howitt St *HEANOR* DE75 ....6 C5
LGEAT NG10 ....73 H1
Hoylake Crs *WOL/BIL/BRX* NG8 ..40 C1
Hoyland Av *NOTTE* NG7 ....56 B1
Hubert St *NOTTE* NG7 ....42 C1
Huckerby Rd *ILK* DE7 ....25 F3
Hucknall Cl *WOL/BIL/BRX* NG8 ..28 C3
Hucknall Crs *CARL* NG4 ....33 F3
Hucknall La *BLWL* NG6 ....17 H2
Hucknall Rd *ARN* NG5 ....31 E2
BLWL NG6 ....18 A2
Hudson St
MAPPK/POR/STA NG3 ....44 A2
Hufton's Ct *HEANOR* DE75 ......12 D3
Hugessen Av *HUCK/RAV* NG15 ..5 H4
Humber Cl *WBRGFD* NG2 ......57 F1
Humber Ldg
BSTN/STPLFD * NG9 ....55 F4
Humber Rd *BSTN/STPLFD* NG9 ..55 F4
LGEAT NG10 ....62 D5
Humber Rd South
BSTN/STPLFD NG9 ....55 H5
Humberston Rd
WOL/BIL/BRX NG8 ....40 B5
Hungerhill Rd
MAPPK/POR/STA NG3 ....43 G1
Hungerton St *NOTTE* NG7 ......42 C5
Hunston Cl *WOL/BIL/BRX* NG8 ..41 F1
Hunt Av *HEANOR* DE75 ....6 B5
Hunter Rd *ARN* NG5 ....20 D4
Hunters Cl *CFTN/RUD* NG11 ..56 D5
Huntingdon Dr *NOTTE* NG7 ....2 B5
Huntingdon St *NOTT* NG1 ......2 C1
Huntingdon Wk *LGEAT* NG10 ..62 C1
Huntingdon Wy
BSTN/STPLFD NG9 ....63 G4
Huntly Cl *CFTN/RUD* NG11 ....66 C5
Hurcomb St
MAPPK/POR/STA NG3 ....44 A1
Hurley Cl *ILK* DE7 ....24 B5
Hurts Cft *BSTN/STPLFD* NG9 ..64 C2
Hurts Yd *NOTT* NG1 ....2 E4
Huss's La *LGEAT* NG10 ....73 G2
Hutchinson Gn
MAPPK/POR/STA NG3 ....3 H1
Hutton Cl *BSTN/STPLFD* NG9 ..54 C2
Hutton St *WBRGFD* NG2 ....44 A4
Huxley Cl *WOL/BIL/BRX* NG8 ..40 C1
Hyde Cl *CFTN/RUD* NG11 ......66 C2
Hyde Park Cl *WBRGFD* * NG2 ..67 F1
Hyson Cl *NOTTE* NG7 ....30 C5
Hyson St *NOTTE* NG7 ....42 C1

I

Ian Gv *CARL* NG4 ....33 F5
Ilam Sq *ILK* DE7 ....15 H5
Ilford Cl *ILK* DE7 ....25 G2
Ilkeston Rd *BSTN/STPLFD* NG9 ..53 H2

HEANOR DE75 ....12 C2
ILK DE7 ....38 A5
ILK DE7 ....52 D3
NOTTE NG7 ....2 A4
Imperial Av BSTN/STPLFD NG9 ....54 D5
CARL NG4 ....33 F4
Imperial Rd BSTN/STPLFD NG9 ....18 A4
BSTN/STPLFD NG9 ....54 D5
Inchwood Cl BSTN/STPLFD NG9 ....63 G4
Incinerator Rd WBRGFD NG2 ....57 H1
Independent St NOTTE NG7 ....42 C2
Ingham Gv NOTTE NG7 ....42 B5
Ingham Rd LGEAT NG10 ....62 D4
Ingleborough Gdns LGEAT NG10 ..72 B1
Ingleby Cl COT/KEY/RAD NG12 ....70 D4
WOL/BIL/BRX NG8 ....40 A4
Ingleby Rd LGEAT NG10 ....72 A4
Inglefield Rd ILK DE7 ....38 A2
Inglewood Rd CFTN/RUD NG11 ....66 B5
Ingram Rd BLWL NG6 ....18 A4
Inham Circ BSTN/STPLFD NG9 ....54 B5
Inham Cl BSTN/STPLFD NG9 ......63 H1
Inham Rd BSTN/STPLFD NG9 ......63 H1
Innes Cl CARL NG4 ....44 D1
Instow Ri MAPPK/POR/STA NG3 ....3 H2
Intake Rd COT/KEY/RAD NG12 ....82 A1
Iona Dr BSTN/STPLFD NG9 ....39 E5
Ipswich Circ
MAPPK/POR/STA NG3 ....44 B3
Ireland Av BSTN/STPLFD NG9 ....65 F1
Ireland Cl BSTN/STPLFD NG9 ....65 F1
Iremonger Rd WBRGFD NG2 ......57 G1
Ireton Gv BSTN/STPLFD NG9 ......64 C4
Ireton St BSTN/STPLFD NG9 ......54 D5
NOTTE NG7 ....2 B3
Irwin Dr BLWL NG6 ....17 E5
Isaac's La BSTN/STPLFD NG9 ....53 E4
Isabella St NOTT NG1 ....2 E7
Isandula Rd NOTTE NG7 ....30 C3
Islay Cl ARN NG5 ....20 A1
BSTN/STPLFD NG9 ....53 E1
Ivatt Dr WBRGFD NG2 ....44 A5
Ives Cl WBRGFD NG2 ....67 F2
Ivy Cl EWD/SEL/PNX NG16 ....15 G5
Ivy Gv CARL NG4 ....45 E1
NOTTE NG7 ....30 D5
Ivy La EWD/SEL/PNX NG16 ....7 H5

J

Jackson Av ILK DE7 ....25 H4
LGEAT NG10 ....52 B5
James St ARN NG5 ....19 H2
EWD/SEL/PNX NG16 ....15 G4
Japonica Dr BLWL NG6 ....29 G1
The Jardines BSTN/STPLFD NG9 ..54 B2
Jarvis Av MAPPK/POR/STA NG3 ....44 C2
Jasmine Cl BSTN/STPLFD NG9 ....65 H5
CFTN/RUD NG11 ....65 H5
WOL/BIL/BRX NG8 ....28 D4
Jasmine Ct HEANOR DE75 ....13 E1
Jasmine Rd ARN NG5 ....30 B3
Jasper Cl COT/KEY/RAD NG12 ....60 D1
Jayne Cl CARL NG4 ....33 H3
WOL/BIL/BRX NG8 ....40 D2
Jedburgh Cl
MAPPK/POR/STA NG3 ....3 H2
Jedburgh Wk
MAPPK/POR/STA NG3 ....3 H2
Jenner St ARN NG5 ....31 E5
Jenness Av ARN NG5 ....18 B1
Jennison St BLWL NG6 ....17 H3
Jenny Burton Wy
HUCK/RAV NG15 ....11 H2
Jermyn Dr ARN NG5 ....18 D1
Jersey Gdns
MAPPK/POR/STA NG3 ....3 K2
Jesmond Rd BLWL NG6 ....18 A4
Jessop's La CARL NG4 ....33 G2
Joan Av HEANOR DE75 ....6 B5
John Carroll Ct
MAPPK/POR/STA NG3 ....44 A2
Johnson Av HUCK/RAV NG15 ....11 G2
Johnson Cl EWD/SEL/PNX NG16 ..15 H3
Johnson Dr HEANOR DE75 ....6 C5
Johnson Rd NOTTE NG7 ....42 B4
Johns Rd COT/KEY/RAD NG12 ....47 F5
John St HEANOR DE75 ....6 A5
ILK DE7 ....26 A4
NOTTE NG7 ....30 C4
Joyce Av ARN NG5 ....31 G1
BSTN/STPLFD NG9 ....63 F3
Joyce Cl ARN NG5 ....31 G1
Jubilee Rd ARN NG5 ....19 H4
Jubilee St EWD/SEL/PNX NG16 ..15 F3
WBRGFD NG2 ....44 A4

Judson Av BSTN/STPLFD NG9 ....53 G5
Julian Cl ILK DE7 ....38 B2
Julian La COT/KEY/RAD NG12 ....35 H4
Julian Rd WBRGFD NG2 ....58 C3
Julie Av HEANOR DE75 ....13 E1
Junction Rd LGEAT NG10 ....73 C3
Juniper Cl CFTN/RUD NG11 ......65 H5
Juniper Ct EWD/SEL/PNX NG16 ..14 D2
NOTTE NG7 ....2 A2
Juniper Gdns BING/VBLV NG13 ..49 F3

K

Kappler Cl CARL NG4 ....45 H1
Karen Gdns BSTN/STPLFD NG9 ..64 C2
Karen Ri ARN NG5 ....20 B1
Katherine Dr BSTN/STPLFD NG9 ..63 G3
Kayes Wk NOTT * NG1 ....3 G6
Keats Cl ARN NG5 ....19 G3
EWD/SEL/PNX NG16 ....16 A4
LGEAT NG10 ....72 C4
Keats Dr HUCK/RAV NG15 ....10 C1
Kedleston Cl BSTN/STPLFD NG9 ..64 B1
LGEAT NG10 ....72 B5
Kedleston Dr ILK DE7 ....25 G2
Keeling Cl BSTN/STPLFD NG9 ....64 C1
Keighton HI NOTTE NG7 ....55 H1
Keilder Dr BING/VBLV NG13 ....48 B3
Kelfield Cl BLWL NG6 ....18 B5
Kelham Gn
MAPPK/POR/STA NG3 ....44 A2
Kelham Wy EWD/SEL/PNX NG16 ..7 H4
Kelling Cl ARN NG5 ....18 D4
Kelsey Cl BSTN/STPLFD NG9 ....64 D3
Kelso Gdns WBRGFD NG2 ....57 E1
Kelstern Cl WOL/BIL/BRX NG8 ..29 G2
Kelvedon Gdns
MAPPK/POR/STA NG3 ....3 J2
Kelvin Cl BSTN/STPLFD NG9 ....62 D1
Kelvin Rd MAPPK/POR/STA NG3 ..44 B1
Kemmel Rd BLWL NG6 ....18 A5
Kempsey Cl ARN NG5 ....18 B2
Kempson St CFTN/RUD NG11 ....77 F3
Kempton Cl
EWD/SEL/PNX NG16 ....15 F3
Kempton Dr ARN NG5 ....20 B1
Kendal Cl HUCK/RAV NG15 ......5 E4
Kendal Ct WBRGFD NG2 ....58 C3
Kendal Dr BSTN/STPLFD NG9 ....54 C3
Kenia Cl CARL NG4 ....33 G3
Kenilworth Ct
BSTN/STPLFD NG9 ....55 F3
NOTTE NG7 ....2 C7
Kenilworth Cl ILK DE7 ....37 F3
Kenilworth Rd
BSTN/STPLFD NG9 ....55 F4
NOTTE NG7 ....2 C7
Kenmore Gdns
MAPPK/POR/STA NG3 ....3 H2
Kennedy Av LGEAT NG10 ....72 D4
Kennedy Cl ARN NG5 ....19 G3
Kennedy Dr BSTN/STPLFD NG9 ..53 F2
Kennington Rd
WOL/BIL/BRX NG8 ....42 A3
Kenrick Rd
MAPPK/POR/STA NG3 ....32 B4
Kenrick St CARL NG4 ....45 H1
Kensington Cl
BSTN/STPLFD NG9 ....63 H5
Kensington Gdns CARL NG4 ......45 F1
ILK DE7 ....38 A1
Kensington Park Cl
WBRGFD * NG2 ....67 F1
Kensington Rd LGEAT NG10 ......62 C2
Kensington St ILK DE7 ....38 A2
Kenslow Av NOTTE NG7 ....42 B1
Kent Av BSTN/STPLFD NG9 ......65 E2
Kentmere Cl WBRGFD NG2 ......58 D4
Kenton Av COT/KEY/RAD NG12 ..28 C2
Kent Rd EWD/SEL/PNX NG16 ....14 D1
MAPPK/POR/STA NG3 ....32 B3
Kent St NOTT NG1 ....3 G4
Kentwood Rd WBRGFD NG2 ......44 A4
Kenyon Rd NOTTE NG7 ....42 A5
Kersall Ct BLWL NG6 ....18 A4
Kersall Dr BLWL NG6 ....18 A5
Kersall Gdns HUCK/RAV NG15 ..5 G5
Kestrel Cl CARL NG4 ....32 C4
ILK DE7 ....38 A4
Kestrel Dr BING/VBLV NG13 ....49 E4
Keswick Cl BSTN/STPLFD NG9 ..54 C3
ILK DE7 ....37 G3
WBRGFD NG2 ....58 D4
Keswick Ct LGEAT NG10 ....62 C4
WBRGFD NG2 ....3 J5
Keswick St WBRGFD NG2 ....3 J5

Kett St BLWL NG6 ....17 G4
Keverne Cl BSTN/STPLFD NG9 ..29 H3
Kevin Rd WOL/BIL/BRX NG8 ....54 C1
Kew Cl CFTN/RUD NG11 ....67 F3
Kew Crs HEANOR DE75 ....13 E1
Kew Gdns WOL/BIL/BRX NG8 ....28 D2
Keys Cl BLWL NG6 ....17 F3
Key St MAPPK/POR/STA NG3 ....44 A3
Keyworth Rd CARL NG4 ....33 E2
Kibworth Cl ARN NG5 ....30 C1
Kiddier Av ARN NG5 ....20 C3
Kilbourne Rd ARN NG5 ....20 C1
Kilburn Cl
MAPPK/POR/STA NG3 ....2 E1
Kilburn Cl BSTN/STPLFD NG9 ....54 A1
Kilburn Dr ILK DE7 ....25 G2
Kildare Rd
MAPPK/POR/STA NG3 ....32 A5
Kildonan Cl WOL/BIL/BRX NG8 ..28 C3
Killarney Cl CFTN/RUD NG11 ....76 B2
Killerton Park Dr
CFTN/RUD NG11 ....67 E2
Killisick Rd ARN NG5 ....20 C2
Kiln Cl ILK DE7 ....24 B4
Kilnwood Cl
MAPPK/POR/STA NG3 ....44 B2
Kilsby Rd CFTN/RUD NG11 ......66 C4
Kilverston Rd LGEAT NG10 ......52 B4
Kilverton Cl WOL/BIL/BRX NG8 ..41 H4
Kilvington Rd ARN NG5 ....20 C3
Kimber Cl WOL/BIL/BRX NG8 ....40 C2
Kimberley Cl
EWD/SEL/PNX NG16 ....15 G5
Kimberley Rd
EWD/SEL/PNX NG16 ....16 A5
WBRGFD NG2 ....44 B4
Kimbolton Av NOTTE NG7 ....42 C4
Kindlewood Dr
BSTN/STPLFD NG9 ....64 A5
King Charles St NOTT * NG1 ....2 D6
King Edward Ct NOTT NG1 ......3 G4
King Edward St
HUCK/RAV NG15 ....11 F1
LGEAT NG10 ....52 C5
NOTT NG1 ....3 G4
Kingfisher Cl
BSTN/STPLFD NG9 ....65 G1
Kingfishers Ct
COT/KEY/RAD NG12 ....68 D2
Kingfisher Whf BSTN/STPLFD NG9 ..56 C1
King George Av ILK DE7 ....25 H5
Kinglake Pl WBRGFD NG2 ....57 F1
Kingrove Av BSTN/STPLFD NG9 ..54 C5
Kings Av CARL NG4 ....33 F3
Kingsbridge Av
MAPPK/POR/STA NG3 ....20 D4
Kingsbridge Wy
BSTN/STPLFD NG9 ....54 B5
Kingsbury Dr WOL/BIL/BRX NG8 ..29 F5
Kingsdale Cl LGEAT NG10 ....72 B4
Kingsdown Mt
WOL/BIL/BRX NG8 ....54 D1
Kingsford Av NOTTE NG7 ....42 B2
Kingsley Crs LGEAT NG10 ....72 C5
Kingsley Dr CARL NG4 ....45 H1
Kingsley Rd WBRGFD NG2 ......44 B4
Kingsmead Av
BSTN/STPLFD NG9 ....53 E1
King's Meadow Rd
WBRGFD NG2 ....56 D1
Kings Moor ARN NG5 ....18 B3
King's Pl NOTT NG1 ....3 G5
Kings Rd LGEAT NG10 ....52 C5
Kingsthorpe Cl
MAPPK/POR/STA NG3 ....32 A4
Kingston Av ILK DE7 ....38 B4
Kingston Ct
COT/KEY/RAD * NG12 ....47 E5
ILK DE7 ....24 A5
WBRGFD NG2 ....3 K5
Kingston Rd WBRGFD NG2 ......57 H5
King St BSTN/STPLFD NG9 ......55 F5
EWD/SEL/PNX NG16 ....8 A5
ILK DE7 ....26 A4
LGEAT NG10 ....73 E1
NOTT NG1 ....2 E5
Kingsway COT/KEY/RAD NG12 ..60 D1
HEANOR DE75 ....6 A5
ILK DE7 ....38 B3
Kingsway Gdns
HUCK/RAV NG15 ....10 D3
Kingsway Rd HUCK/RAV NG15 ..10 D3
Kingswell Rd ARN NG5 ....20 A3
Kingswood Rd WBRGFD NG2 ....67 G1
WOL/BIL/BRX NG8 ....41 G3
Kinlet Rd ARN NG5 ....18 D4
Kinross Crs WOL/BIL/BRX NG8 ..41 F2

Kipling Cl CFTN/RUD NG11 ......75 H1
Kipps St NOTT NG1 ....3 G4
Kirby Cl EWD/SEL/PNX NG16 ....8 B4
Kirby Rd EWD/SEL/PNX NG16 ....8 B4
Kirkby Av ILK DE7 ....38 A2
Kirkby Gdns WBRGFD NG2 ......57 G1
Kirk Cl BSTN/STPLFD NG9 ......64 C3
Kirkdale Cl WOL/BIL/BRX * NG8 ..40 A4
Kirkdale Gdns LGEAT NG10 ......72 C3
Kirkdale Rd LGEAT NG10 ....72 C3
Kirkewhite Av LGEAT NG10 ......73 E2
Kirkewhite Ct WBRGFD NG2 ....57 G1
Kirkfell Cl WBRGFD NG2 ....68 D1
Kirkham Cl HEANOR DE75 ......12 A1
Kirkham Dr BSTN/STPLFD NG9 ..63 G4
Kirkhill BING/VBLV NG13 ....48 D2
Kirkland Dr BSTN/STPLFD NG9 ..64 A4
Kirk La CFTN/RUD NG11 ....77 G2
Kirkley Gdns ARN NG5 ....20 B2
Kirk Rd MAPPK/POR/STA NG3 ..32 B3
Kirkstead St NOTTE NG7 ....42 C1
Kirkstone Av HEANOR DE75 ....13 E1
Kirkstone Ct LGEAT NG10 ....62 C4
Kirkstone Dr WBRGFD NG2 ......58 D2
Kirtle Cl WOL/BIL/BRX NG8 ....41 G1
Kirtley Dr WBRGFD NG2 ....56 D1
Kirton Av LGEAT NG10 ....73 E2
Kittiwake Ms NOTTE NG7 ....42 B4
Kiwi Cl HUCK/RAV NG15 ....10 C2
Knapp Av EWD/SEL/PNX NG16 ..14 A1
Kneesall Gv HUCK/RAV NG15 ..5 G5
Kneeton Cl ARN NG5 ....31 F1
CARL NG4 ....33 E1
Kneeton V ARN NG5 ....31 F1
Knighton Rd ARN NG5 ....19 G5
Knightsbridge Dr
WBRGFD NG2 ....67 F2
WOL/BIL/BRX NG8 ....28 D2
Knightsbridge Gdns
HUCK/RAV NG15 ....5 E2
Knights Cl ARN NG5 ....18 C2
BSTN/STPLFD NG9 ....63 G4
WBRGFD NG2 ....67 F3
Knight St CARL NG4 ....45 H2
Kniveton Pk ILK DE7 ....37 G1
Knole Rd WOL/BIL/BRX NG8 ....40 D3
Knoll Av HUCK/RAV NG15 ....10 D3
Knowle HI EWD/SEL/PNX NG16 ..15 H5
Knowle La EWD/SEL/PNX NG16 ..27 H1
Knowle Pk EWD/SEL/PNX NG16 ..15 H5
Krebs Cl CFTN/RUD NG11 ....65 H5
Kyle Vw ARN NG5 ....18 D1
Kyme St NOTTE NG7 ....42 C3
Kynance Gdns CFTN/RUD NG11 ..67 E4

L

Laburnum Av
COT/KEY/RAD NG12 ....82 D2
Laburnum Cl LGEAT NG10 ....52 C4
Laburnum Gv
BSTN/STPLFD NG9 ....65 G1
Laburnum St
MAPPK/POR/STA NG3 ....43 G1
Lace Rd BSTN/STPLFD NG9 ......55 E4
Lace St NOTTE NG7 ....56 A2
Lacey Av HUCK/RAV NG15 ......11 E2
Lacey Cl ILK DE7 ....25 F2
Lacey Fields Rd HEANOR DE75 ..12 D1
Ladbrooke Crs BLWL NG6 ....29 H2
Ladybank Ri ARN NG5 ....20 D2
Lady Bay Av WBRGFD * NG2 ....58 A2
Lady Bay Br WBRGFD NG2 ......57 H1
Lady Bay Rd WBRGFD NG2 ......58 B2
Ladybridge Cl
BSTN/STPLFD NG9 ....64 D3
Ladycroft Av HUCK/RAV NG15 ..5 F5
Ladylea Rd LGEAT NG10 ....72 B5
Ladysmith St WBRGFD NG2 ......44 B4
Ladysmock Gdns WBRGFD NG2 ..57 G1
Ladywood Rd ILK DE7 ....36 C4
Lakeland Av HUCK/RAV NG15 ..11 H2
Lakeside Av LGEAT NG10 ....72 D5
Lakeside Crs LGEAT NG10 ....72 C4
Lake St NOTTE NG7 ....42 C2
Lamartine St
MAPPK/POR/STA NG3 ....3 H3
Lamb Close Dr
EWD/SEL/PNX NG16 ....8 B3
Lambert Gdns
WOL/BIL/BRX NG8 ....29 H5
Lambert St NOTTE NG7 ....42 B1
Lambie Cl WOL/BIL/BRX NG8 ..41 H3
Lambley Av
MAPPK/POR/STA NG3 ....32 C2

Lambley Bridle Rd
 CALV/BJ NG14 ....22 C4
Lambley La CARL NG4 ....33 G2
Lambley Rd CALV/BJ NG14 ....23 F2
Lambourne Dr
 WOL/BIL/BRX NG8 ....41 E3
Lambourne Gdns ARN NG5 ....20 B5
Lambton Cl ILK DE7 ....25 H2
Lamcote Gdns
 COT/KEY/RAD NG12 ....46 C5
Lamcote Gv WBRGFD NG2 ....57 G2
Lamcote Ms
 COT/KEY/RAD NG12 ....46 C5
Lamcote St WBRGFD NG2 ....57 G2
Laming Gap La
 COT/KEY/RAD NG12 ....80 C5
Lammas Gdns WBRGFD NG2 ....57 G1
Lamorna Gv CFTN/RUD NG11 ....57 E5
Lamplands
 COT/KEY/RAD * NG12 ....70 D3
Lanark Cl WOL/BIL/BRX NG8 ....41 H5
Lancaster Av BSTN/STPLFD NG9 ..53 F5
 LGEAT NG10 ....62 B2
Lancaster Rd HUCK/RAV NG15 ....10 C3
 MAPPK/POR/STA NG3 ....44 B1
Lancaster Wy
 WOL/BIL/BRX NG8 ....28 C3
Lancelot Dr EWD/SEL/PNX NG16 ..15 G1
Lancelyn Gdns WBRGFD NG2 ....67 H2
Landcroft Crs ARN NG5 ....18 D4
Landmere Cl ILK DE7 ....25 H2
Landmere Gdns
 MAPPK/POR/STA NG3 ....32 A4
Landmere La CFTN/RUD NG11 ......67 E3
Landsdown Gv LGEAT NG10 ....63 C5
Landseer Cl NOTTE * NG7 ....42 B2
Landseer St NOTTE * NG7 ....42 B2
The Lane EWD/SEL/PNX NG16 ......14 C4
Laneham Av ARN NG5 ....20 B3
Laneside Av BSTN/STPLFD NG9 ....63 F4
Laneward Cl ILK DE7 ....25 F1
Langar Cl ARN NG5 ....31 F1
Langar Rd BING/VBLV NG13 ....48 D3
Langbank Av ARN NG5 ....18 B1
Langdale Dr LGEAT NG10 ....72 B4
Langdale Gv BING/VBLV NG13 ......48 A3
Langdale Rd
 MAPPK/POR/STA NG3 ....44 C3
Langdon Cl LGEAT NG10 ....62 B5
Langdown Cl BLWL NG6 ....17 F2
Langford Rd ARN NG5 ....20 C3
Langham Av
 MAPPK/POR/STA NG3 ....44 B2
Langham Dr CALV/BJ NG14 ....23 E5
Langley Av ARN NG5 ....20 A4
 ILK DE7 ....13 C5
Langstrath Dr
 COT/KEY/RAD NG12 ....68 D1
Langstrath Rd
 CFTN/RUD NG11 ....66 B5
Langton Cl CARL NG4 ....45 F2
Langtree Gdns BING/VBLV NG13 ....49 E2
Langtry Gv NOTTE NG7 ....30 D4
Lansdown Cl BSTN/STPLFD NG9 ....64 A2
Lansdowne Dr WBRGFD NG2 ....67 G2
Lansdowne Rd BLWL NG6 ....30 D1
Lansing Cl CFTN/RUD NG11 ....76 C1
Lanthwaite Cl CFTN/RUD NG11 ......66 B5
Lanthwaite Rd CFTN/RUD NG11 ....66 B5
Lapford Cl
 MAPPK/POR/STA NG3 ....21 E4
Larch Cl ARN NG5 ....19 F2
 BING/VBLV NG13 ....49 F3
 HUCK/RAV NG15 ....11 G2
Larch Crs BSTN/STPLFD NG9 ....54 C4
 EWD/SEL/PNX NG16 ....7 H5
Larchdene Av
 WOL/BIL/BRX NG8 ....40 C5
Larch Dr LGEAT NG10 ....52 C4
Larch Wy COT/KEY/RAD NG12 ......82 D2
Largs Cl ARN NG5 ....18 B1
Lark Cl BSTN/STPLFD NG9 ....63 H1
Larkdale St NOTTE NG7 ....2 A2
Larkfield Rd
 EWD/SEL/PNX NG16 ....16 A5
Larkland's Av ILK DE7 ....38 B1
Larwood Gv ARN NG5 ....31 F1
Lascelles Av CARL NG4 ....33 E3
Latham St BLWL NG6 ....17 G3
Lathkill Av ILK DE7 ....13 H5
Lathkill Cl BLWL NG6 ....17 G3
 ILK DE7 ....24 B5
Lathkilldale Crs LGEAT NG10 ....72 B4
Latimer Cl BLWL NG6 ....17 H4
Latimer Dr BSTN/STPLFD NG9 ......40 A5
Laughton Av WBRGFD NG2 ....67 G4
Laughton Crs HUCK/RAV NG15 ....10 D3

Launceston Crs
 CFTN/RUD NG11 ....66 D2
Launder St WBRGFD NG2 ....57 F1
Laurel Av COT/KEY/RAD NG12 ......82 C2
Laurel Crs EWD/SEL/PNX NG16 ....16 A4
 LGEAT NG10 ....72 D2
Laurel Rd CARL NG4 ....32 D5
Laurie Av NOTTE NG7 ....42 C1
Laurie Cl NOTTE NG7 ....30 D5
Lavender Cl WOL/BIL/BRX NG8 ......28 D4
Lavender Crs CARL NG4 ....33 E4
Lavender Gdns HEANOR DE75 ....13 E1
Lavender Gv BSTN/STPLFD NG9 ....65 G1
Lavender Wk
 MAPPK/POR/STA NG3 ....43 G1
Laver Cl ARN NG5 ....20 C3
Lawdon Rd ARN NG5 ....20 B1
Lawley Av BSTN/STPLFD NG9 ....55 F2
Lawn Cl HEANOR DE75 ....6 C5
Lawn Mill Rd
 EWD/SEL/PNX NG16 ....15 G3
Lawrence Av CARL NG4 ....45 F3
 EWD/SEL/PNX NG16 ....8 A5
 EWD/SEL/PNX NG16 ....14 D5
Lawrence Cl
 COT/KEY/RAD NG12 ....71 E3
Lawrence Ms
 EWD/SEL/PNX * NG16 ....8 B4
 LGEAT NG10 ....73 E1
Lawrence St LGEAT NG10 ....52 C4
Lawrence Wy WBRGFD NG2 ....56 D1
Lawson Av LGEAT NG10 ....73 F2
Lawson St NOTTE NG7 ....2 A1
Lawton Dr BLWL NG6 ....17 H1
Laxton Av BLWL NG6 ....18 A5
Laxton Dr HUCK/RAV NG15 ....10 D1
Leabrook Cl CFTN/RUD NG11 ....65 H3
Leabrook Gdns HUCK/RAV NG15 ....5 H4
Leacroft Rd WOL/BIL/BRX NG8 ......30 A5
Leadale Av HUCK/RAV NG15 ....5 H4
Leafe Cl BSTN/STPLFD NG9 ....64 B4
Leafield Gn CFTN/RUD NG11 ....66 B4
Leafy La HEANOR DE75 ....12 C1
Leahurst Gdns WBRGFD NG2 ....58 C5
Leahurst Rd WBRGFD NG2 ....68 C1
Leamington Dr
 BSTN/STPLFD NG9 ....64 B2
Leander Cl CFTN/RUD NG11 ....57 E5
The Leas CALV/BJ NG14 ....23 C5
Lechlade Cl ILK DE7 ....24 A5
Lechlade Rd ARN NG5 ....18 D4
Ledbury V WOL/BIL/BRX NG8 ....29 C5
Lee Crs ILK DE7 ....26 C5
Lee La HEANOR DE75 ....13 E1
Leen Cl HUCK/RAV NG15 ....5 H4
Leen Dr BLWL NG6 ....17 H1
 HUCK/RAV NG15 ....5 G4
Leen Gate NOTTE NG7 ....56 B1
Leen Mills La HUCK/RAV NG15 ....5 G5
Leen Pl NOTTE NG7 ....42 B3
Leen Valley Wy HUCK/RAV NG15 ..11 H2
Lees Barn Rd
 COT/KEY/RAD NG12 ....60 C1
Lees Hill St WBRGFD NG2 ....3 K6
Lees Rd MAPPK/POR/STA NG3 ......32 B4
Leicester St LGEAT NG10 ....73 F3
Leigh Rd BSTN/STPLFD NG9 ....63 G3
Leighton St
 MAPPK/POR/STA NG3 ....44 A2
Leiston Gdns ARN NG5 ....18 D2
Leivers Av ARN NG5 ....20 A2
Lema Cl BLWL NG6 ....18 A2
Lendal Cl NOTTE NG7 ....2 A1
Lendrum Ct CALV/BJ NG14 ....35 E1
Lennox St NOTT NG1 ....3 H4
Lenton Av COT/KEY/RAD NG12 ......68 D5
 NOTTE NG7 ....2 A6
Lenton Bvd NOTTE NG7 ....42 C4
Lenton Cl NOTTE * NG7 ....42 C4
Lenton Hall Dr NOTTE NG7 ....55 G2
Lenton La NOTTE NG7 ....56 C1
Lenton Mnr NOTTE NG7 ....42 B5
Lenton Rd NOTTE NG7 ....2 A7
Lenton St LGEAT NG10 ....52 D5
Leonard Av ARN NG5 ....31 E3
Leonard Cheshire Cl
 HEANOR DE75 ....13 E1
Leonard St BLWL NG6 ....18 A1
Leopold St LGEAT NG10 ....73 E1
Leroy Wallace Av NOTTE NG7 ......42 C2
Lerwick Cl CFTN/RUD NG11 ....66 D5
Leslie Av BSTN/STPLFD NG9 ....65 E1
 EWD/SEL/PNX NG16 ....15 G5
 NOTTE NG7 ....30 D5
Leslie Rd NOTTE NG7 ....30 D5
Letchworth Crs
 BSTN/STPLFD NG9 ....64 B2

Letcombe Rd CFTN/RUD NG11 ......66 B3
Levens Cl WBRGFD NG2 ....68 D1
Leverton Gn CFTN/RUD NG11 ....66 B4
Lewcote La ILK DE7 ....24 D4
Lewindon Ct ARN NG5 ....31 H1
Lewis Cl MAPPK/POR/STA NG3 ......3 G2
Leybourne Dr ARN NG5 ....18 B4
Leyland Cl BSTN/STPLFD NG9 ....63 G4
The Leys CFTN/RUD NG11 ....66 A4
Leys Rd CFTN/RUD NG11 ....77 F3
 COT/KEY/RAD NG12 ....79 C2
Ley St CARL NG4 ....45 H1
Leyton Crs BSTN/STPLFD NG9 ......65 G1
Library Rd NOTTE NG7 ....55 H2
Lichfield Cl BSTN/STPLFD NG9 ......63 F3
Lichfield Rd WBRGFD NG2 ....44 B4
Liddell Gv WOL/BIL/BRX NG8 ....41 E3
Liddington St NOTTE NG7 ....30 C4
Lilac Av CARL NG4 ....32 D5
Lilac Cl COT/KEY/RAD NG12 ....82 D2
 WOL/BIL/BRX NG8 ....28 D4
Lilac Crs BSTN/STPLFD NG9 ....65 G1
 HEANOR DE75 ....12 B1
Lilac Ms ILK DE7 ....25 G2
Lilac Rd HUCK/RAV NG15 ....11 G2
Lilleker Ri ARN NG5 ....19 H1
Lillington Rd BLWL NG6 ....5 H4
Lily Av CARL NG4 ....45 H1
Lily Gv BSTN/STPLFD NG9 ....65 G1
Lime Cl COT/KEY/RAD NG12 ....47 E5
 EWD/SEL/PNX NG16 ....15 H4
Lime Gv BSTN/STPLFD NG9 ....63 E1
 LGEAT NG10 ....52 C5
 LGEAT NG10 ....73 E1
Lime Grove Av
 BSTN/STPLFD NG9 ....64 D1
The Limes ILK DE7 ....24 B2
Lime St BLWL NG6 ....17 G3
 ILK DE7 ....38 A1
Lime Ter LGEAT NG10 ....73 E1
Lime Tree Av WOL/BIL/BRX NG8 ..29 F4
 WOL/BIL/BRX NG8 ....41 F5
Limetree Cl COT/KEY/RAD NG12 ..82 C2
Limetree Ct ILK * DE7 ....37 F2
Limetree Ri ILK DE7 ....37 F2
Lime Tree Rd HUCK/RAV NG15 ......11 G3
Limmen Gdns
 MAPPK/POR/STA NG3 ....3 K2
Linby Av HUCK/RAV NG15 ....5 G5
Linby Cl ARN NG5 ....19 G5
 CARL NG4 ....33 F3
Linby Dr WOL/BIL/BRX NG8 ....28 C3
Linby Gv HUCK/RAV NG15 ....5 G4
Linby La HUCK/RAV NG15 ....5 C1
Linby Rd HUCK/RAV NG15 ....5 G4
Linby St BLWL NG6 ....17 H2
Linby Wk HUCK/RAV NG15 ....5 H2
Lincoln Av LGEAT NG10 ....62 B2
Lincoln Circ NOTTE NG7 ....2 A6
Lincoln Cl BSTN/STPLFD NG9 ....63 F5
Lincoln Gv COT/KEY/RAD NG12 ....47 E5
Lincoln St BLWL NG6 ....30 B2
 NOTT NG1 ....3 F4
Lindale Cl WBRGFD NG2 ....58 D5
Lindbridge Rd
 WOL/BIL/BRX NG8 ....29 E3
Linden Av CFTN/RUD NG11 ....65 H5
Linden Gv BSTN/STPLFD NG9 ....53 F5
 BSTN/STPLFD NG9 ....53 F5
 CARL NG4 ....34 A4
 LGEAT NG10 ....73 E1
Linden St MAPPK/POR/STA NG3 ..43 G1
Lindfield Cl WOL/BIL/BRX NG8 ......29 E3
Lindfield Rd WOL/BIL/BRX NG8 ....29 E3
Lindley St EWD/SEL/PNX NG16 ....8 C2
Lindum Gv WBRGFD NG2 ....44 A5
Lindum Rd BLWL NG6 ....30 A2
Linford St BSTN/STPLFD NG9 ....40 A4
Ling Crs CFTN/RUD NG11 ....77 G2
Lingford COT/KEY/RAD NG12 ....71 F3
Lingford St HUCK/RAV NG15 ....11 G1
Lings La COT/KEY/RAD NG12 ....82 B4
Linkin Rd BSTN/STPLFD NG9 ....54 B5
Linkmel Cl WBRGFD NG2 ....56 D2
Linkmel Rd WBRGFD NG2 ....58 D5
Linkmel Rd EWD/SEL/PNX NG16 ....7 G4
Linksfield Ct CFTN/RUD NG11 ......67 F4
Linsdale Cl WOL/BIL/BRX NG8 ......40 A3
Linsdale Gdns CARL NG4 ....33 E1
Linton Ri MAPPK/POR/STA NG3 ....44 B2
Linwood Crs
 EWD/SEL/PNX NG16 ....14 A1
Lion Cl WOL/BIL/BRX NG8 ....29 H3
Lismore Cl NOTTE NG7 ....43 H3
Lissett Av ILK DE7 ....37 H3
Lister Ga NOTT NG1 ....3 F6

Listowel Crs CFTN/RUD NG11 ....76 B1
Litchen Cl ILK DE7 ....26 A3
Litchfield Cl LGEAT NG10 ....73 H2
Littlegreen Rd ARN NG5 ....32 A1
Little Hallam Hi ILK DE7 ....37 H3
Little Hallam La ILK DE7 ....38 A2
Little Hayes WBRGFD NG2 ....67 G2
Little John Wk
 MAPPK/POR/STA NG3 ....43 G1
Little La COT/KEY/RAD NG12 ....69 F3
 EWD/SEL/PNX NG16 ....15 H5
Little Lunnon CFTN/RUD NG11 ......74 D4
Little Meadow
 COT/KEY/RAD NG12 ....71 F4
Little Ox CARL NG4 ....45 G4
Little Tennis St WBRGFD NG2 ....44 B5
Little Tennis St South
 WBRGFD NG2 ....58 B1
Littlewell La ILK DE7 ....52 A2
Litton Cl ARN NG5 ....31 H1
 ILK DE7 ....25 H1
Liverpool St
 MAPPK/POR/STA NG3 ....3 J4
Llanberis Gv WOL/BIL/BRX NG8 ....29 F4
Limekiln Cl BLWL NG6 ....17 F2
Lloyd St ARN NG5 ....31 F3
Lobelia Cl MAPPK/POR/STA NG3 ..43 G1
Lock Cl ILK DE7 ....37 F2
Lockerbie St CARL NG4 ....45 G2
Lock La LGEAT NG10 ....62 C1
 LGEAT NG10 ....72 C5
Locksley La CFTN/RUD NG11 ....66 B2
Lockton Av HEANOR DE75 ....12 B2
Lockwood Cl ARN NG5 ....19 E1
 BSTN/STPLFD NG9 ....65 H2
Lodge Cl WOL/BIL/BRX NG8 ....30 A5
Lodge Farm La ARN NG5 ....19 H1
Lodge La EWD/SEL/PNX NG16 ....6 B1
Lodge Rd EWD/SEL/PNX NG16 ......14 B2
 ILK DE7 ....24 B2
 LGEAT NG10 ....72 D4
Lodgewood Cl BLWL NG6 ....17 F4
Lodore Cl WBRGFD NG2 ....58 D5
Logan St BLWL NG6 ....18 A4
Lois Av NOTTE NG7 ....42 C5
Lombard Cl NOTTE NG7 ....42 C4
London Rd WBRGFD NG2 ....43 G5
Longacre ARN NG5 ....32 A1
Long Acre BING/VBLV NG13 ....49 E3
 HUCK/RAV NG15 ....4 C5
Long Acre East BING/VBLV NG13 ..49 E3
Longbeck Av
 MAPPK/POR/STA NG3 ....32 B4
Longbridge La HEANOR DE75 ....6 A4
Longdale Rd ARN NG5 ....19 G4
Longden Cl BSTN/STPLFD NG9 ......53 G5
Longden St NOTT NG1 ....3 J4
Longfellows ARN NG5 ....19 E2
Longfield Crs ILK DE7 ....38 A3
Longfield La ILK DE7 ....38 A3
Longford Crs BLWL NG6 ....11 H5
Long Hill Ri HUCK/RAV NG15 ....11 E1
Longlands Dr WBRGFD NG2 ....69 E1
Longlands Rd
 BSTN/STPLFD NG9 ....65 G3
Long La BSTN/STPLFD NG9 ....64 C4
 EWD/SEL/PNX NG16 ....10 A5
 ILK DE7 ....13 G4
Longleat Crs BSTN/STPLFD NG9 ....64 B2
Longmead Cl ARN NG5 ....19 F4
Longmead Dr ARN NG5 ....19 F4
Longmoor Gdns LGEAT NG10 ....62 C4
Longmoor La LGEAT NG10 ....62 C1
Longmoor Rd LGEAT NG10 ....62 B4
Longore Sq WOL/BIL/BRX NG8 ......42 A4
Longridge Rd ARN NG5 ....32 A1
Long Rw NOTT NG1 ....2 E5
Longwall Av WBRGFD NG2 ....56 D2
Lonscale Cl WBRGFD NG2 ....68 D1
Lonsdale Dr BSTN/STPLFD NG9 ....63 F4
Lonsdale Rd NOTTE NG7 ....42 B2
Lord Haddon Rd ILK DE7 ....25 H4
Lord Nelson St WBRGFD NG2 ....44 A4
Lord St WBRGFD NG2 ....3 K5
Lorimer Av CARL NG4 ....33 G3
Lorne Cl MAPPK/POR/STA NG3 ....43 F1
Lorne Gv COT/KEY/RAD NG12 ....47 E5
Lorne Wk MAPPK/POR/STA NG3 ..43 F1
Lortas Rd ARN NG5 ....30 C3
Loscoe Mount Rd ARN NG5 ....31 F3
Loscoe Rd ARN NG5 ....31 F3
 HEANOR DE75 ....6 A4
Lothian Rd COT/KEY/RAD NG12 ....68 D5
Lothmore Ct WBRGFD * NG2 ....57 E1
Lotus Cl MAPPK/POR/STA NG3 ......43 H1
Loughborough Av
 WBRGFD NG2 ....44 A4

Loughborough Rd
CFTN/RUD NG11 ....**77** G2
WBRGFD NG2.....................**57** H3
Loughrigg Cl *WBRGFD* NG2 .....**57** E2
Louis Av *BSTN/STPLFD* NG9 .....**54** D4
Louise Av *CARL* NG4 ....**33** H5
Lovelace Wk *HUCK/RAV* NG15 .....**5** C4
Lovell Cl *BLWL* NG6 ....**17** E5
Lowater Ct *CARL* NG4 ....**44** C1
Lowdham Rd *CARL* NG4 ....**32** D2
Lowdham St
MAPPK/POR/STA NG3 ....**3** J4
Lower Beauvale
EWD/SEL/PNX NG16 ....**8** B4
Lower Bloomsgrove Rd *ILK* DE7 ...**26** A3
Lower Brook St *LGEAT* NG10 ......**73** F2
Lower Chapel St *ILK* DE7 ....**26** A4
Lower Clara Mount Rd
HEANOR DE75 ....**12** D1
Lower Ct *BSTN/STPLFD* NG9 ....**55** F4
Lower Dunstead Rd
EWD/SEL/PNX NG16 ....**6** D4
Lower Eldon St *WBRGFD* NG2 .....**3** K6
Lower Gladstone St
HEANOR DE75 ....**6** B5
Lower Granby St *ILK* DE7 ....**26** A3
Lower Maples *HEANOR* DE75 ......**12** D2
Lower Middleton St *ILK* DE7 ......**26** B4
Lower Nelson St *HEANOR* DE75....**6** A5
Lower Orchard St
BSTN/STPLFD NG9 ....**53** E4
Lower Park St
BSTN/STPLFD NG9 ....**52** D5
Lower Parliament St *NOTT* NG1 ....**3** F4
Lower Regent St
BSTN/STPLFD NG9 ....**55** F5
Lower Rd *BSTN/STPLFD* NG9 ....**55** G4
Lower Stanton Rd *ILK* DE7..........**38** A2
Lower Whitworth Rd *ILK* DE7 ......**38** A2
Loweswater Ct *WBRGFD* NG2 ......**58** D4
Lowlands Dr
COT/KEY/RAD NG12 ....**79** G5
Lowlands Lea *HEANOR* DE75 ....**6** C5
Low Pavement *NOTT* NG1 ....**3** F6
Low's La *ILK* DE7 ....**52** B1
Low Wood Rd *BLWL* NG6 ....**17** E5
Lucerne Cl *CFTN/RUD* NG11 ....**57** E5
Lucknow Av
MAPPK/POR/STA NG3 ....**31** G5
Lucknow Ct
MAPPK/POR/STA NG3 ....**31** G5
Lucknow Dr
MAPPK/POR/STA NG3 ....**31** G5
Lucknow Rd
MAPPK/POR/STA NG3 ....**31** G5
Ludford Rd *BLWL* NG6 ....**17** H2
Ludham Av *BLWL* NG6 ....**17** G5
Ludlam Av *EWD/SEL/PNX* NG16 .....**14** B3
Ludlow Cl *BSTN/STPLFD* NG9 ......**54** C2
Ludlow Hill Rd *WBRGFD* NG2 ......**68** A1
Lulworth Cl *WBRGFD* NG2 ....**67** F1
Lulworth Ct
EWD/SEL/PNX NG16 ....**15** G3
Lune Cl *BSTN/STPLFD* NG9 ....**64** D3
Lupin Cl *MAPPK/POR/STA* NG3 .....**43** G1
Luther Cl *MAPPK/POR/STA* NG3 ....**43** H1
Luton Cl *WOL/BIL/BRX* NG8 ....**30** A4
Lutterell Ct *WBRGFD* NG2 ....**67** G1
Lutterell Wy *WBRGFD* NG2 ....**68** D1
Lybster Ms *WBRGFD* * NG2 ....**57** E1
Lydia Gdns *EWD/SEL/PNX* NG16 ....**13** H1
Lydney Pk *WBRGFD* NG2 ....**67** E1
Lyle Cl *EWD/SEL/PNX* NG16 ....**15** F3
Lyme Pk *CFTN/RUD* NG11 ....**67** E1
Lymington Gdns
MAPPK/POR/STA NG3 ....**44** A2
Lymn Av *CARL* NG4 ....**33** G3
Lyncombe Gdns
COT/KEY/RAD NG12 ....**79** G5
Lyndale Rd *BSTN/STPLFD* NG9 .....**53** H3
Lynden Av *LGEAT* NG10 ....**73** E3
Lyndhurst Gdns *WBRGFD* NG2 .....**67** G2
Lyndhurst Rd *WBRGFD* NG2 ....**44** B4
Lynham Ct *BLWL* * NG6 ....**17** G3
Lynmouth Crs *NOTTE* NG7 ....**42** B1
Lynmouth Dr *ILK* DE7 ....**25** G2
Lynncroft *EWD/SEL/PNX* NG16 .....**8** B5
Lynstead Dr *HUCK/RAV* NG15.......**10** B2
Lynton Gdns *ARN* NG5..............**20** B2
Lynton Rd *BSTN/STPLFD* NG9 ......**54** B3
Lyons Cl *CFTN/RUD* NG11 ....**77** E1
Lytham Dr *COT/KEY/RAD* NG12 .....**68** D1
Lytham Gdns *ARN* NG5 ....**18** D1
Lythe Cl *CFTN/RUD* NG11 ....**66** D1
Lytton Cl *MAPPK/POR/STA* NG3....**3** J3

M

Mabel Gv *WBRGFD* NG2...............**58** B3
Mabel St *WBRGFD* NG2..............**57** G1
Macdonald Sq *ILK* DE7 ....**37** G3
Mackinley St *BSTN/STPLFD* NG9.....**53** F2
Maclaren Gdns *CFTN/RUD* NG11 ....**77** G4
Maclean St *CARL* NG4................**44** D1
Mafeking St *WBRGFD* NG2...........**44** B4
Magdala Rd
MAPPK/POR/STA NG3 ....**31** F5
Magnolia Cl *WOL/BIL/BRX* NG8 .....**28** D4
Magnolia Ct *BSTN/STPLFD* NG9......**54** C2
Magnolia Gv *HUCK/RAV* NG15 ....**11** G3
Magson Cl *MAPPK/POR/STA* NG3 ...**3** K3
Maiden La *NOTT* NG1................**3** H5
Maidens Dl *ARN* NG5 ....**19** G2
Maid Marian Wy *NOTT* NG1 ....**2** D5
Maidstone Dr
BSTN/STPLFD NG9 ....**54** C1
Main La *COT/KEY/RAD* NG12 ....**35** H4
Main Rd *BSTN/STPLFD* NG9 ....**55** H5
CARL NG4 ....**33** C4
CFTN/RUD NG11 ....**57** E4
COT/KEY/RAD NG12 ....**35** H5
COT/KEY/RAD NG12 ....**46** D5
COT/KEY/RAD NG12 ....**70** D2
COT/KEY/RAD NG12 ....**79** F2
EWD/SEL/PNX NG16 ....**15** G1
Main St *BLWL* NG6..................**17** H3
CALV/BJ NG14 ....**35** E1
CARL NG4 ....**22** A3
COT/KEY/RAD NG12 ....**82** B3
EWD/SEL/PNX NG16 ....**8** D5
EWD/SEL/PNX NG16 ....**14** A1
EWD/SEL/PNX NG16 ....**14** D5
EWD/SEL/PNX NG16 ....**15** G4
HUCK/RAV NG15 ....**5** F1
ILK DE7 ....**24** B2
ILK DE7 ....**52** A3
LGEAT NG10 ....**73** G2
WBRGFD NG2......................**58** D4
WOL/BIL/BRX NG8 ....**28** A4
Maitland Av *ARN* NG5...............**32** A1
Maitland Rd *ARN* NG5...............**32** A1
Major St *NOTT* NG1.................**2** E3
Malbon Cl *MAPPK/POR/STA* NG3 ...**31** H5
Malcolm Cl
MAPPK/POR/STA NG3 ....**43** F1
Maldon Cl *BSTN/STPLFD* NG9 ....**64** A2
Malin Hl *NOTT* NG1 ....**3** H6
Malkin Av *COT/KEY/RAD* NG12......**47** F4
Mallard Cl *BING/VBLV* NG13 ....**49** F4
Mallard Ct *BSTN/STPLFD* * NG9 .....**65** G1
Mallard Rd *CARL* NG4 ....**46** A2
Mallow Wy *BING/VBLV* NG13 ....**48** B4
Malmesbury Rd
MAPPK/POR/STA NG3 ....**32** B1
Maltby Cl *WOL/BIL/BRX* NG8 ....**29** G3
Maltby Rd
MAPPK/POR/STA NG3 ....**32** B1
Malt Cottages *NOTTE* NG7 ....**30** C4
Malthouse Cl
EWD/SEL/PNX NG16 ....**14** A1
Malthouse Rd *ILK* DE7...............**38** A4
Malting Cl *CFTN/RUD* NG11 ....**77** F3
Maltmill La *NOTT* NG1 ....**3** F6
Malton Rd *NOTTE* NG7 ....**30** C3
Malvern Cl *MAPPK/POR/STA* NG3 ...**31** H4
Malvern Crs *WBRGFD* NG2 ....**68** A1
Malvern Gdns *LGEAT* NG10 ....**72** B1
Malvern Rd *WBRGFD* NG2 ....**67** H1
Manchester St *LGEAT* NG10 ....**73** E3
Mandalay St *BLWL* NG6.............**30** A1
Manesty Crs *CFTN/RUD* NG11 ....**76** B2
Manifold Gdns *WBRGFD* NG2........**57** F1
Manly Ct *ARN* NG5...................**18** B2
Manners Av *ILK* DE7 ....**25** G4
Manners Rd *ILK* DE7 ....**25** H4
Manners St *ILK* DE7 ....**38** B2
Manning St
MAPPK/POR/STA NG3 ....**43** G1
Manning Vw *ILK* DE7 ....**26** A3
Mannion Crs *LGEAT* NG10 ....**72** C4
Manns Leys *COT/KEY/RAD* NG12 ....**70** D4
Mann St *NOTTE* NG7................**30** C5
Manor Av *BSTN/STPLFD* NG9 ....**53** E3
BSTN/STPLFD NG9 ....**55** E5
BSTN/STPLFD NG9 ....**64** D3
WBRGFD NG2......................**3** K6
Manor Farm La
CFTN/RUD NG11 ....**66** B1
Manor Fields Dr *ILK* DE7 ....**37** G1
Manor Green Ct *CARL* NG4 ....**33** G5
Manor Green Wk *CARL* NG4 ....**33** G5
Manor House Rd *LGEAT* NG10 ......**73** G3
Manor Pk *CFTN/RUD* NG11..........**77** E2
Manor Rd *BING/VBLV* NG13 ....**49** E3
CARL NG4 ....**33** G5
COT/KEY/RAD NG11 ....**74** D3
COT/KEY/RAD NG12 ....**35** H3
COT/KEY/RAD NG12 ....**82** B1
EWD/SEL/PNX NG16 ....**14** A1
ILK DE7 ....**25** H4
Manor St *WBRGFD* NG2..............**44** A5
Manorwood Rd
COT/KEY/RAD NG12 ....**71** E4
Mansell Cl *EWD/SEL/PNX* NG16 .....**14** C1
Mansfield Gv *NOTT* NG1 ....**2** D2
Mansfield Rd *ARN* NG5 ....**31** G1
EWD/SEL/PNX NG16 ....**7** H2
HEANOR DE75......................**6** C5
NOTT NG1..........................**2** E1
MAPPK/POR/STA NG3 ....**31** F3
Manston Ms *NOTTE* * NG7 ....**42** C2
Manthorpe Crs *ARN* NG5 ....**32** A2
Manton Crs *BSTN/STPLFD* NG9 .....**55** E3
Manvers Ct *WBRGFD* NG2 ....**3** J5
Manvers Gv
COT/KEY/RAD NG12 ....**47** E5
Manvers Rd *WBRGFD* NG2 ....**58** A5
Manvers St *CARL* NG4 ....**45** H2
ILK DE7 ....**25** H1
NOTT NG1..........................**3** J5
Manville Cl *BSTN/STPLFD* NG9 ......**40** A1
WOL/BIL/BRX NG8 ....**41** H2
Maori Av *HUCK/RAV* NG15 ....**10** C3
Maple Av *BSTN/STPLFD* NG9 ....**65** G1
LGEAT NG10 ....**52** C4
Maplebeck Rd *ARN* NG5 ....**20** B3
Maple Cl *BING/VBLV* NG13 ....**49** F3
COT/KEY/RAD NG12 ....**61** E1
COT/KEY/RAD NG12 ....**82** D2
Maple Ct *NOTTE* * NG7 ....**42** C5
Mapledene Crs
WOL/BIL/BRX NG8 ....**40** B5
Maple Dr *CARL* NG4 ....**34** A3
EWD/SEL/PNX NG16 ....**16** A4
HUCK/RAV NG15 ....**10** D2
Maple Gdns *HEANOR* DE75 ....**12** A1
Maples St *NOTTE* NG7 ....**42** C1
Maplestead Av *CFTN/RUD* NG11.....**57** F3
Mapletree Cl *ARN* NG5..............**19** E3
Mapperley Crs
MAPPK/POR/STA NG3 ....**31** H3
Mapperley Hall
MAPPK/POR/STA NG3 ....**31** G4
Mapperley Hall Dr
MAPPK/POR/STA NG3 ....**31** G4
Mapperley La *ILK* DE7 ....**24** B3
Mapperley Orch *ARN* NG5 ....**20** D3
Mapperley Plns
MAPPK/POR/STA NG3 ....**20** D3
Mapperley Ri *ARN* NG5 ....**31** H3
Mapperley Rd
MAPPK/POR/STA NG3 ....**43** F1
Mapperley St *ARN* NG5 ....**31** G1
March Cl *ARN* NG5...................**18** B3
Marchesi Cl *HUCK/RAV* NG15 ....**10** D3
Marchwood Cl
WOL/BIL/BRX NG8 ....**42** A3
Mardale Cl *WBRGFD* NG2 ....**68** D1
Margaret Av *ILK* DE7 ....**26** A5
LGEAT NG10 ....**62** C2
LGEAT NG10 ....**63** G5
Margaret Crs *CARL* NG4 ....**33** F3
Margaret Pl *BING/VBLV* NG13 ......**48** C2
Margaret's Ct
BSTN/STPLFD NG9 ....**53** H3
Marham Cl *WBRGFD* NG2 ....**3** K7
Marhill Rd *CARL* NG4................**45** G1
Maria Ct *NOTTE* NG7................**2** B7
Marie Gdns *HUCK/RAV* NG15 ....**11** F2
Marina Av *BSTN/STPLFD* NG9 ......**65** E1
Marina Rd *WBRGFD* NG2 ....**56** D1
Marion Av *HUCK/RAV* NG15 ....**5** H4
Maris Cl *CFTN/RUD* NG11 ....**65** H4
Maris Dr *CALV/BJ* NG14 ....**34** D2
Market Pl *HEANOR* DE75 ....**12** B1
ILK DE7 ....**25** H5
LGEAT NG10 ....**73** F1
Market St *BING/VBLV* NG13 ....**48** D3
HEANOR DE75......................**6** B5
ILK DE7 ....**26** A5
NOTT NG1..........................**2** E4
Markham Crs *ARN* NG5 ....**31** F1
Markham Rd
BSTN/STPLFD NG9................**54** C2
Mark St *LGEAT* NG10 ....**62** D1
Marlborough Rd *ARN* NG5 ....**19** G5
BSTN/STPLFD NG9 ....**55** E4
Marlborough St *NOTTE* NG7 ....**56** B2
Marldon Cl *WOL/BIL/BRX* NG8 .....**40** A3
Marlow Av *BLWL* NG6 ....**30** B3
Marlow Crs *ILK* DE7.................**24** A5
Marl Rd *COT/KEY/RAD* NG12 ....**47** C5
Marlwood *COT/KEY/RAD* NG12 .....**71** F4
Marmion Rd
MAPPK/POR/STA NG3 ....**44** B2
Marnham Dr
MAPPK/POR/STA NG3 ....**31** H4
Marple Sq
MAPPK/POR/STA * NG3 ....**3** F1
Marriott Av *BSTN/STPLFD* NG9 .....**63** H1
Marriott Cl *BSTN/STPLFD* NG9 .....**63** H1
Marshall Dr *BSTN/STPLFD* NG9 .....**53** H3
Marshall Hill Dr
MAPPK/POR/STA NG3 ....**32** C4
Marshall Rd *CARL* NG4..............**32** B4
Marshall St *ARN* NG5...............**31** F3
HEANOR DE75......................**6** C5
Marston Rd
MAPPK/POR/STA NG3 ....**44** C1
Martin Cl *BLWL* NG6.................**17** E5
Martindale Cl *WBRGFD* NG2........**58** D4
Martinmass Cl *NOTTE* NG7 ....**56** B1
Martins Hl *CARL* NG4 ....**45** F1
Marton Rd *BLWL* NG6 ....**17** H1
BSTN/STPLFD NG9 ....**64** B3
Marvin Rd *BSTN/STPLFD* NG9 ......**55** E5
Marwood Crs *CARL* NG4 ....**32** D3
Marwood Rd *CARL* NG4 ....**32** D4
Maryland Ct *BSTN/STPLFD* NG9.....**53** F2
Mary Rd *EWD/SEL/PNX* NG16 ......**14** C1
Masonic Pl *NOTT* NG1 ....**2** D4
Mason Rd *ILK* DE7 ....**25** G3
Massey Cl *CALV/BJ* NG14 ....**34** D2
Massey Gdns
MAPPK/POR/STA NG3 ....**3** K1
Matlock Ct *NOTT* NG1 ....**2** E3
Matlock St *CARL* NG4...............**45** G1
Mattingly Rd *BLWL* NG6 ....**17** F4
Maud St *NOTTE* NG7................**30** D4
Maun Av *NOTTE* NG7...............**42** A2
Maurice Dr
MAPPK/POR/STA NG3 ....**31** H3
Maws La *EWD/SEL/PNX* NG16 ......**15** F3
Maxtoke Rd *NOTTE* NG7 ....**2** A7
Maxwell Ct *NOTTE* NG7 ....**42** C5
Maxwell St *BWSH/BRSTN* DE72 ....**72** A1
LGEAT NG10 ....**73** F2
May Av *WOL/BIL/BRX* NG8 ....**40** D4
May Ct *ARN* NG5....................**31** E4
Maycroft Gdns
MAPPK/POR/STA NG3 ....**44** B1
Maydene Cl *CFTN/RUD* NG11 ....**66** A5
Mayfair Gdns *ARN* NG5 ....**18** C5
Mayfield Av *CALV/BJ* NG14 ....**23** E5
HEANOR DE75......................**12** B1
Mayfield Dr *BSTN/STPLFD* NG9 .....**53** G1
Mayfield Gv *LGEAT* NG10 ....**63** F5
Mayfield Rd *CARL* NG4..............**44** C1
Mayflower Ct *WBRGFD* NG2.........**58** B4
Mayflower Rd
EWD/SEL/PNX NG16 ....**14** C2
Mayo Rd *ARN* NG5..................**31** E4
Maypole *CFTN/RUD* NG11 ....**66** B3
Maypole Yd *NOTT* NG1 ....**3** F4
Mays Av *MAPPK/POR/STA* NG3 .....**45** E2
Mays Cl *MAPPK/POR/STA* NG3 .....**44** D2
May St *ILK* DE7 ....**25** H1
Maythorn Cl *CFTN/RUD* NG11 ......**67** F3
Mcintosh Rd *CARL* NG4 ....**33** F2
Meadfoot *BLWL* NG6 ....**29** G1
Meadowbank Ct
EWD/SEL/PNX NG16..............**7** G4
Meadowbank Wy
EWD/SEL/PNX NG16..............**7** G4
Meadow Cl *EWD/SEL/PNX* NG16 ....**8** A3
HUCK/RAV NG15 ....**10** C3
WBRGFD NG2......................**57** H2
Meadow Cottages *CARL* NG4........**45** G1
Meadow Ct *WBRGFD* * NG2 ....**58** A1
Meadow Dr
COT/KEY/RAD NG12 ....**82** D1
Meadow End
COT/KEY/RAD NG12 ....**47** H5
Meadow Gdns
BSTN/STPLFD NG9 ....**64** D2
HEANOR DE75......................**13** H1
Meadow Gv *WBRGFD* NG2 ....**57** H1
Meadow La *BSTN/STPLFD* NG9 .....**64** D2
LGEAT NG10 ....**73** H3
WBRGFD NG2......................**57** H1
Meadow Ri
EWD/SEL/PNX NG16 ....**17** E4
Meadow Rd *BSTN/STPLFD* NG9......**65** G1
CARL NG4 ....**45** G2

EWD/SEL/PNX NG16 ....14 D5
The Meadows *HEANOR* DE75....12 B1
Meadow St *ILK* DE7 ....26 A4
Meadows Wy *WBRGFD* NG2......57 E2
Meadowsweet Hl
  BING/VBLV NG13 ....48 B3
Meadowvale Crs
  CFTN/RUD NG11 ....66 B5
Medawar Cl *CFTN/RUD* NG11....65 H5
Meden Cl *CFTN/RUD* NG11 ......66 B3
Medina Dr *COT/KEY/RAD* NG12..69 E5
Medway St *BSTN/STPLFD* NG9....64 A1
Medway St *WOL/BIL/BRX* NG8....42 A3
Meeks Rd *ARN* NG5 ....20 C2
Meerbrook Pl *ILK* DE7 ....37 F3
Meer Rd *BSTN/STPLFD* NG9 ......63 H1
Melbourne Rd
  BSTN/STPLFD NG9 ....53 F1
  WBRGFD NG2..............58 B2
  WOL/BIL/BRX NG8 ....29 H4
Melbury Rd *ARN* NG5 ....32 A1
  WOL/BIL/BRX NG8 ....28 C5
Meldreth Rd *WOL/BIL/BRX* NG8....40 D1
Melford Hall Dr *WBRGFD* NG2....67 F2
Melford Rd *WOL/BIL/BRX* NG8....28 C5
Melksham Rd *ARN* NG5 ....19 F2
Mellbreak Cl *WBRGFD* NG2......58 D5
Mellors Rd *WBRGFD* NG2........68 A1
Melrose Av *ARN* NG5 ....31 F2
  BSTN/STPLFD NG9 ....65 F1
Melrose Gdns *WBRGFD* * NG2....67 G2
Melrose St *ARN* NG5 ....31 F3
Melton Ct *LGEAT* NG10 ....62 B1
Melton Gdns
  COT/KEY/RAD NG12 ....68 B2
Melton Gv *WBRGFD* NG2 ....57 H4
Melton Rd *COT/KEY/RAD* NG12....68 B5
  WBRGFD NG2..............57 H4
Melville Ct
  MAPPK/POR/STA * NG3 ....31 F5
Melville Gdns
  MAPPK/POR/STA NG3 ....3 K2
Melville St *NOTT* NG1 ....3 F7
Melvyn Dr *BING/VBLV* NG13......48 D3
Mendip Cl *LGEAT* NG10 ....62 B5
Mensing Av *COT/KEY/RAD* NG12....70 D3
Merchant St *BLWL* NG6 ....17 G2
Mercury Cl *ARN* NG5 ....18 B5
Meredith Cl *WBRGFD* NG2........57 E2
Meredith Ct *BSTN/STPLFD* NG9....53 F1
Meregill Cl *ARN* NG5 ....18 C1
Merevale Av *CFTN/RUD* NG11....66 C2
Mere Wy *CFTN/RUD* NG11 ....77 G4
Meriac Cl *ARN* NG5 ....18 C2
Meriden Av *BSTN/STPLFD* NG9....55 F3
Meridian Cl *ILK* DE7 ....25 H1
Merlin Cl *CFTN/RUD* NG11........66 A4
Merlin Dr *HUCK/RAV* NG15 ......10 C3
Merlin Wy *ILK* DE7 ....38 B5
Merrivale Ct
  MAPPK/POR/STA NG3 ....31 F5
Mersey St *BLWL* NG6 ....17 G3
Merton Cl *ARN* NG5 ....20 C1
Merton Ct *BSTN/STPLFD* NG9....55 F3
Metcalf Rd *EWD/SEL/PNX* NG16....8 C4
Mettham St *NOTT* NG7 ....42 C5
The Mews *LGEAT* * NG10 ....62 C1
Meynell Gv *NOTT* NG7 ....30 D4
Meynell Rd *LGEAT* NG10 ....73 E4
Miall Ct *NOTT* NG7 ....42 B3
Miall St *NOTT* NG7 ....42 B3
Mickleborough Av
  MAPPK/POR/STA NG3 ....32 A5
Mickleborough Wy
  CFTN/RUD NG11 ....67 F3
Mickleden Cl *WBRGFD* NG2......57 E1
Mickledon Cl *LGEAT* NG10......72 C1
Middle Av *CARL* NG4 ....32 D5
Middlebeck Av *ARN* NG5..........20 D2
Middlebeck Dr *ARN* NG5 ....20 D2
Middledale Rd *CARL* NG4 ....45 H2
Middlefell Wy *CFTN/RUD* NG11....66 A5
Middle Furlong Gdns
  WBRGFD NG2..............57 E1
Middle Furlong Ms
  WBRGFD NG2..............57 E1
Middle Hl *NOTT* NG1 ....3 F7
Middle La *BSTN/STPLFD* * NG9....41 D1
Middlemore Cottages
  ILK * DE7..............52 A2
Middle Nook *WOL/BIL/BRX* NG8....40 D3
Middle Pavement *NOTT* NG1 ....3 H6
Middle St *BSTN/STPLFD* NG9....55 F5
Middleton Bvd
  WOL/BIL/BRX NG8 ....41 H4
Middleton Cl
  EWD/SEL/PNX NG16 ....16 B4

Middleton Crs
  BSTN/STPLFD NG9 ....54 D2
Middleton Rd *ILK* DE7 ....38 B3
Middleton St
  BSTN/STPLFD NG9 ....54 D4
  EWD/SEL/PNX NG16 ....26 D1
  ILK DE7..............26 B4
Midhurst Cl *BSTN/STPLFD* NG9....64 B2
Midhurst Wy *CFTN/RUD* NG11....66 B4
Midlame Gdns *BLWL* NG6 ....17 E3
Midland Rd *BSTN/STPLFD* NG9....62 D1
  CARL NG4..............45 H1
  NOTTE NG7..............42 B5
Midland Crs *CARL* NG4..............45 G1
Midland Gv *CARL* NG4 ....33 H5
Midland Rd *CARL* NG4 ....45 G1
  EWD/SEL/PNX NG16..............8 A5
  HEANOR DE75..............6 B5
Midland St *LGEAT* NG10..............73 F1
The Midway *NOTTE* NG7..............56 B3
Mikado Rd *LGEAT* NG10..............72 D4
Milburn Gv *BING/VBLV* NG13....48 B3
Mildenhall Crs *ARN* NG5..............19 F2
Mile End Rd *CARL* NG4..............45 F3
Milford Av *LGEAT* NG10..............62 C3
Milford Cl *BLWL* NG6 ....17 F2
Milford Dr *ILK* DE7 ....25 G2
  MAPPK/POR/STA NG3..............44 D1
The Mill Cl *BLWL* NG6..............30 B2
Mill Acre Cl *ILK* DE7..............25 F3
Millbank *ILK* DE7..............25 G2
Millbeck Av *WOL/BIL/BRX* NG8....40 C4
Millbeck Cl *WBRGFD* NG2........58 D5
Mill Ct *LGEAT* * NG10..............73 F2
Mill Crs *ARN* NG5..............19 H2
Milldale Cl *CFTN/RUD* NG11......65 H4
Milldale Rd *LGEAT* NG10........72 C3
Millennium Cl *ILK* DE7..............25 H2
Millennium Wy East *BLWL* NG6....29 F1
Millennium Wy West
  EWD/SEL/PNX NG16..............29 F1
Miller Hives Cl
  COT/KEY/RAD NG12 ....70 D3
Millers Br *COT/KEY/RAD* NG12....70 D2
Millers Ct *COT/KEY/RAD* NG12....35 H4
Millers Ct *NOTT* NG7..............42 B2
Millersdale Av *ILK* DE7..............13 H5
Mill Field Cl *CALV/BJ* NG14........34 D2
Millfield Cl *ILK* DE7 ....25 F2
Millfield Rd *EWD/SEL/PNX* NG16....15 F3
  ILK DE7..............38 B1
Mill Hill Rd *BING/VBLV* NG13....48 C4
Millicent Gv *WBRGFD* NG2........58 A3
Millicent Rd *WBRGFD* NG2........57 H3
Mill La *CARL* NG4..............22 A3
  COT/KEY/RAD NG12..............70 D2
  EWD/SEL/PNX NG16..............26 D4
  LGEAT NG10..............52 C5
Mill Rd *BSTN/STPLFD* NG9........53 E3
  EWD/SEL/PNX NG16..............8 C4
  HEANOR DE75..............12 D2
Mill St *BLWL* NG6..............30 A2
  ILK DE7..............26 A4
Mill View *WBRGFD* * NG2..........44 A4
Milner Av *ARN* NG5..............31 F3
  LGEAT NG10..............73 E1
Milnhay Rd *EWD/SEL/PNX* NG16....7 F5
  HEANOR DE75..............13 E1
Milton Av *ILK* DE7..............25 H1
Milton Cl *ARN* NG5..............20 C3
Milton Crs *BSTN/STPLFD* NG9....64 C4
Milton Ri *HUCK/RAV* NG15........10 C2
Milton St *ILK* DE7..............25 H1
  ILK DE7..............26 A1
  LGEAT NG10..............73 E2
  NOTT NG1..............3 F3
Milverton Rd *ARN* NG5 ....19 F2
Mimosa Cl *CFTN/RUD* NG11......65 H5
Minerva St *BLWL* NG6..............17 G2
Minster Cl *HUCK/RAV* NG15......5 G4
Minster Gdns
  EWD/SEL/PNX NG16..............14 C1
Mint Gv *LGEAT* NG10..............72 B2
Minton Cl *BSTN/STPLFD* NG9....64 A4
Minver Crs *WOL/BIL/BRX* NG8....29 G4
Mirberry Ms *NOTTE* * NG7........42 B5
Misk Hollows *HUCK/RAV* NG15....5 E4
Misk Vw *EWD/SEL/PNX* NG16 ....8 C5
Mission St
  MAPPK/POR/STA NG3..............31 H3
Mitchell Av *EWD/SEL/PNX* NG16....6 D4
Mitchell Cl *BLWL* NG6..............16 D3
Mitchell St *LGEAT* NG10..............73 F4
Mitchell Ter *ILK* DE7..............38 B3
Moffat Cl
  MAPPK/POR/STA * NG3..............44 A1
Mollington Sq *BLWL* NG6........29 G1
Monarch Wy *HEANOR* DE75......6 A5

Mona Rd *WBRGFD* NG2 ....58 B2
Mona St *BSTN/STPLFD* NG9......55 F5
Monks Cl *ILK* DE7..............26 B5
Monksway *CFTN/RUD* NG11......66 D2
Monkton Cl *ILK* DE7..............25 G2
Monkton Dr *WOL/BIL/BRX* NG8....40 D1
Monmouth Cl
  WOL/BIL/BRX NG8..............40 A4
Monroe Wk *ARN* NG5..............18 D3
Monsaldale Cl *LGEAT* NG10......72 C3
Monsall Av *ILK* DE7..............13 H5
Monsall St *NOTTE* NG7..........30 C4
Monsell Dr *ARN* NG5..............19 H1
Montague Rd *HUCK/RAV* NG15....5 F4
Montague St *BLWL* NG6..........17 H3
  BSTN/STPLFD NG9..............54 D4
Montfort Crs *ARN* NG5..............31 G1
Montfort St *NOTT* NG7..............2 A4
Montgomery Cl
  BSTN/STPLFD NG9..............64 B4
Montgomery St *NOTT* NG7 ......2 B2
Montpelier Rd *NOTTE* NG7........56 B2
Montrose Ct
  BSTN/STPLFD NG9..............53 F2
Monyash Cl *ILK* DE7..............25 H2
Moor Br *BLWL* NG6..............18 A1
Moorbridge La
  BSTN/STPLFD NG9..............52 D2
Moorbridge Rd
  BING/VBLV NG13..............48 D2
Moorbridge Rd East
  BING/VBLV NG13..............49 E2
Moore Cl *WBRGFD* NG2..........58 C2
Moore Ga *BSTN/STPLFD* NG9....55 F5
Moore Rd *MAPPK/POR/STA* NG3....33 B3
Moores Av *LGEAT* NG10..........52 D4
Moor Farm Inn La
  BSTN/STPLFD NG9..............53 H1
Moorfield Ct
  BSTN/STPLFD NG9..............53 F2
Moorfield Crs *LGEAT* NG10......62 C1
Moorfields Av
  EWD/SEL/PNX NG16..............8 A4
Moorgate St *NOTTE* NG7..........2 A3
Moorgreen *EWD/SEL/PNX* NG16....8 D2
Moorgreen Dr
  WOL/BIL/BRX NG8..............28 C3
Moorhouse Rd
  WOL/BIL/BRX NG8..............40 D2
The Moorings *WBRGFD* NG2......56 C1
Moorland Av *BSTN/STPLFD* NG9....53 E5
Moorlands Cl *LGEAT* NG10......62 C4
Moor La *BING/VBLV* NG13........48 D2
  BSTN/STPLFD NG9..............54 A1
  CFTN/RUD NG11..............77 E3
  ILK DE7..............50 C1
Moor Rd *WOL/BIL/BRX* NG8......28 C4
Moorsholm Dr
  WOL/BIL/BRX NG8..............40 C4
Moor St *CARL* NG4..............45 H1
Moray Ct *EWD/SEL/PNX* NG16....15 G3
Morden Cl *WOL/BIL/BRX* NG8....28 C5
Morden Rd *EWD/SEL/PNX* NG16....14 D2
Moreland Ct *WBRGFD* * NG2......43 H5
Moreland St *WBRGFD* NG2........44 A5
Morello Av *CARL* NG4..............45 H4
Moreton Rd *CFTN/RUD* NG11....76 B2
Morgan Ms *CFTN/RUD* * NG11....66 A4
Morkinshire La
  COT/KEY/RAD NG12..............70 D2
Morley Av *MAPPK/POR/STA* NG3....31 H1
Morley Ct *WBRGFD* NG2..........3 J5
Morley Dr *ILK* DE7..............25 G2
Morley Rd
  MAPPK/POR/STA NG3..............32 B5
Morley St *ARN* NG5..............19 G4
Mornington Cl *LGEAT* NG10......52 C5
Mornington Crs
  EWD/SEL/PNX NG16..............28 C2
Morrell Bank *ARN* NG5..............18 C4
Morris Av *BSTN/STPLFD* NG9....55 F5
Morris Rd *WOL/BIL/BRX* NG8....28 C4
Morris St *CARL* NG4..............45 H1
Morton Cl *COT/KEY/RAD* NG12....47 H5
Morton Gdns
  COT/KEY/RAD NG12..............47 H5
Morval Rd *WOL/BIL/BRX* NG8....40 D1
Morven Av *HUCK/RAV* NG15......11 G1
Mosley St *HUCK/RAV* NG15......11 F1
  NOTTE NG7..............30 C5
Moss Cl *ARN* NG5..............19 F2
Mosscroft Av *CFTN/RUD* NG11....66 A5
Mossdale Rd *ARN* NG5..............19 F5
Moss Dr *BSTN/STPLFD* NG9......54 A4
Moss Rd *HUCK/RAV* NG15........5 E5
  ILK DE7..............37 H1
Moss Side *CFTN/RUD* NG11......66 D3
Mosswood Crs *ARN* NG5..........19 E3

Mottram Rd *BSTN/STPLFD* NG9....54 B5
The Mount *ARN* NG5..............19 G1
  BSTN/STPLFD NG9..............53 E5
  MAPPK/POR/STA NG3..............32 C3
Mountbatten Gv *CARL* NG4......33 F3
Mountbatten Wy
  BSTN/STPLFD NG9..............64 A4
Mountfield Av *LGEAT* NG10......62 B2
Mountfield Dr *ARN* NG5..........18 D3
Mount Hooton *NOTT* NG1........2 B1
Mount Hooton Rd *NOTT* NG7....42 D1
Mount Pleasant *BLWL* NG6......30 A3
  CARL NG4..............45 F1
  COT/KEY/RAD NG12..............46 D5
  COT/KEY/RAD NG12..............82 C1
  ILK DE7..............25 H1
Mountsorrel Dr *WBRGFD* NG2....58 C5
Mount St *BSTN/STPLFD* NG9......53 F4
  BWSH/BRSTN DE72..............72 A2
  HEANOR DE75..............12 B1
  NOTT NG1..............2 D5
  NOTTE NG7..............30 C4
Mowbray Ct
  MAPPK/POR/STA NG3..............3 H2
Mowbray Gdns *WBRGFD* NG2....68 A3
Mowbray Ri *ARN* NG5..............20 A2
Moyra Dr *ARN* NG5..............19 F3
Mozart Cl *NOTTE* NG7..............42 B2
Mozart St *NOTTE* * NG7............42 B2
Mudpie La *WBRGFD* NG2..........58 D2
Muir Av *COT/KEY/RAD* NG12......79 E1
Muirfield Rd *ARN* NG5..............18 D1
Mulberry Cl *WBRGFD* NG2........67 E1
Mulberry Gv *HUCK/RAV* NG15....11 G3
Mundella Rd *WBRGFD* NG2......57 G2
Mundy's Dr *HEANOR* DE75........12 C2
Mundy St *HEANOR* DE75..........12 B1
  ILK DE7..............26 A3
Munford Circ *WOL/BIL/BRX* NG8....29 F2
Munks Av *HUCK/RAV* NG15........5 E5
Murby Crs *BLWL* NG6..............17 G2
Murden Wy *BSTN/STPLFD* NG9....55 G5
Muriel Rd *BSTN/STPLFD* NG9....55 E4
Muriel St *BLWL* NG6..............17 G3
Muskham Av *ILK* DE7..............26 A2
Muskham St *WBRGFD* NG2........57 G2
Musters Crs *WBRGFD* NG2........68 A1
Musters Cft *CARL* NG4..............45 G5
Musters Rd *BING/VBLV* NG13....48 C3
  CFTN/RUD NG11..............77 E3
  WBRGFD NG2..............57 H3
Muston Cl *MAPPK/POR/STA* NG3....32 A4
Myrtle Av *BSTN/STPLFD* NG9....53 F5
  LGEAT NG10..............72 D3
  NOTTE NG7..............31 E5
Myrtle Gv *HUCK/RAV* NG15......55 F4
Myrtle Rd *CARL* NG4..............32 D5
Myrtus Cl *CFTN/RUD* NG11......65 H4

N

Nabbs La *HUCK/RAV* NG15........10 C1
Nairn Cl *ARN* NG5..............20 C1
Nansen St *BLWL* NG6..............17 H4
Naomi Crs *BLWL* NG6..............17 H1
Narrow La *EWD/SEL/PNX* NG16....15 G1
Naseby Cl *ARN* NG5..............30 C1
Nathaniel Rd *LGEAT* NG10........73 F4
Nathans La *COT/KEY/RAD* NG12....59 G4
Naworth Cl *BLWL* NG6..............18 A5
Neal Ct *EWD/SEL/PNX* NG16......6 D4
Neale St *LGEAT* NG10..............73 F2
Near Meadow *LGEAT* NG10......73 F4
Nearsby Dr *WBRGFD* NG2........58 C5
Needham Rd *ARN* NG5..............20 B2
Needham St *BING/VBLV* NG13....48 D3
Need Wood Av
  BSTN/STPLFD NG9..............53 E1
Neighwood Cl
  BSTN/STPLFD NG9..............63 F4
Nell Gwyn Crs *ARN* NG5..........19 F1
Nelper Crs *ILK* DE7..............38 B3
Nelson Rd *ARN* NG5..............19 H3
  BLWL NG6..............17 H3
  BSTN/STPLFD NG9..............65 F2
Nelson St *ILK* DE7..............26 A1
  LGEAT NG10..............73 E2
  NOTT NG1..............3 H5
Nene Cl *HUCK/RAV* NG15..........10 C4
Nesfield Ct *ILK* DE7..............25 H4
Nesfield Rd *ILK* DE7..............25 H4
Neston Dr *BLWL* NG6..............29 G1
Nether Cl *EWD/SEL/PNX* NG16....8 A4
  MAPPK/POR/STA NG3..............44 B2
Netherfield Rd *LGEAT* NG10......72 C5
Nethergate *CFTN/RUD* NG11....65 H4

Nether Pasture CARL NG4 ......45 H2
Nether St BSTN/STPLFD NG9 ......55 F5
Nettlecliff Wk ARN NG5 ......18 B2
Newall Dr BSTN/STPLFD NG9 ......64 B4
Newark Av WBRGFD NG2 ......3 K6
Newark Cl ARN NG5 ......18 C5
Newark Crs WBRGFD NG2 ......3 K6
Newark St WBRGFD NG2 ......3 K6
Newbery Av LGEAT NG10 ......73 G3
Newbury Cl
  MAPPK/POR/STA NG3 ......32 B1
Newbury Dr
  EWD/SEL/PNX NG16 ......28 C2
Newcastle Av
  BSTN/STPLFD NG9 ......55 E5
  CARL NG4 ......33 F4
Newcastle Circ NOTTE NG7 ......2 A6
Newcastle Ct NOTTE NG7 ......2 A6
Newcastle Dr NOTTE NG7 ......2 A5
Newcastle Farm Dr
  WOL/BIL/BRX NG8 ......29 H4
Newcastle St BLWL NG6 ......17 H3
  NOTT NG1 ......3 F4
Newcastle Ter NOTTE NG7 ......2 B4
  WOL/BIL/BRX * NG8 ......30 A4
Newcombe Dr ARN NG5 ......20 D3
New Derby Rd
  EWD/SEL/PNX NG16 ......7 G5
Newdigate Rd
  EWD/SEL/PNX NG16 ......15 H3
Newdigate St
  EWD/SEL/PNX NG16 ......15 H4
  ILK DE7 ......38 B2
  NOTTE NG7 ......2 A3
Newdigate Vls NOTTE NG7 ......2 A3
New Eaton Rd
  BSTN/STPLFD NG9 ......63 E1
New Farm La
  EWD/SEL/PNX NG16 ......16 B4
Newfield Rd ARN NG5 ......30 C2
Newgate Cl CARL NG4 ......45 F1
Newgate Ct NOTTE * NG7 ......42 C4
Newgate St BING/VBLV NG13 ......48 D3
Newhall Gv WBRGFD NG2 ......58 A2
Newham HEANOR DE75 ......12 D1
Newland Cl BSTN/STPLFD NG9 ......63 H4
  WOL/BIL/BRX NG8 ......41 H3
Newlands Cl
  COT/KEY/RAD NG12 ......68 D2
Newlands Dr CARL NG4 ......33 G4
  HEANOR DE75 ......6 B4
New Lawn Rd ILK DE7 ......25 H5
Newlyn Dr WOL/BIL/BRX NG8 ......30 A5
Newlyn Gdns
  WOL/BIL/BRX NG8 ......29 H5
Newmanleys Rd
  EWD/SEL/PNX NG16 ......13 H2
Newmanleys Rd (South)
  EWD/SEL/PNX NG16 ......13 H1
Newmarket Rd BLWL NG6 ......17 G4
Newmarket Wy
  BSTN/STPLFD NG9 ......63 G4
Newport Dr WOL/BIL/BRX NG8 ......30 A4
Newquay Av NOTTE NG7 ......42 B1
New Rd BSTN/STPLFD NG9 ......53 E2
  COT/KEY/RAD NG12 ......47 E5
  EWD/SEL/PNX NG16 ......9 E3
  NOTTE NG7 ......42 A2
Newstead Av
  COT/KEY/RAD NG12 ......47 F4
  MAPPK/POR/STA NG3 ......32 D3
Newstead Dr WBRGFD NG2 ......58 C4
Newstead Gv BING/VBLV NG13 ......48 B3
  NOTT NG1 ......2 D1
Newstead Rd LGEAT NG10 ......62 C3
Newstead Rd North ILK DE7 ......25 G2
Newstead Rd South ILK DE7 ......25 G2
Newstead St ARN NG5 ......31 F2
Newstead Ter HUCK/RAV NG15 ......5 F4
Newstead Wy
  WOL/BIL/BRX NG8 ......28 C3
New St ARN NG5 ......31 H4
  LGEAT NG10 ......73 F1
New Ter LGEAT NG10 ......52 C5
Newthorpe Common
  EWD/SEL/PNX NG16 ......14 B2
Newthorpe St WBRGFD NG2 ......57 G1
Newton Av BING/VBLV NG13 ......48 C3
  COT/KEY/RAD NG12 ......47 F4
Newton Cl ARN NG5 ......20 C4
Newtondale Cl
  WOL/BIL/BRX NG8 ......30 A4
Newton Dr BSTN/STPLFD NG9 ......53 F5
  WBRGFD NG2 ......67 F2
Newton Rd CARL NG4 ......33 E2
Newtons La EWD/SEL/PNX NG16 ......26 B2

EWD/SEL/PNX NG16 ......26 C2
Newton St BSTN/STPLFD NG9 ......54 D5
New Tythe St LGEAT NG10 ......73 G2
New Vale Rd CARL NG4 ......45 E3
Nicholas Rd BSTN/STPLFD NG9 ......54 C2
Nicker HI COT/KEY/RAD NG12 ......82 D1
Nidderdale WOL/BIL/BRX NG8 ......40 B4
Nidderdale Cl
  WOL/BIL/BRX NG8 ......40 B5
Nightingale Cl
  EWD/SEL/PNX NG16 ......16 C4
Nightingale Wy
  BING/VBLV NG13 ......49 F4
Nile St NOTT NG1 ......3 H4
Nilsson Rd BSTN/STPLFD NG9 ......64 A3
Nine Acre Gdns BLWL NG6 ......17 E3
Nine Corners
  EWD/SEL/PNX NG16 ......15 G4
Nixon Ri HUCK/RAV NG15 ......10 C2
Nobel Rd CFTN/RUD NG11 ......75 H1
Noel St EWD/SEL/PNX NG16 ......15 H4
  NOTTE NG7 ......30 C5
No Man's La ILK DE7 ......51 E3
The Nook BSTN/STPLFD NG9 ......64 D2
  WOL/BIL/BRX NG8 ......40 B4
Nook End Rd HEANOR DE75 ......12 A1
Norbett Cl BSTN/STPLFD NG9 ......64 A3
Norbett Rd ARN NG5 ......20 B2
Norbreck Cl WOL/BIL/BRX NG8 ......29 G3
Norburn Crs BLWL NG6 ......30 C2
Norbury Wy LGEAT NG10 ......52 B5
Nordean Rd ARN NG5 ......20 B5
Norfolk Av BSTN/STPLFD NG9 ......63 H5
Norfolk Cl HUCK/RAV NG15 ......10 C2
Norfolk Pl NOTT NG1 ......2 C3
Norfolk Rd LGEAT NG10 ......63 G5
Norfolk Wk LGEAT NG10 ......62 C1
Norland Cl
  MAPPK/POR/STA NG3 ......43 H1
Normanby Rd
  WOL/BIL/BRX NG8 ......40 B5
Norman Cl BSTN/STPLFD NG9 ......64 B1
  MAPPK/POR/STA NG3 ......3 F1
Norman Crs ILK DE7 ......25 H2
Norman Dr EWD/SEL/PNX NG16 ......8 C5
  HUCK/RAV NG15 ......10 D3
Norman Rd
  MAPPK/POR/STA NG3 ......32 B5
Norman St CARL NG4 ......45 H2
  EWD/SEL/PNX NG16 ......15 G3
  ILK DE7 ......25 C2
Normanton La
  COT/KEY/RAD NG12 ......79 G5
Northall Av BLWL NG6 ......17 G4
Northampton St
  MAPPK/POR/STA NG3 ......3 K1
North Av LGEAT NG10 ......72 D4
North Church St NOTT NG1 ......2 E3
North Circus St NOTT NG1 ......2 C5
Northcliffe Av
  MAPPK/POR/STA NG3 ......32 C3
Northcote St LGEAT NG10 ......73 F2
Northcote Wy BLWL NG6 ......17 H5
Northdale Rd
  MAPPK/POR/STA NG3 ......44 D1
Northdown Dr
  BSTN/STPLFD NG9 ......64 A2
Northdown Rd
  WOL/BIL/BRX NG8 ......41 H2
North Dr BSTN/STPLFD NG9 ......54 D5
Northern Dr EWD/SEL/PNX NG16 ......39 E5
Northern Rd HEANOR DE75 ......6 A5
Northfield Av
  COT/KEY/RAD NG12 ......47 H4
  ILK DE7 ......25 H3
  LGEAT NG10 ......72 B5
Northfield Crs
  BSTN/STPLFD NG9 ......63 H2
Northfield Rd
  BSTN/STPLFD NG9 ......63 H2
Northfields LGEAT NG10 ......72 C5
North Ga NOTTE NG7 ......30 C4
Northgate St ILK DE7 ......25 H4
North Hill Av HUCK/RAV NG15 ......5 E4
North Hill Crs HUCK/RAV NG15 ......5 E4
Northolme Av BLWL NG6 ......17 H3
Northolt Dr WOL/BIL/BRX NG8 ......28 C2
North Rd CFTN/RUD NG11 ......77 E1
  LGEAT NG10 ......72 D3
  NOTTE NG7 ......2 A5
  WBRGFD NG2 ......57 H5
North Sherwood St NOTT NG1 ......43 E1
North St BSTN/STPLFD NG9 ......54 D5
  EWD/SEL/PNX NG16 ......7 E4
  EWD/SEL/PNX NG16 ......8 D5
  ILK DE7 ......26 A4
  WBRGFD NG2 ......3 J5

Northumberland Cl
  MAPPK/POR/STA NG3 ......3 G2
Northwold Av WBRGFD NG2 ......57 G5
Northwood Crs ARN NG5 ......19 F4
Northwood Rd ARN NG5 ......19 F4
Northwood St
  BSTN/STPLFD NG9 ......53 E3
Norton St NOTTE NG7 ......42 C3
Norwich Gdns BLWL NG6 ......17 G1
Norwood Rd NOTTE NG7 ......42 B3
Nointontone St WBRGFD NG2 ......3 K6
Nottingham Rd ARN NG5 ......19 H4
  BING/VBLV NG13 ......48 C3
  BLWL NG6 ......30 B2
  BSTN/STPLFD NG9 ......38 D4
  BSTN/STPLFD NG9 ......53 F4
  CALV/BJ NG14 ......34 C3
  COT/KEY/RAD NG12 ......60 C1
  COT/KEY/RAD NG12 ......82 B2
  EWD/SEL/PNX NG16 ......8 A5
  EWD/SEL/PNX NG16 ......16 C5
  EWD/SEL/PNX NG16 ......29 F1
  HUCK/RAV NG15 ......11 H2
  ILK DE7 ......38 A1
  LGEAT NG10 ......73 F1
  NOTTE NG7 ......30 C3
Nuart Rd BSTN/STPLFD NG9 ......55 E4
Nugent Gdns
  MAPPK/POR/STA NG3 ......3 J2
The Nurseries
  EWD/SEL/PNX NG16 ......8 B5
Nursery Av BSTN/STPLFD NG9 ......64 B1
  BWSH/BRSTN DE72 ......62 A1
  ILK DE7 ......36 B1
Nursery Cl COT/KEY/RAD NG12 ......47 G5
  HUCK/RAV NG15 ......11 F3
Nursery Dr CARL NG4 ......33 G5
Nursery Hollow ILK DE7 ......37 H2
Nursery La BLWL NG6 ......30 B1
Nursery Rd ARN NG5 ......20 A3
  BING/VBLV NG13 ......49 G2
  COT/KEY/RAD NG12 ......47 G5
Nutbrook Crs ILK DE7 ......37 G4
Nutbrook Trail ILK DE7 ......25 F2
Nuthall Cir ILK DE7 ......37 F4
Nuthall Gdns WOL/BIL/BRX NG8 ......30 A5
Nuthall Rd WOL/BIL/BRX NG8 ......29 G2

O

Oackland Ter LGEAT NG10 ......72 D4
Oak Acres BSTN/STPLFD NG9 ......63 H4
Oak Apple Crs ILK DE7 ......37 H2
Oak Av BING/VBLV NG13 ......49 F3
  COT/KEY/RAD NG12 ......46 D4
  EWD/SEL/PNX NG16 ......7 G2
  LGEAT NG10 ......52 B4
Oakdale Dr BSTN/STPLFD NG9 ......64 B2
Oakdale Rd ARN NG5 ......20 C2
  MAPPK/POR/STA NG3 ......44 C2
Oak Dr EWD/SEL/PNX NG16 ......7 H5
Oakenhall Av HUCK/RAV NG15 ......5 H5
Oakfield Cl WOL/BIL/BRX NG8 ......40 B5
Oakfield Dr LGEAT NG10 ......62 C3
Oakfield Rd BSTN/STPLFD NG9 ......53 E4
  HUCK/RAV NG15 ......11 G1
  WOL/BIL/BRX NG8 ......40 B5
Oakfields Rd WBRGFD NG2 ......58 B2
Oak Flatt BSTN/STPLFD NG9 ......63 H1
Oakford Cl WOL/BIL/BRX NG8 ......29 E4
Oak Gv HUCK/RAV NG15 ......11 G3
Oakham Cl ARN NG5 ......18 C3
Oakham Wy ILK DE7 ......25 G2
Oakington Cl ARN NG5 ......19 E5
Oakland Av LGEAT NG10 ......72 D4
Oakland Ct BSTN/STPLFD NG9 ......53 H2
Oaklands Av HEANOR DE75 ......6 D5
Oakland St NOTTE NG7 ......42 B1
Oakleigh Av
  MAPPK/POR/STA NG3 ......32 D3
Oakleigh St BLWL NG6 ......30 A1
Oakley Ms BLWL NG6 ......17 E4
Oakley's Rd LGEAT NG10 ......73 F3
Oak Lodge Dr
  EWD/SEL/PNX NG16 ......15 G3
Oakmead Av WOL/BIL/BRX NG8 ......41 H1
Oakmere Cl COT/KEY/RAD NG12 ......68 D2
Oak Tree Av COT/KEY/RAD NG12 ......47 E4
Oaktree Cl HUCK/RAV NG15 ......10 C3
Oak Tree Cl WBRGFD NG2 ......58 B3
Oak Tree Dr CARL NG4 ......33 H3
Oakwell Crs ILK DE7 ......25 H5
Oakwell Dr ILK DE7 ......25 H5
Oakwood Dr WOL/BIL/BRX NG8 ......41 H1

Oban Rd BSTN/STPLFD NG9 ......54 B5
Occupation Rd BLWL NG6 ......17 G5
  HUCK/RAV NG15 ......11 F2
Ockbrook Ct ILK * DE7 ......26 A2
Ockerby St BLWL NG6 ......17 H4
Odesa Dr BLWL NG6 ......29 G1
Ogdon Ct MAPPK/POR/STA NG3 ......44 A2
Ogle Dr NOTTE NG7 ......2 C6
Ogle St HUCK/RAV NG15 ......5 F5
Okehampton Crs
  MAPPK/POR/STA NG3 ......20 D4
Old Brickyard
  MAPPK/POR/STA NG3 ......44 B1
Oldbury Cl CFTN/RUD NG11 ......76 A2
Old Church St NOTTE NG7 ......56 B1
Old Coach Rd WOL/BIL/BRX NG8 ......41 E2
Old Coppice Side HEANOR DE75 ......12 B3
Old Derby Rd
  EWD/SEL/PNX NG16 ......7 G4
Old Dr BSTN/STPLFD NG9 ......54 C3
Old Farm Rd ARN NG5 ......18 C2
Old Hall Dr
  MAPPK/POR/STA NG3 ......31 G4
Oldknow St NOTTE NG7 ......42 C2
Old Lenton St NOTT NG1 ......3 G1
Old Lodge Dr ARN NG5 ......31 G1
Old Main Rd CALV/BJ NG14 ......23 G5
Old Melton Rd
  COT/KEY/RAD NG12 ......79 F3
Old Mill Cl BSTN/STPLFD NG9 ......63 H4
  NOTTE NG7 ......42 C3
Oldoak Rd CFTN/RUD NG11 ......66 C4
The Old Pk COT/KEY/RAD NG12 ......71 E2
The Old Pond HEANOR DE75 ......12 D2
Old Rd COT/KEY/RAD NG12 ......67 G5
Old School La
  EWD/SEL/PNX NG16 ......14 D5
Old St NOTT NG1 ......3 F3
Old Tollerton Rd WBRGFD NG2 ......58 D4
Olga Rd MAPPK/POR/STA NG3 ......44 A2
Olive Av LGEAT NG10 ......63 E5
Olive Gv CALV/BJ NG14 ......23 E5
Oliver Cl HEANOR DE75 ......7 E5
  NOTTE NG7 ......2 B2
Oliver Rd ILK DE7 ......37 F3
Oliver St NOTTE NG7 ......2 B2
Olton Av BSTN/STPLFD NG9 ......55 E3
Olympus Ct HUCK/RAV NG15 ......10 C4
Onchan Av CARL NG4 ......45 F2
Onchan Dr CARL NG4 ......45 F2
Orange Gdns WBRGFD NG2 ......57 G1
Orby Cl MAPPK/POR/STA NG3 ......44 A2
Orby Wk
  MAPPK/POR/STA NG3 ......44 A2
The Orchard ILK * DE7 ......52 A2
Orchard Av BING/VBLV NG13 ......48 C3
  CARL NG4 ......45 F1
Orchard Cl CALV/BJ NG14 ......23 E5
  CFTN/RUD NG11 ......65 H4
  COT/KEY/RAD NG12 ......46 D5
  COT/KEY/RAD NG12 ......79 E1
  ILK DE7 ......36 A1
  WBRGFD NG2 ......57 H1
Orchard Ct EWD/SEL/PNX * NG16 ......7 E4
Orchard Crs BSTN/STPLFD NG9 ......64 B1
Orchard Gv ARN NG5 ......19 F4
Orchard Ri CARL NG4 ......22 A3
The Orchards CARL NG4 ......33 H4
Orchard St BSTN/STPLFD NG9 ......53 E4
  EWD/SEL/PNX NG16 ......7 E4
  EWD/SEL/PNX NG16 ......14 B1
  EWD/SEL/PNX NG16 ......15 G4
  HUCK/RAV NG15 ......11 F1
  ILK DE7 ......38 A1
  LGEAT NG10 ......73 F2
Orchard Wy LGEAT NG10 ......62 B3
Orchid Cl CFTN/RUD NG11 ......67 F2
Orford Av CFTN/RUD NG11 ......66 C3
  COT/KEY/RAD NG12 ......46 D5
Orion Cl WOL/BIL/BRX NG8 ......40 C1
Orion Dr WOL/BIL/BRX NG8 ......40 C1
Orlando Dr CARL NG4 ......33 G5
Ormonde St EWD/SEL/PNX NG16 ......7 E3
Ormonde Ter
  EWD/SEL/PNX NG16 ......7 E3
Orpean Wy BSTN/STPLFD NG9 ......63 F4
Orston Av ARN NG5 ......20 B3
Orston Dr WOL/BIL/BRX NG8 ......41 H4
Orston Gn WOL/BIL/BRX * NG8 ......42 A5
Orston Rd East WBRGFD NG2 ......58 A2
Orston Rd West WBRGFD NG2 ......57 H2
Orton Av BSTN/STPLFD NG9 ......54 B5
Ortzen St NOTTE NG7 ......42 C2
Orville Rd ARN NG5 ......18 B5
Osborne Av ARN NG5 ......31 F2
Osborne Cl LGEAT NG10 ......62 C4
Osborne Gv ARN NG5 ......31 F3

Osborne St *NOTTE* NG7 ....42 B2
Osbourne Cl
  EWD/SEL/PNX NG16 ....16 A3
Osgood Rd *ARN* NG5 ....20 D5
Osier Rd *WBRGFD* NG2 ....57 F2
Osman Cl *WBRGFD* NG2 ....57 E2
Osmaston Cl *LGEAT* NG10 ....72 A4
Osmaston St *LGEAT* NG10 ....62 D1
  NOTTE NG7 ....42 C5
Osprey Cl *CFTN/RUD* NG11 ....65 H5
Ossington Cl *NG1* 2 E2
Ossington St *NOTT* NG7 ....42 C2
Osterley Gv *WOL/BIL/BRX* NG8 ....28 C3
Oulton Cl *ARN* NG5 ....20 A4
Oundle Dr *ILK* DE7 ....38 B1
  WOL/BIL/BRX NG8 ....41 H5
Ousebridge Crs *CARL* NG4 ....33 H5
Ouse Bridge Dr *CARL* NG4 ....33 H5
Oval Gdns *WOL/BIL/BRX* NG8 ......30 A5
Overdale Cl *LGEAT* NG10 ....72 A3
Overdale Rd *BLWL* NG6 ....29 H2
Overstrand Cl *ARN* NG5 ....20 A4
Owen Av *LGEAT* NG10 ....73 H3
Owers Av *HEANOR* DE75 ....12 C3
Owlston Cl *EWD/SEL/PNX* NG16 ....8 A4
Owsthorpe Cl *ARN* NG5 ....18 D2
Owthorpe Gv *ARN* NG5 ....31 E3
Owthorpe Rd
  COT/KEY/RAD NG12 ....71 E4
Oxborough Rd *ARN* NG5 ....19 F3
Oxbow Cl *WBRGFD* NG2 ....57 F2
Oxbury Rd *EWD/SEL/PNX* NG16 ...15 G2
Oxclose La *ARN* NG5 ....19 F4
Oxendale Cl *WBRGFD* NG2 ....58 D5
Oxengate *ARN* NG5 ....19 E4
Oxford Rd *WBRGFD* NG2 ....58 B4
Oxford St *CARL* NG4 ....33 F4
  EWD/SEL/PNX NG16 ....8 A5
  ILK DE7 ....38 A1
  LGEAT NG10 ....73 E1
  NOTT NG1 ....2 C5
Oxton Av *ARN* NG5 ....31 F1
Ozier Holt *CARL* NG4 ....45 F4
  LGEAT NG10 ....42 D3

P

Packman Dr *CFTN/RUD* NG11 ......77 G1
Paddington Ms
  MAPPK/POR/STA NG3 ....44 B1
Paddock Cl *BLWL* NG6 ....17 G5
  COT/KEY/RAD NG12 ....60 D1
The Paddocks
  COT/KEY/RAD NG12 ....68 C3
  EWD/SEL/PNX NG16 ....16 A5
  LGEAT NG10 ....62 B1
Paddocks Vw *LGEAT* NG10 ....72 B1
The Paddock *BING/VBLV* NG13 ....48 D3
  BSTN/STPLFD NG9 ....64 C4
Padge Rd *BSTN/STPLFD* NG9 ......55 G5
Padleys La *CALV/BJ* NG14 ....22 D5
Padstow Rd *ARN* NG5 ....18 C4
Paget Crs *CFTN/RUD* NG11 ....77 F1
Paignton Cl *WOL/BIL/BRX* NG8 ....29 G3
Paisley Gv *BSTN/STPLFD* NG9 .....64 B5
Palatine St *NOTTE* NG7 ....2 C7
Palin Ct *NOTTE* NG7 ....42 C1
Palin Gdns *COT/KEY/RAD* NG12 ...47 F5
Palin St *NOTTE* NG7 ....42 C1
Palmer Av *HUCK/RAV* NG15 ....5 F4
Palmer Crs *CARL* NG4 ....45 E1
Palmer Dr *BSTN/STPLFD* NG9 .....63 E1
Palmer Rd *BSTN/STPLFD* NG9 .....64 A4
Palmerston Gdns
  MAPPK/POR/STA NG3 ....3 G5
Palm St *NOTTE* NG7 ....30 C5
Papplewick La *HUCK/RAV* NG15 ....5 G5
The Park *COT/KEY/RAD* NG12 .....71 E2
Park Av *ARN* NG5 ....19 H5
  CALV/BJ NG14 ....34 D1
  CARL NG4 ....33 G5
  COT/KEY/RAD NG12 ....79 G5
  COT/KEY/RAD NG12 ....82 A1
  EWD/SEL/PNX NG16 ....7 H5
  EWD/SEL/PNX NG16 ....14 C5
  EWD/SEL/PNX NG16 ....15 H5
  HUCK/RAV NG15 ....5 E5
  ILK DE7 ....26 A5
  MAPPK/POR/STA NG3 ....31 G5
  WBRGFD NG2 ....58 A3
Park Av East
  COT/KEY/RAD NG12 ....82 A1
Park Av West
  COT/KEY/RAD NG12 ....82 A1
Park Cl *ILK* DE7 ....52 A3
  MAPPK/POR/STA NG3 ....31 H3

WBRGFD NG2 ....67 F1
Park Ct *HEANOR* * DE75 ....12 C1
Park Crs *EWD/SEL/PNX* NG16 ....8 A3
  ILK DE7 ....26 B5
  WOL/BIL/BRX NG8 ....40 B4
Parkcroft Rd *WBRGFD* NG2 ....58 A5
Parkdale Rd
  MAPPK/POR/STA NG3 ....44 D2
Park Dr *HUCK/RAV* NG15 ....11 F2
  ILK DE7 ....38 A1
  LGEAT NG10 ....62 B3
  NOTTE NG7 ....2 B6
Parker Cl *ARN* NG5 ....20 D2
Parker Gdns *BSTN/STPLFD* NG9 ...53 G3
Parker St *HUCK/RAV* NG15 ....5 C5
Parkgate *HUCK/RAV* NG15 ....5 C3
Park Hall La *ILK* DE7 ....24 A3
Parkham Rd
  EWD/SEL/PNX NG16 ....15 G3
Park Hl *EWD/SEL/PNX* NG16 ....14 C5
Park House *NOTT* * NG1 ....2 E6
Park House Gates
  MAPPK/POR/STA NG3 ....31 G4
Parkland Cl *CFTN/RUD* NG11 ....65 H3
Parklands Cl *ARN* NG5 ....19 E1
Park La *BLWL* NG6 ....30 B1
  CALV/BJ NG14 ....23 E2
Park Ms *MAPPK/POR/STA* * NG3 ..31 F5
Park Ravine *NOTTE* NG7 ....2 B7
Park Rd *ARN* NG5 ....19 H5
  BSTN/STPLFD NG9 ....53 H3
  BSTN/STPLFD NG9 ....54 D5
  CARL NG4 ....33 G5
  COT/KEY/RAD NG12 ....47 E4
  COT/KEY/RAD NG12 ....79 G5
  HUCK/RAV NG15 ....5 E5
  ILK DE7 ....38 B1
  NOTTE NG7 ....42 C5
Park Rd North
  BSTN/STPLFD NG9 ....54 D5
Park Rw *NOTT* NG1 ....2 D6
Parkside *COT/KEY/RAD* NG12 ......79 G5
  WOL/BIL/BRX NG8 ....40 D5
Parkside Av *LGEAT* NG10 ....72 C1
Parkside Dr *LGEAT* NG10 ....72 C1
Parkside Gdns North
  WOL/BIL/BRX NG8 ....40 D5
Parkside Gdns South
  WOL/BIL/BRX NG8 ....54 D1
Parkside Ri *WOL/BIL/BRX* NG8 ....54 D1
Parkstone Cl *WBRGFD* NG2 ....67 E1
Park St *BSTN/STPLFD* NG9 ....52 D5
  BSTN/STPLFD NG9 ....54 D5
  BWSH/BRSTN DE72 ....72 A1
  HEANOR DE75 ....6 A5
  LGEAT NG10 ....62 D5
  NOTTE NG7 ....42 C4
Park Ter *COT/KEY/RAD* NG12 ......79 G4
  NOTT NG1 ....2 C5
Park Va *NOTTE* NG7 ....2 C6
Park Vw *HEANOR* DE75 ....12 A1
  MAPPK/POR/STA NG3 ....31 H3
Park View Ct *NOTT* * NG1 ....3 F3
Parkview Rd *ARN* NG5 ....18 C3
Park Whf *NOTTE* NG7 ....2 D7
Parkwood Ct *BLWL* NG6 ....18 B5
Parkyn Rd *ARN* NG5 ....19 G4
Parkyns St *CFTN/RUD* NG11 ....77 F3
Parr Ga *BSTN/STPLFD* NG9 ....63 H1
The Parrs *BSTN/STPLFD* NG9 ......55 G5
Parry Wy *ARN* NG5 ....20 C2
Parsons Meadow *CARL* NG4 ....45 F4
Pasture Cl *WBRGFD* NG2 ....45 F4
Pasture La *CFTN/RUD* NG11 ....76 C4
  LGEAT NG10 ....73 H5
Pasture Rd *BSTN/STPLFD* NG9 ....53 E2
The Pastures
  EWD/SEL/PNX NG16 ....14 C2
Pastures Av *CFTN/RUD* NG11 ......76 A1
Pateley Rd *ARN* NG5 ....32 B1
Paton Rd *ARN* NG5 ....18 B5
Patricia Dr *ARN* NG5 ....20 B1
Patrick Rd *WBRGFD* NG2 ....57 H3
Patterdale Cl *WBRGFD* NG2 ....58 D5
Patterdale Rd *ARN* NG5 ....20 A5
Patterson Rd *NOTTE* NG7 ....42 C1
Pavilion Cl *WBRGFD* NG2 ....57 G2
Pavilion Rd *ARN* NG5 ....19 E1
  ILK DE7 ....13 H5
  WBRGFD NG2 ....57 H2
Paxton Gdns
  MAPPK/POR/STA NG3 ....3 J3
Payne Rd *BSTN/STPLFD* NG9 ......63 H3
Peache Wy *BSTN/STPLFD* NG9 ....54 A4
Peachey St *NOTT* NG1 ....2 E3
Peach St *HEANOR* DE75 ....12 A1
Peacock Cl *CFTN/RUD* NG11 ....77 E3
Peacock Crs *CFTN/RUD* NG11 .....66 D3

Peacock Pl *ILK* DE7 ....25 G1
Peakdale Cl *LGEAT* NG10 ....72 B3
Pearce Dr *WOL/BIL/BRX* NG8 ......41 G2
Pearmain Dr
  MAPPK/POR/STA NG3 ....44 A1
Pearson Av *BSTN/STPLFD* NG9 ....64 A1
Pearson Crs *ARN* NG5 ....19 H5
Pearson St *CARL* NG4 ....45 H2
  NOTTE NG7 ....30 C5
Peartree Orch *CFTN/RUD* NG11 ...77 F2
Peary Cl *ARN* NG5 ....18 C4
Peas Hill Rd
  MAPPK/POR/STA NG3 ....3 G1
Peatfield Rd *BSTN/STPLFD* NG9 ...53 E2
Pedley St *ILK* DE7 ....38 A1
Pedmore Va *ARN* NG5 ....18 D3
Peel St *EWD/SEL/PNX* NG16 ....7 E4
  LGEAT NG10 ....73 F1
  NOTT NG1 ....2 D2
Peel Vls *MAPPK/POR/STA* NG3 ....31 H3
Pelham Av *ARN* NG5 ....31 E5
  ILK DE7 ....25 H4
Pelham Cottages *NOTTE* * NG7 ....42 C4
Pelham Crs *BSTN/STPLFD* NG9 ....55 G4
  NOTTE NG7 ....42 C4
Pelham Rd *NOTTE* NG7 ....31 E5
Pelham St *ILK* DE7 ....25 H4
  NOTT NG1 ....3 F5
Pemberton St *NOTT* NG1 ....3 H6
Pembrey Cl *BSTN/STPLFD* NG9 ....53 E1
Pembridge Cl *BLWL* NG6 ....30 A3
Pembury Rd *WOL/BIL/BRX* NG8 ...40 D3
Penarth Gdns
  MAPPK/POR/STA NG3 ....31 H2
Penarth Ri *ARN* NG5 ....31 H2
Pendennis Cl *CARL* NG4 ....34 A4
Pendine Cl *ARN* NG5 ....19 C1
Pendle Crs
  MAPPK/POR/STA NG3 ....32 A4
Penhale Dr *HUCK/RAV* NG15 ....10 B2
Penhurst Cl *CFTN/RUD* NG11 ......66 D2
Penllech Cl *ARN* NG5 ....18 D3
Pennant Rd *BLWL* NG6 ....30 A3
Penn Av *NOTTE* NG7 ....56 B1
Pennhome Av *ARN* NG5 ....31 F3
Pennie Cl *LGEAT* NG10 ....73 E5
Pennine Cl *ARN* NG5 ....19 E1
  LGEAT NG10 ....62 B5
Penn Moor Cl *LGEAT* NG10 ....72 B3
Pennyfields Bvd *LGEAT* NG10 ......72 B2
Pennyfoot St *NOTT* NG1 ....3 J6
Penrhyn Cl *MAPPK/POR/STA* NG3 ..3 H1
Penrhyn Crs *BSTN/STPLFD* NG9 ...64 A2
Penrith Av *COT/KEY/RAD* NG12 ...47 E4
Penrith Crs *WOL/BIL/BRX* NG8 ....29 H3
Penshore Cl *CFTN/RUD* NG11 ......66 A5
Pentland Gdns *LGEAT* NG10 ....62 B5
Pentridge Dr *ILK* DE7 ....25 F2
Peoples Hall Cottages
  NOTT * NG1 ....3 G4
Pepper La *ILK* DE7 ....51 E1
Percival Rd *ARN* NG5 ....31 F3
Percy St *BLWL* NG6 ....30 A2
  EWD/SEL/PNX NG16 ....8 B5
  ILK DE7 ....38 A1
Peregrine Cl *NOTTE* NG7 ....42 B4
Perivale Cl *EWD/SEL/PNX* NG16 ..28 C2
Perlethorpe Av *CARL* NG4 ....33 E3
  WBRGFD NG2 ....3 K6
Perlethorpe Cl *CARL* NG4 ....33 F3
Perlethorpe Crs *CARL* NG4 ....33 F3
Perlethorpe Dr *CARL* NG4 ....33 E3
  HUCK/RAV NG15 ....5 G5
Perry Gdns *ARN* NG5 ....31 E2
Perry Gv *BING/VBLV* NG13 ....49 E3
Perry Rd *ARN* NG5 ....30 C2
Perth Dr *BSTN/STPLFD* NG9 ....53 F2
Perth St *NOTT* NG1 ....3 F3
Peters Cl *ARN* NG5 ....20 D4
  EWD/SEL/PNX NG16 ....8 D5
Petersfield Cl *ARN* NG5 ....18 C3
Petersgate *LGEAT* NG10 ....62 B5
Petersgate Cl *LGEAT* NG10 ....62 B4
Petersham Ms *NOTTE* NG7 ....42 A4
Petersham Rd *LGEAT* NG10 ....62 B5
Petworth Av *BSTN/STPLFD* NG9 ..63 H3
Petworth Dr *ARN* NG5 ....30 C1
Peveril Crs *ILK* DE7 ....25 G3
  LGEAT NG10 ....72 A4
Peveril Dr *ILK* DE7 ....25 C3
  NOTTE NG7 ....2 C7
  WBRGFD NG2 ....67 H3
Peveril Ms *NOTTE* * NG7 ....2 A6
Peveril Rd *BSTN/STPLFD* NG9 .....55 E3
Peveril St *HUCK/RAV* NG15 ....5 F4
  NOTTE NG7 ....42 C2
Philip Av *EWD/SEL/PNX* NG16 .....16 B4
  EWD/SEL/PNX NG16 ....14 B1

Philip Gv *CARL* NG4 ....33 F3
Phoenix Av *CARL* NG4 ....33 F3
Phoenix Cl *WBRGFD* NG2 ....57 E1
Phoenix Pl *BLWL* NG6 ....29 G1
Phyllis Gv *LGEAT* NG10 ....73 G2
Piccadilly *BLWL* NG6 ....18 A4
Pickering Av
  EWD/SEL/PNX NG16 ....8 A5
Pieris Dr *CFTN/RUD* NG11 ....65 H5
Pierrepont Av *CARL* NG4 ....33 F4
Pierrepont Rd *WBRGFD* NG2 ....58 B3
Pilcher Ga *NOTT* NG1 ....3 F6
Pilkington Rd
  MAPPK/POR/STA NG3 ....32 B4
Pilkington St *BLWL* NG6 ....17 G3
Pimlico *ILK* DE7 ....25 H5
Pimlico Av *BSTN/STPLFD* NG9 ....40 A5
Pimlico Cl *BSTN/STPLFD* NG9 .....57 H1
Pinder St *WBRGFD* NG2 ....3 H6
Pine Av *EWD/SEL/PNX* NG16 ....6 D4
Pine Gv *HUCK/RAV* NG15 ....11 G3
Pine Hill Cl *ARN* NG5 ....18 C1
Pinehurst Av *HUCK/RAV* NG15 ....10 B2
Pine Vw *NOTTE* NG7 ....42 C2
Pinewood Av *ARN* NG5 ....20 C1
Pinewood Gdns
  CFTN/RUD NG11 ....76 A1
Pinfold *BING/VBLV* NG13 ....49 E3
Pinfold Cl *COT/KEY/RAD* NG12 ....71 E3
Pinfold La *BSTN/STPLFD* NG9 .....53 F4
  COT/KEY/RAD NG12 ....35 H4
Pinfold Rd *EWD/SEL/PNX* NG16 ...14 C2
The Pingle *LGEAT* NG10 ....73 E1
Pingle Crs *ARN* NG5 ....18 C2
Pintail Cl *CARL* NG4 ....46 A3
Piper Cl *HUCK/RAV* NG15 ....5 G3
Pippin Cl *MAPPK/POR/STA* NG3 ...44 A1
Pitcairn Cl *WBRGFD* NG2 ....57 F2
Pit La *HEANOR* DE75 ....13 E4
Plackett Cl *BSTN/STPLFD* NG9 ....53 G3
Plains Farm Cl
  MAPPK/POR/STA NG3 ....20 D5
Plains Gv *MAPPK/POR/STA* NG3 ..32 B1
Plains Rd *MAPPK/POR/STA* NG3 ..32 B1
Plane Cl *BLWL* NG6 ....17 E3
Plantagenet Ct
  MAPPK/POR/STA NG3 ....3 H2
Plantagenet St
  MAPPK/POR/STA NG3 ....3 H3
Plantation Cl *ARN* NG5 ....19 E1
Plantation Rd
  COT/KEY/RAD NG12 ....82 A1
  WOL/BIL/BRX NG8 ....40 A4
Plantation Side *NOTTE* NG7 ....30 B5
The Plantations *LGEAT* NG10 ....72 B4
Plant La *LGEAT* NG10 ....72 B5
Platt La *COT/KEY/RAD* NG12 ....79 H5
Player Ct *NOTTE* * NG7 ....42 B2
Player St *NOTTE* NG7 ....42 B2
Plaza Gdns *BLWL* NG6 ....30 C1
Pleasant Ct *NOTTE* * NG7 ....42 C1
Pleasant Row *NOTTE* NG7 ....42 C1
Plough La *WBRGFD* NG2 ....3 J6
Plover Whf *WBRGFD* NG2 ....56 D1
Plowman Ct *BSTN/STPLFD* NG9 ...53 E5
Plowright Ct
  MAPPK/POR/STA NG3 ....43 G1
Plowright St
  MAPPK/POR/STA NG3 ....43 F1
Plumb Rd *HUCK/RAV* NG15 ....5 F4
Plumptre Cl
  EWD/SEL/PNX NG16 ....14 A1
Plumptre Flats *NOTT* * NG1 ....3 H6
Plumptre Pl *NOTT* NG1 ....3 G5
Plumptre Rd
  EWD/SEL/PNX NG16 ....7 E2
Plumptre Sq *NOTT* NG1 ....3 H6
Plumptre St *NOTT* NG1 ....3 G6
Plumptre Wy
  EWD/SEL/PNX NG16 ....14 A1
Plumtree Rd
  COT/KEY/RAD NG12 ....70 C5
Plungar Cl *WOL/BIL/BRX* NG8 .....41 G2
Podder La
  MAPPK/POR/STA NG3 ....20 D4
The Point *MAPPK/POR/STA* NG3 ..31 G5
  WBRGFD * NG2 ....57 H3
Polperro Wy *HUCK/RAV* NG15 .....10 B2
Pond Hills La *ARN* NG5 ....20 A1
Poole Meadow *CARL* NG4 ....45 G4
Pooles Cnr *CALV/BJ* * NG14 ....35 E1
Popham Ct *NOTT* NG1 ....3 G6
Popham St *NOTT* NG1 ....3 G6
Poplar Av *ARN* NG5 ....30 D4
  LGEAT NG10 ....52 B4
Poplar Cl *BING/VBLV* NG13 ....49 E4
  CARL NG4 ....45 E2
Poplar Crs *EWD/SEL/PNX* NG16 ..15 H4

Poplar Rd *BWSH/BRSTN* DE72 ......62 A5
The Poplars *BSTN/STPLFD* NG9 .....55 F5
Poplars Av *CALV/BJ* NG14 ....23 F5
Poplars Cl *COT/KEY/RAD* NG12 ....79 G5
Poplar St *NOTT* NG1 ....3 H6
Poplar Wy *ILK* DE7 ....37 G3
Porchester Cl *HUCK/RAV* NG15 ......5 H5
Porchester Rd *BING/VBLV* NG13 ....48 C3
  MAPPK/POR/STA NG3 ....32 B4
Porlock Cl *LGEAT* NG10 ....72 B1
Portage Cl *COT/KEY/RAD* NG12 ....60 D1
Port Arthur Rd *WBRGFD* NG2 ......44 B4
Porter Cl *COT/KEY/RUD* NG11 .....75 H1
Porters Wk
  MAPPK/POR/STA NG3 ....44 B1
Portinscale Cl *WBRGFD* NG2 ....68 D1
Portland Ct *ARN* NG5 ....19 E5
Portland Crs *BSTN/STPLFD* NG9 ...53 F5
Portland Gra *HUCK/RAV* NG15 ....4 D5
Portland Hl *NOTT* NG7 ....55 H2
Portland Rd *BSTN/STPLFD* NG9 ....63 H5
  CARL NG4 ....32 D3
  EWD/SEL/PNX NG16 ....14 C2
  HUCK/RAV NG15 ....11 H1
  ILK DE7 ....26 A2
  LGEAT NG10 ....72 B5
  NOTTE NG7 ....2 B3
  WBRGFD NG2 ....58 A5
Portland St *ARN* NG5 ....19 G4
  BSTN/STPLFD NG9 ....55 F4
Postern St *NOTT* NG1 ....2 D5
Potato Pit La *ILK* DE7 ....50 D2
Potomac Ms *NOTTE* * NG7 ....2 B6
Potters Cl *ARN* NG5 ....18 D3
Poulter Cl *NOTTE* NG7 ....42 A1
Poulton Dr *WBRGFD* NG2 ....44 A5
The Poultry *NOTT* NG1 ....3 F5
Powis St *BLWL* NG6 ....17 G3
Powtrell Pl *ILK* DE7 ....38 C2
Premier Rd *NOTTE* NG7 ....30 D5
Prendwick Gdns *ARN* NG5 ....5 H4
Prestwick Cl *WOL/BIL/BRX* NG8 ....28 C3
Prestwood Dr
  WOL/BIL/BRX NG8 ....41 G1
Previn Gdns
  MAPPK/POR/STA NG3 ....44 A2
Primrose Bank *BING/VBLV* NG13 ....48 C3
Primrose Cl
  MAPPK/POR/STA NG3 ....43 C1
Primrose Crs *CARL* NG4 ....45 G1
Primrose Hl *ILK* DE7 ....25 H2
Primrose Ri
  EWD/SEL/PNX NG16 ....14 B2
Primrose St *CARL* NG4 ....45 G1
  ILK DE7 ....25 H2
Primula Cl *CFTN/RUD* NG11 ....65 H4
Prince Edward Crs
  COT/KEY/RAD NG12 ....60 C1
Princess Av *BSTN/STPLFD* NG9 .....55 F5
Princess Cl *CARL* NG4 ....33 F3
Princess Dr *LGEAT* NG10 ....62 C2
Princess St *LGEAT* NG10 ....73 E1
Princes St *EWD/SEL/PNX* NG16 ......8 A4
Prince St *ILK* DE7 ....25 H1
  LGEAT NG10 ....73 E1
Prioridge *COT/KEY/RAD* NG12 ......71 F4
Prior Rd *ARN* NG5 ....19 G4
Priors Cl *BING/VBLV* NG13 ....49 F2
Priory Av *COT/KEY/RAD* NG12 ......68 D5
Priory Circ *COT/KEY/RAD* NG12 ....68 D5
Priory Cl *ILK* DE7 ....37 F2
Priory Crs *CARL* NG4 ....33 G4
Priory Ms *NOTTE* NG7 ....56 B1
Priory Rd *CARL* NG4 ....33 G4
  EWD/SEL/PNX NG16 ....14 A1
  HUCK/RAV NG15 ....4 D5
  WBRGFD NG2 ....58 B3
Priory St *NOTTE* NG7 ....56 B1
Pritchard Dr *BSTN/STPLFD* NG9 ....55 H3
Private Rd *HUCK/RAV* NG15 ....4 D5
  MAPPK/POR/STA NG3 ....31 K3
Prize Cl *CFTN/RUD* NG11 ....65 H5
Promenade
  MAPPK/POR/STA NG3 ....3 H4
Prospect Pl *NOTTE* NG7 ....42 C5
Prospect Rd *CARL* NG4 ....32 B4
  HEANOR DE75 ....12 D2
Prospect St *NOTTE* NG7 ....42 B2
Providence Pl *ILK* DE7 ....25 H4
Pulborough Cl *ARN* NG5 ....30 C1
Pullman Rd *WBRGFD* NG2 ....44 A4
Purbeck Cl *LGEAT* NG10 ....72 B1
Purbeck Dr *WBRGFD* NG2 ....67 F1
Purdy Meadow *LGEAT* NG10 ....72 A4
Pyatt Cl *WBRGFD* NG2 ....57 F5
Pym Leys *LGEAT* NG10 ....72 A1
Pym St *MAPPK/POR/STA* NG3 ....44 A2
Pym Wk *MAPPK/POR/STA* NG3 ....3 K2

Q

Quantock Gv *BING/VBLV* NG13 .....48 B3
Quarry Av *BLWL* NG6 ....17 G4
Quarry Dl *HUCK/RAV* NG15 ....15 E3
Quarry Hl *ILK* DE7 ....52 A3
Quarry Hill Rd *ILK* DE7 ....38 A3
Quayside Cl *WBRGFD* NG2 ....57 H2
Queen's Av *CARL* NG4 ....33 F3
  HEANOR DE75 ....6 A5
  ILK DE7 ....38 B3
Queensberry St *BLWL* NG6 ....30 B1
Queen's Bower Rd *ARN* NG5 ....19 F2
Queen's Bridge Rd
  WBRGFD NG2 ....43 F5
Queensbury Av *WBRGFD* NG2 ....67 G3
Queens Dr *BSTN/STPLFD* NG9 ......55 H1
  EWD/SEL/PNX NG16 ....16 A4
  ILK DE7 ....37 H1
  LGEAT NG10 ....62 C2
  WBRGFD NG2 ....56 D4
  WBRGFD NG2 ....57 E1
Queens Gv *WBRGFD* * NG2 ....43 F5
Queens Rd *BSTN/STPLFD* NG9 ......65 F1
  COT/KEY/RAD NG12 ....47 E4
  WBRGFD NG2 ....43 G5
Queens Rd East
  BSTN/STPLFD NG9 ....55 G4
Queens Rd North
  EWD/SEL/PNX NG16 ....8 A5
Queens Rd South
  EWD/SEL/PNX NG16 ....14 A1
Queens Rd West
  BSTN/STPLFD NG9 ....64 D2
Queen's Sq *EWD/SEL/PNX* NG16 ......8 A5
Queen St *ARN* NG5 ....20 A1
  EWD/SEL/PNX NG16 ....7 F4
  HUCK/RAV NG15 ....5 E4
  ILK DE7 ....25 H5
  LGEAT NG10 ....73 E2
  NOTT NG1 ....2 E4
Queen's Wk
  WBRGFD NG2 ....57 E2
Querneby Av
  MAPPK/POR/STA NG3 ....31 K3
Querneby Rd
  MAPPK/POR/STA NG3 ....31 H3
Quinton Cl *CFTN/RUD* NG11 ....66 D1
Quorn Cl *BSTN/STPLFD* NG9 ....64 D3
Quorndon Crs *LGEAT* NG10 ....73 E4
Quorn Gv *ARN* NG5 ....30 D2
Quorn Rd *ARN* NG5 ....30 D3

R

Racecourse Rd *WBRGFD* NG2 ......44 C4
Radbourne Rd *WBRGFD* NG2 ....44 A5
Radburn Ct *BSTN/STPLFD* NG9 ....53 F2
Radcliffe Gdns *CARL* NG4 ....35 E5
Radcliffe Mt *WBRGFD* NG2 ....58 A2
Radcliffe Rd *BSTN/STPLFD* NG9 ...57 H2
  WBRGFD NG2 ....57 G2
Radcliffe St *WBRGFD* NG2 ....58 A2
Radford Bvd *NOTTE* NG7 ....42 B2
Radford Bridge Rd
  WOL/BIL/BRX NG8 ....41 H3
Radford Crs *CARL* NG4 ....33 F3
Radford Grove La *NOTTE* NG7 ......42 B2
Radford Rd *NOTTE* NG7 ....30 C4
Radley Sq *BLWL* NG6 ....18 A5
Radmarsh Rd *NOTTE* NG7 ....42 B5
Rad Mdw *LGEAT* NG10 ....72 D3
Radnor Gv *BING/VBLV* NG13 ....48 B3
Radstock Rd
  MAPPK/POR/STA NG3 ....44 B1
Radway Dr *CFTN/RUD* NG11 ....66 D1
Raeburn Dr *BSTN/STPLFD* NG9 ....63 F4
Ragdale Rd *BLWL* NG6 ....17 G2
Raglan Cl *MAPPK/POR/STA* NG3 ....43 C1
Raglan Dr *CARL* NG4 ....34 A4
Raglan St *EWD/SEL/PNX* NG16 .....14 B1
Raibank Gdns *ARN* NG5 ....19 H5
Rainham Gdns *CFTN/RUD* NG11 ....77 E3
Raithby Cl *ARN* NG5 ....18 D4
Raleigh Cl *CFTN/RUD* NG11 ....65 H5
  ILK DE7 ....26 A2
Raleigh Sq *NOTTE* NG7 ....2 B3
Raleigh St *NOTTE* NG7 ....2 B3
Ralf Cl *WBRGFD* NG2 ....67 H2
Ramblers Cl *CARL* NG4 ....45 F3
Ramsdale Crs *ARN* NG5 ....31 G3
Ramsdale Rd *CARL* NG4 ....33 F4
Ramsey Dr *BSTN/STPLFD* NG9 .....53 F1

Ramsey Dr *ARN* NG5 ....20 D4
Ranby Wy
  MAPPK/POR/STA NG3 ....44 A2
Rancliffe Av
  COT/KEY/RAD NG12 ....79 E5
Randal Gdns *NOTTE* NG7 ....42 C1
Randal St *NOTTE* NG7 ....42 C1
Ranelagh Gv *WOL/BIL/BRX* NG8 ....41 F3
Ranmere Rd *WOL/BIL/BRX* NG8 ....41 F1
Ranmoor Rd *CARL* NG4 ....33 C4
Ranmore Cl *BSTN/STPLFD* NG9 ....54 A1
Rannerdale Cl *WBRGFD* NG2 ....58 D5
Rannoch Ri *ARN* NG5 ....20 A1
Ransom Dr
  MAPPK/POR/STA NG3 ....31 H3
Ransom Rd
  MAPPK/POR/STA NG3 ....31 H4
Ranson Rd *BSTN/STPLFD* NG9 .....64 B5
Ratcliffe St *EWD/SEL/PNX* NG16 ....8 A4
Rathgar Cl *WOL/BIL/BRX* NG8 .....40 C4
Rathmines Cl *NOTTE* NG7 ....42 B5
Raven Av *ARN* NG5 ....31 E1
Ravenhill Cl *BSTN/STPLFD* NG9 ...64 A2
Ravens Ct *ARN* NG5 ....19 E5
Ravensdale Av *LGEAT* NG10 ....62 C4
Ravensdale Dr
  WOL/BIL/BRX NG8 ....40 B5
Ravensmore Rd *ARN* NG5 ....31 E3
Ravenswood Rd *ARN* NG5 ....20 A3
Ravensworth Rd *BLWL* NG6 ....17 G2
Rawson St *NOTTE* NG7 ....30 C4
Raymede Cl *ARN* NG5 ....18 C4
Raymede Dr *ARN* NG5 ....18 B4
Raymond Dr *BING/VBLV* NG13 .....49 F3
Rayneham Rd *ILK* DE7 ....25 F1
Rayner Ct *NOTTE* NG7 ....42 C3
Raynford Av *BSTN/STPLFD* NG9 ....64 B2
Ray's Av *HEANOR* DE75 ....12 B1
Ray St *HEANOR* DE75 ....12 B1
Read Av *BSTN/STPLFD* NG9 ....55 F5
Readman Rd *BSTN/STPLFD* NG9 ....63 H3
Rearsby Cl *WOL/BIL/BRX* NG8 .....40 C3
Recreation Rd *LGEAT* NG10 ....52 C5
Recreation St *LGEAT* NG10 ....73 G1
Recreation Ter
  BSTN/STPLFD NG9 ....53 E5
The Rectory Dr *CARL* NG4 ....33 G3
Rectory Av *WOL/BIL/BRX* NG8 .....40 D4
Rectory Gdns
  WOL/BIL/BRX NG8 ....41 E4
Rectory Pl *CFTN/RUD* NG11 ....74 D3
Rectory Rd *CARL* NG4 ....45 E3
  COT/KEY/RAD NG12 ....70 D3
  WBRGFD NG2 ....58 A4
Redbourne Dr
  WOL/BIL/BRX NG8 ....41 H2
Redbridge Dr
  EWD/SEL/PNX NG16 ....28 C2
Redcar Cl *CARL* NG4 ....33 F3
Redcliffe Rd
  MAPPK/POR/STA NG3 ....31 F5
Redfield Rd *NOTTE* NG7 ....56 B3
Redfield Wy *NOTTE* NG7 ....56 B3
Redhill Lodge Dr *ARN* NG5 ....19 G1
Redhill Rd *ARN* NG5 ....19 H1
Redland Av *CARL* NG4 ....33 G5
Redland Cl *BSTN/STPLFD* NG9 ....64 B2
  ILK DE7 ....26 A3
Redland Dr *BSTN/STPLFD* NG9 ....64 B3
Redland Gv *CARL* NG4 ....33 F5
Redmays Dr *CALV/BJ* NG14 ....23 G4
Redmile Rd *WOL/BIL/BRX* NG8 ....29 H3
Redoubt St *NOTTE* NG7 ....42 B5
Redruth Cl *WOL/BIL/BRX* NG8 .....40 B2
Redwood *WBRGFD* NG2 ....57 F5
Redwood Av *WOL/BIL/BRX* NG8 ....40 C5
Redwood Crs *BSTN/STPLFD* NG9 ...65 F1
Reedman Rd *LGEAT* NG10 ....72 C5
Rees Gdns *ARN* NG5 ....18 D1
Regatta Wy *WBRGFD* NG2 ....58 D3
Regents Park Cl *WBRGFD* NG2 .....67 F1
Regents Pl *CFTN/RUD* NG11 ....57 E5
Regent St *BSTN/STPLFD* NG9 ......55 F4
  EWD/SEL/PNX NG16 ....7 E4
  EWD/SEL/PNX NG16 ....15 C4
  ILK DE7 ....38 A1
  LGEAT NG10 ....62 D1
  LGEAT NG10 ....73 E1
  NOTT NG1 ....2 D4
  NOTTE NG7 ....30 D4
Regina Cl *COT/KEY/RAD* NG12 .....59 G2
Reid Gdns *EWD/SEL/PNX* NG16 ....16 A4
Reigate Cl *BSTN/STPLFD* NG9 .....64 D3
Reigate Dr *BSTN/STPLFD* NG9 .....64 D3
Reigate Rd *NOTTE* NG7 ....30 C3

Rempstone Dr *BLWL* NG6 ....18 A5
Renfrew Dr *WOL/BIL/BRX* NG8 ....40 D4
Rennie Hogg Rd *NOTTE* NG7 ......56 C5
Repton Dr *ILK* DE7 ....38 C1
Repton Rd *BLWL* NG6 ....18 A4
  LGEAT NG10 ....72 A5
  WBRGFD NG2 ....67 H1
Retford Rd *ARN* NG5 ....30 D2
Retlaw St *BSTN/STPLFD* * NG9 .....64 C1
Revelstoke Av *ARN* NG5 ....18 A1
Revelstoke Wy *ARN* NG5 ....18 A1
Revena Cl *CARL* NG4 ....45 G2
Revesby Gdns
  WOL/BIL/BRX NG8 ....41 H1
Revesby Rd *ARN* NG5 ....20 A5
Revill Cl *ILK* DE7 ....25 F3
Revill Crs *BSTN/STPLFD* NG9 .....53 G3
Reydon Dr *WOL/BIL/BRX* NG8 .....30 A4
Reynolds Dr *WOL/BIL/BRX* NG8 ....41 E3
Rhyl Crs *CARL* NG4 ....33 G3
Ribblesdale *ILK* DE7 ....37 F3
Ribblesdale Rd *ARN* NG5 ....19 G5
  LGEAT NG10 ....72 B4
Riber Cl *ILK* DE7 ....24 B5
  LGEAT NG10 ....73 E4
Riber Crs *ARN* NG5 ....18 C5
Richardson Cl *CFTN/RUD* NG11 ....65 H5
Richborough Pl
  WOL/BIL/BRX NG8 ....54 C1
Richey Cl *ARN* NG5 ....20 C3
Richmond Av
  BWSH/BRSTN DE72 ....72 B1
  EWD/SEL/PNX NG16 ....26 A1
  ILK DE7 ....26 A1
  LGEAT NG10 ....62 B2
  MAPPK/POR/STA NG3 ....44 A1
Richmond Cl *ILK* DE7 ....24 A5
Richmond Dr *BSTN/STPLFD* NG9 ...64 D1
  COT/KEY/RAD NG12 ....47 E4
  MAPPK/POR/STA NG3 ....31 C3
Richmond Gdns *ARN* NG5 ....19 H1
Richmond Rd *WBRGFD* NG2 ....58 A2
Richmond Ter
  COT/KEY/RAD NG12 ....47 E5
Rick St *NOTT* NG1 ....3 G4
Ridding Ter
  MAPPK/POR/STA NG3 ....3 F2
Ridge La *COT/KEY/RAD* NG12 ......47 F3
Ridgeway *ARN* NG5 ....18 C3
  HEANOR DE75 ....12 C2
Ridgeway Dr *ILK* DE7 ....37 E3
Ridgeway St
  MAPPK/POR/STA NG3 ....3 K1
Ridgewood Dr
  BSTN/STPLFD NG9 ....64 B2
Ridgmont Wk *CFTN/RUD* NG11 .....76 A1
Ridgway Cl *WBRGFD* NG2 ....68 D1
The Ridings *CALV/BJ* NG14 ....23 F5
  COT/KEY/RAD NG12 ....82 D1
Ridsdale Rd *ARN* NG5 ....19 F5
Rifle St *NOTTE* NG7 ....42 B3
Rigley Av *ILK* DE7 ....26 A4
Rigley Dr *ARN* NG5 ....18 B3
Ring Leas *COT/KEY/RAD* NG12 .....71 E4
Ringstead Cl *WBRGFD* NG2 ....67 F1
Ringwood Crs
  WOL/BIL/BRX NG8 ....41 H3
Ringwood Rd *BING/VBLV* NG13 ....48 B3
Ripon Rd *MAPPK/POR/STA* NG3 ....44 C3
The Rise *ARN* NG5 ....31 G2
Riseborough Wk *BLWL* NG6 ....17 C1
Risegate *COT/KEY/RAD* NG12 ......71 E3
Risegate Gdns
  COT/KEY/RAD NG12 ....71 E3
Riseholme Av
  WOL/BIL/BRX NG8 ....40 B5
Rise Park Rd *ARN* NG5 ....18 A1
Risley Ct *ILK* * DE7 ....26 A2
Risley Dr *WBRGFD* NG2 ....57 E1
Riste's Pl *NOTT* NG1 ....3 G5
Ritchie Cl *COT/KEY/RAD* NG12 ....71 F4
Ritson Cl *MAPPK/POR/STA* NG3 .....3 C1
Riverdale Rd *BSTN/STPLFD* NG9 ...64 C4
Rivergreen *CFTN/RUD* NG11 ....66 B4
Rivergreen Cl
  BSTN/STPLFD * NG9 ....54 B1
Rivergreen Crs
  BSTN/STPLFD NG9 ....54 B1
Rivermead *COT/KEY/RAD* NG12 ....71 E4
  WBRGFD NG2 ....57 G4
River Vw *WBRGFD* NG2 ....57 H2
Rivington Rd *BSTN/STPLFD* NG9 ...63 F4
Road No 1 *CARL* NG4 ....45 G3
Road No 2 *CARL* NG4 ....45 G5
Road No 3 *CARL* NG4 ....45 H3

Road No 4 CARL NG4 ......46 B4
Road No 5 CARL NG4 ......46 A3
Road No 7 CARL NG4 ......45 G2
Road No 8 CARL NG4 ......45 G3
Robbie Burns Rd ARN NG5 ...19 F2
Robert's La HUCK/RAV NG15 ......4 D5
Roberts St ILK DE7 ......38 B2
  WBRGFD NG2......3 K5
Robey Cl HUCK/RAV NG15 ......5 C3
Robey Dr EWD/SEL/PNX NG16......8 A4
Robey Ter NOTTE * NG7 ......42 C1
Robina Dr EWD/SEL/PNX NG16 ......14 C2
Robinet Rd BSTN/STPLFD NG9...65 E1
Robin's Wood Rd
  MAPPK/POR/STA NG3 ......32 A2
Robin Hood Cha
  MAPPK/POR/STA NG3 ......3 H1
Robin Hood Cl
  EWD/SEL/PNX NG16 ......14 A1
Robin Hood Dr HUCK/RAV NG15 ...10 D3
Robin Hood Rd ARN NG5 ......19 F2
Robin Hood St
  MAPPK/POR/STA NG3 ......3 J4
Robin Hood Ter
  MAPPK/POR/STA NG3 ......3 H3
Robin Hood Wy
  BSTN/STPLFD NG9 ......53 H1
  EWD/SEL/PNX NG16 ......15 G5
  HUCK/RAV NG15 ......11 H4
  NOTT NG1 ......2 D7
  WBRGFD NG2 ......57 E2
Robinia Cl WBRGFD NG2......68 B1
Robinson Gdns CFTN/RUD NG11...65 H5
Robinson Rd
  MAPPK/POR/STA NG3 ......32 A2
Robin's Wood Rd
  WOL/BIL/BRX NG8 ......41 G1
Rob Roy Av NOTTE * NG7 ......42 C5
Roche Cl ARN NG5 ......20 D4
Rochester Av CARL NG4 ......45 H4
Rochester Cl LGEAT NG10 ......72 B2
Rochester Ct
  EWD/SEL/PNX NG16 ......17 E4
Rochester Wk CFTN/RUD NG11...66 C5
Rochford Cl
  EWD/SEL/PNX NG16 ......15 G1
Rock Cl BLWL NG6 ......30 A2
Rock Dr NOTT NG7......2 B7
Rocket Cl EWD/SEL/PNX NG16 ...15 H3
Rockford Rd BSTN/STPLFD NG9...53 F2
Rockford Rd ARN NG5 ......30 C2
Rockingham Gv
  BING/VBLV NG13 ......48 B3
Rockley Av COT/KEY/RAD NG12 ...47 E4
  EWD/SEL/PNX NG16 ......14 B1
Rockley Cl HUCK/RAV NG15 ...10 B1
Rock St BLWL NG6 ......17 G2
Rockwood Crs HUCK/RAV NG15 ...10 C1
Rockwood Wk HUCK/RAV NG15 ...10 D1
Rodel Ct MAPPK/POR/STA NG3 ...3 G2
Roden St MAPPK/POR/STA NG3 ...3 J4
Rodney Rd WBRGFD NG2 ......58 B5
Rodney Wy ILK DE7 ......26 A1
Rodwell Cl WOL/BIL/BRX NG8 ...41 G2
Roebuck Cl ARN NG5 ......19 E1
Roecliffe WBRGFD NG2 ......67 H2
Roehampton Dr
  BSTN/STPLFD NG9 ......53 E1
Roker Cl WOL/BIL/BRX NG8 ......29 F4
Roland Av CFTN/RUD NG11 ......77 F2
  EWD/SEL/PNX NG16 ......14 C2
Rolleston Cl HUCK/RAV NG15...10 C2
Rolleston Crs
  EWD/SEL/PNX NG16 ......15 G1
Rolleston Dr ARN NG5 ......20 B3
  EWD/SEL/PNX NG16 ......14 B2
  NOTTE NG7 ......42 C4
Roman Dr BLWL NG6 ......30 B1
Romans Ct BLWL NG6 ......30 B1
Romilay Cl BSTN/STPLFD NG9 ...55 F2
Romney Av WOL/BIL/BRX NG8 ...54 C1
Rona Ct BLWL NG6 ......18 B4
Ronald St NOTTE NG7 ......42 C3
Rookery Gdns ARN NG5 ......20 A2
Rookwood Cl
  BSTN/STPLFD * NG9 ......54 D5
Roosa Cl BLWL NG6 ......17 G4
Roosevelt Av LGEAT NG10 ......72 D4
Roper Av HEANOR DE75 ......12 C2
The Ropewalk ILK DE7 ......26 B4
  NOTT NG1......2 C5
Ropewalk Ct NOTT * NG1 ......2 C5
Ropsley Crs WBRGFD NG2......58 B2
Roseacre BSTN/STPLFD NG9 ......65 F1
Rose Ash La ARN NG5 ......19 G2
Rose Av ILK DE7 ......25 H3
Rosebank Dr ARN NG5 ......20 C1

Roseberry Gdns
  HUCK/RAV NG15 ......11 H1
Rosebery Av WBRGFD NG2 ......57 H2
Rosebery St BLWL NG6 ......30 B1
Rose Cl MAPPK/POR/STA NG3 ...43 G1
Rose Ct LGEAT NG10 ......72 C1
Rosecroft Dr ARN NG5 ......19 F4
Rosedale Cl LGEAT NG10 ......72 C3
Rosedale Dr WOL/BIL/BRX NG8...40 A4
Rosedale Rd
  MAPPK/POR/STA NG3 ......44 D2
Rosegarth Wk BLWL NG6 ......30 A1
Rose Gv BSTN/STPLFD NG9 ......65 G1
  COT/KEY/RAD NG12 ......79 G5
Rosegrove Av ARN NG5 ......20 A1
Rose HI COT/KEY/RAD NG12......82 B1
Roseland Cl COT/KEY/RAD NG12...82 A2
Roseleigh Av
  MAPPK/POR/STA NG3 ......32 C3
Rosemary Cl WOL/BIL/BRX NG8 ...28 D4
Roseneath Av ARN NG5 ......18 B1
Rosetta Rd NOTTE NG7 ......30 C4
Rosewall Ct ARN NG5 ......20 C3
Rosewood Crs HEANOR DE75 ......7 E5
Rosewood Gdns WBRGFD NG2 ...67 F3
Roslyn Av CARL NG4 ......33 F4
Rossell Dr BSTN/STPLFD NG9...63 F1
Rossendale ILK DE7 ......25 H1
Rossett Cl WBRGFD NG2 ......59 E5
Rossington Rd WBRGFD NG2......44 A3
Ross La CARL NG4 ......22 B3
Rosslyn Dr HUCK/RAV NG15......5 H4
  WOL/BIL/BRX NG8 ......29 F3
Rosthwaite Cl WBRGFD NG2 ......68 D1
Rothbury Av BSTN/STPLFD NG9 ...53 E1
Rothbury Gv BING/VBLV NG13......48 B2
Rothesay Av NOTTE NG7 ......42 C4
Rothley Av
  MAPPK/POR/STA NG3 ......44 A3
Rothwell Cl CFTN/RUD NG11 ......66 D2
Roughs Wood La
  HUCK/RAV NG15 ......10 C3
Roundwood Rd ARN NG5 ......19 F3
Rowan Av BSTN/STPLFD NG9 ......53 F2
Rowan Cl BING/VBLV NG13 ......49 F3
  ILK DE7 ......38 A3
Rowan Crs EWD/SEL/PNX NG16 ...16 A4
Rowan Dr CFTN/RUD NG11 ......66 D2
  COT/KEY/RAD NG12 ......82 D2
Rowan Gdns BLWL NG6 ......17 G3
Rowe Gdns BLWL NG6 ......18 A4
Rowland Av
  MAPPK/POR/STA NG3 ......32 B3
Rowland Ms
  MAPPK/POR/STA NG3 ......43 H1
Rowsley Av LGEAT NG10 ......72 B4
Roxton Ct EWD/SEL/PNX NG16...15 G3
Royal Av LGEAT NG10 ......63 E5
Royal Ms BSTN/STPLFD NG9......64 B3
Roy Av HUCK/RAV NG15 ......10 D3
Royce Av HUCK/RAV NG15 ......10 D3
Royston Cl WBRGFD * NG2 ......57 E2
Ruby Paddocks
  EWD/SEL/PNX NG16 ......15 G5
Ruddington La CFTN/RUD NG11...67 E1
Rudge Cl WOL/BIL/BRX NG8......41 E3
Ruffles Av
  MAPPK/POR/STA NG3 ......20 C5
Rufford Av BSTN/STPLFD NG9...53 H3
  CARL NG4 ......33 E3
Rufford Cl HUCK/RAV NG15 ......11 H1
Rufford Gv BING/VBLV NG13 ......48 C3
Rufford Rd ARN NG5 ......31 F2
  CFTN/RUD NG11 ......77 G2
  LGEAT NG10 ......72 C5
Rufford Wy WBRGFD NG2......58 C5
Ruffs Dr HUCK/RAV NG15 ......10 D2
Rugby Cl ARN NG5 ......18 B3
Rugby Rd WBRGFD NG2 ......67 F1
Rugby Ter NOTTE * NG7 ......42 C1
Ruislip Cl EWD/SEL/PNX NG16 ...15 F3
Runcie Cl COT/KEY/RAD NG12 ...71 E4
Runnymede Ct NOTTE NG7 ......2 B3
Runswick Dr ARN NG5 ......20 A2
  WOL/BIL/BRX NG8 ......41 F3
Runton Dr BLWL NG6 ......30 C1
Rupert Rd BING/VBLV NG13 ......48 C3
Rupert St ILK DE7 ......26 B4
Ruscombe Pl
  MAPPK/POR/STA NG3 ......3 G1
Rushcliffe Av CARL NG4 ......33 G5
  COT/KEY/RAD NG12 ......47 E5
Rushcliffe Ct BLWL NG6 ......18 A4
Rushcliffe Ri HUCK/RAV NG15 ...19 G5
Rushcliffe Rd HUCK/RAV NG15 ...10 D1
Rushford Dr WOL/BIL/BRX NG8...40 B4
Rush Leys LGEAT NG10 ......73 E4

Rushton Gdns
  MAPPK/POR/STA * NG3 ......43 H1
Rushworth Av WBRGFD NG2 ......57 H5
Rushworth Cl
  MAPPK/POR/STA NG3 ......43 H1
Rushy Cl WOL/BIL/BRX NG8 ......40 C3
Rushy La LGEAT NG10 ......62 A1
Ruskin Av BSTN/STPLFD NG9 ......64 C2
  LGEAT NG10 ......72 C4
Ruskin St NOTTE NG7 ......42 B3
Russell Av WOL/BIL/BRX NG8......41 E3
Russell Crs WOL/BIL/BRX NG8......41 E3
Russell Dr WOL/BIL/BRX NG8......40 D3
Russell Gdns BSTN/STPLFD NG9 ...64 B4
Russell Rd NOTTE NG7......30 C5
Russell St LGEAT NG10 ......63 E5
  NOTTE NG7......2 A2
Russet Av CARL NG4 ......45 G1
Russley Rd BSTN/STPLFD NG9 ...53 H3
Ruth Dr ARN NG5 ......20 B1
Rutland Av BSTN/STPLFD NG9 ...63 H4
Rutland Gv LGEAT NG10 ......62 D1
Rutland Rd BING/VBLV NG13 ......49 E2
  CARL NG4 ......33 E2
  WBRGFD NG2......58 B2
Rutland St ILK DE7 ......26 A4
  NOTT NG1......2 D6
Rutland Ter LGEAT NG10 ......26 A3
Rydal Av BSTN/STPLFD NG9 ......54 C3
  HUCK/RAV NG15 ......5 E4
Rydale Rd ARN NG5 ......19 F5
Rydal Gdns WBRGFD NG2 ......68 A2
Rydal Gv BLWL NG6 ......30 B2
Ryecroft St BSTN/STPLFD NG9 ...53 F3
Ryehill Cl WBRGFD NG2 ......57 G1
Ryehill St WBRGFD NG2 ......57 G1
Ryeland Gdns WBRGFD NG2 ......57 F1
Ryemere Cl EWD/SEL/PNX NG16...7 E4
Rye St NOTTE NG7 ......30 C5
Rylands Cl BSTN/STPLFD NG9 ...65 G2
Ryton Sq WOL/BIL/BRX NG8 ......29 G4

S

Saddlers Yd COT/KEY/RAD NG12...79 F2
Saffron Gdns WBRGFD NG2 ......57 E1
St Albans Cl LGEAT NG10 ......73 F4
St Albans Ms BLWL NG6 ......18 A4
St Albans Rd ARN NG5 ......19 G3
  BLWL NG6......18 A3
St Albans St ARN NG5 ......31 F2
St Andrews Cl BLWL NG6 ......17 H3
St Andrew's Dr ILK DE7 ......25 H5
St Andrew's Rd NOTT NG1 ......43 E1
St Anns Gdns
  MAPPK/POR/STA NG3 ......43 H1
St Ann's HI
  MAPPK/POR/STA NG3 ......43 F1
St Ann's Hill Rd
  MAPPK/POR/STA NG3 ......2 E1
St Ann's St NOTT NG1 ......3 F3
St Ann's Va
  MAPPK/POR/STA NG3 ......3 J1
St Ann's Wy
  MAPPK/POR/STA NG3 ......2 E1
St Ann's Well Rd
  MAPPK/POR/STA NG3 ......3 G3
St Anthonys Ct NOTTE NG7 ......56 B1
St Augustines Ct NOTTE NG7......30 D4
St Austell Dr CFTN/RUD NG11 ...67 E1
St Austins Ct CARL NG4......33 G5
St Austins Dr CARL NG4......33 G5
St Bartholomew's Rd
  MAPPK/POR/STA NG3 ......44 A1
St Catherines St
  COT/KEY/RAD NG12 ......60 D1
St Cecilia Gdns
  MAPPK/POR/STA NG3 ......3 G1
St Chad's Rd
  MAPPK/POR/STA NG3 ......3 K4
St Christopher St WBRGFD NG2 ...44 A4
St Cuthbert's Rd
  MAPPK/POR/STA NG3 ......3 K3
St Ervan Rd CFTN/RUD NG11 ......57 E5
St George's Dr WBRGFD NG2 ......57 E1
St Helen's Crs
  BSTN/STPLFD NG9 ......38 D4
  CALV/BJ NG14 ......34 D2
St Helen's Gv CALV/BJ NG14......34 D2
St Helen's Rd WBRGFD NG2 ......58 A5
St Helen's St NOTTE NG7 ......2 B4
St James Av ILK DE7 ......38 B1
St James St LGEAT NG10 ......62 C3
St James's St BSTN/STPLFD NG9 ...53 E5
  NOTT * NG1 ......2 D6

St James's Ter NOTT NG1 ......2 D6
St John's Crs HUCK/RAV NG15 ...11 H2
St John's Rd CFTN/RUD NG11 ......77 F2
  ILK DE7 ......38 B1
St John's St LGEAT NG10 ......73 E2
St Jude's Av
  MAPPK/POR/STA NG3 ......31 G3
St Laurence Ct LGEAT NG10 ......73 F3
St Lawrence Bvd
  COT/KEY/RAD NG12 ......60 C1
St Lawrence CI HEANOR DE75 ......6 C5
St Leonard's Dr
  WOL/BIL/BRX NG8 ......41 E4
St Leven Cl WOL/BIL/BRX NG8...28 C5
St Luke's Cl WBRGFD * NG2 ......68 C1
St Luke's St
  MAPPK/POR/STA NG3 ......3 J4
St Luke's Wy CALV/BJ NG14 ......35 E5
St Margarets Av
  WOL/BIL/BRX NG8 ......29 H5
St Marks St NOTT NG1 ......3 G3
St Martin's Rd
  WOL/BIL/BRX NG8 ......28 D5
St Mary's Av CARL NG4 ......33 F3
St Mary's Cl ARN NG5 ......20 A1
  BSTN/STPLFD NG9 ......64 C5
St Mary's Crs CFTN/RUD NG11...77 F2
St Mary's Ga NOTT NG1 ......3 G5
St Mary's Pl NOTT * NG1 ......3 G5
St Mary's Rd BING/VBLV NG13 ......49 E2
St Mary St ILK DE7 ......25 H5
St Mary's Wy HUCK/RAV NG15...5 F4
St Matthias Rd
  MAPPK/POR/STA NG3 ......3 K2
St Mawes Av CFTN/RUD NG11......57 E5
St Michael's Av CARL NG4......33 F3
  WOL/BIL/BRX NG8 ......28 C5
St Michael's Sq
  BSTN/STPLFD NG9 ......54 A3
St Nicholas Cl ARN NG5 ......19 H3
St Nicholas St NOTT NG1 ......2 E6
St Norbert Dr ILK DE7 ......37 G3
St Patrick's Rd
  EWD/SEL/PNX NG16 ......16 A4
St Paul's Av NOTTE NG7 ......42 C1
St Paul's St WOL/BIL/BRX NG8......42 A4
St Peter's Crs CFTN/RUD NG11 ...77 F2
St Peter's Ga NOTT NG1 ......3 F5
St Peter's St NOTTE NG7 ......42 B3
St Saviour's Gdns WBRGFD NG2 ...57 G1
St Stephen's Av WBRGFD * NG2 ...44 A4
St Stephen's Rd WBRGFD NG2......3 K6
St Vincent Cl LGEAT NG10 ......73 F3
St Wilfrid's Sq ILK DE7 ......36 B1
Salamander Cl CARL NG4 ......33 E4
Salcey Dr BSTN/STPLFD NG9 ......53 E1
Salcombe Circ ARN NG5 ......19 G1
Salcombe Cl
  EWD/SEL/PNX NG16 ......14 D1
Salcombe Crs CFTN/RUD NG11 ...77 F1
Salcombe Dr ARN NG5 ......19 G1
Salcombe Rd ARN NG5 ......30 C2
Salford Gdns
  MAPPK/POR/STA NG3 ......3 H3
Salisbury Sq NOTTE NG7 ......42 B4
Salisbury St BSTN/STPLFD NG9 ...55 G4
  LGEAT NG10 ......73 F2
  NOTTE NG7 ......42 B4
Salmon Cl BLWL NG6 ......17 E3
Salop St ARN NG5 ......19 G3
Saltburn Rd WOL/BIL/BRX NG8 ...41 F1
Saltby Gn CFTN/RUD NG11 ......67 G3
Salterford Rd HUCK/RAV NG15 ...10 D2
Saltford Cl CARL NG4 ......33 G3
Salthouse Cl BSTN/STPLFD NG9 ...55 F3
Salthouse La BSTN/STPLFD NG9 ...55 F3
Saltney Wy CFTN/RUD NG11 ......66 D3
Samson Ct CFTN/RUD NG11 ......77 E1
Sandale Cl WBRGFD NG2......58 D5
Sandays Cl WBRGFD NG2 ......57 F2
Sandby Ct BSTN/STPLFD NG9......64 B1
Sandfield Ms ARN NG5 ......20 A4
  BSTN/STPLFD NG9 ......63 F4
  NOTTE NG7 ......42 C4
Sandford Av LGEAT NG10 ......73 F2
Sandford Rd
  MAPPK/POR/STA NG3 ......32 A3
Sandgate CFTN/RUD NG11 ......66 D3
Sandhurst Dr BSTN/STPLFD NG9...64 A4
  CFTN/RUD NG11 ......77 E3
Sandhurst Rd BLWL NG6 ......17 G1
Sandiacre Rd BSTN/STPLFD NG9 ...62 D5
Sandon St NOTTE NG7 ......30 D4
Sandown Rd BSTN/STPLFD NG9 ...63 H4
Sandpiper Cl BING/VBLV NG13......49 E4
Sandpiper Wy NOTTE NG7 ......42 B4
Sandringham Av WBRGFD NG2 ...57 H3

Sandringham Crs
  WOL/BIL/BRX NG8 ...40 B3
Sandringham Dr
  BSTN/STPLFD NG9 ...54 B2
Sandringham Pl ILK DE7 ...37 C3
Sandringham Rd LGEAT NG10 ...62 C2
  WBRGFD NG2 ...44 A4
Sands Cl CARL NG4 ...45 F3
Sandside Cl COT/KEY/RAD NG12 ...71 E4
Sandwell Cl LGEAT NG10 ...72 B3
Sandyford Cl BLWL NG6 ...29 H2
Sandy La BSTN/STPLFD NG9 ...54 C2
  COT/KEY/RAD NG12 ...60 A1
  HUCK/RAV NG15 ...5 F5
Sanger Cl CFTN/RUD NG11 ...75 H1
Sankey Dr BLWL NG6 ...17 E5
Sapele Cl CARL NG4 ...33 H3
Sargent Gdns
  MAPPK/POR/STA NG3 ...44 A2
Saskatoon Cl
  COT/KEY/RAD NG12 ...60 D1
Saunby Cl ARN NG5 ...20 C3
Saunton Cl COT/KEY/RAD NG12...68 D2
Savage's Rd CFTN/RUD NG11 ...77 F1
Saville Cl BSTN/STPLFD NG9 ...53 F3
Saville Rd ARN NG5 ...20 A5
Sawmand Cl LGEAT NG10 ...72 D3
Saxelby Gdns BLWL NG6 ...17 G2
Saxondale Dr BLWL NG6 ...18 A5
Saxon Gn NOTTE NG7 ...42 B5
Saxon Wy COT/KEY/RAD NG12 ...71 F5
Saxton Av HEANOR DE75 ...6 C5
Saxton Cl BSTN/STPLFD NG9 ...55 G4
Scafell Wy CFTN/RUD NG11 ...76 A2
Scalby Cl EWD/SEL/PNX NG16 ...7 G5
Scalford Dr WOL/BIL/BRX NG8 ...41 H5
Scarborough Av ILK DE7 ...25 G5
Scarborough St
  MAPPK/POR/STA NG3 ...3 H3
Scarfell Cl WBRGFD NG2 ...68 D1
Scargill Av EWD/SEL/PNX NG16..14 C1
Scargill Cl EWD/SEL/PNX NG16 ...14 C1
Scargill Rd ILK DE7 ...24 B5
Scargill Wk EWD/SEL/PNX NG16 ...8 A4
Scarrington Rd WBRGFD NG2 ...58 A2
Sceptre St ARN NG5 ...31 F3
School Cl WBRGFD NG2 ...57 G2
School La BING/VBLV NG13 ...48 D3
  BSTN/STPLFD NG9 ...64 B2
  LGEAT NG10 ...52 A4
School Sq ILK DE7 ...36 B1
Science Rd NOTTE NG7 ...56 A2
Scotland Rd ARN NG5 ...30 C3
Scott Av BSTN/STPLFD NG9 ...55 E5
Scott Cl BLWL NG6 ...17 E5
Scrimshire La
  COT/KEY/RAD NG12 ...70 D3
Script Dr BLWL NG6 ...30 B1
Scrivelsby Gdns
  BSTN/STPLFD NG9 ...64 C2
Seaburn Rd BSTN/STPLFD NG9 ...63 F3
Seaford Av WOL/BIL/BRX NG8..41 G3
Seaford Wy ILK DE7 ...14 A5
Seagrave Ct
  WOL/BIL/BRX * NG8 ...28 C4
Seagrave Rd EWD/SEL/PNX NG16 ...15 G3
Seamer Rd EWD/SEL/PNX NG16 ...15 G3
Seatallan Cl WBRGFD NG2 ...58 D5
Seathwaite Cl
  COT/KEY/RAD NG12 ...68 D2
Seatoller Cl WBRGFD NG2 ...68 D1
Seaton Crs WOL/BIL/BRX NG8 ...29 F4
Second Av BLWL NG6 ...17 G3
  BSTN/STPLFD NG9 ...56 A4
  CARL NG4 ...32 D5
  CARL NG4 ...33 G5
Sedgebrook Cl BLWL NG6 ...29 H1
Sedgeley Rd
  COT/KEY/RAD NG12 ...79 E1
Sedgewood Gv CFTN/RUD NG11..66 B3
Sedgley Av WBRGFD NG2 ...44 A3
Sedgwick St
  EWD/SEL/PNX NG16 ...7 E4
Sedley Av EWD/SEL/PNX NG16 ...16 B4
Seely Rd NOTTE NG7 ...2 A4
Sefton Av BSTN/STPLFD NG9 ...53 F3
Sefton Dr MAPPK/POR/STA NG3 ...31 G4
Selby Cl BSTN/STPLFD NG9 ...63 F3
Selby La COT/KEY/RAD NG12 ...82 C2
Selby Rd WBRGFD NG2 ...68 A1
Selhurst Ct NOTTE * NG7 ...42 C1
Selhurst St NOTTE NG7 ...42 C1
Sellars Av CFTN/RUD NG11 ...77 F3
Seller's Wood Dr BLWL NG6 ...17 F4
Seller's Wood Dr
  West BLWL NG6 ...16 D3
Selside Ct BSTN/STPLFD NG9 ...63 H2
Selston Dr WOL/BIL/BRX NG8 ...41 H5

Selwyn Cl BLWL NG6 ...18 B5
Serlby Ri MAPPK/POR/STA NG3..44 A2
Serlby Rd EWD/SEL/PNX NG16 ...8 B4
Seven Oaks Crs
  BSTN/STPLFD NG9 ...54 A1
Seven Oaks Rd ILK DE7 ...52 B2
Seventh Av BSTN/STPLFD NG9 ...65 H1
Severals BSTN/STPLFD NG9 ...53 G4
Seymour Rd
  EWD/SEL/PNX NG16 ...14 A1
  HUCK/RAV NG15 ...10 C2
  WBRGFD NG2 ...58 C3
Seymour St
  MAPPK/POR/STA NG3 ...3 K3
Shackleton Cl
  WOL/BIL/BRX NG8 ...28 C3
Shadwell Gv
  BSTN/STPLFD NG9 ...46 D5
Shady La BSTN/STPLFD NG9...64 C5
Shaftesbury Av CALV/BJ NG14 ...23 F5
  LGEAT NG10 ...62 B1
Shaftesbury St NOTTE NG7 ...30 B4
Shakespeare Cl CARL NG4 ...45 F3
Shakespeare Rd
  EWD/SEL/PNX NG16 ...14 D5
Shakespeare St LGEAT NG10 ...62 D5
  NOTT NG1 ...2 D3
Shakespeare Vls NOTT NG1 ...2 E3
Shaldon Cl ARN NG5 ...18 C1
Shanklin Dr BSTN/STPLFD NG9 ...53 E4
Shanwell Cl WOL/BIL/BRX NG8 ...28 C3
Sharnford Wy
  BSTN/STPLFD NG9 ...40 A4
Sharp Cl ILK DE7 ...37 F2
  LGEAT NG10 ...72 D3
Sharphill Rd
  COT/KEY/RAD NG12 ...68 C2
Shaw Crs HUCK/RAV NG15 ...10 D3
Shaw St CFTN/RUD NG11 ...77 F1
Shaw St East ILK DE7 ...38 B2
Shaw St West ILK DE7 ...38 B2
Shearing Cl CARL NG4 ...33 H4
Shearing Hl CARL NG4 ...33 H4
Sheepfold La CFTN/RUD NG11...77 F3
Shelby Cl NOTTE NG7 ...42 B4
Sheldon Cl LGEAT NG10 ...62 C3
Shelford Cl BSTN/STPLFD NG9 ...64 C2
Shelford Crs CALV/BJ NG14 ...23 F5
Shelford Dr BING/VBLV NG13 ...48 C3
Shelford Hl COT/KEY/RAD NG12 ...35 H5
Shelford Ri
  MAPPK/POR/STA NG3 ...44 B2
Shelford Rd CARL NG4 ...32 D2
  COT/KEY/RAD NG12 ...47 E5
Shelley Av CFTN/RUD NG11 ...66 B3
Shelley Cl EWD/SEL/PNX NG16 ...16 A4
  HUCK/RAV NG15 ...10 C1
Shelley Rd ARN NG5 ...19 G3
Shelton Gdns CFTN/RUD NG11 ...77 E2
Shelton St MAPPK/POR/STA NG3 ...3 G2
Shenfield Gdns BLWL NG6 ...18 A1
Shepard Cl BLWL NG6 ...17 E4
Shepherds Cl WOL/BIL/BRX NG8..41 F1
Shepherds Wood Dr
  WOL/BIL/BRX NG8 ...41 H1
Shepton Cl ILK DE7 ...25 G2
Shepton Crs WOL/BIL/BRX NG8...29 E4
Sheraton Dr WOL/BIL/BRX NG8...40 D5
Sherborne Rd WBRGFD NG2 ...68 A1
  WOL/BIL/BRX NG8 ...29 F4
Sherbrook Av ARN NG5 ...19 G4
Sherbrooke Rd ARN NG5 ...31 E4
Sherbrook Rd ARN NG5 ...19 F4
Sherbrook Ter ARN NG5 ...19 G4
Sheridan Ct BSTN/STPLFD NG9 ...53 F2
Sheriff's Lea BSTN/STPLFD NG9 ...63 F4
Sheriffs Wy WBRGFD * NG2 ...43 F5
Sheringham Cl ARN NG5 ...20 A4
Sherman Dr BSTN/STPLFD NG9 ...64 B4
Sherrington Cl CFTN/RUD NG11 ...75 H1
Sherwin Cl MAPPK/POR/STA NG3 ...3 F2
Sherwin Gv NOTTE * NG7 ...42 B5
Sherwin Rd BSTN/STPLFD NG9 ...53 G2
  NOTTE NG7 ...42 B5
Sherwood Gv BING/VBLV NG13 ...48 C3
Sherwood Ri
  EWD/SEL/PNX NG16 ...14 A1
  NOTTE NG7 ...31 E5
Sherwood St HUCK/RAV NG15...11 H1
Sherwood V ARN NG5 ...31 H2
Sherwood Wk HUCK/RAV NG15...5 F2
Shilling Wy LGEAT NG10 ...72 B2
Shipley Common La ILK DE7 ...25 F1
Shipley La ILK DE7 ...24 C2
Shipley Ri CARL NG4 ...45 F1
Shipley Rd WOL/BIL/BRX NG8 ...29 E3
Shipstone St ILK DE7 ...38 C2

  NOTTE NG7 ...30 C5
Shirebrooke Cl BLWL NG6 ...29 H2
Shirley Dr ARN NG5 ...20 C3
Shirley Rd
  MAPPK/POR/STA NG3 ...31 F5
Shirley St LGEAT NG10 ...72 B5
Shoreswood Cl ARN NG5 ...19 E2
Shortcross Av ARN NG5 ...32 A1
Short Hl NOTT NG1 ...3 H6
Short Stairs NOTT * NG1 ...3 H6
Shortwood Av HUCK/RAV NG15 ...11 E2
Shortwood Cl NOTT NG1 ...3 G6
Shorwell Rd CARL NG4 ...44 C4
Shrewsbury Rd WBRGFD NG2 ...44 B4
Shrimpton Ct CFTN/RUD NG11 ...77 G3
The Shrubberies ARN * NG5 ...31 E3
Sidlaw Ri ARN NG5 ...19 E1
Sidmouth Cl
  COT/KEY/RAD NG12 ...79 F5
Sidney Rd BSTN/STPLFD NG9 ...54 B1
Sidney St EWD/SEL/PNX NG16...15 G4
  LGEAT NG10 ...73 E3
Silbury Cl CFTN/RUD NG11 ...76 A2
Silver Birch Cl BLWL NG6 ...29 G1
Silverdale BSTN/STPLFD NG9 ...63 F1
Silverdale Rd NOTTE NG7 ...30 C3
Silver Hill Cl WOL/BIL/BRX NG8 ...28 C3
Silverhow St NOTT NG1 ...2 E6
Silverwood Rd
  BSTN/STPLFD NG9 ...54 D5
Simons Ct BSTN/STPLFD NG9 ...54 C2
Sinclair Cl NOTTE NG7 ...30 C3
Sir John Robinson Wy ARN NG5 ...19 H3
Sisley Av BSTN/STPLFD NG9 ...53 F5
Sixth Av BSTN/STPLFD NG9 ...65 H1
Skeavington's La ILK DE7 ...11 F4
Skelwith Cl COT/KEY/RAD NG12 ...68 D1
Sketchley St
  MAPPK/POR/STA NG3 ...3 K1
Skiddaw Cl WBRGFD NG2 ...68 D1
Skipton Circ
  MAPPK/POR/STA NG3 ...44 B3
Skipton Cl ILK DE7 ...25 G2
Skylark Dr BING/VBLV NG13 ...49 E4
Skylark Dr BLWL NG6 ...30 A1
Slack La HEANOR DE75 ...12 B2
Slack Rd BLWL NG6 ...24 C2
Slade Cl ILK DE7 ...38 A3
Slade Rd BSTN/STPLFD NG9 ...66 A1
Slaidburn Av CFTN/RUD NG11 ...66 D1
Sloan Dr BSTN/STPLFD NG9 ...54 A1
Sloane Ct WBRGFD NG2 ...67 F3
Smalley Av ILK DE7 ...38 B1
Smedley Cl WOL/BIL/BRX NG8 ...29 G3
Smedley's Av LGEAT NG10 ...62 C1
Smeeton St HEANOR DE75 ...13 E1
Smith Dr EWD/SEL/PNX NG16 ...6 D4
Smithfield Av
  BSTN/STPLFD NG9 ...39 E4
Smithson Dr WOL/BIL/BRX NG8 ...40 D4
Smithurst Rd
  EWD/SEL/PNX NG16 ...14 C2
Smithy Cl CFTN/RUD NG11 ...66 A4
Smithy Crs ARN NG5 ...20 A2
Smithy Rw NOTT NG1 ...2 E5
Snape Wood Rd BLWL NG6 ...17 E3
Sneinton Bvd WBRGFD NG2 ...44 A4
Sneinton Dl WBRGFD NG2 ...44 A4
Sneinton Hermitage
  WBRGFD NG2 ...3 K7
Sneinton Hollows WBRGFD NG2...44 A4
Sneinton Rd WBRGFD NG2 ...3 J5
Snowdon Cl ARN NG5 ...19 E1
Soarbank Cl
  EWD/SEL/PNX NG16 ...15 F3
Sobers Gdns ARN NG5 ...20 C4
Softwood Cl BLWL NG6 ...17 E3
Soloman Rd
  EWD/SEL/PNX NG16 ...26 C3
Solway Cl BSTN/STPLFD NG9 ...64 D1
Somerby Ct BSTN/STPLFD NG9 ...40 A4
Somersby Rd ARN NG5 ...20 B5
Somerset Cl LGEAT NG10 ...73 H1
Somerton Av CFTN/RUD NG11 ...66 D2
Songthrush Av BLWL NG6 ...30 A1
Sophie Rd NOTTE NG7 ...42 C1
Sorrel Dr BING/VBLV NG13 ...48 B3
Soudan Dr WBRGFD NG2 ...57 E2
Southampton St
  MAPPK/POR/STA NG3 ...3 J1
South Av COT/KEY/RAD NG12 ...47 G4
Southchurch Dr
  CFTN/RUD NG11 ...76 B1
Southcliffe Rd CARL NG4 ...45 E1
Southdale Dr CARL NG4 ...45 E1
Southdale Rd CARL NG4 ...45 E1
South Devon Av
  MAPPK/POR/STA NG3 ...32 C3

Southey St NOTTE NG7 ...2 A1
Southfield Rd
  WOL/BIL/BRX NG8 ...42 A2
Southglade Rd ARN NG5 ...18 B4
Southlea Rd CARL NG4 ...45 E1
South Pde NOTT NG1 ...2 E5
South Rd BSTN/STPLFD NG9 ...65 F2
  NOTTE NG7 ...2 B7
  WBRGFD NG2 ...57 H5
South Sherwood St NOTT NG1 ...2 E2
Southside ARN NG5 ...20 D3
South Snape Cl BLWL NG6 ...17 E3
South St EWD/SEL/PNX NG16 ...7 H5
  EWD/SEL/PNX NG16 ...14 D2
  HUCK/RAV NG15 ...5 F5
  ILK DE7 ...25 H5
  LGEAT NG10 ...73 F2
South View Rd CARL NG4 ...33 E3
Southwell Ri
  EWD/SEL/PNX NG16 ...14 C3
Southwell Rd NOTT NG1 ...3 H5
Southwold Dr
  WOL/BIL/BRX NG8 ...41 H5
Sovereign Gv LGEAT NG10 ...72 C2
Sovereign Wy HEANOR DE75 ...12 A1
Sowbrook La ILK DE7 ...37 H5
Spalding Rd
  MAPPK/POR/STA NG3 ...44 A3
Spaniel Rw NOTT NG1 ...2 E6
Sparrow Cl ILK DE7 ...38 B3
Spean Dr WOL/BIL/BRX NG8 ...41 G1
Speedwell Cl BING/VBLV NG13...48 B3
Spencer Av LGEAT NG10 ...52 C4
  MAPPK/POR/STA NG3 ...20 D5
Spencer Cl CFTN/RUD NG11 ...77 E2
Spencer Crs BSTN/STPLFD NG9 ...53 C3
Spencer Dr EWD/SEL/PNX NG16 ...16 B4
Spey Cl HUCK/RAV NG15 ...10 C4
Spicer Cl BSTN/STPLFD NG9 ...64 B4
Spindle Gdns BLWL NG6 ...17 F3
The Spinney ARN NG5 ...31 H1
  CALV/BJ NG14 ...23 G5
  ILK DE7 ...37 H2
  ILK DE7 ...52 A3
Spinney Cl COT/KEY/RAD NG12 ...71 E4
  WBRGFD NG2 ...68 D2
Spinney Crs BSTN/STPLFD NG9 ...63 G3
Spinney Dr LGEAT NG10 ...62 D4
Spinney Ri BSTN/STPLFD NG9 ...63 F3
Spinney Rd BING/VBLV NG13 ...48 C3
  COT/KEY/RAD NG12 ...82 A1
  ILK DE7 ...37 H2
  LGEAT NG10 ...62 D4
Spinney Wy CFTN/RUD NG11 ...66 D2
Spondon St ARN NG5 ...31 F3
Spray Cl CARL NG4 ...45 F3
Spridgeon Cl LGEAT NG10 ...62 C4
The Spring LGEAT NG10 ...73 E4
Spring Dale Gdns
  BSTN/STPLFD NG9 ...53 E1
Springfield Av
  EWD/SEL/PNX NG16 ...8 B5
  LGEAT NG10 ...62 B3
  LGEAT NG10 ...73 G1
Springfield Dr
  EWD/SEL/PNX NG16 ...17 E4
Springfield Gdn ILK DE7 ...26 A3
Springfield Rd ARN NG5 ...19 H1
  HUCK/RAV NG15 ...10 C1
Springfields WBRGFD NG2 ...57 G5
Springfield St NOTTE NG7 ...30 C4
Spring Garden Ter ILK DE7 ...26 A3
Spring Gn CFTN/RUD NG11 ...76 B2
Spring Hl EWD/SEL/PNX NG16...15 G5
Springhill Cl BLWL NG6 ...17 G1
Spring La CARL NG4 ...21 G5
  HEANOR DE75 ...12 B1
Spring Meadow
  COT/KEY/RAD NG12 ...71 F3
Spring Moor WBRGFD NG2 ...45 E3
Spring Rd BLWL NG6 ...17 H3
Spring St HUCK/RAV NG15 ...5 F4
Springwood Gdns ARN NG5 ...32 A2
Spruce Gv HUCK/RAV NG15 ...11 G2
Sprydon Wk CFTN/RUD NG11 ...76 C2
The Square COT/KEY/RAD NG12 ...82 B2
Squires Av BLWL NG6 ...17 G1
Squires Wy WBRGFD NG2 ...57 G5
Stacey Av ARN NG5 ...18 C3
Stafford Ct BLWL NG6 ...17 E5
Stafford St LGEAT NG10 ...73 G1
Stagsden Crs WOL/BIL/BRX NG8...40 B3
Staindale Dr WOL/BIL/BRX NG8 ...30 A4
Stainmore Gv BING/VBLV NG13...48 B3
Stainsborough Rd
  HUCK/RAV NG15 ...10 B1
Stainsby Av HEANOR DE75 ...12 B1
Stamford Cl LGEAT NG10 ...73 E5

Stamford Rd *WBRGFD* NG2 ....58 B5
Stamford St
  EWD/SEL/PNX NG16 ....14 D1
  EWD/SEL/PNX NG16 ....26 D1
  HEANOR DE75 ....6 B5
  ILK DE7 ....25 H4
Stancliffe Av *BLWL* NG6 ....17 H3
Standard Ct *NOTT* * NG1 ....2 D6
Standard Hi *NOTT* 1 ....2 D6
Standhill Av *CARL* NG4 ....32 C5
Standhill Rd
  MAPPK/POR/STA NG3 ....32 B4
Stanesby Ri *CFTN/RUD* NG11 .....66 B5
Stanford Gdns
  COT/KEY/RAD NG12 ....47 E4
Stanford St *NOTT* NG1 ....2 E6
Stanhome Dr *WBRGFD* NG2 ....67 G2
Stanhome Sq *WBRGFD* NG2 ....67 G3
  CALV/BJ NG14 ....47 E1
Stanhope Crs *ARN* NG5 ....19 H2
  CARL NG4 ....33 E1
Stanhope Rd *ARN* NG5 ....19 H2
  CARL NG4 ....33 E1
Stanhope St *ILK* DE7 ....38 B2
  ILK DE7 ....51 H3
  LGEAT NG10 ....73 H1
  NOTT NG1 ....3 H5
Stanhope Wy *BING/VBLV* NG13 ...48 D3
Stanier Wy *EWD/SEL/PNX* NG16 ...15 H3
Staniland Ct *BSTN/STPLFD* NG9 ..64 B4
Stanley Av *NOTTE* NG7 ....30 D5
Stanley Cl *ILK* DE7 ....37 H1
Stanley Dr *BSTN/STPLFD* NG9 ....53 H3
Stanley Pl *NOTT* NG1 ....2 D4
Stanley Rd
  MAPPK/POR/STA NG3 ....32 B3
  NOTTE NG7 ....30 C4
  WBRGFD NG2 ....58 A5
Stanley St *ILK* DE7 ....38 A1
  LGEAT NG10 ....73 F2
Stanmore Cl *WOL/BIL/BRX* NG8 ...28 D2
Stanmore Gdns *ARN* NG5 ....19 H4
Stansfield St *NOTTE* NG7 ....42 B3
Stanstead Av *ARN* NG5 ....18 A1
  COT/KEY/RAD NG12 ....79 E1
Stanthorne Cl *CFTN/RUD* NG11 ...66 D2
Stanton Ga *ILK* DE7 ....52 D2
Stanton La *COT/KEY/RAD* NG12 ...83 E2
Stanton Rd *ILK* DE7 ....38 A2
  LGEAT NG10 ....52 A4
Stanway Cl
  MAPPK/POR/STA NG3 ....44 D2
Stanwick Cl *WOL/BIL/BRX* NG8 ...28 D5
Stapleford La
  BSTN/STPLFD NG9 ....63 G3
Stapleford Rd
  BSTN/STPLFD NG9 ....38 D4
Staplehurst Dr *ARN* NG5 ....30 D1
Stapleton Rd *ILK* DE7 ....25 H1
Starch La *LGEAT* NG10 ....52 C4
Starthe Bank *HEANOR* DE75 ....6 C5
Starth Wood Rd
  HUCK/RAV NG15 ....10 C5
Stathern Wk *ARN* NG5 ....19 E3
Station Av *CARL* NG4 ....33 H4
Station Rd *BLWL* NG6 ....17 H4
  BSTN/STPLFD NG9 ....55 F5
  CALV/BJ NG14 ....35 E2
  CARL NG4 ....45 G1
  COT/KEY/RAD NG12 ....79 F3
  EWD/SEL/PNX NG16 ....7 E5
  EWD/SEL/PNX NG16 ....14 D5
  EWD/SEL/PNX NG16 ....15 G4
  HUCK/RAV NG15 ....10 A4
  ILK DE7 ....26 A4
  LGEAT NG10 ....62 C1
  LGEAT NG10 ....73 G1
Station St *BING/VBLV* NG13 ......49 E2
  LGEAT NG10 ....73 G2
Station Ter *COT/KEY/RAD* NG12 ..47 E5
  HUCK/RAV NG15 ....10 A3
Staunton Dr *ARN* NG5 ....31 F1
Staverton Rd *WOL/BIL/BRX* NG8 ...40 D1
Steadfold Cl *BLWL* NG6 ....17 G4
Steads Cl *CARL* NG4 ....45 G1
Steedman Av
  MAPPK/POR/STA NG3 ....32 B1
Steeles Wy *CARL* NG4 ....22 A3
Steinbeck Rd *CARL* NG4 ....44 D1
Stella Av *COT/KEY/RAD* NG12 ....79 E1
Stella Gv *COT/KEY/RAD* NG12 ....79 E1
Stepney Ct *WOL/BIL/BRX* NG8 ....29 E4
Sterndale Rd *LGEAT* NG10 ....73 H2
Steven Cl *BSTN/STPLFD* NG9 .....63 G2
Stevenholme Crs *ARN* NG5 ....18 D4
Stevenson Gdns
  CFTN/RUD NG11 ....77 G3
Stevens Rd *LGEAT* NG10 ....62 B1
Stiles Rd *MAPPK/POR/STA* NG3 ..20 D5

Stinsford Cl *ARN* NG5 ....19 F2
Stirling Gdns *BSTN/STPLFD* NG9 ..64 A4
Stirling Gv *CFTN/RUD* NG11 ....76 C1
Stockgill Cl *WBRGFD* NG2 ....58 D5
Stockhill Circ *BLWL* NG6 ....29 H2
Stockhill La *BLWL* NG6 ....29 H1
Stocks Rd *EWD/SEL/PNX* NG16 ...15 F1
Stock Well *BLWL* NG6 ....17 G4
Stoddard Dr *HEANOR* DE75 ....6 C1
Stoke Ferry La
  COT/KEY/RAD NG12 ....35 F4
Stoke La
  CALV/BJ NG14 ....35 E2
  CARL NG4 ....34 E4
Stolle Cl *ARN* NG5 ....20 D3
Stoneacre *ARN* NG5 ....19 E2
Stone Bridge Rd
  MAPPK/POR/STA NG3 ....3 J3
Stonehaven Cl *ARN* NG5 ....20 C1
Stoneleigh St *NOTTE* NG7 ....2 B3
Stonepit Cl
  MAPPK/POR/STA NG3 ....32 A5
Stonesby V *CFTN/RUD* NG11 ....67 E3
Stoneycroft Rd *BLWL* NG6 ....18 B5
Stoney Houghton Gdns
  BLWL NG6 ....17 G2
Stoney La *BSTN/STPLFD* NG9 .....38 C3
  EWD/SEL/PNX NG16 ....7 F1
Stoney St *NOTT* NG1 ....3 G5
Stoppard Cl *ILK* DE7 ....25 G3
Storey Av *CARL* NG4 ....33 F3
Storth Av *HUCK/RAV* NG15 ....11 F1
Story Gdns *HUCK/RAV* NG15 ......11 H2
Stotfield Rd *WOL/BIL/BRX* NG8 ...40 A3
Stourdale Cl *LGEAT* NG10 ....72 B3
Stowe Av *WBRGFD* NG2 ....67 G1
St Patrick's Rd *HUCK/RAV* NG15 ...5 G5
The Strand *BSTN/STPLFD* NG9 ....64 C5
Stratford Cl *CARL* NG4 ....45 F3
Stratford Rd *WBRGFD* NG2 ....58 A4
Stratford St *ILK* DE7 ....26 A1
Strathglen Cl
  EWD/SEL/PNX NG16 ....15 F3
Strathmore Cl *HUCK/RAV* NG15 ...10 D2
Stratmore Rd *ARN* NG5 ....20 C1
Strelley Rd *WOL/BIL/BRX* NG8 ....28 D5
Strelley St *BLWL* NG6 ....17 G3
The Stretton *NOTTE* * NG7 ....56 B1
Striding Edge Cl *LGEAT* NG10 ....62 C4
Strome Cl *WBRGFD* NG2 ....57 F1
Stuart Cl *ARN* NG5 ....20 C2
Studland Wy *WBRGFD* NG2 ....67 F1
Sturgeon Av *CFTN/RUD* NG11 .....66 C2
Sturton St *NOTTE* NG7 ....30 D5
Styring St *BSTN/STPLFD* NG9 .....55 F5
Sudbury Av *ILK* DE7 ....38 B1
  LGEAT NG10 ....52 B4
Sudbury Ms
  EWD/SEL/PNX NG16 ....13 H1
Suez St *NOTTE* NG7 ....30 C4
Suffolk Av *BSTN/STPLFD* NG9 ....65 H2
  HUCK/RAV NG15 ....10 B2
Sullivan Cl
  MAPPK/POR/STA NG3 ....44 A1
Sullivan St *NOTTE* NG7 ....42 B3
Sumburgh Rd *CFTN/RUD* NG11 ...66 C5
Summerfields Wy *ILK* DE7 ....25 F2
Summerfields Wy South
  ILK DE7 ....25 G3
Summer Leys La *WBRGFD* NG2 ...43 G5
Summer Wy
  COT/KEY/RAD NG12 ....46 D4
Summerwood La
  CFTN/RUD NG11 ....76 A2
Sunbourne Ct *NOTTE* NG7 ....42 C2
Sunbury Gdns *ARN* NG5 ....20 B1
Sunderland Gv
  WOL/BIL/BRX NG8 ....28 C3
Sunlea Crs *BSTN/STPLFD* NG9 ....63 G1
Sunnindale Dr
  COT/KEY/RAD NG12 ....69 E5
Sunningdale Av *HEANOR* DE75 ...12 C2
Sunningdale Dr *ILK* DE7 ....37 E3
Sunninghill Cl *ILK* DE7 ....24 A5
Sunninghill Dr *CFTN/RUD* NG11 ..66 B1
Sunninghill Ri *ARN* NG5 ....20 B1
Sunnydale Rd
  MAPPK/POR/STA NG3 ....44 C2
Sunnyside Rd
  BSTN/STPLFD NG9 ....54 A5
Sunrise Av *ARN* NG5 ....18 C5
Surbiton Ct *ILK* DE7 ....24 A5
Surbiton Sq *WOL/BIL/BRX* NG8 ...29 G2
Surfleet Cl *WOL/BIL/BRX* NG8 ....40 B5
Surgey's La *ARN* NG5 ....20 B1
Susan Cl *HUCK/RAV* NG15 ....5 G3
Susan Dr *BLWL* NG6 ....30 A1
Sussex St *EWD/SEL/PNX* NG16 ....14 B2

Sussex Wy *LGEAT* NG10 ....62 C1
Sutherland Dr *WBRGFD* NG2 ......68 B2
Sutherland Rd
  MAPPK/POR/STA NG3 ....44 C1
Sutton Ct *EWD/SEL/PNX* NG16 ......8 A5
Sutton Gdns *CFTN/RUD* NG11 .....77 F3
Sutton Passeys Crs
  WOL/BIL/BRX NG8 ....41 G5
Swain's Av
  MAPPK/POR/STA NG3 ....44 A1
Swallow Cl *BLWL* NG6 ....30 A2
Swallow Dr *BING/VBLV* NG13 .....49 H4
Swallow Gdns *CARL* NG4 ....32 C4
Swan Meadow *CARL* NG4 ....45 G4
Swansdowne Dr
  CFTN/RUD NG11 ....66 C4
Sweet Leys Rd *WBRGFD* NG2 ......57 E2
Swenson Av *NOTTE* NG7 ....56 B1
Swift Ct *EWD/SEL/PNX* NG16 ....8 A5
Swigert Cl *BLWL* NG6 ....17 E5
Swinburne St
  MAPPK/POR/STA NG3 ....44 A2
Swinburne Wy *ARN* NG5 ....19 F4
Swindon Cl *EWD/SEL/PNX* NG16 ..14 C3
Swiney Wy *BSTN/STPLFD* NG9 ....63 H4
Swingate *EWD/SEL/PNX* NG16 ....15 H5
Swinstead Cl *WOL/BIL/BRX* NG8 ..41 E2
Swithland Dr *WBRGFD* NG2 ....67 H2
Sycamore Cl *BING/VBLV* NG13 ....49 F3
  COT/KEY/RAD NG12 ....61 E1
  HUCK/RAV NG15 ....10 D2
Sycamore Crs *LGEAT* NG10 ....52 B4
Sycamore La *ILK* DE7 ....38 C1
Sycamore Pl
  MAPPK/POR/STA NG3 ....31 F5
Sycamore Ri *BLWL* NG6 ....29 H1
Sycamore Rd
  EWD/SEL/PNX NG16 ....26 C1
  LGEAT NG10 ....72 D4
The Sycamores
  EWD/SEL/PNX NG16 ....13 H2
Sydney Gv *COT/KEY/RAD* NG12 ...46 D5
Sydney Rd *WOL/BIL/BRX* NG8 .....41 G3
Syke Rd *ARN* NG5 ....18 C2
Synge Cl *CFTN/RUD* NG11 ....75 H1
Syon Park Cl *WBRGFD* NG2 ....67 F1

T

Taft Av *LGEAT* NG10 ....52 C5
Talbot Ct *COT/KEY/RAD* NG12 ....46 D5
Talbot Dr *BSTN/STPLFD* NG9 ......53 E1
Talbot St *NOTT* NG1 ....2 C4
Tamarix Cl *CARL* NG4 ....33 H3
Tame Cl *CFTN/RUD* NG11 ....66 D3
Tamworth Gv *CFTN/RUD* NG11 ...66 C4
Tamworth Rd *LGEAT* NG10 ....72 C5
Tangmere Crs
  WOL/BIL/BRX NG8 ....28 D4
Tansy Wy *BING/VBLV* NG13 ....48 B3
Tanwood Rd *BSTN/STPLFD* NG9 ..24 A5
Tarbert Cl *WBRGFD* NG2 ....57 E1
Target St *NOTTE* NG7 ....42 B3
Tatham's La *ILK* DE7 ....25 H3
Tattershall Dr
  BSTN/STPLFD NG9 ....55 G4
  NOTTE NG7 ....2 A5
Tattle Hi *ILK* DE7 ....50 C1
Taunton Rd *WBRGFD* NG2 ....58 A5
Taupo Dr *HUCK/RAV* NG15 ....10 B2
Tavern Av *WOL/BIL/BRX* NG8 .....29 H3
Tavistock Av
  MAPPK/POR/STA NG3 ....31 F4
Tavistock Cl *HUCK/RAV* NG15 .....10 C2
Tavistock Dr
  MAPPK/POR/STA NG3 ....31 F4
Tavistock Rd *WBRGFD* NG2 ....58 A5
Taylor Cl *WBRGFD* NG2 ....44 B4
Taylor Crs *BSTN/STPLFD* NG9 ....53 F3
Taylor La *HEANOR* DE75 ....6 A4
Taylor St *ILK* DE7 ....26 A4
Teak Cl *MAPPK/POR/STA* NG3 ....43 G1
Tealby Cl *BLWL* NG6 ....17 E3
Teal Cl *CARL* NG4 ....46 A1
Teal Whf *WBRGFD* * NG2 ....56 D1
The Teasels *BING/VBLV* NG13 .....48 C4
Technology Rd
  BSTN/STPLFD NG9 ....65 F1
Teesbrook Dr *WOL/BIL/BRX* NG8 ..40 A4
Teesdale Ct *BSTN/STPLFD* NG9 ...63 H2
Teesdale Rd *ARN* NG5 ....30 D3
  LGEAT NG10 ....72 B3
Telford Dr *EWD/SEL/PNX* NG16 ...8 C4
Templar Rd *BSTN/STPLFD* NG9 ...55 G5
Temple Crs *EWD/SEL/PNX* NG16 ..28 C1
Temple Dr *EWD/SEL/PNX* NG16 ...28 D1

Templemen Cl *CFTN/RUD* NG11 ...77 E1
Templeoak Dr
  WOL/BIL/BRX NG8 ....40 B5
Tenbury Crs *WOL/BIL/BRX* NG8 ..29 G4
Tennis Dr *NOTTE* NG7 ....2 A5
Tennis Ms *NOTTE* NG7 ....2 B5
Tennyson Av *CARL* NG4 ....33 G4
Tennyson Ct *HUCK/RAV* NG15 ....10 C1
Tennyson Dr *BSTN/STPLFD* NG9 ..64 C4
Tennyson Rd *ARN* NG5 ....31 H1
Tennyson Sq
  EWD/SEL/PNX NG16 ....26 D1
Tennyson St *ILK* DE7 ....25 H2
  NOTTE NG7 ....2 B2
Tenter Cl *ARN* NG5 ....18 C2
  LGEAT NG10 ....73 E4
Terrace St *WBRGFD* NG2 ....58 A4
Terrian Crs *WBRGFD* NG2 ....58 A4
Terton Rd *ARN* NG5 ....18 C2
Tettenbury Rd *ARN* NG5 ....30 C2
Teversal Av *NOTTE* NG7 ....42 C4
Tevery Cl *BSTN/STPLFD* NG9 .....53 F3
Teviot Rd *ARN* NG5 ....18 C5
Tewkesbury Cl *WBRGFD* NG2 ......58 B5
Tewkesbury Dr *BLWL* NG6 ....30 B1
  EWD/SEL/PNX NG16 ....15 F3
Tewkesbury Rd *LGEAT* NG10 ......73 F5
Thackeray's La *ARN* NG5 ....19 H5
Thames St *BLWL* NG6 ....17 G3
Thane Rd *BSTN/STPLFD* NG9 ......56 A5
Thaxted Cl *WOL/BIL/BRX* NG8 ....40 C2
Theatre Sq *NOTT* * NG1 ....2 E4
Thelda Av *COT/KEY/RAD* NG12 ...82 B1
Thetford Dr *ARN* NG5 ....20 B4
Third Av *BLWL* NG6 ....17 F3
  BSTN/STPLFD NG9 ....55 H5
  CARL NG4 ....32 D5
  CARL NG4 ....33 G4
Thirlbeck *COT/KEY/RAD* NG12 ....71 F5
Thirlmere *WBRGFD* NG2 ....68 D1
Thirlmere Cl *LGEAT* NG10 ....62 C4
  MAPPK/POR/STA NG3 ....44 A1
Thirlmere Rd *LGEAT* NG10 ....62 C4
Thistle Cl *EWD/SEL/PNX* NG16 ...14 C2
Thistledown Rd
  CFTN/RUD NG11 ....76 B2
Thistle Rd *ILK* DE7 ....26 C1
Thistle Green Cl *HEANOR* DE75 ...13 E1
Thomas Av *COT/KEY/RAD* NG12 ..47 H4
Thomas Cl *MAPPK/POR/STA* NG3 ...3 G4
Thompson Cl *BSTN/STPLFD* NG9 ..64 B3
Thompson Gdns *ARN* NG5 ....18 D1
Thompson St
  EWD/SEL/PNX NG16 ....7 E4
Thoresby Av *CARL* NG4 ....33 G4
  WBRGFD NG2 ....44 A5
Thoresby Cl *COT/KEY/RAD* NG12 ..47 F4
Thoresby Ct
  MAPPK/POR/STA NG3 ....31 G5
Thoresby Dl *HUCK/RAV* NG15 ......5 G5
Thoresby Rd *BING/VBLV* NG13 ....48 B3
  BSTN/STPLFD NG9 ....54 B2
  LGEAT NG10 ....72 C2
Thornbury Wy *ARN* NG5 ....18 C3
Thorncliffe Rd
  MAPPK/POR/STA NG3 ....31 F5
Thorndale Rd *BLWL* NG6 ....29 H3
Thorndike Cl *BSTN/STPLFD* NG9 ..65 G2
Thorn Dr *EWD/SEL/PNX* NG16 ....14 C2
Thorner Cl *BLWL* NG6 ....18 B5
Thorney Hi
  MAPPK/POR/STA NG3 ....44 A1
Thorneywood Mt
  MAPPK/POR/STA NG3 ....44 A1
Thorneywood Ri
  MAPPK/POR/STA NG3 ....44 A1
Thorneywood Rd *LGEAT* NG10 ....73 G1
Thorn Gv *HUCK/RAV* NG15 ....11 G3
Thornhill Cl *BSTN/STPLFD* NG9 ...54 A1
Thornley St *NOTTE* NG7 ....42 B1
Thornthwaite Cl *WBRGFD* NG2 ...58 D5
Thornton Av *ARN* NG5 ....19 G1
Thorntons Cl
  COT/KEY/RAD NG12 ....71 F4
Thorntree Cl
  BWSH/BRSTN DE72 ....62 A5
Thorn Tree Gdns
  EWD/SEL/PNX NG16 ....8 A3
Thorold Cl *CFTN/RUD* NG11 ....66 B4
Thoroton Rd *WBRGFD* NG2 ....58 A2
Thoroton St *NOTTE* NG7 ....2 A3
Thorpe Cl *ARN* NG5 ....18 D2
  BSTN/STPLFD NG9 ....52 D4
Thorpe Crs
  MAPPK/POR/STA NG3 ....32 C3
Thorpe Hill Dr *HEANOR* DE75 .....12 B3
Thorpe Leys *LGEAT* NG10 ....73 E4
Thorpe Rd *EWD/SEL/PNX* NG16 ....8 B1

Thorpe's Rd *HEANOR* DE75...............12 A1
Thorpe St *ILK* DE7.........................25 H2
Three Tunes Rd
  EWD/SEL/PNX NG16..................8 B5
Threlkeld Cl *WBRGFD* NG2..............58 D5
Thrumpton Av *LGEAT* NG10.............73 G2
Thrumpton Dr *WBRGFD* NG2.............57 E2
Thurgarton Av *WBRGFD* NG2............44 A4
Thurgarton St *WBRGFD* NG2............44 A4
Thurland St *NOTT* NG1.....................3 F4
Thurlby La *COT/KEY/RAD* NG12......83 E3
Thurlestone Dr
  MAPPK/POR/STA NG3................20 D4
Thurloe Ct *CFTN/RUD* NG11.............67 F3
Thurman Dr
  COT/KEY/RAD NG12...................71 E3
Thurman St *ILK* DE7........................38 B2
  NOTT NG7.................................42 C2
Thursby Rd *CFTN/RUD* NG11............66 B3
Thymus Wk *CFTN/RUD* NG11............65 H5
Thyra Gv *BSTN/STPLFD* NG9............55 F5
  MAPPK/POR/STA NG3................31 G4
Tidworth Cl *WOL/BIL/BRX* NG8..........41 F2
Tilberthwaite Cl *WBRGFD* NG2...........58 D5
Tilbury Ri *WOL/BIL/BRX* NG8.............29 C3
Tilford Gdns *BSTN/STPLFD* NG9........53 F5
Tilstock Ct *EWD/SEL/PNX* NG16.........15 H2
Tilton Gv *ILK* DE7...........................37 F3
Tinkersway *WBRGFD* NG2.................56 D1
Tinsley Rd *EWD/SEL/PNX* NG16.........13 G1
Tintagel Gn *CFTN/RUD* NG11.............66 B5
Tintern Dr *WOL/BIL/BRX* NG8.............30 A3
Tippett Ct *MAPPK/POR/STA* NG3.......44 A4
Tip Tree Cl *EWD/SEL/PNX* NG16.........15 G3
Tiree Ct *BSTN/STPLFD* NG9................53 E1
Tishbite St *BLWL* NG6.......................17 G3
Tissington Rd *NOTT* NG7...................30 B2
Titchfield St *HUCK/RAV* NG15.............5 G5
Tithby Dr *ARN* NG5..........................31 G1
Tithby Rd *BING/VBLV* NG13...............48 D5
Tiverton Cl *HUCK/RAV* NG15.............10 C2
  WOL/BIL/BRX NG8......................29 C3
Tobias Cl *ARN* NG5..........................18 C2
Todd Cl *CFTN/RUD* NG11...................75 H1
Toft Cl *COT/KEY/RAD* NG12...............70 D4
Toft Rd *BSTN/STPLFD* NG9................63 H3
Tollerton Gn *BLWL* NG6.....................18 A5
Tollerton La *COT/KEY/RAD* NG12......69 G2
  COT/KEY/RAD NG12...................79 E1
Tollerton Pk
  COT/KEY/RAD * NG12..................69 F1
Tollerton Rd
  COT/KEY/RAD NG12....................59 E5
Tollhouse Hl *NOTT* NG1.....................2 D4
Tonbridge Mt
  WOL/BIL/BRX NG8......................54 C1
Tonnelier Rd *NOTT* NG7....................56 B2
Top Rd *CFTN/RUD* NG11....................77 F3
Top Valley Dr *ARN* NG5.....................18 B2
Top Valley Wy *ARN* NG5....................18 B3
Torbay Crs *ARN* NG5.........................19 E5
Torkard Dr *ARN* NG5.........................18 C2
Torvill Dr *WOL/BIL/BRX* NG8..............40 D3
Toston Dr *WOL/BIL/BRX* NG8.............41 H5
Totland Dr *BLWL* NG6.......................30 A3
Totland Rd *BSTN/STPLFD* NG9...........54 B1
Totley Cl *BLWL* NG6..........................11 H5
Totnes Cl *HUCK/RAV* NG15...............10 C1
Totnes Rd *MAPPK/POR/STA* NG3......44 C3
Toton Cl *BLWL* NG6...........................18 A5
Toton La *BSTN/STPLFD* NG9..............53 F5
Tottle Gdns *NOTT* NG7......................56 B2
Tottle Rd *NOTT* NG7.........................56 C5
Tower Crs *EWD/SEL/PNX* NG16..........27 H1
Towe's Mt *CARL* NG4.........................45 F1
Towle St *LGEAT* NG10.......................72 B5
Towlsons Cft *BLWL* NG6....................30 A2
Townside Cl *LGEAT* NG10..................72 C5
Town St *BSTN/STPLFD* NG9...............54 A3
  LGEAT NG10.............................52 C5
Town Vw *EWD/SEL/PNX* NG16...........15 G4
Towson Av *EWD/SEL/PNX* NG16..........7 F5
Trafalgar Rd *BSTN/STPLFD* NG9.........65 F2
  LGEAT NG10.............................73 F2
Trafalgar Sq *LGEAT* NG10..................73 F2
Trafalgar Ter *LGEAT* NG10.................73 F2
Traffic St *WBRGFD* NG2.....................43 F5
Trafford Gdns
  WOL/BIL/BRX NG8......................42 A1
Tranby Gdns *WOL/BIL/BRX* NG8.........41 E4
Travers Rd *LGEAT* NG10....................52 B5
Treegarth Sq *ARN* NG5.....................19 E1
Tree View Cl *ARN* NG5......................19 F1
Trefan Gdns *ARN* NG5.......................18 D3
Trefoil Cl *BING/VBLV* NG13................48 B4
Trelawn Cl *ARN* NG5.........................31 G3
Tremayne Rd *WOL/BIL/BRX* NG8........40 B2
Trenchham Gdns *CALV/BJ* NG14.........34 C2

Trent Bvd *WBRGFD* NG2....................58 B2
Trent Br *WBRGFD* NG2......................57 H2
Trent Crs *BSTN/STPLFD* NG9..............64 D3
Trentdale Rd *CARL* NG4.....................45 E2
Trent Dr *HUCK/RAV* NG15.................10 C4
Trent Gdns *CALV/BJ* NG14.................35 E1
Trentham Dr *WOL/BIL/BRX* NG8.........41 H1
Trentham Gdns
  WOL/BIL/BRX NG8......................41 H1
Trent La *CALV/BJ* NG14....................35 E1
  LGEAT NG10.............................73 G4
  WBRGFD NG2............................44 A5
Trenton Cl *BSTN/STPLFD* NG9............53 H2
Trenton Dr *LGEAT* NG10....................73 H1
Trent Rd *BSTN/STPLFD* NG9...............65 G2
  ILK DE7...................................37 G4
  WBRGFD NG2............................44 A4
Trentside *WBRGFD* NG2.....................57 H3
Trentside North *WBRGFD* NG2............57 H2
Trent St *LGEAT* NG10........................73 F1
  NOTT NG1.................................3 G7
Trent Vale Rd *BSTN/STPLFD* NG9........65 F2
Trent Valley Wy
  BSTN/STPLFD NG9.....................74 B2
  COT/KEY/RAD NG12....................35 F5
  WBRGFD NG2............................58 D1
Trentview Ct *WBRGFD* * NG2..............58 A1
Trent View Gdns
  COT/KEY/RAD NG12....................47 F3
Tressall Cl *ILK* DE7............................26 B5
Trevelyan Rd *WBRGFD* NG2................58 A3
Trevone Av *BSTN/STPLFD* NG9...........53 F5
Trevor Rd *BSTN/STPLFD* NG9.............65 E1
  WBRGFD NG2............................58 B5
Trevose Gdns *ARN* NG5....................31 G2
Treyford Ct *CFTN/RUD* NG11.............66 D2
The Triangle *ILK* DE7.........................38 B2
Tricornia Dr *BLWL* NG6.....................29 G1
Tring V *ARN* NG5..............................30 D1
The Trinity *NOTTE* * NG7...................56 B1
Trinity Av *BSTN/STPLFD* NG9.............42 B5
Trinity Cl *ILK* DE7.............................25 H2
Trinity Crs *CARL* NG4........................22 B3
Trinity Sq *NOTT* NG1..........................2 E4
Trinity Wk *NOTT* NG1.........................2 E4
Trinstead Wy *ARN* NG5.....................19 F3
Triumph Rd *NOTTE* NG7....................42 A4
Trivett Sq *NOTT* NG1..........................3 H6
Troon Cl *EWD/SEL/PNX* NG16...........15 F3
Trough La *EWD/SEL/PNX* NG16..........15 G2
Trough Rd *EWD/SEL/PNX* NG16..........15 H3
Troutbeck *COT/KEY/RAD* NG12.........71 F3
Troutbeck Crs
  BSTN/STPLFD NG9.....................54 B3
Trowell Av *ILK* DE7...........................38 B3
  WOL/BIL/BRX NG8......................40 A3
Trowell Gv *BSTN/STPLFD* NG9............39 E5
  LGEAT NG10.............................62 C5
Trowell Park Dr
  BSTN/STPLFD NG9.....................53 E1
Trowell Rd *BSTN/STPLFD* NG9............53 E1
  WOL/BIL/BRX NG8......................40 B3
Trueman Gdns *ARN* NG5...................20 C4
Trueman St *ILK* DE7..........................26 A1
Truman Dr *HUCK/RAV* NG15..............11 F1
Truman's Rd *WBRGFD* NG2................57 G2
Truman St *EWD/SEL/PNX* NG16..........15 E3
  ILK DE7...................................26 B4
Truro Crs *NOTTE* NG7.......................42 B1
Tudor Cl *CARL* NG4...........................45 F3
  LGEAT NG10.............................63 F5
Tudor Ct *HUCK/RAV* NG15.................10 B2
Tudor Falls *HEANOR* DE75..................6 B4
Tudor Gv *NOTT* NG1...........................2 D1
Tudor Pl *ILK* DE7..............................37 F3
Tudor Rd *WBRGFD* NG2....................58 A4
Tudor Sq *WBRGFD* NG2....................58 A4
Tudwal Cl *ARN* NG5..........................18 D3
Tulip Av *MAPPK/POR/STA* NG3..........43 C1
Tulip Rd *EWD/SEL/PNX* NG16.............14 C5
Tunnel Rd *NOTTE* NG7........................2 B5
Tunstall Crs *WOL/BIL/BRX* NG8...........29 F4
Tunstall Dr *BLWL* NG6.......................30 C2
Tunstall Rd *ARN* NG5........................32 A1
Turnberry Cl *BSTN/STPLFD* NG9.........54 B5
  ILK DE7...................................25 F3
Turnberry Ct
  COT/KEY/RAD NG12....................68 D3
Turnberry Rd *BLWL* NG6....................18 A4
Turner Av *EWD/SEL/PNX* NG16............6 D4
Turner Cl *BSTN/STPLFD* NG9..............53 F5
Turner Dr *EWD/SEL/PNX* NG16...........14 C3
Turner Rd *LGEAT* NG10.....................72 D5
Turner St *HUCK/RAV* NG15..................5 F5
Turney St *WBRGFD* NG2.....................57 G2
Turnpike La *BSTN/STPLFD* NG9...........55 F3
Turnstone Whf *WBRGFD* NG2.............56 C1

Turpin Av *CARL* NG4.........................33 E2
Turton Cl *EWD/SEL/PNX* NG16............6 D4
Tuxford Wk
  MAPPK/POR/STA NG3................44 A2
Twells Cl *MAPPK/POR/STA* NG3.........44 A1
Twelve Houses *ILK* * DE7...................37 H5
The Twitchell *BSTN/STPLFD* NG9........64 D2
Twycross Rd *ARN* NG5......................19 E3
Twyford Cl *ILK* DE7...........................24 A5
Twyford Gdns *CFTN/RUD* NG11..........66 B2
Twyford Rd *LGEAT* NG10...................72 A5
Tyburn Cl *ARN* NG5..........................18 D1
Tynedale Cl *LGEAT* NG10..................72 B3
  WOL/BIL/BRX NG8......................30 A5
Tyne Gdns *HUCK/RAV* NG15..............10 C4

U

Ulldale Ct *BSTN/STPLFD* NG9.............64 A2
Ullscarf Cl *WBRGFD* NG2...................68 D1
Ullswater Cl *CARL* NG4.....................33 G3
  WBRGFD NG2............................68 D1
Ullswater Crs *BSTN/STPLFD* NG9........54 B2
Ullswater Dr *HUCK/RAV* NG15..............5 E5
Union Cl *HUCK/RAV* NG15...................5 F2
Union Rd *ILK* DE7.............................37 H1
  MAPPK/POR/STA NG3..................3 C1
Union St *BING/VBLV* NG13.................48 D3
  BSTN/STPLFD NG9.....................55 E5
  LGEAT NG10.............................73 F1
Unity Crs *MAPPK/POR/STA* NG3.........32 D3
University Bvd
  BSTN/STPLFD NG9.....................55 G3
Upminster Dr *ARN* NG5....................20 A1
  EWD/SEL/PNX NG16...................28 C1
Upper Barn Cl *HEANOR* DE75.............6 C5
Upper Canaan *CFTN/RUD* NG11.........77 G1
Upper College St *NOTT* NG1................2 C4
Upper Dunstead Rd
  EWD/SEL/PNX NG16....................7 E3
Upper Eldon St *WBRGFD* NG2.............3 K5
Upper Nelson St *HEANOR* DE75..........6 A5
Upper Orchard St
  BSTN/STPLFD NG9.....................53 F4
Upper Parliament St *NOTT* NG1...........2 E4
Upper Wellington St
  LGEAT NG10.............................62 D5
Uppingham Crs *WBRGFD* NG2............67 G1
Uppingham Gdns *WBRGFD* NG2.........57 C1
Upton Cl *HEANOR* DE75....................12 D1
Upton Dr *ARN* NG5...........................19 G5
Utile Gdns *BLWL* NG6.......................17 F3

V

The Vale *ILK* DE7.............................25 H2
Vale Cl *EWD/SEL/PNX* NG16...............8 C5
Vale Crs North
  WOL/BIL/BRX NG8......................42 A2
Vale Crs South
  WOL/BIL/BRX NG8......................42 A2
Vale Gdns *CARL* NG4........................45 E3
Valerian Wy *BING/VBLV* NG13............48 B4
Vale Rd *CARL* NG4............................45 F2
Valeside Gdns *CARL* NG4...................45 F5
Valetta Rd *ARN* NG5.........................20 C3
Valley Dr *EWD/SEL/PNX* NG16...........14 C1
Valley Gdns *WBRGFD* NG2.................68 C1
Valley Rd *ARN* NG5...........................31 F1
  BSTN/STPLFD NG9.....................63 H1
  CARL NG4.................................32 D4
  COT/KEY/RAD NG12....................47 F3
  COT/KEY/RAD NG12....................68 B1
  EWD/SEL/PNX NG16...................15 E3
  ILK DE7...................................37 H3
Valley Vw *ILK* DE7............................37 H3
Valmont Rd *ARN* NG5........................30 D2
  BSTN/STPLFD NG9.....................53 H4
Vancouver Av
  COT/KEY/RAD NG12....................46 D5
Vanguard Rd *LGEAT* NG10.................73 D4
Varden Av *BSTN/STPLFD* NG9............55 F2
Varney Rd *CFTN/RUD* NG11...............66 C3
Vaughan Av *HUCK/RAV* NG15..............5 H3
Vaughan Rd *BSTN/STPLFD* NG9..........63 H2
Vedonis Pk *HUCK/RAV* NG15.............11 F2
Ventnor Ri *ARN* NG5.........................30 C1
Venus Cl *BLWL* NG6..........................18 B5
Verbena Cl
  MAPPK/POR/STA NG3................43 C1
Verder Gv *ARN* NG5..........................18 B2
Vere St *BLWL* NG6............................17 G3
Verne Cl *CARL* NG4..........................44 D1
Vernon Av *BLWL* NG6........................30 B2

BSTN/STPLFD NG9.....................55 E5
CARL NG4.................................33 G5
CFTN/RUD NG11........................57 E3
Vernon Ct *EWD/SEL/PNX* NG16.........29 E2
Vernon Dr *EWD/SEL/PNX* NG16..........29 E2
Vernon Park Dr *BLWL* NG6.................30 B2
Vernon Pl *BLWL* * NG6.......................30 A1
Vernon Rd *BLWL* NG6........................30 A1
Vernon St *ILK* DE7............................26 A1
  NOTT NG1.................................2 C4
Verona Av *CARL* NG4........................45 G2
Veronica Dr *CARL* NG4......................33 E4
  EWD/SEL/PNX NG16...................14 D2
Vicarage Av *ILK* DE7.........................25 G1
Vicarage Cl *ARN* NG5........................30 C2
  MAPPK/POR/STA NG3..................2 E1
Vicarage Dr *CALV/BJ* NG14................34 D1
Vicarage Gdns *HEANOR* DE75...........12 C1
Vicarage Gn
  COT/KEY/RAD NG12....................68 C3
Vicarage La *CFTN/RUD* NG11.............77 E2
  COT/KEY/RAD NG12....................47 E5
Vicarage St *BSTN/STPLFD* NG9...........54 D5
  ILK DE7...................................25 G1
Vickers St *MAPPK/POR/STA* NG3........31 G5
The Victor *NOTTE* * NG7....................56 B1
Victor Crs *LGEAT* NG10.....................62 D2
Victoria Av *WBRGFD* NG2..................44 A4
Victoria Cl *ARN* NG5.........................20 A1
Victoria Ct *ILK* * DE7.........................25 H4
Victoria Crs *ARN* NG5.......................31 G3
Victoria Emb *WBRGFD* NG2...............57 F2
Victoria Park Wy *CARL* NG4...............46 A2
Victoria Rd *ARN* NG5........................31 E2
  BING/VBLV NG13.......................49 F2
  CARL NG4.................................45 H2
  LGEAT NG10.............................62 C1
  WBRGFD NG2............................57 H4
Victoria St *BSTN/STPLFD* NG9............53 E4
  CARL NG4.................................33 G4
  COT/KEY/RAD NG12....................47 E5
  EWD/SEL/PNX NG16....................7 G5
  EWD/SEL/PNX NG16....................8 A4
  EWD/SEL/PNX NG16...................15 H4
  HUCK/RAV NG15..........................5 E4
  ILK DE7...................................26 A2
  LGEAT NG10.............................72 C4
  NOTT NG1.................................3 F5
Victoria Ter *WBRGFD* * NG2................3 K5
Victory Cl *LGEAT* NG10.....................73 E4
Victory Rd *BSTN/STPLFD* NG9............65 F2
The Village *ILK* DE7..........................36 B1
  ILK DE7...................................50 C1
Village Cl *COT/KEY/RAD* NG12...........68 C3
Village Rd *CFTN/RUD* NG11...............65 H4
Village St *COT/KEY/RAD* NG12...........68 B3
Villa Rd *COT/KEY/RAD* NG12.............79 G5
  MAPPK/POR/STA NG3................43 F1
Villa St *BSTN/STPLFD* NG9.................55 E4
Villiers Rd *ARN* NG5.........................31 G1
  WBRGFD NG2............................58 B5
Vincent Av *BSTN/STPLFD* NG9............65 E1
  ILK DE7...................................26 A5
Vincent Gdns *NOTTE* * NG7...............42 B1
Vine Crs *LGEAT* NG10.......................52 C5
Vine Farm Cl
  COT/KEY/RAD NG12....................70 D3
  ILK DE7...................................37 G2
Vines Cross *WOL/BIL/BRX* NG8...........54 C1
Vine Ter *HUCK/RAV* NG15...................5 G5
Violet Av *EWD/SEL/PNX* NG16............14 C1
Violet Cl *BLWL* NG6..........................30 A2
Violet Rd *CARL* NG4..........................33 E4
  WBRGFD NG2............................58 B3
Vivian Av *NOTTE* NG7........................31 E5
Vulcan Cl *BLWL* NG6.........................30 B1
Vyse Dr *LGEAT* NG10........................72 D3

W

Waddington Dr *WBRGFD* NG2............67 G2
Wade Av *ILK* DE7.............................38 B1
Wades Av *NOTTE* NG7......................42 B1
Wadham Rd *ARN* NG5.......................19 H5
Wadhurst Gdns
  MAPPK/POR/STA NG3..................3 G1
Wadhurst Gv *WOL/BIL/BRX* NG8........54 C1
Wadsworth Rd
  BSTN/STPLFD NG9.....................53 G3
Wainfleet Cl *ILK* DE7.........................25 F2
Waingrove *CFTN/RUD* NG11...............66 D3
Wakefield Av
  COT/KEY/RAD NG12....................47 F4
Wakefield Cft *ILK* DE7.......................25 F2
Walbrook Cl *WOL/BIL/BRX* NG8..........29 F2
Walcote Dr *WBRGFD* NG2..................67 G5

Waldeck Rd *ARN* NG5 ....31 E4
Waldemar Gv
  BSTN/STPLFD NG9 ....55 F5
Waldron Cl *WBRGFD* NG2 ....57 G1
Walesby Crs *WOL/BIL/BRX* NG8.....41 H2
Walgrave Wk *ARN* NG5 ....18 D3
Walker Cl *ILK* DE7.............................38 A4
Walker Gv *BSTN/STPLFD* NG9 ......53 F5
Walkers Cl *BING/VBLV* NG13 ....48 D3
Walker St *EWD/SEL/PNX* NG16 ....8 B5
  WBRGFD NG2...................................3 J4
Walker's Yd *COT/KEY/RAD* NG12....47 E5
Walk Mill Dr *HUCK/RAV* NG15.........5 G3
Wallace Av *CARL* NG4 ....45 G1
Wallace Gdns *BSTN/STPLFD* NG9...63 G5
Wallan Cl *NOTTE* NG7......................42 B2
Wallet St *CARL* NG4 ....45 H1
  WBRGFD NG2...................................57 G1
Wallett Av *BSTN/STPLFD* NG9 ....55 E3
Wallett St *WBRGFD* NG2..................57 G1
Wallis St *BLWL* NG6.........................30 B1
Walnut Cl *ILK* DE7............................38 B1
Walnut Dr *BSTN/STPLFD* NG9 ....54 A3
Walnut Gv *COT/KEY/RAD* NG12.....47 E5
Walnut Tree Gdns *BLWL* NG6..........17 E3
Walsham Cl *BSTN/STPLFD* NG9 .....64 A4
Walsingham Rd *ARN* NG5.................20 B5
Walters Av *EWD/SEL/PNX* NG16 ......7 H1
Walter St *NOTTE* NG7........................2 B2
Waltham Cl *WBRGFD* NG2................58 C5
Walton Av
  MAPPK/POR/STA NG3................44 A3
Walton Ct *ILK* DE7............................24 A5
Walton Crs *CARL* NG4 ....45 F1
Walton Dr *COT/KEY/RAD* NG12......82 C1
Walton St *LGEAT* NG10.....................63 E5
Wansbeck Cl *NOTTE* NG7...................2 A3
Wanstead Wy *ARN* NG5....................18 B1
Warburton Ct *HUCK/RAV* NG15 ....11 G1
Ward Av *HUCK/RAV* NG15................5 G3
  MAPPK/POR/STA NG3................32 C2
Wardle Gv *ARN* NG5.........................20 B2
Wardlow Rd *ILK* DE7.........................25 G2
Ward St *NOTTE* NG7..........................30 B5
Wareham Cl *WBRGFD* NG2...............67 F1
  WOL/BIL/BRX NG8......................29 F2
Warkton Cl *BSTN/STPLFD* NG9.......64 B1
The Warren *COT/KEY/RAD* NG12....71 E4
Warren Av *ARN* NG5.........................30 D3
  BSTN/STPLFD NG9......................53 E4
Warren Av Extension
  BSTN/STPLFD NG9......................53 E4
Warren Ct *BSTN/STPLFD* NG9 ....53 E4
Warrender Cl *BSTN/STPLFD* NG9....54 B2
Warrener Gv *ARN* NG5.....................18 B2
Warren Rd *HUCK/RAV* NG15............10 C2
Warrington Rd *BLWL* NG6................17 H3
Warser Ga *NOTT* NG1..........................3 G5
Warton Av
  MAPPK/POR/STA NG3................32 A5
Warwick Av *ARN* NG5.......................19 H5
  BSTN/STPLFD NG9......................55 E3
Warwick Dr *ILK* DE7.........................25 F2
Warwick Gdns
  COT/KEY/RAD NG12...................71 E5
Warwick Rd *LGEAT* NG10.................73 G2
  MAPPK/POR/STA NG3................31 G3
Warwick St *NOTTE* NG7....................56 B1
Wasdale Cl *WBRGFD* NG2.................68 D1
Washdyke La *HUCK/RAV* NG15........4 D4
Washington Dr
  BSTN/STPLFD NG9......................53 G2
Wasnidge Cl
  MAPPK/POR/STA NG3....................3 H3
Wasnidge Wk
  MAPPK/POR/STA NG3....................3 H2
Watcombe Circ *ARN* NG5.................31 E3
Watcombe Rd *ARN* NG5....................31 F4
Watendlath Cl *WBRGFD* NG2...........68 D1
Waterdown Rd *CFTN/RUD* NG11.....66 A5
Waterford St *BLWL* NG6...................30 B2
Waterhouse La *CARL* NG4.................33 H3
Water La *COT/KEY/RAD* NG12.........60 D1
Waterloo Crs *NOTTE* NG7...................2 A1
Waterloo La *BSTN/STPLFD* NG9......39 F2
Waterloo Prom *NOTTE* NG7...............2 A2
Waterloo Rd *BSTN/STPLFD* NG9 .....65 F1
  HUCK/RAV NG15...........................5 F2
  NOTTE NG7....................................2 A1
The Watermeadows
  LGEAT NG10................................72 C1
Water Orton Cl
  BSTN/STPLFD NG9......................63 F3
Waterside Cl *LGEAT* NG10...............62 C3
  WBRGFD NG2..............................58 D5
Waterside Gdns *NOTTE * NG7...........56 B2
The Waterway *LGEAT* NG10.............62 D2

Waterway St *WBRGFD* NG2 ....57 G1
Waterway St West
  WBRGFD NG2..............................57 F1
Watford Rd *WOL/BIL/BRX* NG8.......29 G3
Watkinson St *HEANOR* DE75 ....6 A5
Watkin St *MAPPK/POR/STA* NG3 ......3 F2
Watnall Rd *EWD/SEL/PNX* NG16 .....16 B4
  HUCK/RAV NG15.........................10 D4
Watson Av *HEANOR* DE75..................6 C5
  MAPPK/POR/STA NG3................44 C2
Watson Rd *ILK* DE7...........................25 F3
Waveney Cl *ARN* NG5.......................20 B4
Waverley Av *BSTN/STPLFD* NG9 .....55 F5
  CARL NG4.....................................33 H4
Waverley St *LGEAT* NG10................73 H1
  NOTTE NG7....................................2 B1
Waverley Ter *NOTT* NG1.....................2 D3
Wayne Cl *CFTN/RUD * NG11............66 B5
Weardale Rd *ARN* NG5.....................30 D3
Weaverthorpe Rd *ARN* NG5.............20 B5
Webb Rd *WOL/BIL/BRX* NG8...........41 G2
Webster Av *EWD/SEL/PNX* NG16.....14 A1
Weedon Cl
  MAPPK/POR/STA NG3................44 B2
Weekday Cross *NOTT* NG1..................3 F6
Weightman Dr
  EWD/SEL/PNX NG16...................14 C3
Welbeck Av *CARL* NG4.....................33 E3
  ILK DE7..37 G3
Welbeck Cl
  MAPPK/POR/STA NG3....................3 F1
Welbeck Gdns
  BSTN/STPLFD NG9......................63 G3
Welbeck Gv *BING/VBLV* NG13.........48 B3
Welbeck Rd *COT/KEY/RAD* NG12....47 F4
  LGEAT NG10................................62 C3
  WBRGFD NG2..............................57 H3
Welbeck Wk
  MAPPK/POR/STA NG3....................2 E1
Welby Av *NOTTE* NG7......................42 C4
Welch Av *BSTN/STPLFD* NG9 ....53 F3
Weldbank Cl
  BSTN/STPLFD NG9......................64 A1
Welham Crs *ARN* NG5.......................20 B3
Welland Ct
  MAPPK/POR/STA NG3................44 A2
Wellesley Crs *WOL/BIL/BRX* NG8...28 C3
Wellin Cl *COT/KEY/RAD* NG12........68 C3
Wellington Circ *NOTT* NG1.................2 C5
Wellington Crs *WBRGFD* NG2..........58 A4
Wellington Pl
  EWD/SEL/PNX NG16.....................8 A5
Wellington Rd *CALV/BJ* NG14.........23 F5
Wellington Sq *NOTTE* NG7................2 A4
Wellington St
  BSTN/STPLFD NG9......................52 D5
  EWD/SEL/PNX NG16.....................8 A4
  HEANOR DE75..............................6 A5
  LGEAT NG10................................62 D4
  MAPPK/POR/STA NG3....................3 F2
Wellington Ter *NOTTE * NG7...............2 A4
Wellington Vls *NOTTE* NG7................2 A4
Wellin La *COT/KEY/RAD* NG12........68 C3
The Wells Rd
  MAPPK/POR/STA NG3................32 A3
Wellspring Dl *BSTN/STPLFD* NG9...63 F1
Welstead Av *WOL/BIL/BRX* NG8......29 G3
Welton Gdns *BLWL* NG6...................17 F2
Welwyn Rd *WOL/BIL/BRX* NG8.......40 D3
Wembley Gdns
  BSTN/STPLFD NG9......................54 A1
Wembley Rd *ARN* NG5......................20 C5
Wemyss Gdns
  WOL/BIL/BRX NG8......................56 A1
Wendling Gdns *ARN* NG5.................19 E2
Wendover Dr *WOL/BIL/BRX* NG8....29 G3
Wenlock Cl *EWD/SEL/PNX* NG16.....14 D2
Wensleydale Cl
  WOL/BIL/BRX NG8......................30 A4
Wensleydale Rd *LGEAT* NG10..........72 C3
Wensley Rd *ARN* NG5.......................19 H5
Wensor Av *BSTN/STPLFD* NG9........55 E3
Wentworth Ct
  EWD/SEL/PNX NG16...................15 F4
Wentworth Cft *HEANOR* DE75...........6 D5
Wentworth Rd *ARN* NG5...................31 E3
  BSTN/STPLFD NG9......................54 B5
Wentworth St *ILK* DE7......................26 B3
Wentworth Wy
  COT/KEY/RAD NG12...................68 C3
Wesleyan Chapel Wk
  BSTN/STPLFD NG9......................53 E4
Wesley Pl *BSTN/STPLFD* NG9 ....53 F3
Wesley St *ARN* NG5..........................31 E4
  EWD/SEL/PNX NG16.....................7 F4
  ILK DE7..25 H1
Wesley Wy *CFTN/RUD* NG11............77 G3
Wessex Dr *EWD/SEL/PNX* NG16.....14 B2

West Av *BSTN/STPLFD* NG9 ....53 F3
  LGEAT NG10................................52 B5
  MAPPK/POR/STA NG3................57 H4
Westbury Cl *BSTN/STPLFD* NG9......64 B2
Westbury Rd *ARN* NG5.....................30 C5
Westby La *EWD/SEL/PNX* NG16.......27 E2
Westcliffe Av *CARL* NG4..................33 E2
  MAPPK/POR/STA NG3................47 F4
Westcliffe Ct *NOTTE * NG7................42 D5
West Cl *COT/KEY/RAD* NG12...........82 B2
West Crs *BSTN/STPLFD* NG9............65 G2
Westcross Av *BSTN/STPLFD* NG9....53 F3
Westdale Cl *LGEAT* NG10................72 B4
Westdale Cl *CARL* NG4.....................33 E3
Westdale Crs *CARL* NG4...................33 F4
Westdale La East *CARL* NG4.............32 D3
Westdale La West
  MAPPK/POR/STA NG3................33 D2
West Dr *NOTTE* NG7.........................55 G4
West End *BSTN/STPLFD* NG9 ....65 E1
West End Ar *NOTT* NG1......................2 D5
West End Crs *ILK* DE7.......................25 C5
West End Dr *ILK* DE7........................25 C5
West End *BSTN/STPLFD* NG9...........52 D5
Westerfield Wy
  CFTN/RUD NG11.........................66 D2
Westerham Cl
  WOL/BIL/BRX NG8......................40 C1
Westerham Rd *CFTN/RUD* NG11......77 E3
Westerhope Cl
  COT/KEY/RAD NG12...................68 D2
Westerlands *BSTN/STPLFD* NG9 .....63 G1
Western Av *BING/VBLV* NG13..........48 C2
Western Bvd *WOL/BIL/BRX* NG8....30 A5
Western Dr *HEANOR* DE75................12 C2
Western Flds *CFTN/RUD* NG11.........77 E3
Western Gdns
  WOL/BIL/BRX NG8......................30 A5
Western St *NOTT* NG1........................3 G4
Western Ter *NOTTE* NG7...................2 A5
Westfield Av *HEANOR* DE75.............12 C2
Westfield Cl *ILK* DE7........................37 F2
Westfield Dr *ILK* DE7........................25 G3
West Furlong
  COT/KEY/RAD NG12...................71 F5
West Ga *LGEAT* NG10......................73 F2
Westgate St
  MAPPK/POR/STA NG3....................3 J1
Westhay Ct *WOL/BIL/BRX* NG8.......41 H3
Westholme Gdns
  WOL/BIL/BRX NG8......................41 H2
Westhorpe Dr *LGEAT* NG10..............72 D1
Westland Av *HUCK/RAV* NG15.........10 C3
Westleigh Rd *WOL/BIL/BRX* NG8....28 D3
Westminster Av *LGEAT* NG10...........62 D1
Westminster Cl
  MAPPK/POR/STA NG3................43 H1
West Moor *WBRGFD* NG2.................45 E3
Weston Av *NOTTE* NG7......................2 A1
Weston Cl *ARN* NG5.........................31 H1
Weston Crs *LGEAT* NG10..................72 A5
Weston St *HEANOR* DE75.................12 D2
West Pk *WBRGFD* NG2.....................52 B4
Westray Cl *BSTN/STPLFD* NG9........40 A5
West St *ARN* NG5.............................19 H3
  COT/KEY/RAD NG12...................35 H4
  EWD/SEL/PNX NG16.....................7 E4
  HEANOR DE75..............................6 A5
  HUCK/RAV NG15.........................37 H1
  ILK DE7..37 H1
  WBRGFD NG2...............................3 J5
West Ter *HUCK/RAV* NG15................5 F5
  ILK DE7..25 F4
West Vw *WBRGFD* NG2....................57 G5
Westview Ct *CARL* NG4....................33 G5
West View Rd *CARL* NG4..................33 G5
Westville Dr *HUCK/RAV* NG15.........10 D3
Westville Gdns
  MAPPK/POR/STA NG3................43 G1
West Wk *WBRGFD* NG2......................3 G1
Westway *COT/KEY/RAD* NG12.........71 E4
Westwick Rd *WOL/BIL/BRX* NG8.....40 B2
Westwick St *ILK* DE7........................38 B2
Westwood Rd *WBRGFD* NG2............44 A4
Wetherby Cl
  EWD/SEL/PNX NG16...................15 F3
  WOL/BIL/BRX NG8......................29 G5
Wetherlam Cl *WBRGFD* NG2............57 F1
Weybridge Cl *ILK* DE7......................24 A5
Wharfdale *WOL/BIL/BRX* NG8.........40 A5
Wharfedale Rd *LGEAT* NG10............72 C3
Wharf La *COT/KEY/RAD* NG12.........46 D5
Wharf Rd *NOTTE* NG7......................56 C3
Wharncliffe Rd *ILK* DE7...................25 H5
Wheatacre Rd *CFTN/RUD* NG11......66 C4
Wheat Cl *WOL/BIL/BRX* NG8...........40 C3

Wheatcroft Vw
  CFTN/RUD NG11.........................67 F3
Wheatfields Rd
  MAPPK/POR/STA NG3................44 B1
Wheatgrass Rd
  BSTN/STPLFD NG9......................64 A1
Wheatley Cl *CFTN/RUD* NG11.........77 F4
Wheatley Dr *CARL* NG4....................44 D1
Wheatley Gv *BSTN/STPLFD* NG9.....65 E2
Wheatsheaf Cl *CALV/BJ* NG14........35 E1
Wheeldale Cl *WOL/BIL/BRX* NG8....40 A4
Wheeler Av
  EWD/SEL/PNX NG16...................14 C1
Wheeler Ga *NOTT* NG1.......................2 E5
Wheldon Av *CARL* NG4....................32 D3
Whernside Rd *ARN* NG5...................19 H5
Whetstone Cl
  WOL/BIL/BRX NG8......................28 C2
Whilton Crs *ILK* DE7........................24 A5
Whinfell Cl *CFTN/RUD* NG11...........66 C4
Whinlatter Dr *WBRGFD* NG2...........58 D5
Whiston Cl *ARN* NG5........................18 D4
Whitbread St *NOTTE* NG7................30 C5
Whitburn Rd *BSTN/STPLFD* NG9.....63 F3
Whitby Cl *WOL/BIL/BRX* NG8..........40 A4
Whitby Crs *ARN* NG5........................20 B5
Whitby Rd *EWD/SEL/PNX* NG16.......8 B4
Whitcombe Gdns *ARN* NG5.............18 D2
Whitechapel St
  WOL/BIL/BRX NG8......................30 A3
White Furrows
  COT/KEY/RAD NG12...................70 D4
Whitegate V *CFTN/RUD* NG11.........66 A5
Whitehead Cl *ILK* DE7......................25 G3
Whitelands *COT/KEY/RAD* NG12.....71 F4
White Lodge Gdns
  WOL/BIL/BRX NG8......................40 C1
Whitely Cl *BSTN/STPLFD* NG9.........53 F3
Whitemoor Av
  WOL/BIL/BRX NG8......................30 A5
Whitemoor Rd *BLWL* NG6................30 A3
Whitemoss Cl
  WOL/BIL/BRX NG8......................40 D5
White Rd *ARN* NG5...........................30 B2
White's Av
  MAPPK/POR/STA NG3................44 C2
Whitfield Cl *CFTN/RUD* NG11.........57 E5
Whiting Av *BSTN/STPLFD* NG9........63 G4
Whittaker Rd *BSTN/STPLFD* NG9....63 H5
Whittier Rd *WBRGFD* NG2...............44 B5
Whittingham Rd
  MAPPK/POR/STA NG3................32 B2
Whitton Cl *ARN* NG5........................19 E1
  BSTN/STPLFD NG9......................64 B4
Whitwell Cl *WOL/BIL/BRX* NG8.......28 D4
Whitwell Rd *WOL/BIL/BRX* NG8......28 D4
Whitworth Dr *CALV/BJ* NG14...........34 B3
  COT/KEY/RAD NG12...................60 D1
Whitworth Ri *ARN* NG5....................18 C2
Whitworth Rd *ILK* DE7......................38 A2
Whyburn La *HUCK/RAV* NG15..........4 B5
Whyburn St *HUCK/RAV* NG15.........11 H1
Whysall St *HEANOR* DE75..................6 B5
Whyston Ct *HUCK/RAV* NG15..........10 B2
Wichnor Cl *CFTN/RUD* NG11...........66 C2
Wickens Wk
  MAPPK/POR/STA NG3....................3 K1
Wicket Gv *NOTTE* NG7.....................42 B4
Wickstead Cl
  MAPPK/POR/STA NG3................32 A2
Widdowson Cl *BLWL* NG6................17 E2
Widecombe La *CFTN/RUD* NG11.....76 A1
Widmerpool La
  COT/KEY/RAD NG12...................83 E4
Wighay Rd *HUCK/RAV* NG15............5 E2
Wigley Cl *MAPPK/POR/STA* NG3.....3 K1
Wigman Rd *WOL/BIL/BRX* NG8.......28 C5
Wigwam La *HUCK/RAV* NG15............5 H5
Wilden Crs *CFTN/RUD* NG11............66 B3
Wildman St *NOTTE* NG7....................2 A2
Wilford Crs *CFTN/RUD* NG11...........77 F1
Wilford Crs East *WBRGFD* NG2........57 F2
Wilford Crs West *WBRGFD* NG2.......57 F2
Wilford Gv *WBRGFD* NG2................57 G2
Wilford La *WBRGFD* NG2.................57 F4
Wilford Rd *CFTN/RUD* NG11............67 E3
  WBRGFD NG2..............................57 E1
Wilfrid Gv *WBRGFD* NG2.................67 H3
Wilkins Gdns *CFTN/RUD* NG11........66 A5
Wilkinson Av *BSTN/STPLFD* NG9....55 E5
Wilkinson St *WOL/BIL/BRX* NG8.....30 A4
Willaston Cl *BLWL* NG6....................29 H1
Wilbert Rd *ARN* NG5.........................20 B2
Willerby Rd *ARN* NG5.......................20 B5
Willersley Dr *WBRGFD* NG2............57 F1
Willesden Gn
  EWD/SEL/PNX NG16...................28 C2
William Av *EWD/SEL/PNX* NG16........8 C1

William Booth Rd *WBRGFD* NG2 ....44 B4
William Cl *CARL* NG4 ....34 A5
William Rd *BSTN/STPLFD* NG9 ......53 E4
  WBRGFD NG2..............................57 H3
Williams Rd *BSTN/STPLFD* NG9 ....64 A3
William St *HUCK/RAV* NG15 ....5 F5
  LGEAT NG10 ....62 D4
Willoughby Av *LGEAT* NG10 ....62 D4
Willoughby Cl
  BWSH/BRSTN DE72 ....72 A1
  NOTTE NG7 ....55 G3
Willoughby Ct *NOTTE* * NG7............42 C5
Willoughby Rd *WBRGFD* NG2 ....58 A5
Willoughby St
  BSTN/STPLFD NG9 ....55 F5
  ILK DE7 ....26 B4
  NOTTE NG7 ....42 C5
Willow Av *BSTN/STPLFD* NG9 ....53 E5
  CARL NG4 ....33 H5
  HUCK/RAV NG15 ....10 C2
  LGEAT NG10 ....63 E5
Willow Brook
  COT/KEY/RAD NG12 ....82 D2
Willow Cl *CALV/BJ* NG14 ....23 E5
  COT/KEY/RAD NG12 ....61 E1
Willow Crs *CARL* NG4 ....22 B3
  CARL NG4 ....33 H3
Willowdene *COT/KEY/RAD* NG12...71 F3
Willow Hill Cl *BLWL* NG6 ....17 F4
Willow La *CARL* NG4 ....33 G3
Willow Rd *BING/VBLV* NG13 ....49 F3
  CARL NG4 ....33 G5
  NOTTE NG7 ....56 B2
  WBRGFD NG2..............................67 H3
Willow Vw *NOTTE* NG7 ....42 C2
Willow Wong *CALV/BJ* NG14 ....23 E5
Willwell Dr *WBRGFD* NG2 ....67 F3
Wilmot La *BSTN/STPLFD* NG9 ....65 E1
Wilmot St *HEANOR* DE75 ....12 B1
  ILK DE7 ....25 H4
  LGEAT NG10 ....72 B4
Wilne Cl *LGEAT* NG10 ....72 B5
Wilne Rd *LGEAT* NG10 ....72 A5
Wilson Cl *ARN* NG5........................20 C5
Wilson Rd *EWD/SEL/PNX* NG16 ......14 A1
Wilsthorpe Rd *LGEAT* NG10 ....72 C1
Wilton St *BLWL* NG6......................30 B1
  ILK DE7 ....26 A4
Wimbledon Dr
  EWD/SEL/PNX NG16 ....28 D2
Wimbledon Rd *ARN* NG5 ....30 D2
Wimborne Cl *WBRGFD* NG2............67 F1
Wimbourne Rd *NOTTE* NG7 ....42 C2
Wimpole Rd *BSTN/STPLFD* NG9......54 C2
Winchester Av
  BSTN/STPLFD NG9 ....54 D3
Winchester Ct *ARN* NG5 ....31 H2
Winchester Crs *ILK* DE7 ....26 B5
Winchester St *ARN* NG5 ....31 G2
Windermere Av *ILK* DE7 ....37 F3
Windermere Cl *CARL* NG4..............33 G3
  WBRGFD NG2..............................59 E4
Windermere Rd
  BSTN/STPLFD NG9 ....54 C2
  HUCK/RAV NG15 ....5 E4
  LGEAT NG10 ....62 B4
  NOTTE NG7 ....30 D5
Windley Dr *ILK* DE7 ....25 G3
Windmill Av *HUCK/RAV* NG15........11 F1
Windmill Cl
  MAPPK/POR/STA NG3 ....44 A3
Windmill Ct *COT/KEY/RAD* NG12...82 C2
Windmill Gv *HUCK/RAV* NG15........11 F1
Windmill La
  MAPPK/POR/STA NG3 ....44 A3
  WBRGFD NG2................................3 K5
Windmill Vw *WBRGFD* NG2 ....44 A3
Windrush Cl *BSTN/STPLFD* NG9......54 C2
Windsor Cl *BSTN/STPLFD* NG9........38 C3
  HEANOR DE75..............................6 B4
  HUCK/RAV NG15 ....5 G4
Windsor Ct *BING/VBLV* NG13..........48 B3
  ILK DE7 ....24 A5

  LGEAT NG10 ....62 C2
Windsor Crs *ARN* NG5....................20 C5
  BSTN/STPLFD NG9 ....53 F4
  ILK DE7 ....37 G4
Windsor St *BSTN/STPLFD* NG9 ......53 E4
  BSTN/STPLFD NG9 ....55 F5
Wingate Cl *BSTN/STPLFD* NG9 ......41 E2
Wingbourne Wk *BLWL* NG6 ....17 H1
Wingfield Dr *BSTN/STPLFD* NG9 ....55 F2
  ILK DE7 ....25 G2
Wings Dr *HUCK/RAV* NG15 ....10 C3
Winifred Crs *CALV/BJ* NG14 ....35 E1
Winifred St *HUCK/RAV* NG15 ....11 G1
Winrow Gdns *BLWL* NG6 ....29 H2
Winscale Av *ARN* NG5 ....18 D2
Winscombe Mt *CFTN/RUD* NG11 ....76 A4
Winsford Cl *WOL/BIL/BRX* NG8 ......29 G3
Winster Av *CARL* NG4 ....33 E4
Winster Cl *BSTN/STPLFD* NG9 ......55 E2
Winster Wy *LGEAT* NG10 ....72 A4
Winston Cl *BSTN/STPLFD* NG9 ......53 F3
  MAPPK/POR/STA NG3 ....20 D4
Winterbourne Dr
  BSTN/STPLFD NG9 ....53 F2
Winterton Cl *ARN* NG5....................20 A4
Winterton Ri *ARN* NG5 ....19 E3
Winthorpe Rd *ARN* NG5 ....20 B3
Wintringham Crs *ARN* NG5 ....20 B5
Wirksworth Rd *ILK* DE7 ....37 F4
Wishford Av *NOTTE* NG7 ....42 B5
Wisley Cl *CFTN/RUD* NG11 ....67 F3
Wistow Cl *WOL/BIL/BRX* NG8..........30 B5
Withern Rd *WOL/BIL/BRX* NG8 ......29 E4
Witney Cl *ARN* NG5........................18 B3
Wittering Cl *LGEAT* NG10 ....73 F4
Wiverton Rd *BING/VBLV* NG13........48 D3
  NOTTE NG7 ....30 D5
Woburn Cl *COT/KEY/RAD* NG12 ....68 D2
Woburn Cft *LGEAT* NG10................62 B2
Woburn Ri *ARN* NG5 ....20 C5
Wolds Dr *COT/KEY/RAD* NG12 ......82 C1
Wolds La *COT/KEY/RAD* NG12 ......80 C1
  COT/KEY/RAD NG12 ....82 C4
Wolds Ri *COT/KEY/RAD* NG12 ......82 C1
Wollacombe Cl
  MAPPK/POR/STA NG3 ....21 E5
Wollaton Av *CARL* NG4 ....33 E2
Wollaton Ct *BLWL* NG6 ....18 B4
Wollaton Crs *BSTN/STPLFD* NG9....54 D3
Wollaton Hall Dr
  WOL/BIL/BRX NG8 ....42 A5
Wollaton Paddocks
  WOL/BIL/BRX NG8 ....40 B4
Wollaton Ri *WOL/BIL/BRX* NG8 ......54 D1
Wollaton Rd
  BSTN/STPLFD NG9 ....54 D3
  WOL/BIL/BRX NG8 ....41 F4
Wollaton St *NOTT* NG1 ....2 D4
Wollaton V *WOL/BIL/BRX* NG8........40 A4
Wolsey Av *NOTTE* NG7 ....42 C3
Wood Av *LGEAT* NG10 ....52 B5
Woodbank Dr
  WOL/BIL/BRX NG8 ....54 C1
Woodborough Rd
  MAPPK/POR/STA NG3 ....43 G1
Woodbridge Av
  CFTN/RUD NG11 ....66 B3
Woodchurch Rd *ARN* NG5 ....19 E1
Wood End Rd *HEANOR* DE75............6 B5
Woodfield Rd
  WOL/BIL/BRX NG8 ....28 D4
Woodford Cl *ARN* NG5 ....18 B1
Woodford Rd *ARN* NG5 ....20 B5
  HUCK/RAV NG15 ....11 F1
Woodgate
  COT/KEY/RAD NG12 ....70 D3
Woodgate Ct *NOTTE* NG7 ....2 A4
Woodgate La
  COT/KEY/RAD NG12 ....70 C3
Woodhall Rd *WOL/BIL/BRX* NG8 ....41 G3
Woodhedge Dr
  MAPPK/POR/STA NG3 ....32 B5
Woodhouse St
  MAPPK/POR/STA NG3 ....44 A3

Woodhouse Wy
  EWD/SEL/PNX NG16 ....28 C2
Woodkirk Rd *CFTN/RUD* NG11........66 C4
Woodland Av
  BWSH/BRSTN DE72......................72 A1
  ILK DE7 ....25 G1
Woodland Cl
  COT/KEY/RAD NG12 ....47 G5
  COT/KEY/RAD NG12 ....71 E4
Woodland Dr
  EWD/SEL/PNX NG16 ....29 E1
  MAPPK/POR/STA NG3 ....31 G4
Woodland Gv *ARN* NG5 ....31 G1
  BSTN/STPLFD NG9 ....64 C1
Woodland Rd *WBRGFD* NG2............58 A2
The Woodlands *BLWL* NG6..............17 H5
  COT/KEY/RAD NG12 ....46 D5
Woodlands Farm Cl
  HUCK/RAV NG15 ....10 C3
Woodland Wy
  EWD/SEL/PNX NG16 ....7 H5
Wood La *CARL* NG4 ....33 H4
  HUCK/RAV NG15 ....5 E5
Woodlane Gdns
  MAPPK/POR/STA NG3 ....44 A1
Woodleigh *COT/KEY/RAD* NG12.....82 B2
Woodley Sq *BLWL* NG6 ....11 H5
Woodley St *CFTN/RUD* NG11..........17 H5
Wood Link *BLWL* NG6 ....16 D3
Woodpecker Cl
  BING/VBLV NG13 ....49 E4
Woodpecker HI *ILK* DE7 ....50 D1
Woodrow Av *WOL/BIL/BRX* NG8 ....29 F5
Woodsend Cl *CALV/BJ* NG14..........35 E1
Woodsford Gv *CFTN/RUD* NG11 ....66 B4
Woodside *EWD/SEL/PNX* NG16 ....7 H5
Woodside Av
  COT/KEY/RAD NG12 ....47 G5
  EWD/SEL/PNX NG16 ....15 H4
Woodside Crs *ILK* DE7 ....13 C5
  LGEAT NG10 ....72 C1
Woodside Dr *ARN* NG5 ....19 G2
Woodside Rd *BSTN/STPLFD* NG9....55 E3
  BSTN/STPLFD NG9 ....63 H2
  CALV/BJ NG14 ....34 C2
  COT/KEY/RAD NG12 ....47 G4
  LGEAT NG10 ....62 B1
Woodstock Av *NOTTE* NG7 ....42 B2
Woodstock Rd
  BSTN/STPLFD NG9 ....63 F3
Woodstock St *HUCK/RAV* NG15......11 G1
Wood St *EWD/SEL/PNX* NG16 ....8 A4
  ILK DE7 ....26 A4
Woodthorpe Av *ARN* NG5 ....31 H1
Woodthorpe Ct *ARN* NG5 ....31 H2
Woodthorpe Dr *ARN* NG5 ....31 H1
Woodthorpe Gdns *ARN* NG5 ....31 H2
Woodthorpe Rd *ARN* NG5 ....32 A2
Wood Vw *COT/KEY/RAD* NG12 ......68 C3
Woodview *COT/KEY/RAD* NG12 ......71 F3
Woodville Cl *BSTN/STPLFD* NG9 ....54 B5
Woodville Dr *ARN* NG5 ....31 F2
Woodville Rd *ARN* NG5 ....31 F2
Woodward St *WBRGFD* NG2............57 G2
Woodyard La
  WOL/BIL/BRX NG8........................41 F3
Wooliscroft Wy *ILK* DE7 ....25 F3
Woollaton St *HUCK/RAV* NG15 ....5 G5
Woolmer Rd *WBRGFD* NG2 ....57 F2
Woolpack La *NOTT* NG1 ....3 H5
Woolsington Cl
  WOL/BIL/BRX NG8 ....28 C3
Woolsthorpe Crs *ILK* DE7 ....37 G4
Wootton Cl *WOL/BIL/BRX* NG8 ......40 C1
Worcester Gdns *ARN* NG5 ....19 H5
Worcester Rd *ARN* NG5 ....19 H5
Wordsworth Av
  HUCK/RAV NG15 ....10 C1
Wordsworth Rd *ARN* NG5 ....19 G3
  EWD/SEL/PNX NG16 ....14 D5
  NOTTE NG7 ....42 B2
  WBRGFD NG2..............................57 H5
Worksop Rd
  MAPPK/POR/STA NG3 ....44 A3

Worrall Av *ARN* NG5 ....20 A3
  LGEAT NG10 ....63 E5
Worth St *CARL* NG4 ....33 F5
Wortley Av *BSTN/STPLFD* NG9......39 E5
Wortley Cl *ILK* DE7 ....26 B5
Wortley Hall Cl *NOTTE* NG7 ....55 H1
Worwood Dr *WBRGFD* NG2............67 F1
Woulds Fld *COT/KEY/RAD* NG12 ....71 E5
Wray Cl *MAPPK/POR/STA* NG3 ....3 K3
Wrenthorpe V *CFTN/RUD* NG11......66 B5
Wrights Orch
  COT/KEY/RAD NG12 ....82 B2
Wright St *CARL* NG4 ....45 G1
Wroughton Ct
  EWD/SEL/PNX NG16 ....8 B5
Wroxham Dr
  WOL/BIL/BRX NG8 ....40 C5
Wychwood Dr
  BSTN/STPLFD NG9 ....53 E1
Wychwood Rd
  BING/VBLV NG13 ....48 B3
Wycliffe Gv
  MAPPK/POR/STA NG3 ....31 H3
Wycliffe St *NOTTE* NG7 ....30 C4
Wycombe Cl *CFTN/RUD* NG11 ......76 A1
Wye Gdns *NOTTE* NG7 ....42 A2
Wykeham Rd *ARN* NG5 ....20 B5
Wykes Av *CARL* NG4 ....33 G3
Wymondham Cl *ARN* NG5 ....20 B4
Wynbreck Dr
  COT/KEY/RAD NG12 ....82 C1
Wyndale Dr *ILK* DE7........................37 F2
Wyndham Ms *NOTT* * NG1 ....43 E1
The Wyndings *ARN* NG5..................32 A1
Wynndale Dr *ARN* NG5 ....30 D2
Wynward Cl *ILK* DE7 ....25 F2
Wynwood Cl
  BSTN/STPLFD * NG9 ....64 A4
Wynwood Rd
  BSTN/STPLFD NG9 ....64 A4
Wyrale Dr *WOL/BIL/BRX* NG8 ....28 D4
Wysall La *COT/KEY/RAD* NG12 ......82 A5
Wyton Cl *ARN* NG5........................18 D5
Wyvern Av *LGEAT* NG10 ....73 E3
Wyvern Cl *EWD/SEL/PNX* NG16......14 A1
Wyville Cl *NOTTE* NG7 ....42 B3

Y

Yalding Dr *WOL/BIL/BRX* NG8 ....40 B4
Yalding Gdns *WOL/BIL/BRX* NG8 ....40 B4
Yarwell Cl *MAPPK/POR/STA* NG3 ....44 D1
Yatesbury Crs
  WOL/BIL/BRX NG8 ....28 D5
Yew Barrow Rd *WBRGFD* NG2 ......68 D1
Yew Cl *ARN* NG5............................31 G3
Yewdale Cl *CFTN/RUD* NG11 ....76 A1
  WBRGFD NG2..............................68 D1
Yew Tree Av *ARN* NG5 ....31 F4
Yew Tree Cl
  COT/KEY/RAD NG12 ....60 C1
Yew Tree La *CARL* NG4 ....33 H3
  CFTN/RUD NG11 ....65 H4
Yew Tree Rd *HUCK/RAV* NG15 ......11 G2
Yonge Cl *COT/KEY/RAD* NG12 ......60 D1
York Av *BSTN/STPLFD* NG9............65 E2
  LGEAT NG10 ....62 B1
York Cl *CARL* NG4..........................33 G3
York Dr *WOL/BIL/BRX* NG8 ....28 C3
Yorke St *HUCK/RAV* NG15..............11 F1
York Rd *LGEAT* NG10 ....62 D5
York St *CARL* NG4..........................45 H1
  NOTT NG1 ....3 F2
Young Cl *BLWL* NG6 ....17 E5
Yvonne Crs *CARL* NG4 ....45 G1

Z

Zulla Rd *MAPPK/POR/STA* NG3 ......31 F5
Zulu Rd *NOTTE* NG7 ....30 C3

Index - featured places

Abbey Road Primary School
  WBRGFD NG2..............................58 B5
Acton Road Industrial Estate
  LGEAT NG10 ....73 F3
Adam House Medical Centre
  LGEAT NG10 ....62 C1
Adco Business Centre
  NOTTE NG7 ....42 B1

Albany Infant School
  BSTN/STPLFD NG9 ....53 F3
Albany Junior School
  BSTN/STPLFD NG9 ....53 F3
Albert Hall
  NOTT NG1 ....2 D5
Albion Leisure Centre
  ILK DE7 ....26 A5

Aldercar Infant School
  EWD/SEL/PNX NG16 ....6 D3
Aldercar School
  EWD/SEL/PNX NG16 ....6 D3
Alderman White Lower School
  BSTN/STPLFD NG9 ....55 E3
Alderman White School
  BSTN/STPLFD NG9 ....54 B5

All Hallows CE Primary School
  CARL NG4....................................33 G4
Amber Trading Estate
  EWD/SEL/PNX NG16 ....15 E3
The American Adventure
  Theme Park
  HEANOR DE75..............................13 E5

Annie Holgate Junior School
HUCK/RAV NG15 .... 11 E1
Apex Business Park
CFTN/RUD NG11 .... 67 E3
Arboretum
NOTT NG1 .... 2 C2
Arkwright Primary School
WBRGFD NG2 .... 57 G2
Arnold & Carlton College
ARN NG5 .... 20 A3
Arnold Health Centre
ARN NG5 .... 20 A2
Arnold Hill School
ARN NG5 .... 20 B4
Arnold Leisure Centre
ARN NG5 .... 20 A2
Arts Centre
NOTT NG1 .... 2 C5
Arts Theatre
NOTT NG1 .... 3 F5
Ascot Industrial Estate
LGEAT NG10 .... 52 D5
Ashforth Business Centre
MAPPK/POR/STA NG3 .... 3 G1
Ash Lea Special School
COT/KEY/RAD NG12 .... 71 E4
Assarts Farm Medical Centre
EWD/SEL/PNX NG16 .... 28 C1
Attenborough Nature Reserve
BSTN/STPLFD NG9 .... 65 E3
Attenborough
Preparatory School
BSTN/STPLFD NG9 .... 64 C1
Awsworth Junior School
EWD/SEL/PNX NG16 .... 26 D1
Awsworth Trading Estate
ILK DE7 .... 26 A3
Bailey Brook Industrial Estate
HEANOR DE75 .... 7 E5
Bakersfield Medical Centre
MAPPK/POR/STA NG3 .... 44 D2
Balloon Wood Industrial Estate
BSTN/STPLFD NG9 .... 40 A4
Bar Lane Industrial Estate
BLWL NG6 .... 30 A3
Beardall Street Primary School
HUCK/RAV NG15 .... 5 G5
Beckett RC School
CFTN/RUD NG11 .... 66 D1
Beechdale Swimming Centre
WOL/BIL/BRX NG8 .... 41 H2
Beeston Clinic
BSTN/STPLFD NG9 .... 55 E5
Beeston Fields Golf Club
BSTN/STPLFD NG9 .... 54 C3
Beeston Primary School
BSTN/STPLFD NG9 .... 55 E3
Bennerley School
ILK DE7 .... 26 A1
Bennnerley Fields
Special School
ILK DE7 .... 26 A1
Bentinck Primary School
NOTTE NG7 .... 42 C2
Berridge Infant School
NOTTE NG7 .... 30 B5
Berridge Junior School
NOTTE NG7 .... 42 B1
Bestwood Park Health Centre
ARN NG5 .... 19 E3
Bestwood Swimming Pool
ARN NG5 .... 19 E4
Bilborough Sixth Form College
WOL/BIL/BRX NG8 .... 40 B1
Bingham Health Centre
BING/VBLV NG13 .... 48 D3
Bingham Industrial Park
BING/VBLV NG13 .... 48 D1
Bingham Infant School
BING/VBLV NG13 .... 48 D2
Bingham Sports Arena
BING/VBLV NG13 .... 48 D4
Bingham Sports Centre
BING/VBLV NG13 .... 49 E4
Bingham Swimming Baths
BING/VBLV NG13 .... 49 E3
Bispham Drive Junior School
BSTN/STPLFD NG9 .... 63 F3
Blenheim Industrial Estate
BLWL NG6 .... 16 D2
Blessed Robert RC
Primary School
CFTN/RUD NG11 .... 76 B1
Blue Bell Hill Infant School
MAPPK/POR/STA NG3 .... 44 A2
Bonington Junior School
BLWL NG6 .... 17 G4

Bosworth Primary School
WBRGFD NG2 .... 57 E2
Boulevard Industrial Park
BSTN/STPLFD NG9 .... 55 G4
Brackenfield Special School
LGEAT NG10 .... 62 C5
Bradbury-Midway
Industrial Estate
NOTTE NG7 .... 56 A4
Bramcote CE Primary School
BSTN/STPLFD NG9 .... 54 A3
Bramcote Crematorium
BSTN/STPLFD NG9 .... 39 H5
Bramcote Hill
Comprehensive School
BSTN/STPLFD NG9 .... 54 A1
Bramcote Hills Golf Club
BSTN/STPLFD NG9 .... 54 B1
Bramcote Hills Primary School
BSTN/STPLFD NG9 .... 54 A2
Bramcote Leisure Centre
BSTN/STPLFD NG9 .... 53 H2
Bramcote Park
Comprehensive School
BSTN/STPLFD NG9 .... 53 H2
Brewhouse Yard Museum
NOTT NG1 .... 2 D7
Breydon Industrial Centre
LGEAT NG10 .... 73 G2
Brinkhill Primary School
CFTN/RUD NG11 .... 66 C3
Broad Marsh Shopping Centre
NOTT NG1 .... 3 F6
Broadway Cinema
NOTT NG1 .... 3 G5
Brookhill Leys Infant School
EWD/SEL/PNX NG16 .... 14 B1
Brookhill Leys Junior School
EWD/SEL/PNX NG16 .... 8 B5
Brooklands Infant School
LGEAT NG10 .... 73 E3
Brooklands Junior School
LGEAT NG10 .... 73 E2
Brooksby Primary School
CFTN/RUD NG11 .... 66 C3
Brookside Industrial Units
BSTN/STPLFD NG9 .... 53 E3
Browns Lane Business Park
COT/KEY/RAD NG12 .... 83 F2
Broxtowe College
BSTN/STPLFD NG9 .... 64 D1
Bulwell Business Centre
BLWL NG6 .... 17 F3
Bulwell Forest Golf Club
BLWL NG6 .... 18 A3
Bulwell Health Centre
BLWL NG6 .... 17 G4
Burford Primary School
ARN NG5 .... 19 F4
Burton Joyce Primary School
CALV/BJ NG14 .... 23 E5
Byron Cinema
HUCK/RAV NG15 .... 5 G5
Canal Museum
NOTT NG1 .... 2 E7
Canalside Industrial Estate
LGEAT NG10 .... 52 D4
Carlton Business Centre
CARL NG4 .... 33 G5
Carlton Cemetery
CARL NG4 .... 33 F5
Carlton Digby Special School
MAPPK/POR/STA NG3 .... 32 D2
Carlton Le Willows
Comprehensive School
CARL NG4 .... 34 A4
Carnarvon Primary School
BING/VBLV NG13 .... 49 F3
Carrington Primary School
ARN NG5 .... 31 E4
Castle Clinic
NOTT NG1 .... 2 B4
Castle Industrial Park
HUCK/RAV NG15 .... 10 D1
Castle Meadow Retail Park
WBRGFD NG2 .... 43 E5
Castle Museum & Art Gallery
NOTTE NG7 .... 2 D6
Castle Park Industrial Estate
WBRGFD NG2 .... 57 E2
Caves of Nottingham
NOTT NG1 .... 3 F6
Central Infant School
CARL NG4 .... 33 G5
Centurion Business Park
BLWL NG6 .... 16 D1
Charlotte Infant School
ILK DE7 .... 25 H3

Charlton House Medical Centre
LGEAT NG10 .... 73 G1
Chaucer Infant School
ILK DE7 .... 26 A5
Chaucer Junior School
ILK DE7 .... 26 A4
Chettles Industrial Estate
NOTTE NG7 .... 42 A3
Chetwynd Road Primary School
BSTN/STPLFD NG9 .... 63 H4
The Chilwell Alderman Pounder
Infant School
BSTN/STPLFD NG9 .... 64 A1
Chilwell College House
Junior School
BSTN/STPLFD NG9 .... 64 C1
Chilwell Manor Golf Club
BSTN/STPLFD NG9 .... 64 D2
Chilwell Retail Park
BSTN/STPLFD NG9 .... 64 A5
Chilwell School
BSTN/STPLFD NG9 .... 64 C3
Christ the King RC
Comprehensive School
ARN NG5 .... 20 C3
Church Cemetery
NOTT NG1 .... 43 E1
Churchview Business Park
BLWL NG6 .... 30 B3
City Farm
MAPPK/POR/STA NG3 .... 3 K3
City Golf Course
BLWL NG6 .... 17 F1
Civil Service Sports Ground
WBRGFD NG2 .... 57 F5
Claremont Pimary School
ARN NG5 .... 31 E4
Clarendon City College
NOTT NG1 .... 3 G5
Clarendon College
ARN NG5 .... 31 E5
Clifton Leisure Centre
CFTN/RUD NG11 .... 66 C5
Clifton Medical Centre
CFTN/RUD NG11 .... 76 B1
Cloudside Junior School
LGEAT NG10 .... 52 C5
College of Continuing Education
HUCK/RAV NG15 .... 5 G5
College of Further Education
NOTT NG1 .... 3 H4
College Street Health Centre
LGEAT NG10 .... 62 D5
Colwick Business Park
CARL NG4 .... 45 G3
Colwick Country Park
WBRGFD NG2 .... 45 E4
Colwick Industrial Estate
CARL NG4 .... 45 G2
CARL NG4 .... 46 A3
Concordia Industrial Estate
LGEAT NG10 .... 72 D4
Coppice Primary School
HEANOR DE75 .... 12 B2
Corfield CE Infant School
HEANOR DE75 .... 12 A1
Cornerhouse
NOTT NG1 .... 2 E4
Cossall Industrial Estate
EWD/SEL/PNX NG16 .... 26 C3
Costume Museum
NOTT NG1 .... 2 E6
Cotgrave CE Primary School
COT/KEY/RAD NG12 .... 70 D3
Cotgrave Place Golf &
Country Club
COT/KEY/RAD NG12 .... 60 B5
Cotgrave Shopping Centre
COT/KEY/RAD NG12 .... 71 E3
Cotmanhay County
Junior School
ILK DE7 .... 13 H5
Cotmanhay Infant School
ILK DE7 .... 13 H5
County Archives
WBRGFD NG2 .... 2 E7
County Business Park
WBRGFD NG2 .... 57 H1
County Infant School
COT/KEY/RAD NG12 .... 71 E3
Covenant College
NOTT NG1 .... 2 D1
Cromford Road Industrial Estate
EWD/SEL/PNX NG16 .... 7 E3
Crompton Road Industrial Estate
ILK DE7 .... 38 B4
Crossdale Drive Primary School
COT/KEY/RAD NG12 .... 79 F5

Dagfa House School
BSTN/STPLFD NG9 .... 55 F3
The Dales Medical Centre
ILK DE7 .... 36 B1
Dallimore Primary School
ILK DE7 .... 37 G4
Daybrook Business Centre
ARN NG5 .... 19 G4
Dayncourt School
COT/KEY/RAD NG12 .... 47 F5
Deaf Society
NOTTE NG7 .... 2 B1
Derby Road Industrial Estate
HEANOR DE75 .... 12 A1
LGEAT NG10 .... 62 C1
Derrymount School
ARN NG5 .... 20 A1
Derwent Street Industrial Estate
LGEAT NG10 .... 72 C3
Digby Industrial Estate
EWD/SEL/PNX NG16 .... 15 E3
Djanogly City
Technology College
NOTTE NG7 .... 30 D4
Douglas Primary School
NOTTE NG7 .... 42 C3
Dovedale Primary School
LGEAT NG10 .... 72 B3
Dunkirk Primary School
NOTTE NG7 .... 56 B2
Durban House Heritage Centre
EWD/SEL/PNX NG16 .... 8 A4
East Derbyshire Magistrates
ILK DE7 .... 25 H5
Eastwood Comprehensive
Lower School
EWD/SEL/PNX NG16 .... 8 B4
Eastwood Comprehensive School
EWD/SEL/PNX NG16 .... 7 H4
Eastwood Health Centre
EWD/SEL/PNX NG16 .... 8 B5
Eastwood Infant School
EWD/SEL/PNX NG16 .... 8 A5
Eastwood & Kimberley
Community College
EWD/SEL/PNX NG16 .... 8 A4
EWD/SEL/PNX NG16 .... 15 G4
Eastwood Town Cricket Club
EWD/SEL/PNX NG16 .... 8 B4
Edgewood Primary School
HUCK/RAV NG15 .... 10 C3
Edna G Olds Primary School
NOTTE NG7 .... 42 C5
Edwalton Municipal Golf Club
COT/KEY/RAD NG12 .... 68 D3
Edwalton Primary School
COT/KEY/RAD NG12 .... 68 D2
Ellerslie Cricket Club
WBRGFD NG2 .... 57 H3
Ellesmere Business Park
ARN NG5 .... 31 E3
Elliot Durham Swimming Pool
MAPPK/POR/STA NG3 .... 31 H4
Elliott Durham
Comprehensive School
MAPPK/POR/STA NG3 .... 31 H3
Ellis Guilford
Comprehensive School
WOL/BIL/BRX NG8 .... 29 H3
Elms Primary School
MAPPK/POR/STA NG3 .... 43 F1
English Martyrs RC
Primary School
LGEAT NG10 .... 62 C5
Erewash Museum
ILK DE7 .... 26 A5
Erewash Valley Golf Club
ILK DE7 .... 52 C2
Ernehale Infant School
ARN NG5 .... 20 B4
Eskdale Junior School
BSTN/STPLFD NG9 .... 64 A1
Exchange Arcade
NOTT NG1 .... 3 F5
Fairfield Primary School
BSTN/STPLFD NG9 .... 53 E5
Fairham Community College
CFTN/RUD NG11 .... 76 C2
Farnborough
Comprehensive School
CFTN/RUD NG11 .... 66 D3
Fernwood
Comprehensive School
WOL/BIL/BRX NG8 .... 40 C4
Fernwood J & I School
WOL/BIL/BRX NG8 .... 40 C4
Field House Infant School
ILK DE7 .... 38 A2

Firbeck Primary School
WOL/BIL/BRX NG8 .... **40** A4

Forest Fields Primary School
NOTTE NG7 .... **30** C5

Forest School
NOTTE NG7 .... **42** D1

Foxwood GM School
BSTN/STPLFD NG9 .... **54** A2

Framework Knitters Museum
CFTN/RUD NG11 .... **77** F3

Frederick Harrison Infant School
BSTN/STPLFD NG9 .... **53** G3

Friesland School
LGEAT NG10 .... **62** A1

The Galleries of Justice
NOTT NG1 .... **3** F6

Gateway Christian School
ILK DE7 .... **36** C5

The George Spencer School
BSTN/STPLFD NG9 .... **63** F1

Gilthill Primary School
EWD/SEL/PNX NG16 .... **15** E3

Glaisdale Business Centre
WOL/BIL/BRX NG8 .... **40** C3

Glaisdale Park Industrial Estate
WOL/BIL/BRX NG8 .... **40** C2

Glapton Primary School
CFTN/RUD NG11 .... **66** A4

Glenbrook Primary School
WOL/BIL/BRX NG8 .... **41** E1

Granby Junior School
ILK NG1 .... **25** H3

Grange Primary School
LGEAT NG10 .... **73** C4

Greasley Beauvale DH Lawrence
Infant School
EWD/SEL/PNX NG16 .... **8** C4

Greasley Beau Vale Junior School
EWD/SEL/PNX NG16 .... **8** C5

Greasley Sports Centre
EWD/SEL/PNX NG16 .... **8** C5

Great Central Railway
CFTN/RUD NG11 .... **76** D5

Greencroft Junior &
Primary School
CFTN/RUD NG11 .... **66** C3

Greenholme School
NOTTE NG7 .... **42** B4

Greenwood Dale
Technology School
WBRGFD NG2 .... **44** B4

Greenwood Infant School
WBRGFD NG2 .... **44** B4

Greenwood Junior School
WBRGFD NG2 .... **44** B4

Greenwood & Sneinton
Family Medical Centre
WBRGFD NG2 .... **44** B3

Greythorn Primary School
WBRGFD NG2 .... **67** F1

GX Superbowl
NOTTE NG7 .... **56** B2

Hadden Park High School
WOL/BIL/BRX NG8 .... **41** E1

Haddon Primary School
CARL NG4 .... **33** E3

Hallam Fields Junior School
ILK DE7 .... **38** A3

The Hall
COT/KEY/RAD NG12 .... **46** A5

Harrington Junior School
LGEAT NG10 .... **62** C5

Harvey Hadden Sports Centre
WOL/BIL/BRX NG8 .... **40** D1

Harvey Hadden Stadium
WOL/BIL/BRX NG8 .... **41** E1

Haydn Primary School
ARN NG5 .... **31** F3

Haywood Comprehensive School
ARN NG5 .... **19** F5

Heanor Gate Industrial Estate
HEANOR DE75 .... **12** A1

Heanor Health Centre
HEANOR DE75 .... **12** B1

Heanor Langley Infant School
HEANOR DE75 .... **12** B1

Heanor & Langley Mill District
Memorial Hospital
HEANOR DE75 .... **12** C1

Heanor Leisure Centre
HEANOR DE75 .... **12** C1

Heanor Town Sports Ground
HEANOR DE75 .... **12** B1

Heathfield Primary School
ARN NG5 .... **30** C2

Henry Mellish
Comprehensive School
BLWL NG6 .... **17** H5

Heritage Centre
CFTN/RUD NG11 .... **77** F4

Heymann Primary School
WBRGFD NG2 .... **67** G2

Highbank Primary School
CFTN/RUD NG11 .... **76** A2

Highbury Hospital
BLWL NG6 .... **17** H5

Highfield Primary School
LGEAT NG10 .... **62** D4

High Pavement Sixth
Form College
ARN NG5 .... **18** C5

High School Sports Ground
ARN NG5 .... **30** D1

Hillside Medical Centre
BSTN/STPLFD NG9 .... **53** G4

HM Prison
ARN NG5 .... **31** E2

Hogarth Primary &
Nursery School
MAPPK/POR/STA NG3 .... **44** B1

Holgate School
HUCK/RAV NG15 .... **10** D1

Hollygate Industrial Park
COT/KEY/RAD NG12 .... **71** F2

Hollygirt School
MAPPK/POR/STA NG3 .... **43** F1

Hollywell Primary School
EWD/SEL/PNX NG16 .... **15** F3

Holme Pierrepont
Country Park
COT/KEY/RAD NG12 .... **45** G5

Holy Cross RC School
HUCK/RAV NG15 .... **5** G3

Horsendale Primary School
EWD/SEL/PNX NG16 .... **28** D2

Hucknall Airfield
HUCK/RAV NG15 .... **11** E5

Hucknall Industrial Park
HUCK/RAV NG15 .... **10** D3

Hucknall Leisure Centre
HUCK/RAV NG15 .... **5** G4

Hucknall National Junior School
HUCK/RAV NG15 .... **5** F4

Hucknall Town FC
HUCK/RAV NG15 .... **11** E2

Huntingdon Primary &
Nursery School
MAPPK/POR/STA NG3 .... **3** F1

Ilkeston Bowl
ILK DE7 .... **37** H1

Ilkeston Community Hospital
ILK DE7 .... **25** G1

Ilkeston School
ILK DE7 .... **25** G5

Ilkeston Swimming Pool
ILK DE7 .... **25** H4

Interchange 25 Business Park
BWSH/BRSTN DE72 .... **62** A2

Iona School
MAPPK/POR/STA NG3 .... **44** B3

James Peacock Infant School
CFTN/RUD NG11 .... **77** E2

Jesse Gray Primary School
WBRGFD NG2 .... **67** H1

Jewish Cemetery
WBRGFD NG2 .... **67** H3

John Carroll Leisure Centre
NOTTE NG7 .... **42** C3

John Clifford Primary School
BSTN/STPLFD NG9 .... **55** F5

John Ryle Health Centre
CFTN/RUD NG11 .... **66** B5

John Storer Clinic
NOTT NG1 .... **2** C5

Ken Martin Swimming Pool
BLWL NG6 .... **17** H1

Kensington Junior School
ILK DE7 .... **38** B1

Kestrel Business Park
CARL NG4 .... **45** H3

Keyworth Health Centre
COT/KEY/RAD NG12 .... **82** B2

Keyworth Primary School
COT/KEY/RAD NG12 .... **82** B1

Killisick Junior School
ARN NG5 .... **20** C1

Kimberley Leisure Centre
EWD/SEL/PNX NG16 .... **15** H4

Kimberley Primary School
EWD/SEL/PNX NG16 .... **15** G4

Kimberley School
EWD/SEL/PNX NG16 .... **15** H4

King Edward Park
Primary School
MAPPK/POR/STA NG3 .... **3** K4

The Kings School
WBRGFD NG2 .... **57** F2

Kirk Hallam Community
Technology College
ILK DE7 .... **37** G2

Kirk Hallam Ladywood School
ILK DE7 .... **37** G2

Lace Centre
NOTT NG1 .... **2** D6

Lace Market Theatre
NOTT NG1 .... **3** F6

Lady Bay Primary School
WBRGFD NG2 .... **58** B2

Ladycross Infant School
LGEAT NG10 .... **52** C5

Lakeside Infant School
LGEAT NG10 .... **72** C4

Lambley Primary School
CARL NG4 .... **22** A3

Langley Business Park
EWD/SEL/PNX NG16 .... **7** E5

Langley Mill CE Infant School
EWD/SEL/PNX NG16 .... **7** E4

Langley Mill Junior School
EWD/SEL/PNX NG16 .... **6** D3

Langley Park Industrial Estate
EWD/SEL/PNX NG16 .... **7** E4

Larkfields Junior School
EWD/SEL/PNX NG16 .... **16** A4

Larklands Infant School
ILK DE7 .... **26** B5

The Lawrence Museum
EWD/SEL/PNX NG16 .... **8** A4

Law School
NOTT NG1 .... **2** D3

Leen Mills Primary School
HUCK/RAV NG15 .... **5** G4

Lenton Business Centre
NOTTE NG7 .... **42** B4

Lenton Health Centre
NOTTE NG7 .... **42** C4

Lenton Industrial Estate (East)
NOTTE NG7 .... **56** C3

Lenton Industrial Estate (West)
NOTTE NG7 .... **56** B4

Lenton Leisure Centre
NOTTE NG7 .... **42** C5

Lenton Primary School
NOTTE NG7 .... **42** C5

Linby Cum Papplewick CE
Primary School
HUCK/RAV NG15 .... **5** G1

Lings Bar Hospital
WBRGFD NG2 .... **58** D5

Long Eaton Community School
LGEAT NG10 .... **73** E2

The Long Eaton & District
Arts Council
LGEAT NG10 .... **73** E2

Long Eaton Stadium
LGEAT NG10 .... **73** G1

Longmoor Primary School
LGEAT NG10 .... **62** C3

Lyncroft Primary School
EWD/SEL/PNX NG16 .... **8** B4

Madford Business Park
ARN NG5 .... **19** G4

Manners Industrial Estate
ILK DE7 .... **25** G3

The Manor Surgery
BSTN/STPLFD NG9 .... **55** E5

Manvers Junior School
COT/KEY/RAD NG12 .... **71** E3

Mapperley CE Primary School
ILK DE7 .... **24** C3

Mapperley Park
Medical Centre
MAPPK/POR/STA NG3 .... **43** F1

Mapperley Plains
Primary School
MAPPK/POR/STA NG3 .... **32** C2

Margaret Glen-Bott
Comprehensive School
WOL/BIL/BRX NG8 .... **41** G4

Marlpool Junior School
HEANOR DE75 .... **12** D1

Maywood Golf Club
BWSH/BRSTN DE72 .... **51** G5

Meadowbank Day Hospital
WBRGFD NG2 .... **57** E2

Meadow Brookes
Business Park
LGEAT NG10 .... **73** H3

Meadow Lane Infant School
BSTN/STPLFD NG9 .... **64** D1

Meadows Primary School
WBRGFD NG2 .... **57** F1

Meadow Trading Estate
WBRGFD NG2 .... **57** H1

Media Centre
NOTT NG1 .... **3** G5

Melbourne Park Medical Centre
WOL/BIL/BRX NG8 .... **29** H4

Melbury Primary School
WOL/BIL/BRX NG8 .... **28** C5

Mellers Primary School
NOTTE NG7 .... **42** C3

Mental Health Clinic
BSTN/STPLFD NG9 .... **65** E1

Michael House School
HEANOR DE75 .... **12** D4

Middleton Primary School
WOL/BIL/BRX NG8 .... **41** H4

Milford Primary School
CFTN/RUD NG11 .... **76** B1

Moderns RFC
CFTN/RUD NG11 .... **57** E3

Moorgreen Industrial Park
EWD/SEL/PNX NG16 .... **8** C2

Mornington Primary School
EWD/SEL/PNX NG16 .... **28** C1

Mountford House School
ARN NG5 .... **31** F4

Mundy CE Junior School
HEANOR DE75 .... **12** B1

Museum of Nottingham Lace
NOTT NG1 .... **3** F6

National Ice Centre
NOTT NG1 .... **3** H5

The National School
HUCK/RAV NG15 .... **5** E3

National Water Sports Centre
COT/KEY/RAD NG12 .... **59** F1

Natural History Museum
WOL/BIL/BRX NG8 .... **41** F5

Netherfield Infant School
CARL NG4 .... **45** G2

Netherfield Junior School
CARL NG4 .... **45** H1

Netherfield Medical Centre
CARL NG4 .... **45** H1

Nethergate Special School
CFTN/RUD NG11 .... **66** C5

New College Nottingham
BLWL NG6 .... **29** H1

Newstead Industrial Estate
ARN NG5 .... **20** B3

Northgate Primary School
NOTTE NG7 .... **30** C4

Nottingham Airport
COT/KEY/RAD NG12 .... **69** G1

The Nottingham
Bluecoat School
WOL/BIL/BRX NG8 .... **29** H5

Nottingham City Hospital
ARN NG5 .... **18** D5

Nottingham City
Hospital Mobility Centre
ARN NG5 .... **31** E1

Nottingham Community College
MAPPK/POR/STA NG3 .... **3** J4

Nottingham Forest FC
(City Ground)
WBRGFD NG2 .... **57** H2

Nottingham General Hospital
NOTTE NG7 .... **2** C6

Nottingham High School
NOTT NG1 .... **2** B1

Nottingham High
School for Girls
NOTT NG1 .... **2** D1

Nottingham Industrial Museum
WOL/BIL/BRX NG8 .... **41** F5

Nottingham Magistrates Court
WBRGFD NG2 .... **43** F5

Nottingham Nuffield Hospital
ARN NG5 .... **19** G5

Nottingham Racecourse
WBRGFD NG2 .... **44** D5

Nottingham RFC
BSTN/STPLFD NG9 .... **65** E1

Nottinghamshire County
Cricket Club (Trent Bridge)
WBRGFD NG2 .... **57** H2

Nottingham South & Wilford
Industrial Estate
CFTN/RUD NG11 .... **67** E2

Nottingham Trent University
CFTN/RUD NG11 .... **65** G4
CFTN/RUD NG11 .... **66** A3
NOTT NG1 .... **2** E3
NOTT NG1 .... **2** C2

Nottingham University Hospital
NOTTE NG7 .... **56** A1

Notts County FC (Meadow Lane)
WBRGFD NG2 .... **57** H1
Nutbrook Cricket Club
ILK DE7 .... **25** E5
The Oaks Medical Centre
BSTN/STPLFD NG9 .... **55** E4
Old Basford Health Centre
BLWL NG6 .... **30** B3
The Open University
ARN NG5 .... **31** E5
NOTTE NG7 .... **42** C4
Orchard Business Park
ILK DE7 .... **25** C4
LGEAT NG10 .... **52** C5
Orchard Park Industrial Estate
LGEAT NG10 .... **52** D5
Our Lady of Perpetual Succour
RC Primary School
BLWL NG6 .... **18** A4
Palm Court Industrial Centre
NOTTE NG7 .... **30** C4
Parkdale Primary School
CARL NG4 .... **45** E2
Park House Medical Centre
CARL NG4 .... **33** G5
Parklands Infant School
LGEAT NG10 .... **62** C5
Peoples College of
Tertiary Education
NOTT NG1 .... **2** E6
Phoenix Infant School
CARL NG4 .... **33** G3
Pierrepont Gamston
Primary School
WBRGFD NG2 .... **58** D5
Pinewood Infant School
ARN NG5 .... **20** C1
Pinfold Trading Estate
BSTN/STPLFD NG9 .... **53** F3
Playhouse Theatre
NOTT NG1 .... **2** D5
Playworld
CARL NG4 .... **21** F1
Plumtree School
COT/KEY/RAD NG12 .... **79** F3
Portland Leisure Centre
WBRGFD NG2 .... **57** G2
Portland Primary School
WOL/BIL/BRX NG8 .... **40** B2
Primary School
ARN NG5 .... **31** E4
Priory Junior School
CARL NG4 .... **33** F4
The Priory RC Primary School
EWD/SEL/PNX NG16 .... **14** C1
Puppets Theatre
MAPPK/POR/STA NG3 .... **3** G1
Quarry Hill Industrial Estate
ILK DE7 .... **38** A3
Quarry Hill Industrial Park
ILK DE7 .... **38** A3
Queens Drive Industrial Estate
WBRGFD NG2 .... **56** D2
Queen's Medical Centre
NOTTE NG7 .... **42** A5
Radcliffe on Trent Golf Club
COT/KEY/RAD NG12 .... **61** G1
Radcliffe on Trent
Infant School
COT/KEY/RAD NG12 .... **47** F5
Radcliffe on Trent
Junior School
COT/KEY/RAD NG12 .... **61** E1
Radford Primary School
NOTTE NG7 .... **42** B3
Redhill Leisure Centre
ARN NG5 .... **19** H1
Redhill School
ARN NG5 .... **19** H1
Richard Bonnington
Primary School
ARN NG5 .... **20** A1
Richard Herrod Leisure Centre
CARL NG4 .... **32** D5
Rise Park Junior School
ARN NG5 .... **18** C1
Rise Park Shopping Centre
ARN NG5 .... **18** C1
Riverlyn Medical Centre
BLWL NG6 .... **17** H4
Riverside Retail Park
NOTTE NG7 .... **56** D3
Robert Mellors Primary School
ARN NG5 .... **20** B2
Robert Miles Junior School
BING/VBLV NG13 .... **49** E2
Robert Shaw Primary School
WOL/BIL/BRX NG8 .... **42** A2

Robin Hood Industrial Estate
MAPPK/POR/STA NG3 .... **3** J4
Robin Hood Primary School
ARN NG5 .... **18** D4
Robin Hood Statue
NOTTE NG7 .... **2** D7
Roddington Country Park
CFTN/RUD NG11 .... **77** F5
Ropewalk Industrial Centre
ILK DE7 .... **26** B4
Rosehill Clinic
MAPPK/POR/STA NG3 .... **3** K2
Rosehill Special School
MAPPK/POR/STA NG3 .... **3** K2
Round Hill Primary School
BSTN/STPLFD NG9 .... **55** E4
Ruddington Fields
Business Park
CFTN/RUD NG11 .... **77** G4
Ruddington Grange Golf Cub
CFTN/RUD NG11 .... **67** F4
Ruddington Medical Centre
CFTN/RUD NG11 .... **77** F2
Rushcliffe Arena
WBRGFD NG2 .... **57** G5
Rushcliffe Leisure Centre
WBRGFD NG2 .... **68** A2
Rushcliffe School
WBRGFD NG2 .... **68** A2
Rylands Junior School
BSTN/STPLFD NG9 .... **65** F2
Sacred Heart RC School
CARL NG4 .... **45** E1
St Anns Well Infant School
MAPPK/POR/STA NG3 .... **43** H1
St Augustines RC
Primary School
MAPPK/POR/STA NG3 .... **31** F5
St Barnabas
Catholic Cathedral
NOTT NG1 .... **2** C4
St Edwards' RC School
MAPPK/POR/STA NG3 .... **44** A2
St John Houghton
Catholic School
ILK DE7 .... **37** F2
St Johns CE Primary School
BSTN/STPLFD NG9 .... **53** F4
CARL NG4 .... **45** F3
St Johns College
BSTN/STPLFD NG9 .... **54** A4
St Josephs School
NOTT NG1 .... **2** C4
St Laurence CE Primary School
LGEAT NG10 .... **73** F3
St Mary RC Primary School
NOTTE NG7 .... **30** C5
St Marys CE Primary School
BLWL NG6 .... **17** H2
St Patricks RC Primary School
CFTN/RUD NG11 .... **57** E3
St Peters CE Junior School
CFTN/RUD NG11 .... **67** G5
St Teresas RC Primary School
WOL/BIL/BRX NG8 .... **29** F5
St Thomas Catholic
Primary School
ILK DE7 .... **37** H1
Salutation Inn
NOTT NG1 .... **2** E6
Sandiacre Friesland
Sports Centre
BWSH/BRSTN DE72 .... **62** A1
Savoy Cinema
NOTTE NG7 .... **42** C4
Sawley J & I School
LGEAT NG10 .... **72** B5
Sawmills Industrial Park
HEANOR DE75 .... **6** A4
Scala Cinema
ILK DE7 .... **25** H5
Scargill CE Primary School
ILK DE7 .... **36** A1
Scotholme Primary School
NOTTE NG7 .... **30** C5
Screen Room Cinema
NOTT NG1 .... **3** G4
Seagrave Primary School
WOL/BIL/BRX NG8 .... **28** C3
SGCS Business Park
BSTN/STPLFD NG9 .... **65** F2
Sheet Stores Industrial Estate
LGEAT NG10 .... **73** E4
Shipley Country Park
HEANOR DE75 .... **12** C5
Shipstones Business Centre
NOTTE NG7 .... **30** B4

Showcase Cinema
NOTTE NG7 .... **56** B3
Snape Wood Medical Centre
BLWL NG6 .... **17** E2
Snape Wood Primary School
BLWL NG6 .... **17** F3
S N College
NOTT NG1 .... **2** E5
Sneinton CE Primary School
MAPPK/POR/STA NG3 .... **44** A4
Sneinton Health Centre
WBRGFD NG2 .... **3** J5
South East Derbyshire College
HEANOR DE75 .... **12** C1
ILK DE7 .... **38** A2
Southern Cemetery
WBRGFD NG2 .... **67** G3
South Nottingham College
WBRGFD NG2 .... **67** G1
Southwark Infant School
BLWL NG6 .... **30** A1
Southwark Junior School
BLWL NG6 .... **30** B2
South Wilford Endowed
Primary School
CFTN/RUD NG11 .... **57** E4
Southwold Primary School
WOL/BIL/BRX NG8 .... **42** A3
South Wolds School
COT/KEY/RAD NG12 .... **82** C2
Springfield Primary School
BLWL NG6 .... **17** H1
Spring St Primary School
HUCK/RAV NG15 .... **5** E5
Stadium Industrial Park
LGEAT NG10 .... **73** G1
Standhill Infant School
MAPPK/POR/STA NG3 .... **44** C1
Stanhope Primary School
CARL NG4 .... **33** E2
Stanstead Primary School
ARN NG5 .... **18** B2
Stanton-on-the-Wolds Golf Club
COT/KEY/RAD NG12 .... **83** E2
Stanton Vale Special School
ILK DE7 .... **38** A2
Stapleford Health Centre
BSTN/STPLFD NG9 .... **53** E5
Stenhouse Medical Centre
ARN NG5 .... **19** H2
Stevenson Junior School
BSTN/STPLFD NG9 .... **53** G3
Stonebridge Court
Industrial Estate
MAPPK/POR/STA NG3 .... **3** K3
Stonebridge Mental
Health Centre
MAPPK/POR/STA NG3 .... **3** K3
Strelley Health Centre
WOL/BIL/BRX NG8 .... **28** C4
Sunnyside Primary School
BSTN/STPLFD NG9 .... **54** A5
Sycamore J & I School
MAPPK/POR/STA NG3 .... **3** H1
Sycamore Junior School
MAPPK/POR/STA NG3 .... **43** G1
Tales of Robin Hood
NOTT NG1 .... **2** D5
Tennis Court Industrial Estate
WBRGFD NG2 .... **44** B5
Theatre Royal & Concert Hall
NOTT NG1 .... **2** D4
Thornfield Industrial Estate
MAPPK/POR/STA NG3 .... **44** A3
Thornton's Holt Camping Park
COT/KEY/RAD NG12 .... **60** C3
Thorpes Road Industrial Estate
HEANOR DE75 .... **12** A1
Tollerton Primary School
COT/KEY/RAD NG12 .... **69** E5
Toot Hill School
BING/VBLV NG13 .... **48** D3
Top Valley Health Centre
ARN NG5 .... **18** C2
Top Valley School
ARN NG5 .... **18** B2
Torkard Hill Medical Centre
HUCK/RAV NG15 .... **11** F1
Totan Banks Road Infant School
BSTN/STPLFD NG9 .... **63** G4
Trent Bridge Primary School
WBRGFD NG2 .... **57** G3
Trent Business Centre
LGEAT NG10 .... **62** D4
Trent College
LGEAT NG10 .... **62** D5
Trent Pool Sports Centre
WBRGFD NG2 .... **58** A1

Trent South Industrial Park
WBRGFD NG2 .... **44** B5
Trent Vale Infant School
BSTN/STPLFD NG9 .... **65** G2
The Trinity School
WOL/BIL/BRX NG8 .... **29** F5
Trowell CE Primary School
BSTN/STPLFD NG9 .... **39** E4
Unity Primary &
Nursery School
NOTTE NG7 .... **2** A2
University Chaplaincy
BSTN/STPLFD NG9 .... **55** F4
University of Nottingham
NOTTE NG7 .... **42** A4
NOTTE NG7 .... **55** G2
Vernon Park Trading Estate
BLWL NG6 .... **30** B2
Victoria Business Park
CARL NG4 .... **46** A2
Victoria Health Centre
NOTT NG1 .... **3** F3
Victoria Leisure Centre
NOTT NG1 .... **3** H4
Victoria Shopping Centre
NOTT NG1 .... **3** F3
Walter Halls Primary School
MAPPK/POR/STA NG3 .... **31** H3
Waterside Retail Park
ILK DE7 .... **26** B4
Welbeck Primary School
WBRGFD NG2 .... **57** F1
West Bridgford School
WBRGFD NG2 .... **67** G1
Westbrook Special School
LGEAT NG10 .... **72** D2
Westdale J & I School
MAPPK/POR/STA NG3 .... **32** D2
Westglade Junior School
ARN NG5 .... **18** C2
West Hallam Cricket Club
ILK DE7 .... **36** A1
West Hallam Medical Centre
ILK DE7 .... **36** B1
West Park Leisure Centre
LGEAT NG10 .... **72** C2
The Wheldon School
CARL NG4 .... **32** D4
Whitegate Primary School
CFTN/RUD NG11 .... **76** A1
Whitemoor Court
Industrial Estate
NOTTE NG7 .... **30** B5
Whitemoor Primary School
WOL/BIL/BRX NG8 .... **30** A4
Wholesale Fruit & Flower Market
WBRGFD NG2 .... **43** H5
Whyburn Primary School
HUCK/RAV NG15 .... **5** E5
Wilford Business Park
CFTN/RUD NG11 .... **67** E2
Wilford Hill Crematorium
WBRGFD NG2 .... **67** G3
William Booth
Birthplace Museum
WBRGFD NG2 .... **3** K5
William Booth Infant School
WBRGFD NG2 .... **3** K6
William Crane School
WOL/BIL/BRX NG8 .... **29** G4
William Howitt Junior School
HEANOR DE75 .... **6** A5
William Lilley Infant School
BSTN/STPLFD NG9 .... **53** E5
William Sharp School
WOL/BIL/BRX NG8 .... **40** B1
Willow Brook Primary School
COT/KEY/RAD NG12 .... **83** E2
Willow Farm Primary School
CARL NG4 .... **33** H3
Willow Industrial Estate
BLWL NG6 .... **17** H2
Wollaton Cricket Club
WOL/BIL/BRX NG8 .... **40** D4
Wollaton Park Golf Club
WOL/BIL/BRX NG8 .... **41** G5
Wollaton Vale Health Centre
WOL/BIL/BRX NG8 .... **40** C5
Woodborough Road Clinic
ARN NG5 .... **31** G3
Woodview Business Centre
ARN NG5 .... **18** D1
Ye Old Trip To Jerusalem Inn
NOTT NG1 .... **2** E7

Notes

Notes